African Systems of Thought

GENERAL EDITORS

Charles S. Bird
Ivan Karp

CONTRIBUTING EDITORS

James W. Fernandez
Luc de Heusch
John Middleton
Roy Willis

IRON, GENDER, AND POWER

Rituals of Transformation in African Societies

EUGENIA W. HERBERT

INDIANA UNIVERSITY PRESS
Bloomington and Indianapolis

Manufactured in the United States of America

Library of Congress Cataloging-in-Publication Data
Herbert, Eugenia W.
Iron, gender, and power : rituals of transformation in African
societies / Eugenia W. Herbert.
p. cm.—(African systems of thought)
Includes bibliographical references (p.   ) and index.
ISBN 0-253-32733-4 (cloth : alk. paper).—ISBN 0-253-20833-5 (paper : alk. paper)
1. Industries, Primitive—Africa, Sub-Saharan. 2. Rites and ceremonies—Africa, Sub-
Saharan. 3. Iron industry and trade—Africa, Sub-Saharan. 4. Iron—Africa, Sub-Saharan—Folklore. 5. Cosmology, African. 6. Power (Social sciences) 7. Sex role—Africa, Sub-Saharan. I. Title. II. Series.
GN645.H43 1993
303.3′72′096—dc20
93-16102

1 2 3 4 5 97 96 95 94 93

CONTENTS

MAPS

Figures 1–27 follow page 40; figures 28–47 follow page 187.

PREFACE

Bi oran ba sou okounkoun, a be wo l'abbe.
The more obscure an affair is, the more one endeavors to get to the heart of it.

Proverb, Atakpamé, Togo

Every spring a ritual takes place at Mount Holyoke, a women's college in western Massachusetts. Alumnae returning for reunion participate in a parade, all of them dressed in white and accompanied by a male marching band. The oldest classes come first, followed by progressively younger women. The graduating seniors (also in white) bring up the rear, carrying a chain of laurel leaves. The parade ends at the grave of Mary Lyon, who founded the college in 1837. Here the seniors pass through the ranks of all of the alumnae, drape the laurel chain over the iron fence that surrounds the gravesite, and conclude by singing "Bread and Roses."

The ceremony is a classic rite of passage by which those about to graduate are symbolically incorporated into the community of their predecessors as fully fledged adult women in named age-grades. Their new identity is given not simply by the bestowal of a diploma but through their metaphorical rebirth from the collective womb of the previous graduates, validated by the founding ancestress whose vitality is reinforced by the offering of medicinal leaves associated with victory and longevity. The ritual is overseen by two priestesses, the president of the college and the president of the alumnae association.

If one asked any of the participants what the ceremony was all about, probably none would describe it as I have done. They would see it as little different from other alumnae and alumni parades that are standard fare at American college reunions. And yet, looked at more closely, it *is* different because of the details of its choreography. The comparable event at a sister college (Wellesley), for example, does call for white attire but does not include the nubile initiates (the seniors have already graduated and left town), the founding benefactor, music, or a laurel chain, and it ends up in a mass meeting in which class gifts are announced to general applause, each class trying to top the others in the amount of money subscribed.

I cite this ritual for several reasons, most of all because it raises questions common to all field research. How does the observer understand what she or he is seeing? Am I justified in bringing to the Mount Holyoke parade an exegesis that would startle most of the "natives"? Why are two roughly similar ceremonies structured so differently? Why isn't a comparable wealth of symbolism evident in the alumnae/alumni ceremonies of Wellesley and other institutions that were founded about the same time and that have the same interest in cementing bonds of sisterhood and brotherhood in a higher loyalty as well as venerating the founding ancestors? Have these rites been simplified and shorn of earlier elements that would indicate a more extensive core of common belief, or did they never have them? Or have I overlooked aspects that are in fact more essential than those I have singled out as significant?

I would probably not have thought much about the Mount Holyoke parade had I not been wrestling with African rituals of transformation that also seem to be structured along the twin axes of gender and age, rituals that fit intriguing paradigms only to come up with anomalies or discrepant variants when one extends the comparison farther afield. At the same time, the event cited serves to remind us that ways of looking at the world, indeed of being in the world (to borrow a phrase from Karen McCarthy Brown), in a distant continent such as Africa have their parallels in our own culture. As well they might: for of all the human experiences, is not the interplay of gender and of age the most fundamental?

This study comes out of my earlier work on the history of copper in African cultures, *Red Gold of Africa*. In the course of that research, I came across hints that metals and the processes that produced them were sometimes genderized. I probably would not have pursued this line of research had I not been prodded by my colleagues to think more seriously about gender in Africa and to think about it, naturally, in the arena I knew best, metallurgy. At the same time, I realized that iron should be the focus of the study since it is the primary metal in Africa, as it has been in the West and in Asia.

After the appearance of the copper book, the late H. M. Friede, whose contribution to the historical metallurgy of South Africa has been so extraordinary, suggested I tackle a sequel on the cultural history of iron. This is not that book. It does not propose to cover the technology itself nor the economic, social, political, and artistic uses of iron. Rather, its topic is the belief system underlying the working of iron, especially iron smelting, and the extent to which this belief system also underlies other core acts of transformation: the investiture of chiefs, hunting, and pottery. The mapping of one process can be carried over into others because of an overarching similarity in how they are perceived to operate (cf. Barley 1983:11). The model of transformation that emerges from this comparative study invokes above all the interplay of gender and age, mirroring quite understandably their preeminence in lived experience.

The conceptualization proposed here challenges the tendency to treat the ironworker as someone apart and metallurgy as an activity unlike others. To some extent it is a reaction against the earlier preoccupation with the status of the smith: was he an insider or an outsider, respected or despised, feared or honored? These are useful questions, but they have led to a neglect of what the smith actually does and how he is believed to do it. Furthermore, the very adjectives that became the staple of these studies pose real problems of cultural translation, just as do accompanying terms such as *purity* and *pollution*.

The opportunity to pursue this line of inquiry was provided at a propitious moment by the Mount Holyoke Project on Gender in Context, generously supported by a grant from the William H. Donner Foundation. My colleagues in the project, as heterogeneous a lot as one could imagine, offered an intellectual community and shrewd insights in the early stages of the work, as did the workshop visitors who assembled early each summer for four years to explore a vast range of exciting questions raised in the burgeoning field of gender studies. The Donner Foundation also helped to fund field research in Togo in 1985 and the film that was made of iron smelting, *The Blooms of Banjeli: Technology and Gender in West African Iron Making*.

This book owes a primary debt to the people of Banjeli, Togo, and Lopanzo, Zaïre, for their hospitality and assistance in documenting metallurgical practices. In Togo, my thanks go especially to the Ministère de l'Education Nationale et de la Recherche Scientifique, Dovi Kuevi, the late Chief Sertchi Magnibo, master smelter Belam Diyambo and his équipe, to Sertchi Gmanimbe, Kwabena Attah, and Phil de Barros. Above all, I am grateful to Candice Goucher for making me aware of the research possibilities in Banjeli and for sharing her knowledge and company. In Zaïre I was privileged to work with Kanimba Misago and with the staff of the Institut des Musées Nationaux du Zaïre. We were also much aided by Pr Honoré Vinck of the Centre Bamanya (Equateur) and Boilo Mbula, and were delighted to be joined by Colleen Kriger. In both countries the staffs of the Centre Culturel Américain did much to facilitate our research, especially John Treacey and Morgan Kulla in Togo and Kate Delaney in Zaïre. On our return trip to Togo in 1992, Tammy Holtan was a wonderful host in Kabou-Sara and Johanna Kowitz in Lomé, and Louis Firmin and his Bretons provided indispensable assistance.

Research in Zaïre in 1989 was assisted by a grant from the Joint Committee on African Studies of the Social Science Research Council and the American Council of Learned Societies with funds provided by the National Endowment for the Humanities and the Ford Foundation. I am also grateful to Mount Holyoke College for faculty grants that helped defray the costs of a brief trip to Dakar in 1989 and research in Togo in 1992. In addition, I would like to thank the staff of the Williston Library at Mount Holyoke, particularly the Interlibrary Loan Department for their unfailing ingenuity in tracking down obscure publications: they triumphantly confirmed that it is indeed possible to carry out an ambitious research agenda without direct access to a major research library. What the library did for the mind, the Kendall pool did for the body and soul: communing with the *bisimbi* of the watery deep helped me over many a block and confusion, and I thank the personnel and student guards.

The Bellagio Conference and Workshop on African Material Culture in May 1988 offered an ideal opportunity to try out the germs of the ideas in this book, and I thank the organizers, Christraud Geary, Kris Hardin, and Mary Jo Arnoldi, as well as the participants for their critiques and suggestions. For more than a decade Dave Killick has enriched my understanding of metallurgical technology in Africa; he is an ideal colleague and very special friend with whom I could swap sources and ideas. Over the same period, Carlyn Saltman has been my companion on four trips to Africa as photographer, film maker, and friend. Thomas Jacob has provided most of the photographs in this book: over the years I have come to count on him for superb quality and enthusiastic participation, whatever the project.

A number of colleagues have shared unpublished work, especially Ian Fowler, Terry Childs, Hans Hahn, Peter Telfair, Cathy Skidmore-Hess, and Zoë Strother. Virginia Lazzati and Diana Wylie offered helpful suggestions on early stages of the manuscript. Subsequently, I have benefited enormously from close readings by Patrick McNaughton, Ian Fowler, Terry Childs, Marla Berns, and anonymous readers for the Indiana University Press, as well as by my husband, Robert L. Herbert.

Bob has been my companion through some four decades of the life cycle. Together we have shared the drama of procreativity; now we are moving together toward ancestorhood. I dedicate this book to him, to our children, and to our grandchild Alexander.

Iron, Gender,
and Power

Map 1. Most frequently cited ethnic groups.

1. Bamana
2. Dogon
3. Minyanka
4. Senufo
5. Hausa
6. Banjeli
7. Tamberma
8. Asante
9. Shai
10. Yoruba
11. Benin
12. Mafa
13. Ga'anda
14. Baguirmi
15. Moundang
16. Babungo
17. Gbaya
18. Mandja
19. Beti
20. Fang
21. Mangbetu
22. Tégué
23. Teke (Tio)
24. Kongo
25. Yaka
26. Lele

27. Lopanzo
28. Chokwe
29. Lunda
30. Ndembu
31. Luchazi
32. Kuba
33. Luba
34. Kwanyama
35. Lega
36. Bashu
37. Dime
38. Ankole
39. Ganda
40. Nyoro
41. Haya
42. Kikuyu
43. Shambaa
44. Fipa
45. Chisinga
46. Bemba
47. Tumbuka
48. Kaonde
49. Chewa
50. Shona
51. Thonga

Techniques and Cosmology

> [Iron] stains the great earth wheresoever you
> can see it, far and wide—it is the colouring sub-
> stance appointed to colour the globe for the
> sight, as well as subdue it for the service of
> man.
>
> John Ruskin (1858)

> Gender can no more be marginalized in the
> study of human societies than can the concept of
> "human action," or the concept of "society."
>
> Henrietta Moore (1988)

This is, ultimately, a book about the cosmologies of sub-Saharan Africa as they
are invoked to explain and control technologies of transformation. Because it
is about cosmologies, it is about power: where it resides; who may invoke it,
by what means and for what ends; and how to protect against it since power
is always double-edged. I will argue that within the systems of belief under-
pinning transformative processes, gender plays a far more important role than
has been commonly realized. Together with age, it structures much of the
conceptualization and manipulation of power.

What do we mean by *power* in this context? Like so many words in common usage, it defies easy definition. Social scientists tend to invoke Weber's
notion of access to and control over people and resources. The widely acknowledged hegemony of male elders or chiefly lineages or other privileged
groups over the rank and file of children, junior males, nubile women, and
slaves in many sub-Saharan societies surely rests on such access and control.
But, as Karp (1989) points out, these are surface features and do not explain
how such access and control are achieved, maintained, and understood. True,
almost every society has had experience of the exercise of power by brute
physical force that enables certain groups to dominate others, but in surveying the historical and anthropological literature one is struck by how rarely
overt coercion actually figures in the maintenance of unequal access to and

control over people and resources once a social order is in place. Coercion may be important in times of turmoil and in imposing new personnel in the apparatus of power, but if physical strength, stamina, and productivity were all that really mattered, young men and women should be the primary players in the drama of power. Instead, that role has fallen preeminently to older men (whose seniority may be reinforced in additional ways) throughout most of world history and, to a lesser extent in the African case, to older women.

This suggests not only that cosmology—beliefs about the nature of the universe—must be invoked to explain what power is and how it operates but also that gender and age are critical constituents of cosmology and therefore of any definition of power, although they are not the only factors. If we see power not simply as a static state or relationship but also as the means by which desired transformations are accomplished (Arens and Karp 1989), the relevance of gender and age becomes much more apparent. Human experience provides the template par excellence of transformation in the cycle of life, the sequence of birth, maturation, and death, the parallel regeneration of the natural and social worlds. Power to control the outcome in one sphere is not different from that which is applied in another; that is, we seem to be confronted with coherent and unified beliefs about the nature of power within individual African societies. These beliefs privilege age and gender because they are the most salient characteristics of lived experience: the most successful individuals are those who live to old age and who abundantly reproduce themselves. By extension, they are even more successful, more "powerful," if they are able to apply this ability to other domains that are seen as inherently similar.

Power therefore involves an understanding of cosmology, the forces that effect outcomes in the world, and with it a knowledge of how to influence them. While social cohesion demands that people living together share the same beliefs and values, there is a vast disparity when it comes to how much different individuals will actually know. To a large extent the concentration of power in the hands of the few depends on the shared assumption that they possess bodies of esoteric knowledge unavailable to the rest of the population. The links between power and secrecy run deep, although the fiction of secrets, the necessity of mystification, may be as important a pillar of power relationships as the reality (cf. S. F. Moore 1976; Vansina 1955; Dupré 1978; Fowler n.d.). To understand who exercises power and how, we must look at who monopolizes the secrets that make things happen and to whom they are selectively or progressively imparted, for there are no secrets if they are not shared with someone else (De Boeck 1991b:45, citing Zempléni). It is a truism that knowledge is power in Africa and therefore not to be lightly dispersed. It is also true that the acquisition of knowledge is largely determined by age and gender, although there are other paths—as, for example, the diviner or healer whose vocation is directly imposed by a spirit or divinity.

The definition of power that I would propose, then, emphasizes the *means* by which selected individuals are thought to gain access to and control over people and resources through their mastery of transformative processes. I focus on sets of ritual actions and prescriptive behaviors, first and foremost those associated with ironworking, and then move to technologies viewed as analogous in order to posit similar structures and underlying patterns, for it is in ritual that beliefs about power are acted out. Neither the actors nor the actions of ritual are arbitrary; they must be consistent with culturally accepted notions about who may mobilize unseen power and how. While such an approach may appear unorthodox in historical studies, it is in keeping with recent trends in anthropology and the history of religion (Jacobson-Widding 1991:10–11). It seems particularly suited to the oft-noted African preoccupation with the human, the concrete, the practicalities of the here and now.

From this perspective, iron technology can be viewed as a multilayered text that reveals its conceptual basis indirectly, through actions, rather than directly as an explicitly articulated system of beliefs. I am looking at what people *do*, not just at what they say. Indeed, when asked why they do what they do, metallurgists usually give a commonsense answer: "Because that is the way we do it" or "Because it works." Few may even be aware of the holistic theory that underlies their actions, just as few who use computers nowadays understand or need to understand how they actually work. It may be, too, that earlier rationales have been lost as ironworking has become marginalized and moribund or simply that these specialists are unwilling to elaborate to outsiders precisely because questions of power are involved.

The would-be observer must therefore take fragments, meaningless in themselves, and put them together so that they form a coherent whole. Further, because the data from a single example would be a shaky base from which to generalize, I have attempted to collate information from across sub-Saharan Africa to see whether, beneath the enormous variability of detail, there are in fact commonalities that allow us finally to make inferences about belief systems, about the forces and laws that Africans believe govern the universe and human destinies, that is, about cosmologies. At the same time, I am assuming that one can use the insights gained from other modes and areas of investigation to illuminate what is happening with metallurgy and vice versa. One body of data can serve to check the other. The wide-angled focus on the ensemble of actors and activities, rather than on a single aspect, gives greater prominence, I believe, to the interlocked and interlocking axes of gender and age than other methods.

But why metallurgy? My reasons are twofold. First, it was practiced throughout the subcontinent wherever suitable ores and fuel were found, and it held a central place in all but purely pastoral and hunting-gathering societies. By African standards, too, it is relatively well documented and is one of the few activities for which one can claim some historical depth. Second, ironworking offers a precious window into African cosmologies and a model for other technologies with similar cosmological grounding. It corresponds to what Clifford (1983) refers to as a "synedochic" representation of culture where one activity can be seen as a microcosm of more general beliefs and practices. In a continent that was virtually without indigenous written records before the nineteenth century, documentation of belief systems is hard to come by, and such strategies are all the more necessary.

While our accounts of ironworking are relatively modern, it is reasonable to assume that the basic beliefs go back much farther, that whatever the changes in specific detail, the composite package of core beliefs and the rituals that derive from them would not have changed radically. This is an important point and a contentious one, so I should emphasize that I am not claiming that there is an unchanging body of "traditional" metallurgical practices, only a set of beliefs that could be expressed in various ways and adapted to new social and economic conditions without losing their integrity. Ironically, smelting is a particularly appropriate object for this study precisely because it died out in most areas in the early decades of this century: the ensemble of its practices were frozen in time in the memory of its last practitioners and were not subjected to the welter of new influences that have so strongly affected other areas of life and belief. Already sensing the effects of change, R. P. Wyckaert entitled his study of Fipa ironworking "Forgerons païens et forgerons chrétiens au Tanganyika," but there were still plenty of "pagan" smelters when he wrote in 1914.

To illustrate the perhaps surprising degree to which older practices have been preserved. In 1985 my colleagues and I arranged for a reconstruction of iron smelting in Banjeli, in northwest Togo. A few furnaces were still active into the 1950s in this area, but large-scale iron production had declined already in the 1920s. We left the procedures entirely in the hands of local specialists. They built a furnace, choosing the site of an older one and incorporating parts of it. The ancestors and the spirits were called upon to bless the enterprise. During the entire process, the smelter kept close watch to see that no women and no men not observing the prohibition against sexual activity came near the furnace. During the smelting itself, food and leaves were offered to the furnace, it was exhorted to be fertile in iron, and a child was beaten and made to cry. In spite of the exclusion of women, the three of us female researchers were allowed to be present throughout, and an old woman with two younger ones also approached the furnace on several occasions.

Like the ceremony cited in the preface, this assemblage of behaviors has many parallels in smelting rituals elsewhere but is not a carbon copy of any that I know of, just as the Banjeli furnace is much like others but not identical even to those found twenty-five miles away—indeed, another reconstruction undertaken just a few years later in the same village was not identical. Nevertheless, the smelting rituals include several key aspects which one might expect to (and, in fact, does) find elsewhere: a careful definition of who can take part, in terms of gender, lineage, or skills, and sexual behavior; an overt linkage with genealogy and ancestral power; and an anthropomorphizing of the furnace itself and of the smelting process. It is immediately obvious that gender is not synonymous with sex since our presence as foreign women was tolerated, while the old woman and her young attendants played a necessary part.

These are the paradigmatic elements. They often occur, however, with significant differences, omissions, and additions, so much so that the problem of interpretation becomes acute and cannot always be resolved, given the gaps in the data. For a historian, the difficulty of following change in any one area is especially frustrating. Nevertheless, the material that is available allows one to propose a model that highlights the close association of iron with fertility and with sources of power seen as both ancestral and female. In fact, ironworking in Africa presents us with the apparent paradox of a male-dominated craft that must invoke elements of female power to succeed. We see this not only in the creation of anthropomorphic furnaces but also in the range of rituals that are structured around the opposition and complementarity of male and female, fertility and sterility, living and dead.

Further, the beliefs underlying iron technology are not unique to this activity; they can be extended to other key enterprises that involve forms of transformation and access to "supernatural" power. I have limited myself here to activities dominated by males—metallurgy, hunting, and royal investiture—not simply to keep the project manageable but to show how a set of beliefs supports male appropriation or replication of female procreativity. Thus, when one turns to a comparable female activity, pottery, the asymmetry with these enterprises becomes clear: pottery simply does not invoke the same "power field" even though the procreative paradigm is applicable. One could just as well look at other basic activities such as agriculture and cattle tending, which seem to be equally gendered and equally structured by principles of age, and I hope others will.

It should not really be surprising that the beliefs encoded in iron technology are equally relevant to other activities, that the most basic paradigm is transferable. It confirms the consistency and comprehensiveness of African thought, its capacity to encompass a range of processes, and, as we will see, its ability to accommodate change. The thesis of this book is that African transformative processes invoke the human model as the measure of all things, giving preeminence to the two most salient aspects of lived experience, gender and age. If we think of gender as one axis—a horizontal axis, so to speak—the other axis is the vertical one of the life cycle, uniting the living with the dead. Both axes define social identity, offering a model based on human experience that can then be projected onto a range of creative enterprises. Most fundamentally, both revolve around complex and inseparable notions of power and fertility. The formulation of these concepts will differ contextually within a culture as well as from culture to culture. If there is any validity to my hypothesis, however, the underlying paradigm will emerge precisely because it is so basic to human existence, at least as it has been lived for most of the world's history.

THE AGE OF IRON

The story of iron has many threads. Throughout the Old World, scholars have labeled that span of history dating from its advent the "Iron Age" in recognition of its revolutionary effect on all aspects of culture. The actors in the story have themselves been just as aware of its profound import, often giving iron and those who shape it a privileged place in myths and legends of genesis. Long before the nuclear age, they had to confront the terrible ambivalence of a technology that promised so much for good and evil, for increased productivity and increased destruction.

Iron Age peoples have had to find ways to understand the technology and to fit it into social, political, and economic systems. They must explain just how the smelter is able to transform stone into workable metal, why it succeeds at times and fails at others, and how the smith forms raw material into objects of use, adornment, and ritual. How does the smith/smelter gain and preserve the power he so evidently displays? Who is he apt to antagonize by it, and how can he protect himself? Who should benefit from the output of the furnace and forge and in what ways?

These questions are not unique to metalworking and not unique to Africa; they lead us to the most basic beliefs about the nature of the world and the place of humans in it, especially the means by which they can hope to exert control over the forces that govern their lives. What is true for Africa may well have wider application to other Iron Age peoples before the industrial and scientific revolutions.

Iron Working in Africa

Lamenting the wanton destruction of the monumental slag heaps of Cyprus, the archaeologist, F. L. Koucky, has written, "It is unfortunate that these slag piles have not been treated as important antiquities, for they record an effort greater than the building of the pyramids or the construction of many great cities of the past" (Koucky and Steinberg 1982:150). The same might be said of the vast and visible remains of ironworking in Africa: slag heaps so extensive that in some areas they shape the very contours of the land.

Ironworking spread over all of sub-Saharan Africa in the millennium spanning the period from about the fifth century B.C. to the fifth century A.D. (map 2). There has been much debate about initial as well as secondary routes of diffusion and even some speculation that the technology might have been invented independently in Africa. Without more information, it is impossible to give a definitive answer. The prevailing wisdom, however, is that without antecedent metallurgical experience in the working of copper and its alloys, for which there is no widespread evidence, the more complex technology needed to smelt iron is unlikely to have developed independently in Africa

Map 2. Iron smelting sites identified in sub-Saharan Africa.

south of the Sahara. Be that as it may, virtually the only people left out of the iron revolution were hunter-gatherers, some of whom were in fact incorporated into metal-producing societies.

In some parts of the continent, production remained small-scale, adapted to local needs. In other areas, however, there is clear evidence of intensive or long-term production. Field surveys have identified more than ten thousand smelting sites north and west of Kano in northern Nigeria (Darling 1986), for example, while concentrations of more than one thousand furnaces have been found in the largest settlement sites in the Middle Senegal Valley (McIntosh, McIntosh, and Bocoum 1992). The two areas most carefully studied, Bassar in northwestern Togo (Goucher 1984; de Barros 1986; Hahn 1991b) and the Ndop Plain in the Cameroon Grassfields (Warnier and Fowler 1979; Fowler 1990), present a picture of an industry that reached impressive levels of production in the nineteenth century. The first Germans to reach northern Togo late in the century found hundreds of furnaces in operation in the Banjeli region alone, turning out their trademark iron-shaped blooms (figs. 1 and 2). Other major iron-producing centers in Futa Jallon in central Guinea and Yatenga in Burkina Faso remain to be studied with the same degree of thoroughness (Pole 1983). In more forested areas, slag heaps are harder to find, masking the scale of local metallurgy.

Ironworking consists of a number of separate operations: mining, preparing the ore, manufacturing charcoal or other fuels, constructing the smelting furnace, smelting proper, refining or otherwise treating bloomery iron for forging, and finally smithing the finished objects. Africa is abundantly supplied with iron ores, albeit of differing qualities. The red earth that makes such a strong visual first impression on the traveler to Africa is composed of iron oxides, the lateritic crust that covers so much of the continent. Although different types of ores have been used, the most common were hematite, which was dug close to the surface or in deeper shafts, magnetite, occurring in river sands and gravels, and limonite or bog iron (a hydrated form of hematite), found in swamps or lakes. In some cases different types of ores were deliberately mixed.

Preparation involved selecting the leanest ores, then washing or crushing them to get rid of as much of the inert matrix as possible. River sands might be winnowed like grain to separate the particles of iron from impurities, while hematite ores were often pounded with stones to concentrate the mineral. Ores might also be roasted to drive out excess moisture and to increase their permeability. Sometimes the ore was formed into balls to be fed into the furnace. Fluxes were rarely added except in the form of old slag.

Charcoal was the primary fuel used throughout sub-Saharan Africa. Successful smelting demanded hardwoods that would burn slowly at high temperatures. Among the most commonly used trees were the *Burkea africana*, found in the savannas of west and central Africa, and *Pericopsis angolensis*, also a savanna hardwood. In some cases, grasses were burnt to preheat the furnace. Babungo smelters relied on finely cut and dried wood chips for the bulk of their fuel, rather than on charcoal alone (Fowler 1990:198).

Smelting in Africa depended exclusively on the bloomery process, which was also used in Europe and parts of Asia in antiquity and during the medieval period. Bloomery furnaces must reach temperatures high enough to separate slag from iron (1100°–1300°C), and they must do this in a reducing atmosphere so that iron oxides are reduced to metallic iron. Ore is smelted at temperatures below the melting point to produce a spongy mass of iron—the bloom—rather than the liquid cast iron produced by blast furnaces, which would have been too brittle to forge. In a few exceptional cases cast iron was produced, but it is not clear whether this was intentional. It could have been made forgeable by allowing it to remain for some time in the oxidizing atmosphere of the forge (Childs:pers. comm.)

African metallurgists evolved a mind-boggling array of furnace types capable of meeting these two basic requirements of controlled temperature and reducing atmosphere (Cline 1937:44–51; Kense 1983; Friede 1986). To say that they fall into three main categories—bowl hearths, low shaft, and tall shaft furnaces—does not do justice to the almost infinite variation of size and shape within each category. Heterogeneity often occurred within the same region and even among a single ethnic group. Some furnaces allowed for slag to be tapped or to run off; others did not. Some were meant to serve only for a single smelt and had to be broken down to retrieve the bloom; others could be used for years with only minor repairs. Some produced massive blooms; others, very modest chunks of iron. And, clearly, some were much more efficient than others, although "efficiency" itself needs to be defined in ways that would have made sense to the people involved. To some extent, furnace design may have been intentionally adapted to local technological needs. Thus, the differences in furnace size within the Bassar region have been explained by reference to the varying mineral content of the ores available. The rich ores of Banjeli and its immediate environs, for example, did not require the massive furnaces of Nangbani, with its inferior ores, to produce the same amount of bloom (Hupfeld 1899). In general, however, attempts to correlate furnace design with local conditions have not been very convincing (Célis 1988:270), leaving us without a satisfactory explanation for the proliferation of furnace shapes and sizes. Nor does a mapping of furnace types offer convincing evidence for the diffusion of ironworking throughout sub-Saharan Africa.

The construction of smelting furnaces will be described at some length below. Usually they were built out of clay, using the same sort of building techniques as houses. Sometimes, however, they incorporated earth from termite hills or kaolin. In certain areas, they were provided with a thatched roof shelter. Tuyeres, providing for air intake, were also made of clay and termite mounds, but in some cases they were fired for added strength.

Among the shaft furnaces, the most interesting division, technologically speaking, is between those that depended on bellows to reach smelting tem-

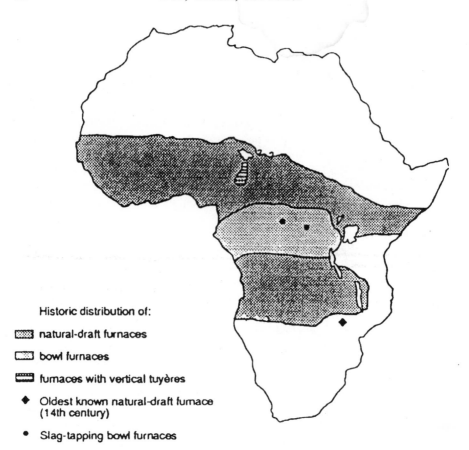

Historic distribution of:

▓ natural-draft furnaces

▢ bowl furnaces

▤ furnaces with vertical tuyères

♦ Oldest known natural-draft furnace (14th century)

● Slag-tapping bowl furnaces

Map 3. Historic distribution of natural-draft, vertical-tuyere, and slag-tapping bowl furnaces (Killick 1991b).

peratures and those that accomplished this by induced or natural draft, that is, by air being drawn in at the base of the furnace and rising as it was heated (figs. 3 and 4). Except for a single example in Burma, Africa is the only place in the world where natural draft furnaces have been documented with certainty, although there is speculation that they may have existed in Europe in earlier times. The most unusual arrangement among the bellows-driven furnaces, found only in northern Cameroon and northeastern Nigeria, employed a vertical tuyere running the height of the shaft and connected with bellows operated on a raised platform (map 3) (Killick 1991b).

While some blooms were pure enough to forge directly, others needed to be refined in a furnace much smaller than that used in smelting or in the forge by hammering to remove slag and charcoal. This also tended to remove carbon from the metal in the case of carbon steels produced in the smelting process. Once reduced to a relatively pure if not necessarily homogeneous metal, the iron was ready for the blacksmith.

Where smelting paraphernalia and process showed a dizzying variety, smithing was pretty much the same everywhere until the advent of imported, industrially produced tools, and even these have not changed it radically. Essentially the smithy consists of an open charcoal hearth, bellows, a hammer, and an anvil. Interestingly enough, metal tools did not necessarily make stone ones obsolete. A stone anvil might remain the cornerstone of the forge, and unhafted stone hammers often were more efficient for removing impurities from bloom and for preliminary forging than iron ones (cf. Dugast 1986). In other areas the primary tool might be an iron implement with a rounded head at one end and a tapered spike at the other that could serve as either hammer or anvil—in the latter case it was usually embedded in a log resting on the ground.

Iron bars were imported from Europe into coastal areas of West Africa in increasing quantities from the seventeenth century on and undoubtedly had a severe impact on smelting in these areas, but it is difficult to say how far inland this impact extended. Certainly Denis Williams (1974) is correct in suggesting that demand for iron imports reflected an "iron hunger" in much of Africa, a demand exceeding supply from indigenous sources. Nevertheless, I cannot accept his thesis that the revolutionary consequences of iron were felt in Africa *only* with the advent of this import trade, nor that the ritualization of the metal dates from this period. The evidence is far too slim to support his claims and is refuted by massive amounts of counterevidence for the ritualization of iron in interior areas unaffected by imports before the late nineteenth century. As with his interpretations of Nigerian bronzes, his eagerness to postulate outside influences on African belief and technology goes well beyond the data. Incidentally, virtually all reports concur that African-produced iron tools were believed by their users to be stronger and more durable than imports.

In spite of competition from imported metal in coastal areas, bloomery furnaces, whether driven by bellows or reliant on natural draft, were still in operation throughout the continent in the first decades of the colonial period. Indeed, iron industries in some areas were conducting interesting experiments (Fowler 1990; Célis 1988), both in adaptive technologies and in new forms of labor organization, experiments which unfortunately were cut short by the imposition of colonial rule and integration into the colonial economy. In most regions indigenous iron smelting was hard hit by the flood of cheap imported scrap metal early in the present century; by the 1920s the industry was moribund, persisting until after World War II in only a few remote regions. The last regularly functioning smelting furnace ceased production in 1985 at Koni in northern Ivory Coast (*Fraternité Matin*, 15 July 1985), although there are reports that hard times have brought about a revival in northern Ghana. Essentially, however, African ironworking locales are now "archaeological sites." All that separates them for the moment from "absolute archaeology" is the fact that one can still find actors in this industry and with their help reconstruct its outlines (see the appendix). Unfortunately, even this will no longer be possible within a few years (Gouletquer 1983:186); it may already be too late.

The same is not true for smithing. Smiths are still much in demand, both to make objects out of scrap metal and to repair everything from hoes to automobiles. The village smithy is still apt to be a hub of activity, a place where people—primarily men and boys—congregate to watch, to take their turn at the bellows, and to exchange the news.

THE SMITH AS CULTURE HERO

The working of metals is a crucial enterprise, as the voluminous literature on the smith attests, and precisely because of this it has usually been viewed as exceptional. The smith is a culture hero of Promethean proportions, living outside society, mediating between the natural and supernatural domains.[1] This is an image that contains a great deal of truth for many African societies but is hardly recognizable in others. Attempts to generalize about the role and social status of the smith in Africa have foundered in the face of seemingly unmanageable diversity: here the smith is simply an artisan, there he is not only metalworker but also circumciser, burier of the dead, diviner, musician, maker of charms, peacemaker, and counselor of kings. The Mafa (Cameroon) smith is the *maître de deuil*, overseeing all the activities of death and burial (Podlewski 1965:14–17); the Hausa smith of the Ader region (Niger) is associated only with the ceremonies of life, never with those of death (Echard 1965:367). Here, anyone can learn the trade through payment and apprenticeship; there, one must be born a smith and marry only within other smithing lineages. Here, the smith differs little from anyone else socially; there, he is a polluted outsider. Or, in a total reversal, he is—at least on a symbolic level—the king himself. Among the Gbaya of the Central African Republic, the metallurgist is exceptional only while he is smelting (Moñino 1983:288).

No doubt much of this variability has existed as long as metals have been worked in Africa, that is, for more than two thousand years in some areas, and is thoroughly consistent with the diversity of African cultures and their interactions with each other over time. Even within a single ethnic group one cannot assume either a uniformity of technology or of social roles (Sutton 1985:165–66). Unfortunately, given the absence of written records and the imprecision of oral traditions on such matters, the documentation does not exist to follow this historical evolution very far back in most societies. The problem is compounded by the extinction of smelting in our own century, which has undoubtedly skewed the record radically. The knowledge of smelting is rapidly being lost so that only smithing survives.

---

1. Barley (1984) attacks the "smithing obsession" as largely a fiction of western observers, but I am not convinced. See Chapter 8.

And yet many traditions emphasize that the quintessential smith was he who not only forged iron but knew the secrets of smelting:

> Eee blacksmiths are numerous,
> Ah but blacksmiths who can melt stone into iron have grown rare.
> Bee hunters are numerous, lion killers are scarce.
> (McNaughton 1982:9–10)

Iron smelting was the "apex of traditional technology" (ibid.:15);[2] the smelter, the "grand forgeron" (Zahan 1980:141). There were, of course, many societies in areas without workable ores that therefore never smelted and had to obtain their iron from those who did, a circumstance which no doubt heightened the mystique of smelting. Even today indigenously smelted iron and remains of slag are still important in certain ritual contexts—especially those concerned with healing and infertility (Berglund 1991:269–70; Pole 1982:511; McNaughton 1988:114; Iroko 1989:13; Ramona Austin pers. comm. 1991). The smith, too, has found his role changing until he has become less a creator than a repairman. Some have given up the craft altogether: among the Matakam (Cameroon), a fourth of the smiths no longer forge at all (Podlewski 1966:13). Just how these changes have affected the remembered past and the ensemble of beliefs about metalworking is often difficult to fathom.

The distinction between smith and smelter is often blurred (vid. Dupré 1981–82:196), but it is a crucial one. Referring to the mosaic of populations south of Lake Chad, Wente-Lukas (1972:126) calls attention to the greater role of "magico-religious practices" in cultures that smelt iron as opposed to those that simply forge. The same observation could be extended to other parts of the continent. In Babungo in the Cameroon Grassfields there is, in fact, an "ideological separation of smith and smelter": not only is what they do different, it is also conceptualized and organized differently (Fowler 1990:287). Indeed, the belief that smelting provides the primary arena in which ideas of transformation are played out has determined the emphasis in this book.

In practice, however, the distinction is impossible to adhere to strictly, above all because of the changes in the past century and the ambiguities of the sources. Even the detailed exegesis of Dogon myths by Griaule and Dieterlen fails to take account of the difference, perhaps because smelting had died out among the Dogon by the 1930s. In common usage, *smith* is a generic term, covering the gamut of metallurgical activities. Nevertheless, it is difficult to generalize about African metallurgy because there is so much variation in degrees of specialization. Sometimes, it is true, a single technologist will mine and prepare metallic ores, manufacture charcoal, build a furnace and carry out smelting in it, perform the vital rituals himself, and forge the raw iron into finished implements. Usually, however, the smith/smelter calls on a

---

2. *Pace* Pole (1982), who argues for the preeminence of the smith over the smelter.

work force that may be limited to peers and apprentices or that may include a larger contingent of kin and nonkin assistants. And where metallurgy is intensive, specialist groups will parcel out activities such as mining, smelting, refining, and forging. At the risk of occasional repetition, I will try to clarify the distinction between roles in what follows.

So much attention has been paid to who the smith is—to his social status and his multiple roles—that what he does as a metallurgist has often been neglected. Examining more closely what he does and then how it parallels other activities can provide a dimension that has frequently been missing in earlier studies. Above all, by reinserting the smith into a specific context, we can hope to see in what ways and at what moments he is exceptional and with whom he shares this exceptionality. This in turn will provide clues to more general beliefs about access to and manipulation of power.

TECHNOLOGY, GENDER, AND AGE

Since metallurgy is an arena where gender concepts seem often to be writ large, a study of the convergence of metalworking and gender illuminates both subjects. What I have only gradually come to realize is that concepts of age and the relationship between the living and the dead are equally important. Together they provide a framework of interpretation that makes intelligible the transformation of ore into implements with which to dominate the natural world by casting it into the language of primary social relationships: most obviously those of male and female, human and spirit, or, to be more precise, husband and wife, parent and child, and ancestor and living descendants because they always involve cultural definitions and, implicitly, cultural norms, not purely biological ones.

Precisely because gender concepts are so fundamental in any society they are rarely articulated as such. They are part of the "tacit knowledge" (Sperber 1975:x–xi; cf. Douglas 1957:46) of a group, so obvious and so "natural" as not to need any explanation. As Jean Comaroff (1985:124ff.) has commented, cosmological systems—of which gender is a key component—are only translated into "beliefs" when they confront alien views of the world. Here, indeed, is a prime area where we must look to actions and symbols rather than words to see how gender is acted out in everyday and in exceptional situations. And I would agree with Sperber that these actions and the symbolism of which they are a part are more than an instrument of social communication; they "participate in the construction of knowledge and in the functioning of memory" (1975:xii).

The role of age, generational relationships, and the community of the living and the dead as it is formulated in different African societies is harder for westerners to understand, and it was only belatedly that I came to realize its importance to my work. At the risk of oversimplifying, we can say that power augments with age, not simply because of greater wisdom achieved through experience, but because in a world traditionally beset by high mortality, a long life is not an accident—it depends on and gives witness to some degree of control of spiritual forces. The ultimate power is therefore vested in ancestors. But it is not only long life that is valued: the fully human man or woman is also the parent of living children. Here notions of age intersect with those of procreativity, for the ancestors are linked to the family by bonds of reciprocity; Karp (1988) has even referred to them as part of the family "labor force." While they intervene in powerful ways that fundamentally affect the fortunes of their descendants, they are equally dependent on them for their continued vitality through the rituals that must be performed. If a family line comes to an end, the tragedy takes on more than human dimensions—hence the extraordinary premium set on procreativity and efforts devoted to ensuring it.

Ancestors play a vital but not an exclusive role in human events. Most African cultures also see the world populated by a multiplicity of other divinities and spirits who must be placated to obtain their favor and avoid their malevolence. Sometimes specific deities are believed to oversee crafts such as iron, as in the case of the Yoruba Ogun or Irungu in the Bacwezi pantheon (Schmidt 1990:269–70); at other times it is the spirits of the bush and the earth whom one must appease to acquire wood and ore. Like ancestors, these supernatural entities can assist or harm humans and human activities according to how they are treated; much of the knowledge of the specialist, whether smelter, diviner, or "*féticheur*," is devoted to assuring their goodwill and active cooperation. The spirits and deities may themselves be organized in kinship groups, identified by gender and age relationships to one another. Some, however, are androgynous or entirely sexless.

The same knowledge applies equally to combating another category of powerful forces: witches. Witchcraft is so complex and takes so many forms in Africa that one hesitates to speak about it in the singular. Whereas the other forms of supernatural beings are neutral, capable of bringing good or evil, witches are by definition to be feared. In essence, witchcraft is the explanation provided for the evil and misfortune that cannot be understood by reference to other loci of power. It is the power of the envious and of the self-aggrandizing. In some societies it is virtually synonymous with individual success and acquisition of power: the king is, ipso facto, a witch; so may be anyone who manages to live to old age. Laura Bohannan has made us well aware of the Tiv belief that people can only be bewitched by relatives in the male line (1975; cf. idem 1954), while Zoë Strother notes that successful circumcisers among the Pende are automatically deemed to be witches (1992). Though they are not the only characteristics, it is interesting to see that longevity, the rare achievement of old age, in one case, and the circumciser's ability to "create" males, in another, may be attributed to witchcraft. Unfortunately, although accounts may refer to invocation of benign spirits and attempts to protect against malevolent ones, they often do not define them very precisely.

A focus on gender, sexuality, and age as they are manifest in the various aspects of ironworking can enlarge our understanding of African metallurgy and at the same time underscore the commonalities metallurgy shares with other transformational processes such as hunting and investiture. These, too, reveal a preoccupation with fertility and reproduction, with power and vulnerability, and, like ironworking, they are activities monopolized by males— a fact which suggests a special appropriation of procreative powers.

I am aware that some readers may see the argument as a form of neodiffusionism because it postulates a single paradigm underlying the variable epiphenomena. As with my earlier study of copper in Africa, I was surprised when the evidence, so various at first glance, began to point to similarities in basic beliefs explaining transformation throughout sub-Saharan Africa. However, there are some basic differences, and I will discuss them at several points and in my concluding chapter.

Since these beliefs are derived, in my view, from direct experience and its articulation with elementary forms of social structure, it really should not be surprising that they give a primacy to the factors of gender and age. As I will suggest in the conclusion, this model of the world is not unique to Africa and still has vestiges in our own ways of thinking.

THE STATE OF THE PROBLEM
AND THE PLAN OF THIS BOOK

The best sources, few in number, are those that record the metallurgical processes of smelting and refining in their heyday, while they were still part of ordinary praxis. These are uneven, however, in that some of them focus narrowly on technology, ignoring symbolic and social aspects. In others the problem is the reverse, a neglect of the details of the technology.

In more recent times a surprising number of reconstructions have been commissioned and documented (see the appendix). I have participated in two of them, the first in Banjeli, Togo (1985), the second in Lopanzo, Zaïre (1989). Of course, the authenticity of reconstructions is problematic. For starters, the intervention of the western researcher, whether male or female, must be assumed to have an impact on what happens. Participants have to reckon with the alien presence and where he or she fits into the immediate scheme of social and economic relationships and the larger picture of conflicting belief systems. As Ian Fowler has observed: "You, *qua* the reconstructor, are not anything at all like a fly on the wall; rather, you are the flywheel and the engine of what is going on" (pers. comm.).

One must keep in mind, too, that although the activity no longer plays the central role it once did, experts may be unwilling to disclose all of the rituals and medicinal substances because these still represent a considerable repository of power when applied in other realms. Further, in most cases reconstructions have depended on the fallible memories of elders who were young men or even children when they last observed or participated in the process. Nor is memory the only problem: because of their youth they were probably not privy to all the secrets of the trade (Fowler n.d.). Consequently, we must expect that in some cases, at least, there may be a fair amount of ad-libbing going on.[3]

Nevertheless, reconstructions are often the best source we have, the last chance to salvage both technical and ritual practices. Ideally, they can be checked against other sources of information and against comparable activities. The Mafa reconstructions arranged by Nicholas David have been particularly valuable because they have illustrated variability not only within a single culture but by a single smelter, a fact which argues still more against any notion of rigid "traditional" practice. Some of these reconstructions have been well documented in photographs and films (Herbert and Pole 1989).

In addition to studies based on direct observation, a substantial body of oral tradition has been collected by fieldworkers throughout the continent, most notably by Célis, who has done exhaustive research on all aspects of metalworking in Rwanda, Burundi, Equateur (Zaïre), and Ivory Coast. His magnificent *Eisenhütten in Afrika* (1991) became available too late for me to incorporate it into this study, but it represents a major contribution. For technologies themselves I have found the work of David Killick most helpful.

The sexualization of metalworking has struck observers in many parts of the world. It has been developed most broadly by Mircea Eliade in his *Forgerons et Alchimistes* (1956), translated as *The Forge and the Crucible* (1962). Eliade was not an Africanist, and in his treatment of Africa he was also limited by the material available to him and by his own world-historical approach. Inevitably, his narrow emphasis on the sexualization of metalworking and on metallurgy as obstetrics led to monolithic overgeneralization and oversimplification: above all, he missed the larger world of social relationships mirrored in metallurgical processes and the particularities of individual African cultures in his tendency to see something intrinsic in metals that determined attitudes toward them. Nevertheless, he demonstrates that the procreative paradigm is not peculiar to African metalworking but can be found widely among preindustrial societies.

Walter Cline, who pioneered the study of the technical, social, and ritual aspects of metalworking and whose *Mining and Metallurgy in Negro Africa* (1937) remains an indispensable base, was more sensitive to the cultural milieu that shaped African metalworking practices and rituals and much more impressed by the seemingly infinite variety of the evidence. Cline's monograph is surely one of the most influential works ever to exist only in mimeograph form, both for its remarkable command of the then-available literature

---

3. Zoë Strother comes to the same conclusion about Pende investiture. In one area, a chiefly investiture had not occurred in more than thirty years, thanks to the longevity of the incumbent. Consequently, the memory of some of the rituals was clearly hazy (pers. comm.).

and for the judiciousness of its analysis. Cline's work has been the starting point for both of my studies of African metallurgy, and each time I return to it I am impressed anew with his breadth and insights.

More recently the synthesizing work of several writers, most notably Pierre de Maret (1980, 1985), has confirmed the direction of my own thinking about metalworking, procreation, and power. De Maret focuses primarily on Central Africa. Specialized studies of ironworking in other areas such as those of Echard (1965, 1968, 1983), van der Merwe and Avery (1987), Rowlands and Warnier (1988), and Fowler (1990) have also affirmed the intensely sexual and procreative nature of the processes, albeit with significant variants. Childs (1991a) has, in addition, proposed the term *technological style* to embrace the total context of practices such as metalworking. This she defines as "the formal integration of the behaviors chosen during the manufacture and use of material culture which, in its entirety, expresses social information." In the case of iron smelting, technological style embraces both the smelters and the work they perform, the choreographer and the choreography, as she expresses it, offering a theoretical framework for the specifics of belief and the ways in which it affects behavior. To some extent this pursues Cline's conclusion that the varied forms which the ritualization of iron takes "depend rather on other conditions within the culture than on a peculiar set of social and religious attitudes which the craft carries with it"—that is, on some mystical quality ascribed uniquely to iron (1937:114).

The literature on chiefly investiture in Africa and the cosmological basis of political power is as extensive as that on metallurgy. Perhaps in reaction to Frazer, however, it tends to take the form of detailed case studies, many of which provide superbly nuanced explications of the meaning of the much abused term *divine kingship*. I have benefited especially from the researches of Mertens (1942), Vansina (1973, 1978), de Heusch (1975), Packard (1981), Adler (1982), Fortier (1982), Devisch (1988), and Pemberton (1989). In contrast, the literature on hunting is sparse, and the schema proposed has been teased out of a number of works, inspired especially by Mary Douglas's studies of the Lele (1954, 1963) and the work of Victor Turner (esp. 1953, 1968). It is ironic that African pottery, so long a mainstay of archaeology, has been signally neglected by historians, anthropologists, and art historians. Field studies of potting are far less numerous than those of metalworking (reflecting, perhaps, a gender-bias inasmuch as pottery in Africa is predominantly a female activity), but scholars such as Quarcoo and Johnson (1968), Barley (1984), Stössel (1984), David, Sterner, and Gavua (1988), Sterner (1989), Berns (1988, 1989a, 1989b, 1990), Hardin (1988), Kreamer (1989), and Spindel (1989a) are now looking closely at the ways in which pottery practices reflect social values and beliefs.

It is also only recently that scholars have begun adequately to explore the meaning of gender not only in these particular domains but also more broadly (see, e.g., Ardener [1968] 1975; MacCormack and Strathern 1980; Scott 1988; H. L. Moore 1988; di Leonardo 1991). Here I have found Scott's definition the most relevant. She distinguishes two separate but integrally related propositions: first, that "gender is a constitutive element of social relationships based on perceived differences between the sexes," and second, that "gender is a primary way of signifying relationships of power" (1988:42). In other words, it is culturally and historically specific because it derives from perceptions of sexual difference rather than the differences themselves, and it is embedded in a power field. Further, the symbols through which notions of gender are expressed often reflect contradictions within the culture. Thus, the antithetical images of Eve (or Lillith) and Mary in the Judaeo-Christian tradition have their counterpart in the witch/nurturing-mother dichotomy found in African societies. Notions of gender will also change as social and power relationships change, but this is much harder to track, especially in the African context, because of the limited historical material.

The distinction between gender and biological sex has come as something of a revelation to western scholars, and yet the abundant literature on initiation makes clear that Africans have known all along that gender is socially, not biologically, created and that it evolves over the life cycle. Personhood does not come "naturally" but must be achieved though the intervention of relevant groups. By extension, therefore, gender is also an important element in healing rituals as René Devisch shows so beautifully in his book *Se recréer femme* (1984). Indeed, the work of Devisch and his student Filip De Boeck and of the scholars brought together by Anita Jacobson-Widding in Uppsala shows just how rich exegesis can be that combines more traditional themes of body imagery and personhood with gender analysis and semantic exploration.

The same sort of attention needs to be focused on age and death. Just as one does not become an adult by living to puberty, one does not become an ancestor simply by dying: here, too, even when one has the prerequisites of advanced age and successful reproductivity, it is only ritual action that accomplishes the wished-for transformation. Further, the relationship between the living and the dead perpetuates notions of reciprocity that structure social relationships generally and may reinforce distinctions of gender and seniority.

None of the studies of African metallurgy I have cited has had the temerity to look at sub-Saharan Africa as a whole and explore more extensively the implications of the genderization of the process and the significance of the rituals and prohibitions that commonly accompany it, nor have they fully dealt with genealogical aspects. Furthermore, with the exception of Pierre de Maret and Terry Childs, most scholars have tended not so much to integrate iron-working with other transformative processes as to emphasize its exceptionality. My purpose, therefore, is twofold: to put this intersection of technology and gender/age under a microscope and see what it reveals, then to consider whether the model derived from metalworking can help also to illuminate other technologies of transformation, specifically the investiture of chiefs, hunting, and pottery.

Part I of the book provides a detailed overview of metallurgy in sub-Saharan Africa, with a particular focus on iron smelting, which, it is argued, is or was the primary metallurgical activity, the stage on which beliefs were most prominently acted out. It is not a study of the smith per se, that is, not primarily a study of his social status. Rather, it looks at what he does and what that tells us about the transformative process.

I propose to look first at work roles, then at the forms given to the central artifacts of metalworking—furnaces and bellows—and their positioning in space. In the most overt examples, these paraphernalia take on male and female forms and a technological genealogy. What I will also argue is that even when the forms are not overt, genderization and social identity are achieved by other means and reiterated by the rituals, exclusions, prohibitions, and prescriptions surrounding smelting in sub-Saharan Africa as a whole. The totality of the process thus invokes the paradigms of procreation and of the living and the dead, not only as part of the explanatory process but *actively*, to make things happen.

The most obvious advantage of the comparative method, as I have noted, is that it suggests explanations for phenomena that examined in a single case might seem incomprehensible. While an encyclopedic inventory of the statuses and roles assigned to the smith in different societies may indeed be a "sterile" enterprise, I agree with Boyer (1983:60) that when one looks at the symbolic systems—infinitely variable though they may appear to be—and how they are embedded in an ordinary understanding of the world, several relatively simple models may emerge. The basic assumption that guides this method is that there is an intimate relationship between technology and culture.

The disadvantage of the comparative approach is that the reader, especially the non-Africanist reader, may feel overwhelmed by legions of unfamiliar names and excessive detail. This is unfortunately unavoidable since the point is to show how extremely variable practices are even while arguing for underlying patterns. I have tried to provide summary introductions and conclusions to each chapter to make the argument clearer. Certain names will recur more than others, like themes in a piece of music, and I hope that gradually the reader will begin to recognize them as old friends. To aid in the process Map 1 locates the most frequently mentioned ethnic groups and places. It is nonetheless sobering to reflect that perhaps fifty ethnic groups are mentioned in the text out of perhaps a thousand in all of sub-Saharan Africa and that there is no reason to assume homogeneity even within a single ethnic group since we are more and more aware that ethnicity is a fragile and historically suspect category for much of Africa. While many peoples practiced metallurgy only minimally, for the rest, information is simply lacking. This is especially true of cultures south of the Limpopo.

Part II surveys two other masculine activities of transformation that embody many of the same features as metalworking: royal investiture and hunting. It draws on a variety of studies ranging from ethnographic accounts of investiture rituals to structuralist interpretations of myth and legend to propose a more general theory of transformation based on the paradigm of human reproduction that seems to be found in many societies.

Whereas these activities offer fundamental symmetries in underlying conceptualization as well as in details of practice, there is a curious asymmetry when one compares metalworking with pottery. Pottery is often seen as the female analogue of metallurgy since it is usually women's work; particularly in West Africa the potter is commonly the smith's wife. Potting might therefore be expected to be a mirror image of metalworking, and to some extent it is. However, we shall see that ultimately the two activities are disparate in the degree of ritualization and in the power they encode.

Finally, I will discuss the implications such a model has as a vision of gender relations and of power over the natural world. The reader will be aware of a deliberate shift in approach and even style between the two parts: having set up the model in the first in exhaustive detail, I have preferred to carry out the comparisons in the second using a broader brush.

There are, to be sure, major problems in such an agenda. The data on earlier metalworking, it must be emphasized, are often of very mixed quality and above all frustratingly incomparable. This is even more the case when one tries to compare metalworking with other activities: where there is good material on metalworking, there may be little or no information about pottery, hunting, initiation, and so forth, nor about indigenous beliefs concerning conception, pregnancy, birth, or sexuality. I can testify from firsthand experience how difficult it is to obtain data about such beliefs. Skillful female interpreters may be hard to find and informants are often reluctant to talk to outsiders—more basically, one may be at a loss how even to pose questions that are comprehensible. Myths and legends, where they exist, may offer some corroborating evidence, but their meaning is not always clear and their historical value is a matter of much debate.

The converse is equally true. Ethnographers of the Griaule school have been particularly sensitive to the role of gender in African cosmology and to the degree to which it has been used as a primary category of classification, but they have been inclined to idealize their subjects and have neglected technology as such. More troubling, their methodology has been questioned and their data have been viewed with much skepticism by others working in the same areas (van Beek 1991). Germaine Dieterlen's *Essai sur la religion bambara* (1951) is a prime example and will be discussed more fully in Chapter 4.

Finally, even if we postulate a persistence of core beliefs over time, social and political change do alter symbolic systems and make their decoding increasingly difficult—and this is true of historical change before as well as during the colonial and postcolonial periods. The "symbolic cryptographies" embedded in the processes discussed here have inevitably been eroded, leaving fragmented rather than whole structures. In Hunt's words, "historical losses in symbolic structure hide, over time, the structure's total meaning" (1977:32). The task, then, is to reconstruct them as best we can.

The hypotheses presented in the conclusion are therefore meant to be a challenge rather than an assertion, a plea for more work to confirm, refute, or modify them. Let us proceed cautiously, however, heeding the sage dictum that "it is best to look after the data and hope that the paradigms will look after themselves" (Prins 1980:3–4).

Why should we care about a technology that clearly cannot compete with modern industry, that was laborious and often frustrating, that occasionally failed and at times was even dangerous? Why indeed should we care about a technology that relied on a body of expertise, practical and ritual, to exclude women and the less powerful in the service of an often arbitrary authority?

We should care because, with the extinction of so central an enterprise as African iron smelting, we are losing the chance to see beliefs evolved over centuries—social, economic, political, religious—acted out in all their complexity, variability, and adaptability. If metalworking was indeed a microcosm of beliefs and practices, its demise is comparable to the loss of a great work of art or of the Alexandrine library. In societies where traditions were passed on orally and where the most important secrets were handed down only to those who had demonstrated their eligibility, the line of transmission has been abruptly and brutally severed. "Chaque veillard qui meurt dans la brousse," declared the Fulani scholar Hampaté Ba, "c'est une bibliothèque qui brûle." Nowhere is this truer than in the case of the African iron smelter.

Nevertheless, many of the ideas that structured iron technology and analogous transformative activities we will be surveying survive in transmuted form in other arenas. Indeed, the adaptability and resilience of African beliefs has been a leitmotif of recent studies of religion in Africa and the Diaspora. The "fugue of gender" in Bwiti religious rituals of the present-day Fang, for example, although fusing Christian with non-Christian belief and practice, becomes more understandable once we see the connections between gender separation and proscribed sexuality with enhanced fertility in earlier rituals of transformation (Fernandez 1982, 1991; Werbner 1990). And should we really be surprised that a well-educated inspector of schools in Sierra Leone insists that ancestral blessing is the key to children's success in school (Bledsoe 1992:182)?

Ultimately, the story of metallurgy is an excursus about power, and in that respect we would do well to meditate upon its lessons, however removed they may at first seem from life in the modern world. Power is perhaps the least understood concept going, for all that we refer to it incessantly. African cosmologies tried to deal with it head on, and the results are well worth pausing over.

PART ONE

Those Who Play with Fire
African Metallurgy as
Epic Drama

ONE

The Actors and the Artifacts

> If a woman tried to use a smith's tools, he would
> make a fetish that would render her infertile.
>
> Lotoy, smith, Lopanzo, Zaïre

The exuberantly gynecomorphic furnaces of Central Africa first attracted me
to this subject. Surely, something interesting must be going on if metallurgists went to such lengths to adorn their smelting furnaces with breasts, navels, scarification patterns, and beaded belts. But was this only a regional
phenomenon? What about traditions where there were no such external signs—
were there other ways to make the same statement, or was an entirely different ideology at work? These are the questions I will be addressing in this
chapter and the following.

First, however, we must look at the allocation of work roles and the fundamental question of who may become a smith or smelter, since this is essential to any understanding of what metallurgy involves.

WORK ROLES AND THE SEXUAL DIVISION OF LABOR

The smith and smelter are always male. While women may be employed
in parts of the metallurgical process, they are never in control of either the
key technological or ritual procedures. To be sure, there are a few legends
that things were not always thus. Hausa smelters in Ader (Niger) claim that
once upon a time women did the smelting but gave it up because it was such
hard work (Echard 1983:220; cf. idem 1965:354ff.). One of Célis's informants
in Rwanda, an elderly smelter, insisted that ironworking had first been introduced to the country by a female chief (1988:78). The Chokwe have a similar
legend about the introduction of smelting by way of a Lunda woman who
transmitted the knowledge to her husband (Martins 1966:42; Mesquitela Lima
1977:350). Like similar traditions about the origin of secret societies or about
times when women ran things (usually incompetently or oppressively), we
should probably not take them as historical fact. In any event, they refer to
times so firmly in the past that they have no apparent relevance to current
practice.

But this does not mean that every male can become a smith. Whether one is born a smith or becomes one depends on the society in question. Throughout much of west Africa, smiths must be members of endogamous occupational groups, sometimes referred to as "castes" (Tamari 1991; McNaughton 1988:9, 156–60). Members of these groups are not allowed to marry or have sexual relations with noncasted, free individuals of the society. In practice this means that one must be born into a smithing lineage to be a smith (unless one gains access through slave status). Not all males so born actually choose to take up the trade, however, nor do those who do necessarily work at it full time. These endogamous groups are best known among the Mande-speaking peoples, but may be found as well in southeastern Nigeria and parts of Cameroon. Thus, the Amube clan of Amalla village are the only Orba (Ibo) smiths. According to Okafor (1989), they constitute a closed caste; non-Amube are not allowed to become smiths. The Mafa (Matakam) of northwestern Cameroon also form such a group. Absolute endogamy is the rule, with a strict division of the population into smiths and everyone else (Podlewski 1965:9–13). The distinction then extends to their wives, who also fill prescribed roles.

Where smiths form an endogamous group, there has been much discussion of the possible historical origin of such segregation. Do they represent autochthonous or earlier groups than the bulk of the population? Are they later arrivals or itinerants? Is their place in the social hierarchy and the attitude of others toward them a function of who they are (or were) or of what they do (including the roles they play in addition to metalworking, such as circumcision, burial, the preparation of charms)? According to some informants, the Dogon (Mali) explain the endogamy of the smith as the necessary result of a separate creation from the placenta of Nommo, which also conferred on them a mixed blood, made in part from the sacrificial blood of the god (Dieterlen 1965–66:10).

Recently, however, Tal Tamari has presented an exhaustively supported argument that artisan and musician castes developed among peoples of the western Sudan as a result of extensive cross-cultural borrowing: "They appeared among the Malinke no later than 1300, and were present among the Soninke and Wolof no later than 1500," that is, well after the adoption of ironworking technologies throughout the area (1991:221). From these centers castes spread to most other Sudanic peoples through migration. In an intriguing interpretation of the Sundjata epic, she proposes that caste differentiation occurred only after the Sosso-Malinke war, which forms the kernel of all versions of the poem and is usually dated to the early to mid-thirteenth century. This amounted to a deliberate effort to separate sources of power that had previously been concentrated in the person of Sumanguru, the blacksmith king of the Sosso. Smiths and musicians could not be deprived of their magical powers, but they could be redefined as specialist groups who could no longer aspire to kingship and hence posed no threat to the new Malinke dynasty established by Sundjata. The relation of smiths to kings and chiefs is a subject to which we will return in Chapter 6.

Although it may never be possible to explain their historical origins with certainty, what is striking about regions in which smiths form such endogamous groups is a *perception of difference* by both sides, smith and nonsmith. As Vaughan observes in his study of Marghi smiths (northeastern Nigeria): "They and their technology are mysterious because they are socially distinctive" (Vaughan 1973:166–67,190–91). This distinctiveness is not reducible to ordinary stratification, precisely because smiths, like other casted groups, are believed to have unique powers that enable them to fill their particular roles (cf. B. Wright 1989:42); only among some pastoralists such as Tuareg and Masai do they form a distinctly servile population.

In much of Central Africa, by contrast, access to the craft is not exclusively hereditary and smiths' wives play no special role. An aspirant can pay to become apprenticed and be accepted after learning the skills (de Maret 1980). Often his "graduation" and the establishment of a new forge are marked by a ritual akin to an initiation. In practice, to be sure, the trade often ends up being hereditary, passed down from father to son or nephew. A smith will only accept family members as apprentices (Weeks 1913:90) because the apprenticeship/initiation for outsiders is too expensive or simply because the son or nephew has had the advantage of growing up in the trade. Given the importance of ancestor-smiths to the success of smelting, at least a fictive kinship may have been more important than has been realized (see, e.g., Figueiredo Lima 1977:122). Among the Shona, for example, men often believe they are summoned to become smiths by the ancestors who manifest themselves in dreams or through illness (Dewey 1990), but this does not carry with it any obligation to endogamy.

The guildlike smithing organizations found in parts of Nigeria fall between the extremes but lean toward the strictly endogamous occupational groups because recruitment is closely controlled and sets a premium on kinship and residence in smithing quarters (Neaher 1979:357; Nadel 1942:257–74; Dark 1973:45ff.; Jaggar 1973b). Pole (1975:36) makes a similar comment about blacksmithing in northern Ghana: in principle it was open to any males, but in practice it was controlled by single smithing clans.

All of these systems, then, serve to exclude *most* of the population from the specialized knowledge, technical and "magical," that characterizes metallurgy and confers on its practitioners their unusual powers. Smiths everywhere have cultivated secrecy, both to enhance their own status and to protect themselves against sorcery. Control over metallurgy represents control not only over an economically valuable resource but over skills and knowledge that confer substantial power and are vested only in men, especially in the older masters of the craft.

As we have noted, African women are never smelters and never smiths. Paradoxically, however, they may contribute a significant amount of the labor required to prepare for smelting operations (Killick 1990:160; Herbert and Goucher 1987). As with the cultivation of indigenous staple crops, there is often what Guyer (1991:260) refers to as an "interdigitation" of male and female labor. Thus, women may gather or even mine ores, sort them, wash them, and prepare them for smelting. A few writers suggest that women are more apt to do surface gathering of ores while men do underground mining, but the evidence for this distinction is spotty (Martinelli 1982:39, 41; but cf. Gehrts 1915:246). What does seem to be generally true is that there is less ritualization of surface collection than of mining proper, and the greater the degree of ritualization, the more likely it is that women will be excluded or relegated to minor roles. The same proviso would seem to hold also for making charcoal. While women are less commonly charcoal makers than ore gatherers, there are areas such as Bassar where, at least in recent times, they seem to have been the primary manufacturers of charcoal, probably because of a shortage of male labor. And wherever there is carrying to be done, it is women who do it. Only where women were rigidly excluded from all stages of ironworking have they not served as porters (e.g., Carl and Petit 1955:60).

Constructing furnaces of clay is carried out by smelters and hence is a male occupation. Since women frequently participate in house construction, which uses the same techniques, one might expect them to be involved in this work also, but this rarely seems to be the case. Exceptionally, Haberland claims that the potter wives of the Dime of southwestern Ethiopia, like other "paleo-nigritic" peoples of the Sudan, did build the large smelting furnaces of the region (1964a:6). In the reconstruction of Mafa smelting, however, where the smith's wife was also a potter, she did not work on the furnace proper, but she did make the clay pots for the bellows and the crucibles used to refine bloomery iron. In addition, she fabricated the pot representing *zhikile* (God), which was placed by itself on the rocks near the furnace and which was the object of offerings and sacrifices during the smelt (David et al. 1989; cf. Sassoon 1964:177). Wives of Fipa smelters assisted their husbands in smoothing the wet clay on the furnace exteriors, although they were not allowed to work on the interior (Lechaptois 1932:242; Wyckaert 1914:372). Elsewhere, women frequently helped to prepare the clay and carry it to the furnace site but went no further. Even the clay tuyeres, which would seem to be most closely akin to pottery, were made by male smelters. The Fipa themselves, according to Wyckaert, were uncomfortable about this since pottery was woman's work. Their solution was to palm off the job on young men who hid themselves from public view to carry it out—a reminder of the lower status of young men.

Not only are women never smelters or smiths, but as a rule they cannot take part in the smelting process itself nor in the forging of metal. And yet, of course, there are exceptions. Whether these are solely a response to historical pressures is impossible to say, but however firmly gender boundaries seem to be fixed, like everything else in "traditional" societies, they do stretch and change. There are scattered references to women operating bellows for smelting or refining furnaces among the Ewe (Spiess 1899:64), Kabye (Cridel 1967:63), Dime (Todd n.d.), Beti (Guyer 1984:5), Masai (Cline 1937:115), and in southwestern Tanzania (Wright 1985:162). In We (Cameroon) the blacksmith's wife operated the bellows while he forged (Rowlands and Warnier 1988:29).

In some of these areas the scale of iron production may have been responsible for the employment of women in these roles. No doubt this was particularly true where increases in production during the nineteenth century outstripped the male labor supply (MacKenzie 1975:206–7). Wright speculates that iron smelters may have co-opted their daughters for tasks such as operating bellows during refining because by the 1930s and 1940s there were fewer young men available, especially young men who earlier would have performed this as part of brideservice but were now caught up in colonial patterns of labor migrancy. Jaggar (1973b:16) notes that young unmarried daughters of Kano blacksmiths sometimes helped out in the forge like their younger brothers, working bellows or polishing blades. Here, however, I believe the crucial condition is that they were unmarried, that is, in principle asexual.[1] In any case, it seems to have been a reluctant response to labor shortage as in Tanzania and earlier in Zimbabwe.

A quite different principle was probably at play in the structuring of smelting among the Kwanyama of southern Angola. Entire families set up the temporary camps in mining and smelting areas with no exclusion of women from the operation; indeed, women, children, and neighboring San ("Bushmen") would all take a turn at the bellows during the ten- to twelve-hour smelting sequence (Estermann 1976:148; Powell-Cotton 1937). One suspects that the involvement of all these groups was prescriptive as part of the understanding of what made the process successful, a subject we will return to when discussing ritual. On the other hand, given the scale of Kwanyama operations, labor needs may have influenced the organization of work (Angebauer 1927:111).

In northern Ghana, Pole found a remarkable variation in the role of women from site to site over a relatively small area. In the eastern part of the country, smelting was carried out by itinerant Busanga smiths working in family groups, which may or may not explain the integral role of women in all aspects of iron production. At Zanlerigu, on the other hand, the case was more likely to have been personal rather than institutional: the elder sister of the smith gained an ascendancy simply because she was more knowledgeable than her brother as well as physically strong enough to tackle the bellows. Pole suspects, however, that "in the old days," when smelting was done more regularly, women would not have been allowed to be so closely involved, whatever their qualities (pers. comm.). Nonetheless, this example does make more credible the report of the behind-the-scenes role of women in Katangan copper working. "The knowledge of the metallurgic technique," writes Rickard (1927:57), "is retained by the old women of the village, and they are highly regarded. They transmit their knowledge to their successors, mem-

---

1. Girls might also do odd jobs around the foundry before the onset of menstruation in Babungo (Cameroon) (Fowler 1990:153).

bers, as it were, of a guild." We will have more to say about the role of older women later.

While it may seem too obvious to mention, a primary role of women in African ironworking has been as cooks and brewers of beer, no mean feat in areas where teams of metalworkers might number in the scores or even hundreds and where smelting might continue for weeks at a time. Since smelting often took place away from the village, either for reasons of secrecy and seclusion or simply to be near supplies of ore, this also meant carrying food and drink long distances. Provisioning the work sites became enmeshed, in turn, in the rituals, taboos, and prescriptions of metallurgy itself.

Is there an underlying structure to the division of male and female labor in ironworking? Almost two centuries ago, Mungo Park commented that among the Mandingo the washing of gold ores was women's work because it resembles the winnowing of grain (1799:217–18). The same analogy can be made between pulverizing ore and pounding grain or other staples—in some areas the same mortar and pestle are used as for pounding yams (Bellamy and Harbord 1904:103).[2] Surface mining itself seems very close to gathering and other female agricultural activities, especially where the ore is in the form of black magnetite washed out of river sands.

The criteria of physical strength and the need to adapt work to pregnancy, nursing, and the care of small children do not adequately explain the assignment of metalworking roles. First of all, women *do* prepare charcoal, physically a very demanding job. Bassari and Konkomba women, for example, produce charcoal for both smelting and forging and carry the heavy straw baskets long distances on their heads. Mining and gathering ore require that they often travel far from their villages. Meg Gehrts (1915:246) paints a graphic picture of the women miners of Banjeli, in western Togo, digging out ore, their babies at the breast—a scene captured on film, in fact, by Hans Schomburgk.[3] True, Gehrts claims these women were slaves, but local traditions here and in other areas confirm that mining was also done by free women and children.

Working the bellows is extremely strenuous, especially during smelting operations where it may continue for hours—with forging it is not as continuous and may even be done by children—and yet we have seen that it is not beyond women's capacities. Smelting in natural draft furnaces, on the other hand, requires no great physical exertion at all but rather a command of ritual knowledge and an expertise in combining the right quantities of ore and fuel and controlling air flow. One might even say that it requires some of the instincts of the good cook who senses intuitively what is going on in the pot or the oven.

---

2. Dumett (1987:216–17) comments that women pulverized and winnowed gold ore in the Wassa region of Ghana using techniques almost certainly adapted from the traditional method of preparing "kenkey," a type of bread made by crushing maize between two stones.

3. This clip is included in the film *The Blooms of Banjeli* (1986).

Forging, however, does require immense strength in the upper torso. Incidentally, in the Bassar region, three of the four smiths interviewed in 1985 were lame, providing a curious corroboration of Norse and Greco-Roman mythology: what would have been an impossible handicap for farming and hunting was no impediment to smithing since they had powerfully built shoulders and arms. Physiologically women may not be able to develop the same sort of strength, although anyone who has taken a hand with the heavy wooden pestles African women wield year in and year out must wonder . . .[4] The one exception I have come across demonstrates that women were physically capable of smithing. Formerly, Gbaya women who were born as twins could exercise all male occupations and roles except warfare but including forging (Vergiat 1937:50). Here, cultural beliefs about twins clearly predominate over other determinants of gender.

Biology, then, is as unsatisfactory in explaining the allocation of male and female work roles in metalworking as in other areas. Only a few male activities require brute strength, while those commonly performed by women demand a great deal of stamina and often take them far from home. As Guyer has pointed out, the task most universally assigned to women—cooking—has nothing to do with physiology and can be downright dangerous when combined with caring for small children (Guyer 1981). On a cosmological level, however, it has analogies with gestation that are often explicitly recognized.[5]

We must also consider the role of women as wives and daughters of smiths. Not only does this status lead to their inclusion in the work force during metalworking operations where other women might be excluded, but it may also dictate other activities. Most commonly the wives of smiths are potters. This is particularly true in West Africa where smiths form endogamous lineages, but it may also be found elsewhere. There may, in fact, be a correlation with smithing: where any man may become a smith, any woman may become a potter (cf. Pole 1975:35–36); conversely, when a particular clan has a monopoly on metalworking, it may also have a monopoly on potting.

Where smiths are circumcisers, as among the Mande, their wives are excisers (Dieterlen 1951:188; Appia 1965:320) and midwives (Ardouin 1978:17). Among the Mafa of northern Cameroon, both the smith and his wife attend women in childbirth and offer treatment for sterility (Podlewski 1966:32–33)—in the context of their general marginality, gender differences seem less accentuated. It is not clear whether the smith's wife also plays a prominent role in Mafa rituals of death, which are the special province of her husband (cf. Cline 1937:186).

---

4. Cf. Mary Kingsley's description of Fang forging: "The hammers are solid cones of iron, the upper part of the cones prolonged so as to give a good grip, and the blows are given directly downwards, like the blows of a pestle" (1898:260).

5. One of the great ironies of colonial rule in Africa was the transfer of this labor from the female to the male domain among those recruited to work for Europeans.

GYNECOMORPHIC FURNACES

From the gender-specificity of work roles let us turn to the artifacts of iron-working themselves and especially the imposing structures of Central Africa, prominently adorned with breasts and other female appurtenances (fig. 5). These are the most obvious clues to the genderization of the smelting process. Such sexualization is by no means unique to this area, nor even to Bantu Africa. Conversely, not all smelting furnaces in Central Africa conform overtly to this type. But it is the logical starting point for any discussion of the reproductive paradigm as it applies to iron smelting.

Unfortunately, we are sorely frustrated in mapping the extent of these phenomena by incomplete information, compounded by the Victorian prudery of some observers. Melland (1923:138), for example, speaks of Lunda furnaces of "fantastic shapes," generally representing the human figure "with certain members thereof unnecessarily enlarged." This may be paralleled by the reticence of African smelters to talk about the subject. The aged Manyubi smelter, for instance, who emphatically denied that his people made furnaces with breasts and navels, that the furnace represented a woman, and that it was in any way connected with childbirth may have had his own reasons for secrecy (Cooke 1966:86). Baumann's Chokwe informants insisted that breasts were modeled on their furnaces "just for fun" (1935:82, pl. 24). Similarly, because of the sexual symbolism and the fact that she was a woman, Danielle Jonckers was unable to obtain a description of Minyanka (Mali) iron smelting and its associated rites (1979:117).

The area of the overtly gynecomorphic furnace (Cline 1937:53) is extensive, including the Chokwe (Lunda), Luba, Luchazi, Tabwa, and Lozi of eastern Angola, southeastern Zaïre and Barotseland, the Bena and Kinga of the southern highlands of Tanzania, and the Shona of Zimbabwe (map 4). Its antiquity in this region is suggested by Luba genesis myths in which Kalala Ilunga summons a master smelter from lands to the east of the Zaïre River who shows the Luba how to make an iron smelting furnace in the shape of a human being by hollowing out an anthill, an innovation that was seen as more sophisticated than their earlier technology (Reefe 1981:82). Far to the north, Mandja furnaces (Central African Republic) could be either male or female, each distinguished by appropriate features modeled in clay on the front (Vergiat 1937:115). In the western Sudan, the Minyanka also formerly decorated their smelting furnaces with clay bas-reliefs showing "female sexual attributes," although we do not know the details of these (Jonckers 1979:118)—we should not, in fact, assume that they would be purely physiological since they might also include female scarification or other gender-specific decorative details. They may, however, be similar to Malinke furnaces in northwestern Ivory Coast, illustrated by Célis (1991:134–35), with prominent breasts modeled above the tuyere holes.

Unfortunately, no very old examples of such furnaces survive. Like all fur-

Map 4. Area of overtly gynecomorphic smelting furnaces.

naces, the clay superstructure tends to crumble so that only the bowl or pit at the base is left.[6] Often it is not even easy for the archaeologist to distinguish a smelting site from a forging site unless there is an abundance of slag. Nevertheless, furnaces of this type have been identified in three widely separated areas of Zimbabwe at sites that probably date from the nineteenth century. On one of the furnaces, at Chibi, the breasts had been partially broken away (fig. 6). Immediately below them was a "small, well-defined protuberance, probably an umbilicus," and below this, a circular boss with four deep grooves, representing female genitalia (Robinson 1961:20–21; cf. Prendergast 1978:11, 14). In his travels to Great Zimbabwe in the early 1890s, Theodore Bent saw a similar furnace still in common use (fig. 7a), although he simply described the grooves as "furrows" (1893:307–8). Others have referred to them as ethnic scarifications (Bullock 1950:110; Franklin 1945:7; MacKenzie 1975:212).[7]

We are fortunate to have three descriptions of Chokwe smelting furnaces and procedures: Redinha's account is based on fieldwork in southern Lunda in 1946, Bastin's and Martins's in northern Lunda in 1956 and 1962, respectively. They all agree that the furnace represents a woman giving birth but illustrates regional differences and possibly changes over time. Redinha's diagrams (figs. 8 and 9) show the furnace as classically gynecomorphic. What is visible to the eye is confirmed by the terminology, beginning with the Chokwe word for furnace, *lutengo*, which also means vulva (Martins 1966:40). The superstructure represents the trunk of a woman, with chin (*queixo*), prominent breasts (*seios*), navel (*umbigo*), and female scarifications (*tatuagens*). The upper part of the interior chamber is the *goela* (gullet), while the two poles of wood serving as supports for the furnace were designated as arms and the sides of the extracting ditch as legs. The opening of the furnace or hearth "completed the feminine image," that is, of the parturient woman giving birth in a seated position (Redinha 1953:130). Martins adds that the Chokwe term for the opening means pubis (1966:39).

Smelting was preceded by prayers to the ancestors, sacrifices, and an extensive use of medicines to protect the site and the work. A decoction of roots was rubbed in a circle around the furnace, then in a line from the mouth of the tuyere to the top, replicating the practice of making a band with herbs and white clay (*pemba*) on the stomach of a pregnant woman stretching from the middle of the breasts to the abdomen. Pemba is used in rituals throughout Central Africa to assure good fortune. "In the furnace, or more correctly in the womb of the furnace, the block of iron takes shape which they call *muana*, son of the woman. The slag which envelopes the metal they give the name of

---

6. How vulnerable such apparently solid structures are was brought home to us when we learned that the tall clay furnace built for us in Banjeli in January 1985 was virtually destroyed by heavy rains three years later.

7. Sinclair (1991) refers tantalizingly to furnace types in the coastal southern Mozambique-Natal region dating from the early first millennium A.D., "some of which were elaborately decorated," but he gives no further details nor sources for this information.

tchidonje [placenta]." The smelter stands in front, "where the iron is born . . . the place of the midwife" (Redinha 1953:130–37).[8]

Martins (1966) provides a series of photographs that document the construction of the furnace and the accompanying rituals (figs. 10–17). Although similar in the main to Redinha's description, there is one obvious difference (which he does not comment on): the senior wife of the smelter plays an active part in the series of sacrifices to the ancestors and in the offerings of beer and other medicines to the furnace. But she is the only woman allowed to come near, and she does not participate in the actual smelt.

Even within the Lunda region in which the Chokwe live, Redinha (1953:137–39) noted a wide variation in the details of furnace decoration, some lacking breasts, navel, and scars entirely, while Bastin (1974) illustrates much more lavish use of painted motifs on a furnace near Dundo (fig. 18). The welter of furnace types existing in relatively close proximity is in fact typical of other regions as well (cf. Killick 1983; Moñino 1983; Rowlands and Warnier 1988). It may reflect the movement of distinct populations within a given area, no doubt intensified by the upheavals of the nineteenth century, or possibly the overlapping of different traditions.

This makes Bernhard's discovery at Ziwa Farm, Inyanga (Zimbabwe), particularly interesting. He found two distinct furnace types, an older beehive furnace and a larger, more elaborate, and apparently more recent furnace. Each, however, is adorned with a naked female figurine. On the first furnace the figurine is heavily damaged, but on the second it clearly depicts a "woman in the act of giving birth to a child," with the lower parts quite realistically formed (fig. 19). Bernhard points out that "the whole figurine conforms in every detail to the description of childbirth among the Mashona as given by D. M. Gelfand: It is naked save for a string or thin girdle around the waist that apparently represents the *mukonde*, the "string of red, white, and black beads . . . still worn by women in the remoter parts of the country while giving birth to a child" (Bernhard 1963:235–36). Subsequent reconstructions of Shona smelting incorporate these details of breasts, scarification, and women's waist beads (fig. 20) (e.g., Robinson 1961: pl .1b; Dewey 1990), although other sources refer to the belt of beads by the name of *mutimwi*. It marks the stage in a Shona woman's life associated with marriage and motherhood and serves amuletically to enhance her sexuality and ensure fertility (Childs 1991a:349).

In Zambia, the Kaonde evoke childbirth not through such representations but through the "posture" of the iron smelting furnace—a cylindrical body supported on four arched arms and legs with clay feet—suggesting a woman giving birth (Fagan 1971). The Haya furnace in Tanzania is referred to simply as the "breasted one" (O'Neill et al. 1988), although no breasts are visible.

---

8. Among the Luchazi, the word for slag has the same root as that for afterbirth (M. Armor: pers. comm.).

In a variation on the theme, Vergiat (1937:115) found that Mandja (Central African Republic) furnaces were often grouped in twos, one female, the other male, with appropriate attributes fashioned in clay on their fronts.[9] Interestingly enough, a furnace at Gomperi, Lawra, in extreme northwestern Ghana is viewed as purely male, even though its shape is similar to others in the region that are female except for an addition on the top of the shaft representing a man's hairstyle. The bellows stands are the legs, the bellows bowls are the lungs, the air pipes form the penis, the tuyere and slag-tapping hole together constitute the urinary tract, the support for the shaft is the buttocks, the shaft forms the body, and so forth. Pole sees this as an exception to the reproductive paradigm: "Production of iron is therefore not interpreted as giving birth in Gomperi" (pers. comm.). The same might be said of a brass casting furnace in the Brong-Ahafo region, also in northern Ghana, which had no male anatomical characteristics but was recognized as male and named Ebura Kofi (Ray Silverman, lecture 5/11/85). And yet perhaps these contradictions give us the ultimate clue to what may be going on, that is, a male appropriation of reproduction.

There are, by contrast, few overt allusions to age that have been documented. The Mafa furnace reconstructed by Dokwaza carried the effigy head of his father on its shield (David et al. 1989). But this seems to be exceptional. The genealogical motif is more likely to be found in the continuity of older furnaces with new ones. Thus, Bassari (Togo), Ushi (Zambia) (Childs 1991a:343), and Ekonda (Zaïre) furnaces were built on the site of older ones; in addition, the Bassari smelter deliberately incorporated bits of the old in the construction of the new. In the Gbaya reconstruction, one of the smelters transplanted a bush believed to have protective powers from the ruins of his father's furnace to the entrance of the new one (Moñino 1983:303). The Kwanyama (Angola) leave a horseshoe-shaped ring of slag at the site of the pit furnace after smelting for later operations (Powell-Cotton 1937).

The Luo/Kuria furnace (Kenya), on the other hand, emphasized genealogy in a different way. It was built on a generational module, specifically that of the smelter grandfather, using measurements based on human proportions (knuckles, fingers, etc.). Its ultimate referent was the ancestor himself (Ocholla-Ayayo: pers. comm.). Unfortunately, while the invocation of ancestors in smelting rituals is well documented, few observers have paid much attention to how their role is invoked in the artifacts of the process.

---

9. We (Cameroon) smelters also operated two furnaces at once when it was practicable, but they were both seen as female (Rowlands and Warnier 1988:17)—possibly a form of ferrous polygamy. Labouret's (1931:66) cryptic description of a Lobi furnace with "un modelage grossier ressemblant à deux têtes humaines" might refer to a single furnace combining male and female. Similarly, Bertho (1946) describes a tall shaft furnace near Dédougou (Ivory Coast) on which were modeled in clay two human forms, male and female. The female had two breasts and a protruding abdomen, "symbole qui semble indiquer," he comments, "que la fusion du fer est assimilée à une sorte de procréation."

Bellows and Ores

The action of the bellows extends the sexual metaphor embodied in the furnace form. In the Tchiboco (Lunda) furnace described above, bellows connecting with the tuyeres were inserted into the rear of the furnace (fig. 21), their shape and positioning revealing "um certo significado fálico." As the tempo of smelting increased, "the rhythm of the bellows is rather like masculine activity" (Redinha 1953:137; cf. Mesquitela Lima 1971:378). Burton describes Luba smelting in similar terms. The bellows workers started pumping about 4 A.M., continuing until the bloom emerged about sixteen hours later: "Throughout all this time the workers continue in an excited afflatus, swaying their bodies, and accompanying the pumping of the bellows with shouts to the spirits to give them many axes and hoes, or challenging malignant spirits to do their worst" (1961:119; cf. de Rosemond 1943:83). The Njanja (Shona) of Zimbabwe see the bellows and tuyere explicitly as the male organ penetrating the female torso of the furnace. Formerly made from the hide of a goat skinned alive, the bellows "panted" through the clay pipe, producing iron bloom as the result of this copulation (MacKenzie 1975:212; Bullock 1950:110). While all this activity might suggest the "labor" of delivery even more appropriately than the sexual act, this does not seem to be the case in any of the descriptions; instead, there is a telescoping of the process from copulation to birth. Ekonda terms for bellows do not seem to be explicitly sexual, but their arrangement and activity are as suggestive as those involved with more conventional furnaces—and the view from the bellows is nothing short of spectacular.

Natural draft furnaces do not rely on bellows, and yet the plugs that control the intake of air may be equally phallic. Bassari plugs, *mpulo* (fig. 22), are remarkably similar to those used in Burundi: both types are made by modeling wet clay on a stick of wood and then inserting one in each draft hole. They are made and used only by the male smelters. The clay remains in place while the stick is withdrawn as needed. The Bambala (Ila) equivalent are also made of fine clay molded onto poles. The clay is prepared by women (as one might expect) but applied by men. Unlike the Bassari mpulo, these poles are lubricated with a slimy, viscous substance made from washing a particular plant so that they can easily be drawn out of their clay sleeves (Smith and Dale 1920:2,205).

Bellows are not always male, however. Frequently they mirror a male-female complementarity in their pairing. The two tuyeres of the Tsaayi (Teke) smelting furnace, for example, are called "husband and wife" (Dupré 1981–82:213, 220n.3). Pygmy smiths of Buganyuzi (Burundi) refer to their small bellows of dried earth as "my father" and "my mother," emphasizing parental rather than spousal relationships (Célis and Nzikobanyanka 1976:63). For the southern Mbeere (Kenya), it is essential to use skin from both sexes of goats. The right-hand bellows must always be made from a male calf or goat, the left-hand from a female. The tuyeres, formed of clay by the blacksmith, are referred to as male, the nozzle of the bellows as female (J. Brown 1971:38). Among the Ekonda (Zaïre), on the other hand, the word for the clay tuyere connecting the wooden bellows to the bowl furnace is the same as that for vagina, but it is modeled on a wooden pole referred to by the term for penis (Célis 1987:114). In the Bwété initiation rites of the Mitsogho (Gabon), bellows unite both male and female elements: etymologically the word for bellows, *biomba,* derives from that for doors, that is, the female genitalia, but the masculine side derives from the two air chambers (testicles) and the poles used to pump are collectively seen as the penis. The action of the bellows is the " 'sound of the mother Biomba' which corresponds to the panting during the sexual act" (Gollnhofer and Sillans 1978:234).

A comparable anthropomorphism and sexualization of bellows was formerly widespread among the Nyoro and Ganda smelters and smiths in Uganda and possibly among the Toro and Ankole as well. The Nyoro bowl bellows rather graphically represented a glans and penis on the one hand, a clitoris and urethral orifice on the other. A variant was detachable, with the female symbol flatter and blunter than the male and described by informants as decorated with red and black vertical lines. The bellows were used in pairs, converging in the tuyere, and were customarily of unequal size with the larger identified as female (Lanning 1954:167–68).

In the examples from Kenya and Uganda there is then a reduplication of male-female. The same is even more intricately true of Gbaya-'bodoe (Central African Republic) smelting where the ensemble of furnace and bellows consists of "several series of couples: the furnace is female, the block of three bellows male." However, individually these bellows are, from left to right, "the young mother, the mother, and her male child; the last provides the solo rhythm, the mothers respond." Finally, the skin of the bellows is female, "a red antelope who runs while the male [bellows] pole pursues her" (Moñino 1983:304). Again, not only an evocation of female-male in a sexual context but also as mother and child, and yet both relationships suggest that the male is the more active agent.

The bloom as successful outcome of a symbolic *accouchement* figures in a striking ritual reported from the regions of Kayes in western Mali. A two-hundred-pound bloom was dragged still steaming from the furnace. Water was applied to cool it, and townswomen came forward to lift their skirts and absorb its vapors; others collected the liquid that had run over the iron and drank it. Both were ways to absorb the *nyama,* or vital force of the bloom (McNaughton 1988:20–21). The same analogy with female fertility and the fertility of the furnace underlies the custom in Lawra (northern Ghana) whereby women who have suffered difficulties in childbirth and who have had stillborn babies come to the smelting furnace or, more commonly nowadays, to the forge to deliver their babies in order that they may be born strong. A child born by the furnace was called "Sabo," one born by the forge, "Saa" (Pole: pers. comm.).

As to ores, in most cases smelters had access only to a single type. However, in areas where different varieties were available, they, too, might be distinguished by gender. Roscoe (1911:379; idem 1923a:218), who was particularly sensitive to such categories, notes that both Ganda and Kitara (Nyoro) smelters distinguished between male and female ores. The Nyoro believed that the black male ore was of better quality but had the disadvantage of being hard to break up and prepare for smelting, while the red female iron was softer and found in different areas. Ganda smelters were explicit about the need to combine both kinds in smelting.[10] The same belief was common to Jur ironworkers in the Bahr al-Ghazal (Crawhall 1933:41). The majority of Babungo (Cameroon) smelters used two different ore types from different sources (limonite and hematite, which would also differ in color), which they, too, classified as male and female. It was generally believed that the combination of the two was necessary for the production of abundant bloomery iron (Fowler 1990:139, 144).

Rowlands and Warnier (1988:15–16) provide the fullest description of such usage. In the We/Isu smelting industry of Cameroon, male and female ores were fed into the furnace through the chimney, but where the male ore was ferralitic gravel collected in dry areas of the region, the female ore was not an iron ore at all—probably not even a flux—but a clay collected from the banks of a local stream. Here the key distinction was apparently not one of color but of dry and wet. The male ore was never washed; it was said to be "dry" and powerful like semen, in contrast to the female, which was wet and weak "like a woman." We smelters also distinguished two types of clay used in making the tuyeres for the furnace: the female was said to be brown; the male, red (ibid.:17).

CONCLUSION

This chapter has focused primarily on the play of gender in iron smelting. That work roles should be allocated along gender—and to some extent age— lines should come as no surprise since this is a common feature of African life. However essential their contributions may be to many phases of ironworking, women are relegated to those activities that do not carry high status and, above all, do not involve access to what are considered the key bodies of knowledge. And knowledge here, as elsewhere, confers power. On the other hand, most men do not have this access either, so we can see the exclusivity of the craft as a mechanism by which a few males, mostly those of mature years, maintain their monopoly on a crucial enterprise.

When genderization is extended to the primary artifact of iron smelting, the bloomery furnace, it takes several forms. Female sexual characteristics may be modeled directly on the exterior of the furnace; posture, too, may

10. Dime smiths also distinguish between black and red ores and use equal amounts in smelting, but Todd (n.d.) does not say whether they are seen as male and female.

underscore the image of birth. But gender is more than physiology: hence the addition of scarification patterns and other forms of adornment that give the furnace a social, not simply a sexual, identity and at the same time enhance its fertility, just as they do with women themselves. Or, in a variant, this message is conveyed through clay figurines on the furnace wall.

The sexual imagery of the bellows is more complex than might appear at first glance. Often they are not only male but they incorporate both male and female elements, as do ores. This helps us to understand the few cases in the literature where furnaces are considered male or male and female. What is essential is that there is a genderization of the process. The basic paradigm is not necessarily undercut, since the pairing of male and female simply reaffirms the reproductive allusion, while the exceptional unpaired male furnace may simply be carrying the male appropriation of gestation to its ultimate limits.

Sometimes the evidence is not to be found in the visible "anatomy" of the furnace, so to speak, but in the terminology given to its parts and above all in the rituals acted out by the smelters, rituals that bring the furnace to life and create its "gender" and social status.[11] Even where the furnace has obvious sexual characteristics, in fact, rituals vitalize it; the mere act of construction does not suffice to bring the furnace to life and to make it produce iron. The nature of these rituals and what they reveal will be the subject of the following chapters.

---

11. Lest one assume that such gynecomorphizing is peculiar to Africa, the newsletter of the Historical Metallurgy Society of Great Britain (1985:4, 1) informs us that the four "Queen" blast furnaces of the Appleby Frodingham complex in Lincolnshire were named Mary, Bess, Anne, and Victoria.

Fig. 1. Old furnaces in the region of Banjeli (Meyer 1910:2, fig. 3, after Hupfeld).
Photo Thomas Jacob.

Fig. 2. Horseshoe-shaped bloom, Banjeli (Gehrts 1914). Photo Thomas Jacob.

Fig. 3. Cross-section of a draft furnace, Banjeli (Gehrts 1914). Photo Thomas Jacob.

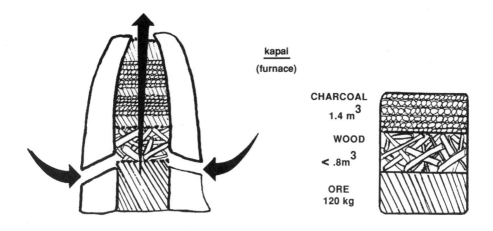

kapai
(furnace)

CHARCOAL
1.4 m^3

WOOD
< .8m^3

ORE
120 kg

Fig. 4. Diagram of a natural draft furnace, Banjeli, Togo (Goucher 1984).

Fig. 5. Chokwe furnace, close-up showing sexual symbolism (Mesquitela Lima 1977, fig. 3). Photo Thomas Jacob.

Fig. 6. Close-up of
iron smelting furnace showing
anthropomorphic decoration.
Chibi Reserve, Zimbabwe
(Robinson 1961, pl. 1a).

Fig. 7a–c. Diagrams of Makalanga (Shona) iron smelting furnace, granaries, and
drums (Bent 1893:308, 46, 70).

Fig. 8. Diagram of Chokwe furnace: Kaparandanda, Alto Zambeze (Redinha 1953, fig. 73).

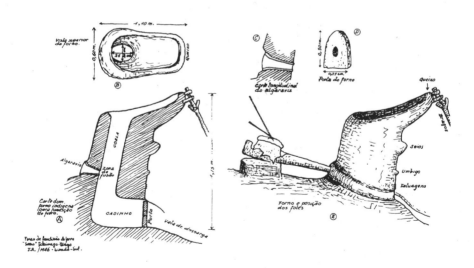

Fig. 9. Diagram of Chokwe furnace: Tchiboco, Lunda-Sul (Redinha 1953, fig. 70).

Fig. 10. Figures 10–17 depict iron smelting in northern
Lunda (Angola) (Martins 1966). All photos Thomas Jacob.
Figure 10 depicts master smelter and wife making
pemba sacrifice to spirits of ancestors and great smelters.

Fig. 11. Another phase of the *pemba* sacrifice.

Fig. 12. Master smelter sacrifices a chicken and drips blood on ore,
bellows, and furnace.

Fig. 13. Smelting furnace ready to be activated. Note
"tchifife" near mouth with head of sacrificed chicken.

Fig. 14. Purification at the smelting site.

Fig. 15. Master Sá Lulende offers prayers to stakes
representing Sá Mbanze, the first Lunda smelter, while
the furnace is in operation.

Fig. 16. Master smelter and assistant remove the bloom.

Fig. 17. Discharge from the furnace.

Fig. 18. Chokwe furnace in operation near Dundo (Bastin 1974, fig. 2).
Photo Thomas Jacob.

Fig. 19. Furnace on Ziwa Farm, Zimbabwe (Bernhard, 1963, pl. 2).

Fig. 20. Shona iron-smelting furnace reconstructed for Centenary Exhibition, Bulawayo, 1953 (Robinson 1961, pl. 1b).

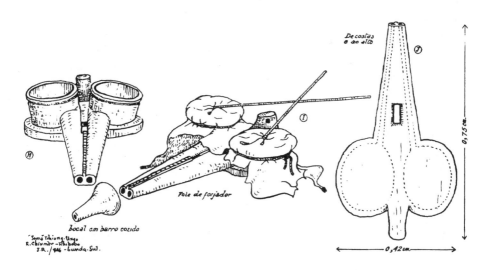

Fig. 21. Diagram of Chokwe bellows (Redinha 1953, fig. 72).

Fig. 22. Plugs *(mpulo)* in place, smelting furnace, Banjeli, 1985.
Photo Carlyn Saltman.

Figs. 23–24. Construction of iron-smelting furnace, Banjeli, 1985.
Photo Carlyn Saltman.

Figs. 23–24. Construction of iron-smelting furnace, Banjeli, 1985.
Photo Carlyn Saltman.

Fig. 25. Slag tapping, Banjeli. Note ring of white ash. Photo Carlyn Saltman.

Fig. 26. Putting tuyere in place, Lopanzo (Equateur), Zaïre, 1989.
Photo Eugenia Herbert.

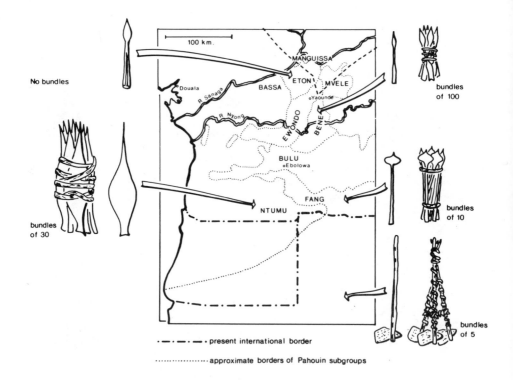

Fig. 27. Iron bridewealth currencies from southern Cameroon (Guyer 1986).

TWO

Rituals of Transformation and Procreation

All the ancestors whose names I have forgotten,
this is your drink.
All the fetishes that I have forgotten, this is your
drink.
We want the fire of this furnace to be a real fire,
not just smoke. You all come and build this furnace, not us.

Belam Diyambo, smelter, Banjeli, Togo

In many cultures of Africa the sexual characteristics and postures of the smelting furnace and its parts are not so explicit as those described above. Initially,
we may be justified at most in seeing the furnace as anthropomorphic rather
than gynecomorphic, since the anatomical terms invoked are gender-neutral:
mouth, chest, navel, stomach. The furnace is fed and given drink and "shits"
slag, which has to be removed from the vents. The clues to how the furnace
and the smelting process are conceptualized—and genderized—must be found
in the actions of the participants. These behaviors are both prescriptive and
proscriptive: what they should do and what they shouldn't do. This chapter
will look at the first aspect of smelting rituals, the positive actions required to
accomplish the transformation of ore into metal, analyzing in particular the
role of words, music, dance, sacrifice, and medicines. Chapter 3 will examine
tabooed behaviors and the exclusion of women from ironworking, which are
considered equally necessary to a successful outcome.

The purpose of ritual is to make something happen. In their classic form,
smelting rituals aim to accomplish a series of transformations: they turn the
furnace first from an inert structure of clay into an undifferentiated human
being and then give it a complete social identity, that is, the identity of a fully
mature woman whose sexuality and fecundity are controlled by the smelter to
produce an abundance of offspring in the form of iron. While the transformation may be made visible by the addition of female sexual characteristics or
adornment to the furnace, these are not essential since it is in any event the
actions of the smelter-creators which are crucial.

Without those visible signs of gender identity, however, the nature of the process is less apparent, so we must look to the details of the ritual process to confirm our interpretation, especially to the words, music, and medicines that accompany the operations. The Phoka (Malawi) furnace, for example, is simply a "pot" while it is being built, but when the basic structure is complete, it becames *mvali*, a nubile young woman. Women and children of the village are invited to a feast of white maize porridge, and songs are sung whose theme is "Be pleased with our young woman." Henceforth, until it is dry and ready for use, the furnace must be protected every night by encircling the top with a sapling, "tying it together." This sapling, which eventually becomes part of the protective wooden fencing around the furnace, is called by the same word as the belt a woman uses to hold up her underwear. Finally, when smelting begins, the furnace is referred to by the smelters as "our wife" (van der Merwe and Avery 1987:159).

SMELTING RITUALS: FOUR CASE STUDIES

The details of the ritual vary considerably, however—almost as much as the furnace forms themselves. This variability can best be illustrated by a detailed look at four cases drawn from very different cultures across the subcontinent. In each case we can follow the entire sequence from the construction of the furnace through the smelting process. Two of them draw on reconstructions in which I participated personally.

Ader Hausa (Niger)

Hausa ironworking in the Ader region of Niger has been superbly described and filmed by Nicole Echard (1965, 1968, 1983). As she demonstrates, the smelting process offers a paradigmatic enactment of "the reduction of iron ore . . . conceived as the equivalent of biological reproduction" (1983:221). It takes place in an isolated, temporary encampment to which only the endogamous *forgerons noirs* (smiths who work ferrous metals) and their families have access. In theory the furnaces should be lit at the full moon and the entire operation completed before the appearance of the new moon.

The number of furnaces depends on the size of the smelting group but ideally numbers between twenty and thirty. The furnaces are lined up in a precise order along a north-south axis: the senior lineages are at the north end, the junior at the south, with the furnace of the *sarkin zango*, the chief of the smelting camp, in the middle; his is larger than the others and has an additional tuyere. The furnace is a truncated cone, made of clay and strengthened with horizontal bands, placed over seven tuyeres (eight in the case of the sarkin zango) radiating from a hole in the ground. These tuyeres provide the natural draft for the smelting process. The furnace shafts are portable and are moved after a smelt to a new hearth, following a path from east to west.

At the extreme west of the camp is the place of sacrifice, which has two components: a wooden pole from a particular tree with a bunch of bush grasses at its top and a newly made calabash containing nineteen different medicines, both vegetal and animal. These are only put in place the morning of the day that smelting is to begin, immediately after a ram is sacrificed and its meat consumed by the smelters. During the smelting sequence, the sarkin zango accomplishes a series of ritual movements patterned spatially and numerically. He follows a circular course from furnace to furnace in the direction west-south-east-north, repeating this three times (three is the masculine number). This circular movement will be replicated later by the metal as it fuses and is repeated for each of the furnaces. He also touches each of the seven tuyeres on each furnace with the medicines in the calabash before depositing them on the pile of charcoal.

While performing these movements, the sarkin zango also pronounces a set of brief, metaphoric phrases that allude to the process, its mythic origins, and its desired results. These *paroles noires* clarify the symbolic aspects of the operation. They identify the iron bloom as the daughter of the hearth. The paroles noires also prescribe the ideal qualities of the iron being produced: like the vulva and clitoris of a woman, it should be light and luminous; like the vulva it should swell from desire and become like the rounded belly. "When sperm and blood swirl without stopping, rolling up like a tapeworm— just as the fire and molten matter swirl—the womb swells bit by bit" (Echard 1983:221). These words are spoken at key moments in the technical process, especially when the smelter adds baskets of freshly pulverized ore from a succession of different points. If he added the mineral from the same spot, the "stones of iron" would form a "ball" prematurely, blocking the rotation of the matter necessary for the creation of a "good" ball, an analogy to the belief that a proper fetus also depends on the creation of a good ball through the swirling of its constituent parts.

Joining the smelter is a child who brings four baskets of ore in succession to the sarkin zango as he orients himself to the four cardinal directions. At each point he places the basket on his head and recites a ritual phrase. The ore is not supposed to touch the ground but touches the head of the child, then the head of the sarkin zango, before being emptied into the furnace. These rituals are performed against a background of music provided by the "griots of the smiths" (sons of mothers from smithing and fathers from non-smithing families) who sing their praises and erotic songs, along with the women of their family who dance.

Beyond these required actions, it is believed that a smelter can assure success by allying himself with a bush spirit. But the cost of this is the death of a member of his family. The spirit gradually appropriates the person's life force, and death comes during the day after the night that smelting begins:

there is a reciprocal exchange in which death is the price of the fertility of the furnace.

In this ritual drama, the movable shaft of the furnace is, in fact, the virgin bride, although the only identifiable "anatomical" characteristics are its two sets of "eyes," which glow from the fire within. "She" is washed and decorated and then deflowered by the smelter. The foundation of the furnace is the nuptial house of the newlyweds, and its emplacement symbolizes the entrance of the bride into her husband's house. The tuyeres placed on a bed of straw and the circular movement of the sarkin zango are all part of the ritual of fertilizing and protecting the bride: she is impregnated by the fire during the single night's duration of the smelt (smelting always begins at dusk and ends before dawn) and in the morning gives birth to a child, the bloom of raw iron.

The running of the molten slag is equated with the rupture of the waters and the beginning of labor pains. The process is accompanied by the music of griots, whose erotic songs make the furnace conceive and grow large. As in the Lunda case described in Chapter 1, the slag is also the placenta. Afterward, it is buried in the foundation hole just as the human placenta is buried under the house floor. Most stunning of all, after the final smelt, young men smash the furnace while the smelter implores them in the name of God to desist. Unfortunately, the full meaning of this startling—and troubling—dénouement has yet to be explained.

Echard summarizes the entire process thus: *"faire coïncider, terme à terme, fabrication du métal et reproduction biologique,* cela au point que la connaissance obstétricale soit considérée comme savoir forgeron" (1983:221, italics hers). That is, the Hausa smelter/smith is a master of obstetrical knowledge but never actually practices. Women deliver alone or with the help of older women. On the obstetrical level he acts out the same isolation observed with regard to nonsmiths in the larger society. And yet it is precisely his understanding of obstetrics that enables him to transform ore into iron.

Fipa (Tanzania)

Fipa iron smelting offers a striking similarity in the treatment of the furnace as a new bride but within a totally different social context (Lechaptois 1913:242; Wyckaert 1914; Grieg 1937; Robert 1949; Wise 1958; Wembah-Rashid 1973; Willis 1981). Unlike the Ader Hausa, Fipa smelters do not form an endogamous occupational group. In theory metalworking could be learned by anyone who apprenticed himself to a master and who then received the indispensable collection of medicines, the *ntangala;* in practice, it tended to be handed down in families. The ingredients of each ntangala varied and were kept secret by the smelter, but Robert's list of one such collection shows a mixture of plant and animal, domestic and wild. Similarly, the prayer addressed to the ntangala before the departure for smelting in the bush called upon the spirits of the house and those of the wild, as well as the ancestral smelters, to grant an abundance of iron. While those assisting in the smelt were subject to strict sexual taboos, the master smelter was required to perform the sex act and to masturbate with his wife the night before furnace construction began, then rise very early and go to the site without washing his hands before any of the others got there—in other words, to begin the work with the odor strongly on his hands in order to neutralize the "harmful influences emanating from those fellow workers who were impure" (Robert 1949:244). A similar ritual precedes sowing in the fields, suggesting that controlled sexuality is seen as the most potent protection against uncontrolled sexuality and, more positively, as "analogous to the social transformation of nature" (Willis 1977:283).

The construction of the furnace was a major undertaking that involved two days of hard work by a force of fifty or more men, women, and children—a real community effort in contrast to the isolation in which Hausa smelters erected their furnaces. The resulting oven was also a much more substantial creation than that of the Hausa and could be used over and over once it was fully dried; it was emphatically not expendable at the end of a single smelting campaign (Wyckaert 1914:372; Grieg 1937:78; Wise 1958:106–9).

The ceremonies marking the completion of the furnace replicated those of a wedding day, when a virgin bride would be brought to her husband's village amidst feasting, drinking, dancing, and song. They brought together all those who had worked on building the furnace to witness the rituals that reinforced its spatial orientation and, at the same time, its sexual identity. The kiln was smeared with oil and adorned with daubs of white millet flour and *nkulo*, the reddish-brown powder made from a tree root and worn by girls at the onset of menstruation and at their weddings. These daubs were painted from east to west, counterclockwise, top to bottom. On the crest of the furnace were placed flowers and feathers. "Bride, walk very steadily," urges the master smelter, to which the assembly responds, "(That we may) take you to your father and mother." With the completion of all rituals, the bride had come home (Wembah-Rashid 1973:18–20).

Aside from preparing the charcoal and ore, the one remaining task before smelting could begin was to cut out the openings at the base of the furnace for the natural air vents. Accounts differ as to the number and terminology of these, but agree that the largest was called the "mother" of the furnace and served as the entrance as well as being fitted with a battery of tuyeres, while the next in size was the "father." According to Wyckaert (1914:372), the rest were referred to as "children." There is also some disagreement about the direction the main holes faced, a reflection no doubt of the different periods of the observers. It seems most probable that the "mother" opening faced the setting sun, the father, the rising sun, consistent with Fipa genderization of space (Wise 1958:234; Willis 1981:28).

Once the holes were made, the furnace was painted black with a mixture of anthill clay, earth, and ash, and the flowers and feathers on its rim were removed. Wembah-Rashid (1973:23) was given conflicting explanations for this,

either because the smelters themselves were becoming fuzzy about the process or because they were being deliberately evasive. The most credible is
that it mimics the veiling of the young wife's body with black cloth in antici-
pation of pregnancy, an interpretation consistent with the smelter's earlier
statement likening the kiln to a bride: "When it is loaded it is just the same
as saying she has conceived. The slag trickling out corresponds to labour time
and the iron obtained is the baby" (ibid.).

Curiously enough, neither Wyckaert (1914) nor Grieg (1937) mention the
decoration of the Fipa furnace or recognize the analogy with the stages of the
female life cycle: bride/wife/mother. Perhaps this is another case where we
are confronting regional differences within a single ethnic group or where
informants were simply reluctant to divulge certain information. Wyckaert
does, however, describe a key ritual involving children that was somewhat
altered in the reenactments reported by Wise (1958) and Wembah-Rashid
(1973). Once the furnace is completed, the tuyeres fashioned, and the wood
prepared for charcoal, the master smelter brings out his *ntangala,* or box of
sacred medicines, without which smelting cannot proceed or succeed and to
which the smelter addresses his prayers that the enterprise will be blessed.
The next day before sunrise the ntangala is carried to the smelting camp by a
child, and no one else is allowed to touch it. The child (sex unspecified—and
possibly unimportant?) is accompanied by another child carrying a pair of
chickens, male and female, to be sacrificed. "These two children, bearers of
sacred objects, must walk like spirits, they cannot scratch or touch their bodies. The rest—men, women and young people—follow in good order, their
foreheads if not purified at least whitened with chalk." Above all, the ntangala
must never touch the ground (Wyckaert 1914:373–74).

Subsequently, the children go alone to the furnace with the chief to cut the
throats of the chickens and drip their blood on it, the wood, the tuyeres, the
ore, and the charcoal. Then one of them goes *inside* the furnace through the
large opening while the other stands outside, both continuing to sprinkle blood
and intoning, "Light the fire yourself. May it burn well!" Guided by the chief,
the child inside places medicines in the basin hollowed out in the floor of the
furnace, adds the heads of the two chickens, and covers the whole with a
layer of earth. The chickens are then cooked and eaten by the children, with
adults strictly forbidden to join the repast. Even the bones and remains have
to be buried so that dogs will not get them. Wyckaert claims that of all the
rituals surrounding ironworking this is, in the eyes of the smelters, the most
important. After this, the master smelter is free to enter the furnace with his
ntangala, load it, and position the tuyeres in each opening, beginning with
the mother and proceeding to the father and then the children (373–76). Wise's
account emphasizes even more strongly the children's ritual crawling in and
out of the mother and father openings (235–36). This is obviously a symbolic
replication of the birth process, but there seems to be much more going on.
Wyckaert comments that the children walk to the smelting camp "like spirits"
and are the only ones allowed to touch the ntangala, to sacrifice the chickens

and then eat them. Are they, in fact, the ancestors themselves who become central actors in the metallurgical drama before being born again?

Banjeli Bassari (Togo)

The Bassari smelting furnace is not female by "anatomy" nor by decoration nor even by terminology. The words used to designate its parts—mouth, chest, lungs, stomach—are generically human, just as when air is drawn through the draft holes, the furnace is said to breathe. Like the *paroles noires* pronounced by the Hausa smelter and the movements he accomplishes, the ritual acts and invocations of the Bassari smelter not only bring the furnace to life but give it a sexual identity and render it fertile. Initially the smelter is the "father" of the furnace; later, he and his assistants become its—her—symbolic husbands.

For whatever reasons, our informants were noncommittal when asked about the sexual aspects of the furnace and smelting. It was only when we obtained a fuller translation from nonparticipant Bassari of the prayers and combined these with the visible rituals that we could confirm our interpretation. Probably some of the rituals that would have made this more evident have been lost with the passage of time: Martinelli's (1982:45) informants told him, for example, that when the foundation of a new furnace was first outlined with pebbles, the head of the smelting lineage would pour out millet flour mixed with water, a symbol here as elsewhere of fertility, while he invoked the High God and the spirits to make the enterprise fruitful. During the reenactment in 1985 only millet beer was used for these libations.[1]

Since the Bassari furnace was used over and over, unlike its Hausa counterpart but like the Fipa structure, the rituals, quite logically, were only performed at the time of the first smelt in a newly constructed furnace, although the taboos and exclusions held for all successive smelts. The site chosen for the new furnace is marked off with a leafy branch to protect it. Kneeling at the site beside a small pile of fragments from an old furnace, the master smelter offers libations of millet beer to the spirits and the ancestors to bless the enterprise and drive away evil spirits. First he calls upon the high god, then on his smelter grandfather and great-grandfather, then on various spirits. At the end he repeats three times: "All the ancestors whose names I have forgotten, this is your drink. We want the fire of the furnace to be a real fire, not just smoke. You all come and build this furnace. It is not we who build it."

He then makes a shallow circular trench, using a string as compass and outlining it with pebbles and the bits of old furnace (figs. 23 and 24). Standing

---

1. The discussion of Bassari ironworking that follows is drawn from fieldwork carried out in Bassar-Banjeli in January–February 1985 with Candice Goucher and Carlyn Saltman and a return visit in July 1992. See also the film *The Blooms of Banjeli* (1986) and its accompanying study guide as well as Herbert (1988), Goucher (1984), Martinelli (1982), Cornevin (1962), de Barros (1986), Kuevi (1975), and Bérard (1951). Hans Hahn arranged a reconstruction of iron smelting in Banjeli in 1988 that differed slightly from that observed in 1985 (Hahn 1991b).

in the middle of the circle and casting sand mixed with medicines in each direction, he repeats: "All buyers, come and buy this iron." In a small calabash he mixes a medicine composed of shaved bark used to protect the future furnace, and he daubs the hands and feet of all the participants with it. No one can approach the site without being purified and protected with this, and once purified they must refrain from sexual relations until the end of the smelt. Additional medicines are incorporated in the clay of the furnace wall during construction: fruits, leaves, porcupine skin, and hippopotamus hide. Once building is well under way, a celebratory meal is brought to the site. It is prepared by an old woman, assisted by two girls.

The most dramatic rituals are those leading up to ignition. When the furnace has been loaded with wood, charcoal, and ore, the master smelter encircles it with a ring of white ash mixed with water, adding an ashen loop above its entrance. He places a leafy sprig in the loop, held in place by fresh clay. The circle, according to one informant, represents the "person" of the furnace, with two arms (around the circumference of the furnace) and mouth (the loop). Such ash circles also decorate shrines of the Bassari and neighboring peoples, indicating periods of liminality and offering protection (Kirby: pers. comm.). They are also found on furnaces in northern Ghana: at Zanlerigu a ring of white wood ash is poured around the pile of ore on the ground, "marking a barrier both for the spirits outside and those inside that may cause harm if they get out." A similar ring of white ash is also spread around the shaft of the furnace to protect pregnant women passing near from the "harmful effects of the structure, which may cause them to have a miscarriage" (Pole 1974a:26, pl. 1). The white ash is analogous to the white clay used in Central Africa.

The old woman brings a basin of specially prepared fufu with mudfish sauce. The smelter sets a gourd of it in front of the furnace mouth, and holding a handful he addresses the furnace: "Give birth to good iron; give birth to good iron." He slaps some of the food on the leaf in the center of the loop and calls on the furnace to be as fertile as the tree that produced the leaf, to bring forth "bracelet iron," that is, iron of the highest quality from which bracelets were once made.

Next, the smelter leads an unsuspecting child to the front of the furnace and beats him with a switch until he cries. He then leaves him to console himself with a calabash of the food, admonishing him to eat the fish in one piece so that the iron will come out in one piece, and joins the other smelters with the rest of the fish.

The smelter stays close to the furnace during most of the three days the smelt is in progress, checking the process through the tuyere holes, monitoring the use of the plugs, tapping slag—and seeing that no one comes near the furnace who has not been purified with the medicines (fig. 25). As time passes he listens for the tell-tale sound of the solidifying bloom dropping onto the bed of sand, reminiscent of the fetus dropping in the womb when birth is near, although this analogy was not drawn by the participants. On the morning of the third day, after the furnace has cooled somewhat, he pries open the entrance wall to the furnace and extracts the bloom. In the past, this would have been broken up manually and the raw iron further refined in a small bellows-driven furnace.

Ekonda (Zaïre)

Ekonda iron smelting, as observed in the village of Lopanzo, differs radically from any of the three examples described above. Like other peoples of the Equatorial forest (as well as the Kwanyama of extreme southern Angola, to whom we have already referred), the Ekonda use a bowl furnace with no shaft at all, only a clay tuyere through which the air of the bellows is channeled. Nevertheless, in the rituals of the smelt it is possible to find analogies to the preceding cases and to posit a genderization of the process.[2]

The smelting atelier is a large rectangular enclosure with a peaked thatched roof supported by posts. The roof, in fact, is similar to that used on houses and palaver huts and is simply taken from one of these for the smelt. While the atelier must be constructed at the full moon, smelting itself must await the new moon. Then the bowl and observation-slag pit, tuyere, and bellows are all made the very day of the smelt. Between the two operations, charcoal is prepared and iron ore is mined, roasted, and pulverized.

Whereas in Kwanyama smelting, San play an active role, Batwa (Pygmies) have an analogous role for the Bantu Ekonda—in spite of the fact that neither San nor Batwa have historically been metalworkers. Although the Batwa stand in a servile relationship to the Ekonda, their indispensability is recognized in both practical and ritual domains. As masters of the forest, they are the charcoal makers. They are also owners of fire, called upon each time a fire has to be lit, and are entitled to a portion of the animals sacrificed and consumed at the smelt. When the *maître de la terre*, that is, the descendant of the oldest son of the oldest son of the Ekonda lineage inhabiting the quarter where smelting occurred, blesses the smelt, he has to be joined by his Batwa counterpart, who is also the oldest son of the oldest son of the corresponding lineage. Together they represent the first occupants of the forest and first, albeit immigrant, masters of the earth. Their intercession is necessary to obtain the permission of the ancestors, "the invisible masters of the earth," before commencing operations and for this we gave them special gifts (Kanimba 1991:3). Again, this illustrates the pivotal role of ancestors and the necessity of establishing the proper mediation with them—in this case, a double mediation given the intertwined history of Bantu and Batwa in the Equatorial forest.

In recognition of its ritual and technological aspects, Ekonda smelting is supervised by a master smelter and a ritual specialist, though they are some-

---

2. This description is based on Célis (1987) and on fieldwork carried out in Lopanzo in July–August 1989.

times combined in a single person. In the case of the 1989 reconstruction, the master smelter claimed the position by virtue of his lineage and age but had no knowledge of the process, so he deferred for all intents and purposes to the ritual specialist to whom he was related but who came from another village (and whose presence was intensely resented by the local citizenry).

In the absence of a true furnace, the key to the sexual interpretation of Ekonda smelting, I would suggest, lies in the form and function of the tuyere/bellows and in the panoply of medicines used. The furnace consists essentially of a hollowed-out depression filled with charcoal and ore, with a tunnel leading to a larger observation pit into which slag is supposed to flow; there is no superstructure as such. Nevertheless, there is a large clay tuyere into which the bellows channel air; it is this tuyere, one may argue, that is analogous to furnaces elsewhere. The tuyere is modeled over a conical wicker basket with a mixture of clay, fiber, and palm oil. The air passage is kept open by inserting a stick, which is only removed when the tuyere is in place. It is positioned on its side so that the small opening is buried in the charge, while the bellows' nozzles send air into the large opening at the rear (fig. 26).

As Célis (1987:114) notes, "Toute une partie du vocabulaire attaché aux fonderies est tirée d'organes ou de caractéristiques sexuels." While the parts of the bellows seem to be generically anthropomorphic (chest, nose, tail), one of the terms for the tuyere is *boongó*, which also designates the vagina: a second term, *nsóngé*, also means moon and menses. The pole inserted in it, *mpoló*, is the same as that for the male sexual organ. With a different tonality—*mpòlo*—the word means vagina. When the slag begins to run from the bowl into the observation pit, it is compared to the menses of a woman. While the associations of moon and menses will be dealt with more fully in Chapter 3, the correspondence of slag and menstruation seems apt: both are the waste products of the creative process. And finally, the smelt begins just before dark, mirroring the prohibition against sexual relations during the day.

The rituals accompanying the smelt follow the common pattern: sacrifices (in this case, a pregnant goat, a female dog, a cock, and a dried fish); prayers to the ancestors and the first smelter, asking them to aid the enterprise; the exclusion of women; the observance of sexual taboos during charcoal making, the construction of the atelier and smelting; and the prescriptive use of certain trees, leaves, and bark, both practically and medicinally. For now, let us look particularly at the last mentioned.

From the outset, the atelier is treated as a sacred precinct. Certain types of trees are indicated for its construction, while one is explicitly forbidden. Particular plants are buried at the base of posts supporting the roof, while others are attached to the post and strung across the open front of the edifice. Some of these plants have recognized apotropaic functions; others more positively ensure a successful outcome; another secures the well-being of a family and symbolizes the alliance of Batwa and Bantu in the village.

On the day of the smelt, these are renewed and more are added, especially to the sides and bottom of the furnace bowl. Their collective purpose is to interdict the site to women and to all who are not observing the taboos against sexual relations and violence. They also drive away evil forces and promote the success of the operation. The kaolin—white clay—applied to the bodies of the smelter and the ritualist at this time serves to attract the help of beneficent spirits (it was also used in the ritual preceding the construction of the atelier). The kaolin and the leaves, creepers, fronds, etc., are used in other contexts for the same purposes.

DISCUSSION

These individual and quite different cases underscore the complex interweaving of discrete but integral elements that make up the fabric of iron smelting. First there is the form of the artifacts involved and the manipulation of the materials: our focus on the rituals of transformation should never let us lose sight of these empirical realities. The master smelters were skilled technicians whose long experience led them to make subtle adaptations to the nuances of each operation, guided by sight and sound.

What concerns us here, however, is the explanatory framework within which they worked, the meaning of "technology" as we can see it played out. In the scenarios sketched out above and in the many other accounts we see, first and foremost, an intricate system of relationships, all of which must be kept in proper balance if the process is to succeed: relationships between ancestors and living, spirits and humans, evildoers and well-wishers, as well as males and females. The rituals of iron smelting have ultimately a very practical purpose: to mobilize all the propitious forces and keep at bay all the malevolent ones so that the operation will be successful. Hence the panoply of sacrifices and medicines, of prescriptive and interdictive behaviors—and of words, music, song, and dance.

Words, Music, and Dance

Often it is the language addressed to the furnace or used by the smelters, in addition to the terminology designating its parts, that explicitly indicates what is believed to be happening, thus, the invocation to the Fipa furnace, "Bride, walk very steadily," or to the Bassari furnace to "Give birth to good iron." The Hausa smelter's *paroles noires* describing the ideal qualities of the female genitalia or the fusion of sperm and blood in the fetus are given cosmological reinforcement in the spatial and numerical orientation of the movements that accompany them, especially since the smelter is known to be a master of obstetrical knowledge.

Examples could be multiplied from throughout Africa. In the early years of the century, a Belgian observer recorded that the "fetisher" who supervised Lega (Zaïre) smelting directed a number of invocations to the furnace, among them "In the morning, before giving birth, you are full of energy; when you have given birth, your strength is exhausted" (Delhaise 1909:136). Or, by extension, the language could suggest that the smelters themselves had given birth. After the smelting in which Yves Moñino participated, he was congratulated by his comrades and fellow villagers: "Tu as accouché du fer" (Moñino 1983:301).

The Gbaya (Central African Republic) furnace was provided with ears "to understand what one told it to do" (ibid.:304, 307); Pole (1975:36) also found ears on some of the furnaces in northern Ghana. With or without them, it—usually she—was expected to hear and to respond, even to the most esoteric references such as those embodied in the sacred poems recited to Ogun by Yoruba (Nigeria) iron smelters (Adeniji 1977). Interestingly enough, although the Yoruba (like most Africans) carried out smelting in secret, they had to build the furnace close enough to human habitation for voices to be heard:

> If the sound of people's voices do not penetrate inside the hearth of the smelter, the iron which is being smelted inside it will become dumb; that is that this iron will not become iron that rings but rather slag—which means that this iron is still-born. (Adeniji 1977:19)

The importance of the human voice as an agent of transformation is paralleled by that of music. We have already noted the part played by the griot in Hausa smelting, singing the praises of the true smelter-smith, the *fils des hommes,* and animating the work of the furnace. Indeed, the role of music is so central to metallurgy that Célis (1987:132) felt called upon to remark on its absence in reconstructions of Ekonda smelting in 1973 and 1974 and to wonder if it had been lost during the forty-odd years since smelting had been abandoned in this region.[3] In fact, it was not at all absent in our reconstruction some fifteen years later. Customarily music has been as common in African metalworking as in the ancient world, where Forbes points out that there was a quasi-universal connection between the smith and music, in myth and legend as well as in practice (1950:81). And music is commonly associated not only with words but also with dance, for is the *sarkin zango* not performing a dance in his circular movements inscribed by the points of the compass and the location of the furnaces?

One thinks immediately of the close association of the smith and the griot throughout the western Sudan and particularly of the unforgettable scene from Camara Laye's *L'Enfant Noir* in which the griot participates intimately in the transformation of raw gold into jewelry: "Il s'échauffait comme s'il eut été l'artisan même, . . . comme si le bijoux fût né de ses propres mains" (1953:39–40). In Cameroon, Gebauer's 1950 film documents the role played by musicians in the Grasslands' brass casting,[4] just as the Powell-Cotton film of 1937 shows the Kwanyama iron smelter dancing as he invokes the ancestors.

---

3. As seems to have been the case in Banjeli in 1985 (cf. Martinelli 1982:65).

4. Clara Gebauer confirms this intimate association between music and metalworking from her observations of smiths at work in the Grasslands during the 1930s (pers. comm.).

Several thousand miles away in Katanga, Bayeke copper smelters sang a hymn to the rhythms of the bellows:

> Ku Mulu wa Kalabi kudi kinonge.
> On the summit of Kalabi rises a high furnace,
> A high furnace with a large womb, the heritage of our father Lupodila,
> A high furnace where copper trickles and billows.
> O my Mother! O my Mother! (de Hemptinne 1926:22)

The antiquity of this association of music and metalworking is evident from an engraving in Cavazzi that shows the Ndongo king forging iron to the accompaniment of a veritable orchestra of musicians (Cavazzi 1687; Bassani 1987) (fig. 27).

Music in this context, as in others, serves multiple purposes. Like work songs generally, it provides a tempo and helps to keep up the morale and energies of the workers, especially the bellows operators during their marathons of pumping. This was clearly the case in the Ekonda reconstruction. The patterning of bellows rhythms is often indistinguishable from that of drums: thus, in Gbaya smelting, the bellows identified as the "male son" provided the lead beat, while the two "mother" bellows played off of it in classic call-and-response. In the rare cultures such as the Bäle and Bari where women were present during iron smelting, they sang or trilled to urge the men on (Fuchs n.d.:9; Cline 1937:136).[5] Similarly the kneading of mud for furnace construction among the Fipa became itself a form of dance: "The wet mud was thrown into a pile on the ground . . . , then twenty or thirty people gathered round and rhythmically began kneading the mud with their feet. A sort of African 'hokey-cokey' ensues" (Wise 1958:107).

Much more is involved than work rhythms, however. The Mafa (Cameroon) considered singing and harp playing indispensable to the production of good iron (Gardi 1954:18). As the 1988 film by David and Le Bléis makes clear, however, the music and dance were part of a precise scenario: It is only when the master smelter Dokwaza dances his return to the smelting furnace in war headdress that it is permissible, indeed requisite, to play music in the vicinity of the furnace. The working of the bellows then becomes itself a musical performance:

> Dokwaza played the bellows like drums, Butay struck up his harp, and they began to sing antiphonally, building to periodic climaxes. This was the first time that music had been allowed near the furnace. From then on, as Dokwaza and Butay alternated their roles, and for much of the time when others took over the bellows, the music continued, its rhythms egging on the bellowsmen. (David et al. 1989:194–95)

---

5. McNaughton describes how Bamana blacksmiths "play" the bellows, and he even reproduces a transcription of some of their rhythms. He too notes that women pounding millet near the forge matched the blacksmith's rhythms with their huge pestles and handclapping routines (1988:25).

When the smelt has been successful, the smelter tunes up his harp and sings to the iron bloom, then passes the harp twice around the bloom; once this is done, the bloom can be crushed and heated in the refining crucible (David 1987: dokforge 1–2).

Smelting songs are often erotic, if not downright bawdy, underscoring the sexual nature of the smelting process. Ekonda smelting songs were accompanied by Elvis-like movements of the hips. We have already noted the extremes of obscenity and insult that characterize Fipa smelting (Robert 1949:244). Among the Haya, also in Tanzania, the female identity of the furnace is, in fact, established not by its form or embellishments but above all through the songs sung by the smelters, which are replete with sexual allusions. The most highly charged are those describing the flow of the *emondo*, a small aquatic animal, used as a metaphor for flowing semen, and the spotted animal that is a metaphor for the penis (Schmidt 1988). The marriage song toward the end of the smelt celebrates the successful union with the reluctant bride (O'Neill et al. 1988). Ila smelting songs also refer explicitly to male and female sex organs (Smith and Dale 1968:2, 207–8). We have already noted the erotic element in the songs of the Hausa griot and their role in smelting. Chulu (Chewa, Malawi) songs, on the other hand, are an "odd mixture" of religious and bawdy—odd perhaps only if one assumes that sex can have no part in the sacred (van der Merwe and Avery 1987:159).

Precise transcriptions of metalworking songs are scanty and their meaning is often obscure. An Ila (Zambia) song, for example, runs: "It is boiling; it is boiling, the medicine; when the physic is ready, I shall free a woman and child; it is boiling, the medicine" (Smith and Dale 1968:2, 209). When cracks appear in a Nyamwezi (Tanzania) smelting furnace, the bellows operators sing, according to Stern's translation (1910:154), "Ein dummes Weib, sie verdirbt den Ofen/ Denn sie hat oder findet nichts auf dem Haufen" ("What a dumb wife, she spoils the furnace/ For she has or finds nothing in the heap"). When the iron bloom is extracted, they sing: "Woman, Ji Ja! Others mound up the stubble in the fields/ Ji! Others mound it up." Working in Burundi, Célis and Nzikobanyanka have collected the most extensive corpus of songs related to ironworking. While their meaning, too, is often elusive, many of those chanted during smelting invoke the "wife of the craftsman" and the mother with a child on her back. Another exhorts: "Choisis, choisis, choisis au-dessus/ Choisis au-dessus, ainsi, le fer au-dessus, le mâchefer en dessous/ *Agenouille-toi et enfante*" (1976:125, italics mine).[6]

Like other aspects of ritual, it is highly likely that the meaning of many of these songs is intentionally esoteric precisely because they are charged with power. The elderly Manyubi (Zimbabwe) smelter who quietly sang the song of the bellows while illustrating their use in smelting and then refused to acknowledge that he had been singing or to repeat the words clearly illus-

---

6. Cf. Delisle's (1884:470) account of smelting at Franceville (Gabon), which suggests that the singing was matched by cries and groans that seem to replicate labor pains.

trates this point: music is at the core of smelting ritual and is not to be shared with the profane (Cooke 1966:86–87).[7]

While some of the songs are unique to metalworking, others may be sung in other contexts, a subject that needs far more investigation. Many Chulu smelting songs, for example, are also part of the repertoire of the men's secret society (van der Merwe and Avery 1987:159). The songs sung to the ancestors by Lopanzo miners were still familiar precisely because they were also used in other settings where the ancestors were invoked for assistance.

The rapport between dance and furnace among the Fang is more complex. According to informants, "The dance *àkòm* and the furnace *(àkùa)* are the same thing"; the dance/song "has been born of the work of the furnace." The same "master of ceremonies" presides over both the dance and the smelting, and only men who have been initiated may participate. In trying to explicate the meaning of this association of dance and furnace, which he sees as conditioning "la mouvance sociale ancienne chez les Fang," Mbot asserts, "To the extent that they intervene in various social activities, the working of iron and the dance *àkòm* bring together the material and social preoccupations of the village." Both play a part in reproducing the social order (1975:59–70). His analysis is, in fact, extraordinarily rich precisely because he considers the ideological and social impact of the cessation of iron smelting among the Fang during the colonial period.

Fang women are never allowed to see the dance nor even to hear the sound of the flutes from a distance. They are excluded from the dance just as they are excluded from smelting because on a certain level the two are identical. At the same time, this incorporation of elements of male initiation connects smelting to the larger context of socialization and is part of the elaborate balancing of social and antisocial forces in Fang cosmology. That is, the smelter must invoke antisocial forces to accomplish his work, but he must hold them in check with more benign forces (Boyer 1983:47–49). In both spheres, iron smelting and initiation, however, the performance of music and dance is part of the arsenal by which transformation is accomplished.

If these songs and dances were directed to the participants and especially to the furnace itself, their ultimate audience was the spiritual forces that have the power to establish the gender of the furnace and assure its fertility: gods and ancestors. In many cases it is the smelter's position in a lineage of metallurgists that confers his authority, and he makes this plain in his prayers. Hence the specificity of the Bassari smelter in naming his grandfather and the great-grandfather he never knew but heard about. Compare the Gbaya ritual in which the smelter runs down a whole list of past furnaces and their builders

---

7. Even sound itself may play a crucial role: Kwanyama (Angola) smelters place a small curved iron plate in the slight space between the opening of the bellows and the tuyere of the smelting furnace, then wrap the joint with a special band of dried grass. The sole purpose of the plate and dried grass, according to the master smelter, is to produce a sibilant sound that can be heard at a considerable distance, "the music of the smelt" (Estermann 1976:146; Estermann and Cunha e Costa [1941]:157).

in relation to those taking part in the construction of a new furnace (Moñino 1983:304). In both cases, the master smelters reiterate and defer to the power of their ancestors: "It is not we who build this furnace." Within the social hierarchy, as Moñino observes, the ancestral dead stand at the top, to be acknowledged and supplicated in any major enterprise (ibid.:307). They have power in their own right to affect the outcome, and they can also intercede with other spiritual forces (Delhaise 1909:135).

Medicines and Sacrifice

"Medicines" are equally critical in the construction of the furnace and in the smelting process itself. We have seen their role in each of the cases described in detail (as well as in Chokwe smelting, described in the preceding chapter): the nineteen vegetal and animal medicines that the sarkin zango applied to each tuyere of the Hausa furnaces and to the pile of charcoal; the equally numerous medicines that went into the Fipa ntangala; the medicines gathered by the Bassari feticheur, going naked to the mountains in the dead of night, to protect the furnace and its workers from contamination and evil forces and to ensure its fertility; the repertoire of medicines employed at every stage of construction of the Ekonda atelier as well as in the furnace before and during smelting. In Bantu Africa, especially, it is common to place a pot of medicines in the base of smelting furnaces. Such a pot has been found in a Congo furnace dated to about the seventh century A.D. (de Maret 1988). The Babungo bury two pots, filled with numerous plants gathered from each type of tree and plant in the chiefdom, including cultivated plants. Their efficacy is believed to be exhaustible; hence, if smelting is no longer going well, the pots are dug up and the medicines replaced (Fowler 1990:222).

Sacrifices, too, play an integral part. In the cases presented, they were absent only in the construction of the Bassari furnace in 1985. There is evidence that this was not so in the past (Martinelli 1982:45), and, in fact, white hens were sacrificed at Hahn's reconstruction in Banjeli three years later. In a sense, the meal of mudfish fufu and the offerings of millet beer are also forms of sacrifice. The optional exchange of a human life for successful smelting in the Hausa example represents a form of sacrifice as well as a reiteration of the intimate link between death and life. The Mangbetu, too, claimed that smelting demanded a human life in the past (Marre, Schildkrout et al. 1990, *Spirits of Defiance;* cf. Schulze 1971:126 and Fowler 1990:162).

As David Livingstone ([1841–56] 1961:64) noted long ago, it is the knowledge of these medicines and sacrifices and of the rituals accompanying their use more than any technical skill that is seen as the key to success in smelting. While sacrifices are more overt and seem to follow common patterns related to type of animal, sex, color, number, etc., as well as offerings of food and drink, medicines belong to the domain of the secret, their precise identity and source kept from rival smelters as much as from profane outsiders (vid., e.g., Killick 1983:B:10, D:20). As a result, we have few inventories of such medicines and even fewer studies that are able to connect them with other uses and associations in a particular society.[8]

Generally speaking, the purpose of medicines is multiple: to protect against human and superhuman agents of evil and against those who transgress sexual and other taboos, and, more positively, to impart to the furnace and its product the ideal qualities inherent by analogy in both. In their study of Phoka (Tumbuka) smelting in Malawi, van der Merwe and Avery (1987:160) were able to document the uses of medicine with unusual thoroughness, noting also which are essential (the hippo skin, for example, which had to be flown in from South Africa and which has its parallel in the Bassari furnace) and which are optional. They conclude:

> Most of the plants have medicinal uses other than that of assisting with smelting and so do some of the animals and minerals. They constitute most of the Phoka pharmacopoeia for dealing with witchcraft; diseases caused by witchcraft and spirit possession; epidemics that threaten a community; or venereal diseases that reduce fertility. Other items are clear symbols of fertility and plenty: millet, peanuts and other edibles, schooling fish, a termite queen, a fish net, a beer strainer, and the like. The final group symbolises the desirable qualities of strength, toughness, hardness, wiliness, and speed—qualities one wishes to impart to the smelting and its product.

Their informants clearly understood the symbolism and homologies involved.

The list of medicines used in We (Cameroon) foundries and smithies is also remarkable for its diversity. While Warnier and Rowlands were able to identify a number of the plants and their use in treating various ills, the connection with smelting is by no means obvious in all cases. When they asked their chief informant if the plants had been "selected for their therapeutic properties in curing human diseases," he replied that the choice was simply empirical: "It is a matter of experience. At the beginning, the dead elders found that those leaves were successful in insuring good smelting, and restoring things into order if there had been something wrong in the workshop." Nevertheless, they noted that some of the plants used in the smelting cocktail and in curing a foundry were also employed to treat barrenness or to ease a difficult accouchement, as we have also seen at Lopanzo. One particular herb used to "cure" a spoilt smithy is the same as that given to women who have suffered a miscarriage because "a mishap in the smithy is likened to a miscarriage" or may cause the iron to "cook" in the fire and disappear, which is a miscarriage of sorts. Other plants used in both the foundry and the smithy were prescribed to cure edema and swelling, symptoms believed to be characteristic of witches who often die with swollen feet or swollen belly. Since witches commonly cause barrenness and death and are sowers of discord,

---

8. For exceptions, however, see Robert 1949; Podlewski 1965; Brelsford 1949; Wyckaert 1914; van der Merwe and Avery 1987; Rowlands and Warnier 1988; and David et al. 1989.

such medicines would have the added function of trapping them and preventing them from spoiling the process (Rowlands and Warnier 1988:19–20, 23–24, app. I; cf. Fowler 1990:158).

Mafa smelters in northern Cameroon also used a variety of grasses, roots, and branches. One root was partly eaten by the smelter, then the rest was buried with another plant at the base of the furnace before construction began to protect both furnace and smelters against impurity, especially that caused by sexual relations. The branch placed in the furnace shaft to drive away evil spirits was the same as one set in the door of buildings under construction. Some of the Mafa medicines were pounded and mixed with daub by the smelter's daughter and then offered to the rising and setting sun before being applied to the furnace and bellows. In a few known cases, the names of the medicines are suggestive: for example, "panther's testicles," "monkey's pubic shield" (David 1987: bldg. fur. 2, 4, 13, 17). Another account of Mafa smelting comments that the smith spits on the furnace in the course of the smelt, just as his *accoucheuse* wife spits on the newborn baby during the naming ceremony (Schaller 1973:57–58): here the saliva itself is a form of life-giving medicine.

One of the most famous medicines to reinforce the fertility of the smelting furnace was employed by the Tonga (Malawi). They allegedly threw a piece of human afterbirth into the furnace to aid in smelting (Cline 1937:139). Like the leafy sprig applied to the Bassari furnace, at least some of the woods and plants used in Ekonda smelting are also known to be associated with fertility. The bark of the *bosengé*, the primary tree used to make charcoal, for example, is one of the ingredients of the potion sprinkled on the smelting furnace; it is also used to wash women to augment their fecundity. Similarly, a creeper that interdicts the atelier and its environs to the profane, *bosèisèi*, is "suspended at the entrance to a house where a newly delivered mother is secluded so that those who enter may admire the infant." The stem of the creeper also may be boiled to make a potion that relieves the pain of childbirth (Hulstaert 1966; cf. Célis 1988:136). There is therefore a multiple identification of the atelier with a house in which a woman has sexual relations (which are forbidden in the bush) and also gives birth.

A second major category of medicines includes those that protect against menstruating women and/or people who are violating sexual taboos. In Zambia, Chisinga smelters buried a medicine in the layers of green wood in the furnace called *chibele*, literally "woman's breast." It consisted of a "conical excrescence chopped from the trunk of the chipolo tree." In addition, they made a medicine from the roots of another shrub mixed with boiling water poured over stones. This ensured that the iron ore would burn properly and not be spoiled because a worker had sexual intercourse the night before or because a worker's wife was menstruating (Brelsford 1949:28). Unfortunately, we have no other information about the shrub that might illuminate its use.

Among the plants used by Burundi smelters to protect the smelt against menstruating women, one reed in particular is etymologically related to the word for a woman's period. Its action is reinforced by sprinkling a solution of ochre and water on the foyer of the furnace (Célis and Nzikobanyanka 1976:88–89). The same plant used by the Fang to guard against menstruating women also functions to make the iron grow together on the analogy of the single fruit uniting with a cluster (Tessmann 1913:1, 226).

While menstrual blood can imperil the smelt, it can be neutralized by homologous medicines, just as other medicines can offer blanket protection against men violating sexual taboos (to say nothing of witches and sorcerers). Thus, if a Fang smelter's wife menstruates during the smelt, a lozenge-shaped figure is carved out of bark on the post of the smelting hut on the side facing the oven. It represents the female sex organ and is rubbed with red dye wood that has been been rubbed against the offending woman and that symbolizes her flow of blood. A sprig of *Myrianthus arboreus* is added to the figure. As Tessmann (1913:1, 226) sees it, this signifies that what is "unclean" has been hidden and rendered harmless. Danger can be appropriated, as it were, by incorporating and controlling it.

How these medicines were collected and by whom might also be important. At We, in the Cameroon Grassfields, it was crucial to collect all medicinal plants when they were young, fresh, and full of moisture. Most, in fact, came from shady, damp areas, explicitly underscoring the associations of water/fertility/female sex/low ground/coolness (Rowlands and Warnier 1988:18–19). In the Babungo case, the owner of the furnace rather than the smelters is the medicinal specialist (Fowler 1992). Among the Bassari, it is the féticheur who goes out at night, entirely naked, to gather plants on the mountainside. At Lopanzo, it was also the féticheur who supervised the abundant use of medicines, both in the construction of the atelier and during the smelting.

Another form of medicine is the white ash applied in rings or bands to furnaces in northern Ghana and the Bassari region of Togo. A band of white ash also runs down the heat shield of Dokwaza's furnace (Mandara Mountains, Cameroon) (David et al. 1988). This practice finds an echo far to the south in the smelting rituals of the Kwanyama Ambo (Angola). In the Powell-Cotton film of 1937, white lines of chalk are painted on the bodies of family members before they leave for the mining camp, then again on the master smelter and his son before the first ore is mined, and finally on the master smelter during smelting operations. Estermann's (1976:147) account of the ritual of the "curing of the stones" among the same group refers to the "sacrifice" of white earth or chalk in which the smelter applies a few marks on his head, nose, and abdomen, on the heads of the bellowsmen, and on the bellows handles themselves. As we have noted, the practice finds a parallel in Ekonda smelting, where the smelter and féticheur apply kaolin to their bodies during the rituals, and in Chokwe smelting, where chalk is applied to the furnace. Such usages tie smelting into the complex world of color symbolism, especially of the connotations of white to mark sacred spaces, invoke the ancestors, and proclaim a state of purity. For example, sacrifice takes place at the point of intersection of the ring of white ash with the vertical rising from it on the Zanlerigu furnace reconstructed in northern Ghana (Pole: pers. comm.).[9] And sacred spaces are dangerous spaces, to be protected and avoided (cf. Kirby 1986:78, 280–81, pl. 15).

Finally, how do we interpret the presence of children in smelting rituals? There have been suggestions that they represent symbolic sacrifices. Eliade, for example, entitles a chapter "Human Sacrifices to the Furnace," and cites among others the Chewa case, where a woman is made to abort and the fetus is then buried with medicines in a hole over which a new furnace will be built ([1956] 1962, ch. 6; Hodgson 1933:163).[10] Does the beating of the Bassari child represent in some sense a symbolic sacrifice? It seems highly unlikely. Rather, he, too, seems to be an equivalent to the iron gestating in the womb of the furnace; perhaps his cries when he is beaten mimic the cries of the newborn child, the bloom that is about to be delivered from the furnace.

Children could simply be viewed as a type of medicine themselves, rein- forcing the procreative potential of the furnace by analogy or correspondence (but cf. Moñino 1983:305). At the same time they represent asexual beings, neutral actors in a highly sexualized drama. This may be the explanation for the Mourdi custom which demands that about an hour after the smelting furnace is lit, a goat must be sacrificed and its meat immediately cooked and eaten by the smelters, who are then fed by a young child who puts the pieces of meat in their mouths and lifts the calabashes of water or milk to their lips (Carl and Petit 1955:68). While Western writers often project their own ideas of "innocence" onto these children, we should avoid the ethnocentric over- tones of this notion and see them more precisely as beings who have not yet acquired a fully sexual and social identity. Jomo Kenyatta (1938: ch. 10), for example, underscores the role of old men and women and children in major Gikuyu rituals such as rainmaking, planting, and purifying crops: the opera- tive principle seems to be that these participants are not in their prime repro- ductive years or, in the case of the men, they are enjoined from sexual activ- ity. Further, as we have noted in the Fipa case, children may at times be viewed as incarnations of the ancestors themselves.

Alternatively, children seem in some cases to be surrogates for the furnace and its offspring. Thus, when the Bassari smelter feeds the child standing by the furnace mouth, he is also feeding the furnace, for he tells the boy to eat the mudfish in one piece just as the ideal bloom should come out of the furnace in one horseshoe-shaped piece. Compare the Tumbuka (Malawi) rit- ual in which flour, medicine, and a white cockerel are sacrificed at the fur- nace, and the blood of the cock is allowed to drip onto the charcoal inside

---

9. At another reconstruction in the same area, sacrifice took place at the protuberance referred to as the "navel" of the furnace (Pole: pers. comm.).

10. Bryant ([1948] 1970:389) claims that Zulu smelters believed it was necessary to incorporate human fat into their operations and they murdered someone to obtain it, but Bryant's information was collected so long after smelting ceased in Zululand that it must be read with caution. How- ever, aborted fetuses and stillborns were reputed to be common ingredients in magical prepara- tions in Barotseland and other parts of Central Africa (Reynolds 1963:43).

before it is given to children to eat on the spot with maize porridge (Killick 1983:A:4). More baffling is the interpretation of the Chokwe ritual in which a child is brought to the front of the furnace where the master smelter smears chewed white clay on her navel, chest, and head; when asked the reason for this, he replied that it was to provide food to the child (Redinha 1953:135)— presumably, by association, to the child gestating in the furnace.

Smelting and Twins

Célis (1987:117) observed that all of the medicines used during the Ekonda smelt "doivent aller par deux," but he offered no explanation for this observation. My hypothesis is that it alludes not only to the reproductive paradigm itself, to male-female doubling and human fertility, but more specifically to the birth of twins, human fertility squared, as it were.[11] The Ekonda look upon twins as very powerful but for good or evil; they can bring either good luck or bad. One must wait to see what happens—for example, whether one of the twins or another member of the family dies. They are therefore treated very carefully. The mother remains in seclusion for several weeks after the birth, naked most of the time. Both parents wear a belt of creepers after the birth, and these creepers, *bososónó*, are also strung around the smelting atelier to ward off evil.

During the smelt, certain foods are prepared which can only be consumed by the smelter himself, by fathers of twins, and by specialists in trapping elephants (Célis 1987:117).[12] The first product of the smelt, furthermore, is referred to as *"l'aîné,"* the elder (as of siblings). The movement Célis calls a "mouvement obscène du bas-ventre" (115)—a swiveling of the hips—is performed at the birth of twins as well as when an unauthorized person touches ore or steps across the smelting bowl and at several other points in the smelting process. It is, of course, not really obscene but is associated with protecting fertility against hostile spirits. When twins are born, too, the Batwa are allowed a license they do not ordinarily have in Ekonda society. In other words, there seems to be a correspondence between smelter, father of twins, and hunter. Hunting and its analogies with smelting will be discussed in Part II. As for the equation of smelting:fathering of twins, each may be seen as extraordinary yet ambivalent events, fraught with danger yet augmenting the power of the man who can pull it off. Both reflect not only the control of male-female powers but also those of Bantu and Batwa.

If this interpretation is correct, it finds parallels in central Africa and in the Cameroon Grassfields. The Tabwa smelting furnace, in extreme southeastern

---

11. Triplets are seen as even more remarkable and are also subject to special treatment, but they are, of course, much rarer.

12. According to Kanimba's informants (1991), the white cock sacrificed over the bowl of the furnace could only be eaten by the smelter, the smith, the father of twins, and the twins themselves.

Zaïre, was sometimes referred to as "mother of twins," and there is evidence that the bloom was extracted at the new moon, alluding to the importance of the new moon in Tabwa thinking and specifically in rituals related to twins (Roberts and Maurer 1985:183). Directly across Lake Tanganyika, the Fipa, according to Robert (1949:244), make the same association of smelting with the birth of twins—the baskets of iron it produces. The insults and obscene songs that punctuate the process are similar to those demanded at the birth of twins.

As for Cameroon, Fowler (1990:38, 131, 160) notes that as the Babungo smelting furnace evolved, the product itself changed from the single bloom delivered from the old furnace type to the twin blooms of the developed Babungo clump furnace. Just as twin children represented the ultimate in human fertility, so the twin blooms were considered a sign of divine favor, specifically a blessing bestowed by Nywi, the spirit or breath manifested in all forms of life. This connection was made in the chanting of praise songs for twins during the erection of the foundry beams and in the "prayers for the reproductive fertility of the chiefdom and the productivity of the foundry" on the occasion of the construction of a new foundry. This view may, in fact, have been more generalized in the Cameroon Grassfields. An informant in We, northwest of Babungo, explained that if the bloom came out in two separate lumps, "it would then be considered that the furnace had delivered twins, and the smelters would perform the same birth celebration as for twins, with twin dances and songs. They would slaughter a goat and the whole ward would rejoice," for twins are believed to possess special powers (Rowlands and Warnier 1988:17).

It would be interesting to see if the association with twins is more widespread than has been recognized; presumably it would only be relevant where the bloom is produced in separate pieces rather than a single bloc as in Bassari smelting, but we can't be certain. In any event, the linkage is highly suggestive. Twins are always looked upon with some ambivalence because they are seen as both blessing and threat to their parents and to society. On the one hand, they represent super fertility; on the other, a heightened risk of mortality. They are usually ascribed more than ordinary power, even as infants, so that, like any anomalous birth, they are regarded with some apprehension. In Tabwa belief, for example, they are held to mediate between nature and humanity, taking on some of the characteristics of chiefs, and precise rituals must be followed at the time of their birth to keep them from making trouble (Roberts and Maurer 1986:29–31). In the case of the Ekonda, this special treatment extends even to marriage. Twins, like iron (and like chiefship, as we will see), become a metaphor for the ambiguities of power.

CONCLUSION

The difficulty in interpreting the discrete elements of ritual is that they have no single or fixed meaning. Some parts of the ritual are direct—the exhortation to the supernatural powers to assist. But many are indirect, making the same statement through multiple layers of correspondences and analogies, where like is thought to reinforce like. Thus, the ancestors' presence and power may be signified in a variety of ways: by calling on them by name, by using bits of their old furnaces in the building of a new one, by making sacrifices to them, by using the color white. Similarly, the affirmation of the furnace as a gestating woman is stated and restated in the sequence, beginning with the construction of the furnace and running through the entire sequence of the rituals of consecration: the choreography of belief.

In this chapter, however, we have looked only at the obligatory actions of the players in the drama of iron smelting. In the next, we need to explore the rationale behind the proscriptive side of ironmaking: the exclusion of women, especially of menstruating women, and the interdiction of sexual relations during smelting and its related activities, as well as a series of nonsexual taboos.

THREE

Rituals of Transformation

EXCLUSIONS AND TABOOS

> If a smelter slept with a woman, he did not go
> near the furnace because of the danger of death.
>
> Tonja Najombe, Nangbani, Togo

> Si une femme en règles s'approche au fourneau,
> elle aura des menstrues infinies.
>
> Amba Mbili, Lopanzo, Zaïre

Murray Armor recalls an occasion when a European woman, on a visit to Kalabo (Barotseland, Zambia) while Luchazi smelters were building a furnace, insisted on going to see the site after being asked not to. The smelters were so upset that they stopped working entirely for a time, then rebuilt the structure several yards away (pers. comm.). The problem was not that she was European but that she was a woman, although had she been African she probably would have had the good sense to stay away. For all their variability, accounts of smelting are almost unanimous on two points: the exclusion of women, and menstruating women in particular, and the prohibition of sexual relations for those participating in the smelt and sometimes in related operations. In many cases, smelting sites were isolated precisely to keep women away and to keep an eye on the men involved.

THE EXCLUSION OF WOMEN

At Musigati in Burundi women were not allowed near the foundry or forge nor could they so much as touch forging implements (Célis and Nzikoban-yanka 1976:19, 34–35). Even the wives of these smelters had to be careful not to taste the food they left for their husbands as long as the smelt was in progress, lest "the block of iron disintegrate at the first blow of the hammer when it emerges from the hearth." Elsewhere, women simply left food for the metallurgists at some distance from the site (e.g., Roscoe 1911:381; Brock and Brock 1965:99). In stricter times Chisinga (Zambia) smelters would not even allow this but relied on young boys to cook for them during the four to five-day smelting period (Brelsford 1949:28). Among the Dime, however, only menstruating women were excluded from the smelting site (Todd n.d., n.p.).

There are at least two important qualifications to this generalized exclusion of women. First, although the sources are too imprecise to draw categorical conclusions, there is evidence that young girls and older women were often exempted from the prohibition (e.g., Cooke 1966:86; Killick 1990:128; van der Merwe and Avery 1987:164; Appia 1965; but cf. Kuntz 1935:186, and Maes 1930:72). At Banjeli, for example, the meals that formed part of the furnace-building and smelting rituals were brought to the site by an elderly widow, a "woman who does not go out," assisted by two young girls who had spent the previous night with her to guarantee that they were not menstruating or engaged in sexual activity. All other women had to stay far away—they were not even supposed to look upon the flames darting from the crest of the furnace.[1] Similarly, the maize flour included in the medicines used in the construction of the Chulu (Chewa) smelting furnace was pounded and ground by an old woman with no husband, that is, a woman both infertile and celibate (van der Merwe and Avery 1987:157).

Our own case at Banjeli provides a further exception to the rule. Why were we, three women, allowed to watch all phases of Bassari smelting, although two of us were clearly postmenarche and premenopausal? The answer seems to be that as foreigners we were in an ambivalent gender category. When we asked our informants about this after the completion of the smelt, they seemed genuinely baffled by the question since the whole reconstruction was undertaken on our initiative. This may seem to contradict the example cited at the beginning of the chapter, but it should be noted that our involvement was fully negotiated, that we followed all of the smelting prescriptions and proscriptions, and that we were daubed with the protective medicines just as were the rest of the crew (Herbert and Goucher 1987). Hence we had what seemed to us a complicated identity—both male and female, insider and outsider—but one that was not at all problematic to our hosts (Herbert 1986).[2]

Clearly, then, it is not women *qua* women who pose a danger to the furnace and the smelting process but women to the extent that their presence undermines the smelters' obligation of abstinence or that they may be menstruating. Adeniji (1977:31) mentions a third possibility, namely, that women may be witches. But we will postpone this subject until Chapter 5. Children, postmenopausal women, and, in some cases, nursing mothers (van der Merwe and Avery 1987:164) are not a threat because they are sexually unavailable or even situationally sexless. We must therefore examine the implications of sex-

1. According to the Brocks (1965:99), Nyika women in southern Tanzania were not allowed near the container of smelting medicine.

2. The fact that he was an outsider may have enabled Patrick McNaughton to be accepted as an apprentice to a Bamana blacksmith, whereas this would have been impossible to an insider not born into a smithing family—except for a slave (McNaughton 1988:xv–xvi, 4).

uality and of menstruation to discover why they are inimical to the smelting process, keeping in mind that these are two very separate aspects of femaleness even though the two taboos frequently occur in tandem.

TABOOS AGAINST SEXUAL RELATIONS

In extreme cases, the sexual taboo has been extended to all phases of smelting, including mining, the construction of the furnace, and the preparation of the charcoal.[3] In theory, during this entire period Bassari smelters should not even have contact with anyone who was sexually active, nor should any of the latter touch anything related to the smelt: furnace, ore, wood, charcoal. Martinelli claims that Bassari work groups were kept small to avoid the possibility that two men might be having sexual relations with the same woman, which would be especially noxious to the smelt (1982:47), a worry also expressed by other informants. In the event, small crews sufficed for the natural draft furnaces. The restriction ended only when the iron bloom fell to the base of the furnace (for the master smelter, only when the bloom was finally extracted).

Ankole smelters had to observe sexual abstinence until the iron had been smelted and the smith had made a hoe from the bloom (Roscoe 1923b:105–6). This could be a very onerous interdiction in areas where smelting extended over a long period of the year and sometimes, as in the case of the Ankole, it was eased by applying only to intercourse with women other than a smelter's wife. Nevertheless, Tessmann comments that the prohibition against all sexual relations for two months before as well as during iron smelting, along with the high cost of necessary medicines, made smelting decidedly unappealing to the Fang of Gabon (1913:224–25).[4]

At Babungo, in the Cameroon Grassfields, all foundry crew members were obligated to refrain from sexual intercourse the day before smelting was due to begin. A worker who had recently taken a new wife was especially dangerous and had to be purified, along with his new spouse, by means of medicines administered by the compound head, who oversaw the ritual rather than technological aspects of smelting. But the most severe restrictions were those imposed on the *woenfiibuu*, the resident supervisor of the foundry, who had to remain celibate and live in the foundry itself for some four to six months at a time and who directed smelting operations. The woenfiibuu was often a son of the compound head or even more commonly a slave, and he was the only full-time metallurgist; unskilled nonspecialists could smelt under his guidance by bringing fuel and helping with the bellows (Fowler 1990:151, 157ff.).

Failure to observe sexual taboos is the most common explanation offered

---

3. According to Fowler's Babungo informants (1990:223), men who had recently had sex were not to walk through split woodchips drying in the sun nor touch iron ore, lest the smelt fail to produce a bloom. Indeed, men preparing woodchips for a smelt were forbidden even to touch a woman and then touch the chips.

4. See, however, Mbot's interesting gloss of this interdiction as part of an ecological strategy (1975:73–75).

for the failure of a smelt in virtually all the information available from all parts of the subcontinent (with witchcraft a close second). This was as true in our experience with reconstructions at Banjeli (Togo) as in Chaplin's (1961:58) with the Kaonde (Zambia). Armor (pers. comm.) notes that Luchazi smelters often bought their charcoal from outsiders whose morals could not always be counted on. If a smelt failed, the usual recourse was to "beat the daylights out of them," even leading to a couple of murders when the alleged culprits refused to confess and submit to rites of purification. In an interesting extension of these beliefs, Senufo smelter/smiths who form an endogamous caste *(Kpäö)* of full-time metallurgists not only interdict sexual relations during mining and smelting but believe that any sexual contact between Kpäö and Fulani or griots would ruin the smelt (Dittmer 1962:6–7, 9).

The vulnerability of the furnace to sexual relations seems to stem directly and logically from the notion that it is a woman—more correctly a wife—impregnated by the smelter husband and gestating a fetus of raw iron in its womb. If we see the relationship as social rather than simply biological, as husband-wife instead of just male-female, the explanation becomes clearer on one level, more complex on another. It becomes clearer because concepts of adultery and socially sanctioned sexual rights to women can be invoked to explain taboos: they guard the furnace against her adultery as well as her husband's, an adultery that can cause the smelt to abort just as a wife's or husband's adultery during pregnancy may cause a difficult labor or a deformed or stillborn infant. Thus, misfortune is believed to befall the womb of a Chewa wife if her husband commits adultery when she is pregnant and then eats out of the same pot with her (Hodgson 1933:129).

Brelsford's Chisinga (Zambia) informant, the headman Kapambwe, was explicit on this parallel. "The furnace, he said, was regarded as the smelter's wife for the period of the work and to sleep with his human wife meant that he was committing adultery as far as the furnace was concerned. Moreover the furnace was pregnant with iron, she was a wife with 'great riches in her womb' and to commit adultery whilst the wife is pregnant means, among other tribes besides the Chisinga, that the child will die, and by analogy the furnace would not produce good iron" (1949:28). The Ushi, south of the Chisinga, make the same analogy: sexual relations on the part of the workers would be regarded as adultery by the kiln, and if any "unclean" people, i.e., those having sexual relations not sanctioned by society, approach the kiln, "then as a woman would be in danger of a miscarriage or a still-birth, so the kiln would not produce good iron" (Kay and Wright 1962:36). The Lamba smith is forbidden to have sex with his wife the night before smelting begins lest the metal stay soft and never harden (Doke 1931:347–48), while the northern Kpelle (Liberia) explain that if the prohibition is violated, slag will stop dropping to the bottom of the furnace (Schulze 1971:124).

The Bassari, who, as we have seen, were strong in their belief that sexual relations on the part of anyone involved in smelting jeopardized the outcome, also had severe penalties for adultery. According to a German observer early in this century, an offended husband had the right to kill the guilty man or even have him castrated (Klose 1903:313). Kuevi's information that the smelting process may thus have served as a kind of ordeal is intriguing, albeit unsubstantiated by other sources (1975:35). An elderly Bassari informant confirmed, however, that there were dangers to participants as well as to the furnace in breaking sexual proscriptions: If a man who was smelting iron slept with a woman, he simply did not go near the furnace because it could cause death—presumably his own (interview: Najomba 1985).

Most of these citations do not go beyond the basic analogy of furnace as gestating wife. Babungo belief, however, adds an important dimension to the prohibition of sexual relations by linking them to witchcraft. Here, adultery by a husband jeopardizes the fetus in his wife's womb because it brings together the "sorcery substance of the wife with that of another mature female. . . . Similarly, the smelting medicines that activate the blessing of Nywi that fecundates the bloom are also the agency that causes the smelt to fail if the sexual proscriptions associated with iron smelting are flouted" (Fowler 1990:158). In both smelting and human pregnancy, "there are associated dangers mediated through the agency of the medicines-sorcery of the furnace-wife." Fowler also schematizes the parallel sets of relationships that inform Grassfields thinking thus:

Mother/Wife	Organ of Sorcery	Child
Furnace	Medicines	Bloom

This view makes explicit the problematic nature of female fecundity.

Not all smelters will volunteer associations between sexual prohibitions in smelting and adulterous relations in pregnancy. When David (1987: dokintro 5) asked a Mafa smelter why sexual abstinence was obligatory during the period beginning with the building of the furnace until after the completion of the smelt, he replied that that was just the way it was. His wife's explanation, on the other hand, "was hypothetic-deductive in its epistemology. She supposed, she said, that a smith had had sex during the tabooed period and the smelt produced no iron. This had been perceived as cause and effect."

We also need to know more about customary regulation of sexual relations between husband and wife during pregnancy to see if these help to explain sexual taboos during smelting. While repeated intercourse may in some or many cultures be considered necessary for proper gestation of the fetus, there may be a corresponding restriction later in pregnancy. Thus, Mandja husbands are expected to cease relations with their wives about the fourth month of pregnancy (when the baby begins to show?) and until the baby is weaned; failure to do so is believed to cause miscarriage (Vergiat 1937:42).

Nevertheless, two other aspects of sexual relations may also be mirrored in these prohibitions: notions of hot and cold and the fear of witchcraft and sorcery. Livingstone observed that Kgatla (Botswana) smelters "refused admittance to those who have had intercourse with the other sex since the period of the year when they annually commence smelting, lest they should bewitch the iron. . . . Iron bewitched is when it is burned to a cinder from a too brisk use of the bellows" (1961:35). In fact, what Livingstone may be recording is not only a literal intervention of witchcraft but also a common belief about the "hotness" of sexual intercourse. At Babungo, the consequences were equally serious but opposite: If sexual taboos were not observed, the fire in the furnace would die away or some other mishap would occur. Tégué beliefs are similar (Dusseljé 1910).

De Heusch (1956) asserts that such taboos may be understood "if one acknowledges that the maximum power of virility is concentrated on extractive technology, coupling of ore and fire, birth of iron." Both hot and cold can be dangerous in specific situations, but the heat of sex seems particularly antithetical to iron smelting, whether it causes the fire to burn too intensely or to go out altogether—what appear to be contradictions in the data are simply variants on the play of fire as a primary force, the reversals that comparative studies often reveal. At the same time these may converge with ideas about conservation of energy, as the quotation from de Heusch implies, a belief in a limited quota of male vitality—an African version of the finite orgasm theory (cf. Jonckers 1979:118). We will return to these ideas in discussing other arenas of transformation: hunting, warfare, rites of passage—all activities, as we shall see, that are marked by the same sexual taboos as smelting.

While the exclusion of women and the taboo against sexual relations during smelting are widespread, they are not quite universal. What are we to make, for example, of the presence of the Mafa smelter's wife at the smelting site during David's 1986 reconstruction (David et al. 1989:187–88; cf. Célis 1988:87, 141)? Or the fact that the Kwanyama smelter *must* sleep with his wife the night before the smelt (Powell-Cotton 1937)? In the absence of explicit evidence, we can only propose some very tentative answers.

Accounts of Mafa smelting, in fact, differ slightly. Schaller (1973:43) states that although smelters must abstain from sexual relations for five days before the smelt, their wives may be present during the operation as long as they are not menstruating. Gardi's log notes only that the smelter's wife appears on the scene twice during the operation, the first time to bring him a calabash of water in which millet meal has been mixed, the second to bring a more substantial meal (1953:14–15). Dokwaza's wife manufactured the bellows pots, fired other parts of the bellows, and with her daughter brewed the beer that was consumed throughout the smelt. She was present throughout much of the process, beside or on the furnace platform (David et al. 1989:187–88). The film shows that twice during the smelt she and her husband, their arms intertwined, took part in a ritual by drinking millet beer out of the same calabash, an act that would seem to underscore male-female interaction analogous to the smelting process.

Among the Mafa, smiths/smelters constitute an endogamous occupational group, the *ngwazla*, or "transformers," who carry out important responsibilities in connection with birth, death, healing, and divination, as well as working in metal. Since they are considered unclean by the *vavai* majority, they live and work largely in isolation (vid. Podlewski 1965). As we have noted, ngwazla women play a prominent role as midwives and potters, producing vessels used in ritual as well as everyday contexts, such as the pot that is incorporated into the furnace itself. Dokwaza, the master smelter, refused to comment on the sexual symbolism of the furnace or sexual aspects of smelting generally; it is hard not to see the removal of the glowing mass of charcoal and bloom from the furnace orifice as a reenactment of birth, however, or the passing of a sheaf of grasses between his legs, touching his genitals, as a ritual of virile procreativity! At the same time, its "nose" and horns/penis as well as the terminology of feeding the furnace, giving it something to drink, and removing slag "turds" from the vent, underscore its essentially anthropomorphic character.[5] It may simply be that the smelter's wife is present because caste solidarity takes precedence over gender distinctions or that Dokwaza's wife is postmenopausal and no longer fertile so that her presence would not contradict the exclusion of sexually active reproductive women.

However, David (1988) suggests another intriguing line of thought, namely that among the Mafa, "men are to women as *Vavai* are to smelters," that is, the smelter as a transformer and converter—perhaps also an outsider—may be seen as a "situational female."[6] Echard (pers. comm.) sees some evidence for this among the Hausa where smiths are equally marginalized by the society in spite of their vital role. Such a view receives possible corroboration from Schmidt's (1988) observation that Haya smelters formerly wore women's raffia skirts. When one factors in Dokwaza's war bonnet and the metaphor of "killing the furnace" and bringing it to life again, the Mafa equation becomes truly mind-boggling: it encapsulates the complete paradigm of male/female, life bestowing and death bringing.

Undoubtedly, different but related notions are involved in the Kwanyama case. Here the entire family group moves to the sources of iron ore and sets up a temporary camp with children, animals, and neighboring San: each ironworking lineage functions as a corporate entity, with no attempt to isolate the activity from women and children. We should note, incidentally, that the obligation of sexual intercourse the night before the smelt (reported by the Powell-Cotton sisters in their film) is not mentioned by Estermann (1976:1, 144–49; Estermann and Cunha e Costa 1941:34–36, 147–61) in his fairly detailed accounts of Kwanyama ironworking. Perhaps as a priest he omitted it out of delicacy. But even assuming that the act *was* obligatory, it may not be as contradictory as it appears. Rather, it confirms the primary fact, namely

5. Rosemary Joyce also comments that David et al.'s argument about pots as persons "may apply equally well to the similarly decorated iron furnace, in which a process of transformation takes place. Analogous decoration would seem to mark transformation" (1988:383), that is, the act of decorating in this case confers a sort of personhood.

6. According to van Beek (1982), the Kapsiki, near neighbors of the Mafa, consider smiths to be not fully adult, even to some degree children. Hence they need nonsmith patrons or alter egos to negotiate brideprice or to appear in court with them. This, however, would presumably be equally true of women, so their marginality might also be interpreted as female.

the analogy of coitus and smelting.[7] Instead of threatening the smelter's reproductive role, here it reinforces it. Indeed, it is by no means uncommon to find in African understandings of causation that like can be both "imical" and inimical to like. As Wilson expresses it in discussing Nyakyusa ritual: "Things which are felt to be alike are taken as causally connected. Both positive actions and avoidances or taboos are based on the assumption that like objects or actions react on one another." While "avoidances come from resemblances," sometimes the opposite is true (1957:10). In other words, like things may in one context be felt to be antagonistic; in another, sympathetic.

MENSTRUATION TABOOS

The same principle arguably underpins menstruation taboos in metalworking, for the evidence makes abundantly clear that menstruation is commonly viewed as a threat to iron smelting no less dangerous than sexual activity—with which it is commonly incompatible as well. In the few areas, indeed, where women are permitted to take part in iron smelting and related activities, it is only on condition that they are not menstruating (Guyer 1984:5; Schaller 1973:59; Todd n.d., n.p.).[8]

Virtually all accounts focus on the baleful effects that the presence of a menstruating woman would have on a smelt. In an extreme example, if a Rwandan smelter's wife was menstruating, he had to postpone the smelt until her period was over even though she would not come near the site; in the case of an assistant's wife, he simply had to cancel out (Célis 1988:62, 87). As we have seen in Chapter 2, a good part of the medicinal arsenal was mobilized to protect against menstruating women as well as against those who had violated the sexual taboo.

When we pressed informants in Lopanzo (Zaïre) about what would happen to the offending woman if she did violate the prohibition and come near the furnace, they at first demurred, saying that the situation simply would not arise. Finally, they acknowledged that she would be doomed to "les menstrues infinies"—menstruation without end—and hence to sterility. This parallels the explanation for the effects on a man violating the taboo against sexual intercourse during smelting: impotence.

The customary explanation, given by many informants as well as by western interpreters, is that both sex and menstruation are "polluting" and therefore incompatible with a process that can only be carried to a successful conclusion by those who are in a state of purity. Words such as *pollution* and *purity* are

---

7. How explicitly this analogy was understood comes out in Killick's fieldnotes (1983:A:6). When Tumbuka smelters described iron smelting and its accompanying sexual restrictions, they commented that once it was over, "we would go home and make ng'anjo [the furnace] with our wives!"—a remark that was followed by "general laughter."

8. Surprisingly, women at Jefisi in northern Ghana are allowed to operate the bellows even when menstruating, but since they must take the appropriate medicines to protect the furnace (Pole: pers. comm.), they do not invalidate the general rule.

loaded with ethnocentric baggage, however, much of which has undoubtedly now affected "traditional" understanding of the terms. As Gottlieb (1982, 1988) has reminded us, the conscious or unconscious pejoratives attached to the notion of pollution have obscured our understanding of what is actually at issue, and this is particularly true in the assumptions about menstrual blood. Since menstrual taboos (like sexual taboos) affect many areas, not just metal-working, they must be studied closely in a cultural context, as Gottlieb has done with the Beng (Ivory Coast). We cannot assume that they carry the same valences even in related cultures. Unfortunately, the few studies that attempt to do this do not concern areas where we have the best information about metallurgy. Therefore, we will borrow the insights, recognizing that specific conclusions may not necessarily lend themselves to transfer.

Gottlieb argues for a return to the notion of pollution as "things out of place" (1982:45n.2; but cf. Buckley and Gottlieb 1988:30–31). Menstrual blood may be out of place, a harmful and alien intrusion in the smelting process, because it represents a failure to conceive, the opposite of the result desired. It is thus essentially different from the sacrificial blood of animals that is frequently a necessary and vitalizing constituent of smelting rituals. While most informants simply say that it "spoils the work," Mbeere (Kenya) smelters were more specific: menstrual blood prevents the iron ore from fusing in the furnace (Brown 1971:39–40; cf. Kay and Wright 1962:36; McCosh 1979:165).[9] Again, like affects like. The menstrual blood that has failed to coagulate into a fetus causes the metal to run out in molten slag rather than solidifying into a bloom. The same analogy is reflected in the Ekonda expression that slag "runs like the menses of a woman" during the smelt (Célis 1987:118).[10]

The incompatibility of menstruation and fire goes beyond the smelting furnace. In many parts of East and Central Africa, menstruating women are hemmed in by fire taboos. They cannot use the common fire, and when their periods are over they must often go through purification rites before they can light a new fire or return to the family hearth. Richards explains that for the Bemba, at least, contact with a menstruating woman, as with a corpse, makes a fire cold; by extension, her "coldness" leads to a range of other prohibitions (1956:30ff.; cf. Roscoe 1923a:263; Smith and Dale 1920:2, 26–27). In this respect, menstruation is the exact opposite of sexual intercourse, which is dangerous precisely because it is hot: there may be danger both in what is like and what is unlike.

Menstruating women are also commonly prohibited from cooking as well as from engaging in sexual relations; conversely, a woman usually is expected to cook for her husband when it is her turn to have sexual relations with him.

---

9. In what may be an allusion to menstruation, the wives of Chisinga smelters do not use red *nkula* dye on their hair or bodies during smelting, since this is believed to make it more difficult for the furnaces to reach the white heat necessary for the production of good iron (Brelsford 1949:28).

10. Gottlieb's Beng material could also suggest an alternative reading: that menstruation implies the same principle of fertility as the smelting furnace and that is why boundaries must be set between the two.

At Lopanzo, informants explicitly stated that menstruating women were not only supposed to keep their distance from the furnace site but also to refrain from cooking for those participating in the smelt.

This linkage raises interesting questions of parallels between smelting, cooking, sexuality, and reproduction. De Heusch ([1972] 1982b:32) asserts that "since the work of Lévi-Strauss, we can no longer doubt the universal equivalence of the sexual act and cooking," but is not the identification of gestation and cooking even closer? For example, Aluund (Lunda) belief (Southwestern Zaïre) affirms that the "raw blood-stuff" contributed by the father is processed and cooked in the womb during pregnancy (De Boeck 1991a:162). In the analogic thinking that makes it possible to see many symbolic levels concurrently, smelting may then be viewed not only as procreation but simultaneously as cooking. Collett points out that this is a common notion in East and Central Africa (the area, incidentally, where fire taboos seem to be most extensive):

> The foetus and iron are linked because both of them involve a transformation of one substance into another and this transformation is mediated by heat. This common method of transformation probably underlies the conceptual linkage between furnaces and women, and smelting and procreation. . . . The inclusion of pots and cooking in this metaphorical grouping is also understandable. Cooking involves a heat-mediated transformation of the raw into the cooked and this takes place inside a vessel, the pot. Not only transformation but irreversible transformation. (1985:121)

Thonga (Mozambique) belief elaborates this close association of fire and birth. A "child is the product of successful firing," which must be followed by a ritual cooking and then a gradual cooling down as it is integrated into the patrilineage. Here the process is equated first with firing a clay pot without cracking and then with a kind of smoking that protects the infant against the dangers of the external world and enables it to move from the interior of the maternal hut to the external social space. According to de Heusch (1980), the catalyst for the intrauterine firing of the embryo is, in fact, the menstrual blood, which gives off heat. Twins, interestingly enough, are viewed as the result of excessive intrauterine firing and carry a death-dealing power.

Killick's Chewa and Tumbuka informants in Malawi were not forthcoming about associations of smelting and gestation, but they did see an explicit analogy with cooking, specifically with porridge. Iron bloom was called *mkute* by the Chewa, the word for "cold cooked maize porridge," a reference, apparently, to the fact that it was cooked in the furnace, then left to cool overnight. Similarly, iron-rich slag collected for resmelting was referred to as "half-cooked iron" (Killick 1990:125, 130n.14). Burton reports a "superstition" among one Luba group that obviously baffled him. No ironworker was allowed to have anything to do with the preparation of food. "Were he even to pick up a stick used in stirring mush, or to lift a pot from the fire, he would be disqualified from taking part in smelting iron," for, it was believed, if he violated this interdiction, the spirits would refuse to allow the iron to leave the ore (1961:119). Just how we are to interpret this taboo is problematic, but it would seem to be intimately connected with the identification of smelting and cooking and the danger of like to like, which we will discuss at greater length below. Normally, however, men are so little involved in cooking in Africa that this does not take the form of a taboo.[11] However, Dusseljé cites the case of his Tégué (Congo) cook whose mayonnaise never succeeded if he had had sexual relations the night before (1910:n.1), thus brilliantly, albeit unwittingly, confirming Lévi-Strauss.

PERIODICITY AND THE PHASES OF THE MOON

Jackson's (1977:92n.9) proposition that periodicity is seen as an oscillation between order and disorder may also help to elucidate the peculiar power attributed to menstrual blood.[12] The menstrual cycle is characterized by such periodicity, signifying both fertility, that is, potential life, and waste or failure, the loss of such life. The fertility of the furnace is equated with conception, smelting failure with the discharge of blood. While most accounts of smelting do not take account of phases of the moon, the phenomenon most obviously related to the menstrual cycle, Echard observes that Hausa smelters in the Ader ideally light their furnaces at the full moon and try to finish the campaign before the moon wanes or at least before the new moon is visible (1965:359). The sequence is reversed for the Ekonda: construction of the smelting hut must begin at the full moon, and smelting must coincide with the new moon, as is also true for the Mambwe, south of Lake Tanganyika (Decle 1898:297–98). Among the Kota, trees used to make charcoal had to be cut at the full moon (Telfair 1987). In Futa Jallon entire smelting families would go into the bush at full moon to look for ore, and when it was found, they would offer sacrifices and dance to the spirits of the mines (Durand 1932:48).

The Bashu of eastern Zaïre greet the first quarter of the moon with the words "The moon appears." The same phrase is used as a euphemism for a woman's menstrual period, which they associate with cleansing, washing away pollutive substances that have built up in a woman's body between her periods. By extension the new moon is also associated with rituals designed to purify those who have been contaminated by forces of the bush during the same lunar phase (Packard 1981:43). Thus, the association of menstruation

---

11. In Burundi, the taboo appropriately concerned smelters' wives, who were allowed to prepare their food but were under no circumstances to taste it while the smelters were working because, as an informant expressed it, "le bloc de minérai se serait pulverisé au premier coup qu'on lui aurait donné au sortir du foyer" (Célis and Nzikobanyanka 1976:35).

12. This power is known in Yoruba as *fuù* (Fadipe [1939]1970:332).

with pollution needs to be qualified since it also represents purification (cf. Feierman 1990:82).

The Ekonda associate the new moon with prosperity, so many activities are synchronized with it: not only smelting but also setting traps in hunting and the emergence from seclusion of the young mother after the birth of her first child. Dances associated with the *levée de deuil*, the final funeral ceremony, are timed for the full moon. The rising of the new moon is a dominant image in Tabwa thought and art. As we have noted, it is connected with the birth of twins and the extraction of bloom from the smelting furnace. Indeed, de Heusch ([1972] 1982b:51–54, 185) sees lunar symbolism as a key element in the myths of central Africa and the beginning of each lunar cycle as a time of intense ritual activity; to some extent lunar cycles are a miniversion of seasonal cycles. The moon is an "unstable" sign, however, and may be associated with both good and ill fortune, fertility and sterility (menstruation). There may be an implicit linkage, too, of conception and/or birth, as well as menstruation, with the phases of the moon (Tessmann 1913:2, 16; Prins 1980:146).[13]

To be sure, there are very down-to-earth reasons to see the new and full moon as propitious times and to coordinate activities with it: the difference between a moonless night and a moonlit one in an African village with no electricity is too obvious to need belaboring. After all, as an old Africa hand, Karen Blixen always set out on safari at the new moon to have the benefit of a whole series of moonlit nights (Dinesen [1937] 1985:90). In general, one can make the equation that sexual activities and menstruating women are inimical to the successful conclusion of key activities, while the new moon is propitious for them.

TABOOS AGAINST VIOLENCE

Rowlands and Warnier (1988) have argued that the prohibition against sexual intercourse and against the presence of menstruating women during metalworking is directly related to the need to make iron production itself a nonviolent process to counter the association of iron implements with war and violence. In fact, prohibitions against violence at the smelting site (or forge) are widespread. But, as a Grassfields informant remarked perceptively, the sexual taboo has less to do with sex itself than with the "avoidance of jealousy and quarrels associated with sex." Rowlands and Warnier see the exclusion of menstruating women as part of the larger need to protect the work site from contamination by blood, itself a signifier of violence.

Whatever its validity for the We case, this explanation is not entirely convincing in the larger picture, or, rather, it is likely to be only one piece in the puzzle and does not necessarily preempt or invalidate explanations related to a reproductive paradigm. Indeed, violence is antithetical to reproduction

---

13. I was assured by the maternity ward nurses at Yale–New Haven Hospital in 1957 that there were always more babies born at the full moon than at any other time.

itself. Violence belongs to the domain of death, not life. Areas such as markets, which are often seen as women's spaces, have similar prohibitions against violence. Even incest taboos may be explained less in terms of sexuality than as a means of minimizing intragroup conflict, including conflict with a defined set of ancestors (cf. Kaberry 1971). In purely commonsense terms, violence is inappropriate wherever people must be able to mix or to concentrate on a difficult activity. Furthermore, the prohibition against violence seems to concern the smithy as a public place more than the foundry as a secluded and secret site, although it does figure among the taboos in Lopanzo smelting. As for the military motif introduced by the smelter Dokwaza during Mafa smelting, it may be less an allusion to violence per se than an analogy between the powers invoked by the smelter and by the warrior. Or, as David et al. (1989:202) speculate, it may be an example of "Mafa baroque, atypical but valuable precisely because the themes it exaggerates are quintessentially Mafa."

We must emphasize, too, that menstrual blood differs from sacrificial blood, and neither can automatically be equated with other forms of blood nor assumed to signify violence (cf. de Heusch 1982b [1972]:168ff.; de Maret 1980:274)—blood is a (the?) primordial symbol precisely because it is so multivalent.

PREGNANCY AND SMELTING

There is still a third attribute of femaleness that may be problematic in smelting and grounds for the exclusion of women: pregnancy. The evidence here is much more fragmentary than for the taboo against sexual relations and menstruating women. This may reflect the real state of things—that ironworkers often did not see pregnant women as a separate category—or it may simply reflect a failure on the part of observers to probe more deeply, especially where sexual and menstrual taboos may have more readily fit preconceived expectations than those concerning pregnancy. And yet with the early age of marriage, the premium put on fecundity, and the virtually universal practice of late weaning, most African women (unlike their sisters in the present-day West) spent as much or more time pregnant and lactating than menstruating (cf. Prins 1980:284–85n.25). This would have made menstruation taboos less onerous than for contemporary western societies but pregnancy taboos more so.

Pregnant women were seen as especially harmful to the smelt by Phoka (Tumbuka) ironworkers in Malawi (van der Merwe and Avery 1987:162). Some of Killick's informants among neighboring northern Tumbuka peoples noted that even husbands of pregnant women could not take part in smelting (1990:132). The same belief holds in Burundi: when the first smelt carried out at Musigati failed, the failure was attributed to the pregnancy of the wife of one of the researchers involved—even worse, he had touched the bellows. To counter this, before the process was repeated, an amulet was added to the charcoal during the second day of the smelt, the same amulet which is believed to bring good fortune to young girls looking for beaux (Célis and Nzikobanyanka 1976:35). De Maret (1980:275) relates this avoidance of pregnancy during smelting to a more generalized fear of prematurity: for the same reason, pregnant (or menstruating) women in Rwanda cannot attend a birth. Ekonda informants simply state that if a pregnant woman were to come near the smelting atelier, her child would have bad luck all its life.

In a few areas pregnant women were allowed to participate in mining (Galloway 1934:500; Radimilahy 1985:35). Among the Bassari, they were forbidden to carry ore from the mines, not because it was hard work but because they were "in a state of impurity" (Martinelli 1982:41). A Kotokoli smith living in Banjeli suggested that the danger might be reciprocal, at least as far as forging is concerned. Thus, even now, women who are pregnant or carrying small babies should not enter the forge for fear that the baby will sicken. Where a menstruating woman would harm the forge, the forge harms the fetus or infant (interview Boukari Saley 1985). This would seem to be implied also in the beliefs cited above from Burundi and Rwanda. Similarly, where the ring of white ash around the Bassari furnace apparently protects the furnace against harm, Pole (pers. comm.) found that the ring around the Jefisi furnace in northern Ghana protected pregnant women against the power of the furnace.

This is clearly another area that needs more investigation, first of all to know how widespread pregnancy taboos are, then to try to understand their foundation. Here, too, the principle of the incompatibility of likes could be invoked as part of the explanation. At the same time, more knowledge about pregnancy beliefs and practices would undoubtedly explain much more about smelting rituals. When Baumann (1935:87) talks about such beliefs among the Chokwe, Luimbi, and Lunda, his remarks could apply equally to smelting processes among the same peoples:

> The pregnant woman . . . is in a very special condition. Protective measures against the malevolent attacks of the nganga, who wish to destroy the fruit of motherlove with their sorcery, join hands with customs which circumscribe the mother-to-be with interdictions and prescriptions because she is perceived as impure.

She is painted with red and white earth and surrounded with taboos that both protect her and others from her. Like the furnace, one might say that she is both vulnerable and powerful: her fertility can go horribly awry or produce great bounty. We have already noted the invocations to the furnace to produce wealth, but there is also the danger of failure or of injury to the participants. Even today, "pregnancy is the most risky thing that an African woman can undertake" (Lucas quoted in "Child Survival," in *Africa News*, 1 May 1989).

How important it is, then, to look more carefully at the exclusion of women from iron smelting. While this is often expressed as a blanket exclusion, it is women of reproductive age who are its primary target and who have to be dealt with explicitly, according to the qualities that directly affect the operation: sexuality, menstruation, pregnancy. Each of these possibilities invokes a different rationale, since each is tied to a different social status and behavior, even to a different cosmological referent; we cannot assume that one explains the other. Yet all are vitally relevant to the smelting process precisely because it shares with them its reproductive function.

NONSEXUAL TABOOS

Although sexual and menstrual taboos have attracted the most attention, there are other types of prescriptive and proscriptive behavior associated with ironworking. The logic of some in the context of smelting beliefs is clear, but in other cases their meaning is often baffling—possibly to the smelters as well as to outside observers.

Dietary Prescriptions and Avoidances

Food and drink play an important part in smelting rituals, especially in the form of offerings to supernatural forces: directly or through the intermediary of the participants. Sometimes certain foods are obligatory, such as the panther's heart and millet gruel laced with fortifying plants of the Mafa (Podlewski 1965:21) or the roasted plantain of the Bagam (Cameroon) (Malcolm 1924:136). Yoruba smelters must chew white kola and alligator pepper, both hot foods, while chanting invocations to Ogun, the patron deity of iron, and to the ore so that it will "burn to become iron." They must avoid red palm oil, normally one of Ogun's favorites, when they first pour iron ore into the fire "because evil powers like red palm oil" (Adeniji 1977).

The Bassari offered no explanation for the mudfish meal that is obligatory during the first smelt in a new furnace, but it is likely that its curled shape is associated with the horseshoe form of the ideal bloom (David: pers. comm.). Following the same sort of associational thought, Tiv boys are given mudfish while they are recovering from circumcision because it is smooth and black, qualities desired in the healed penis (P. Bohannan 1954:5). Because of its ability to move between two different domains, the mudfish is, in fact, a common symbol of liminality. Among the Batammaliba of northern Togo/Bénin it is linked more precisely to the earth and the deity of the underworld, no doubt because of its burrowing habits (Blier 1987:25).

Sometimes the foods in question may be shared only by other designated groups. Thus, among the Ekonda only smelters, hunters specializing in elephant traps, and fathers of twins may consume the prescribed menu of chicken, fish, palm oil, cane rat, and bananas (Célis 1987:117). Elsewhere, the emphasis may be on what cannot be eaten during the smelting period (Roscoe 1923a:221): honey or salt (Stern 1910:153; Robert 1949:242), fish (Vergiat 1937:113), mutton (Brown 1971:39), pork (Wyckaert 1914:371; Robert 1949:242), alcohol, goat, and chicken (Moñino 1983:304), or potatoes (Cline 1937:117). The Powell-Cotton sisters reported that Kwanyama smelters were not supposed to eat or smoke before mining, and they had to fast before smelting until all of the ore was poured into the furnace (1937).

Brelsford (1949:29) is one of the few to offer any gloss of these food taboos. According to his informants, Chisinga smelters abstained from eating anything at all until the furnace fire was burning well. Then they ate only hot food, both staple and relish, for, if the food were cold, the furnace would be cold as well. Similarly they avoided a whole series of foods considered slimy or liquid, such as honey, large mushrooms, relish from the leaves of the *tutwe* tree, and the genet (because of his slitheriness), lest these prevent the iron from solidifying into a solid mass. Interestingly enough, this was exactly the explanation given for the exclusion of menstruating women. In addition, foundry workers were forbidden food cooked by the mother of a newborn baby because this would cause the iron to shrink in size. This last taboo seems neatly to point up the convergence of two paradigms of the smelting process: reproduction and cooking.

While most of the information available concerns food that must or must not be eaten while working metal, the Kapsiki of the Mandara mountains of northwestern Cameroon present an example of smiths who collectively and at all times eat different foods from the rest of the population. Or rather, they eat animals that nonsmiths eat but also others that no one else would think of touching. Here Kapsiki form an endogamous group living very separately from their fellows. Only a small number actually work metal nowadays; more important is their role in everything that has to do with death and burial. They also serve as diviners, healers, and musicians. When Van Beek (1982) classified the foods they eat that others don't, he found that they all had something in common with the smith himself so that in a sense they eat the "[blacksmiths] among the beasts"—animals that are carnivores, carrion-eaters, black, musicians, perform special functions, and have odd rather than even hooves. Is this a unique case, or have other researchers simply overlooked this kind of evidence?

Nakedness and Clothing

Two other taboos recorded in various parts of Africa are related to the body: the requirement of nakedness or special clothing during the work and the prohibition against washing all or parts of the body. Earlier, Ekonda miners worked practically naked. Western Nyamwezi (Tanzania) smelters performed all of the smelting operations entirely naked (Stern 1910:155), as did their Minyanka counterparts in Mali (Jonckers 1979:118) and, according to some accounts, Bassari smelters in Banjeli. Ushi (Zambia) also worked naked when the kilns were fired, which was an additional reason for isolating smelting sites from villages (Kay and Wright 1962:31). According to Martinelli (1982:50), Bassari smelters worked bare-chested with only a leather loincloth and an apron of animal skin. An 1897 account described these aprons as often ornamented with a plaque of brass, the insignia of the profession (cf. Redinha 1953:130; Krieger 1963:319; Killick 1983:D:5). In 1985 there was no sign of the loincloth or apron, but the smelter wore only a pair of shorts. He did, however, don a shirt during the ritual invocation of the ancestors preceding the construction of the furnace (vid. Saltman et al. 1986). Grieg (1937:77) says only that Fipa smelters wore special clothes during the ceremonies attendant on furnace construction, but he does not describe them. The Ekonda master smelter and ritual specialist also donned special costumes for the key phases of smelting in Lopanzo.

Nakedness, special clothing of barkcloth, or animal skin may link the smelter more closely with nature, corresponding to his isolation in the bush during smelting and his mediating role between the wild and the civilized. The only information about prescriptive clothing that seems to relate more directly to reproduction is Schmidt's comment (1988) that Haya (Tanzania) bellows operators traditionally wore grass skirts, dyed maroon (that is, woman's clothing), one of the intriguing hints that those involved in smelting may in some areas have been seen as situationally female.

Miscellaneous Taboos

Several accounts refer to taboos against washing, shaving, or even cutting one's hair during smelting or mining (Killick 1990:147; Brock and Brock 1965:99; Davison and Mosley 1988:80; Bérard [1945] 1951:235; de Rosemond 1943:81; Roscoe 1923a:219), but Brelsford is the only one to link it to other aspects of ritual. He describes how the workers involved in smelting wash their hands, feet, and face in water containing a decoction of medicinal leaves and bark. This cleanses them literally and figuratively, and thereafter they do not go home or bathe until the smelting is completed so as not to lose the power of the medicine (1949:28–29). Since this type of purification is widespread, it would be valuable to discover if similar washing taboos are more common than has been noted in the literature.[14] Interestingly enough, among the Bambala it is the wives of smelters who are forbidden to wash, anoint themselves, or put on any ornaments while their husbands are away in the bush smelting iron; they are, in fact, "in the same state as recently bereaved widows" (Smith and Dale 1920:207). Here, the significance is quite different: the

---

14. Unfortunately, we did not think to inquire about it during our reconstruction in 1985, although Bérard had documented such an interdiction among the Bassari smelters. Our informants at Lopanzo were not aware of any such taboos.

husbands are, for a period, dead to their wives in still another variation on the theme of furnace as spouse.

There are other taboos which are also by no means unique to smelting, such as those against whistling (de Rosemond 1943:81; Moñino 1983:304; Radimilahy 1985:36; Célis 1988:87), stepping over any part of the furnace installation (Célis 1987:114 and 1988:87; Weeks 1913:90; van Overbergh 1907:181–82, 297; Radimilahy 1985:40), or the presence of artificial materials in the area of the furnace or slag heaps (Dittmer 1962:9).[15] Whistling may summon or alert evil spirits and is probably to be understood in terms of more general prescriptions of silence in ritual contexts; it would seem to be different in some way from the human voice or music in its effect on transformative operations (Childs: pers. comm.; cf. Laye 1953:76). Stepping over—*enjambement* in French sources—is clearly a metaphor for sexual intercourse in some if not most cases (e.g., De Boeck 1991a:170–71),[16] but this has not been much studied.

CONCLUSION

The widely recognized exclusion of women from iron smelting needs to be qualified: it refers not to all women but to fertile women who are in theory at least, sexually available to the smelters. It therefore does not necessarily include prepubescent or postmenopausal women or women who for other reasons fall outside the category of potential sexual partner.[17] Consequently, it is intimately linked to the prohibition against sexual activity imposed on the smelters at various stages of their work but most commonly and rigorously during the smelt itself, a prohibition which seems to mirror interdictions against adultery during pregnancy. In the exceptional cases where, on the contrary, intercourse is prescribed, this concerns the smelter and his wife and, rather than undermining the model of gestation, seems to reinforce it by an alternative analogy. On a practical level, the taboo against sexual relations during smelting would keep away most adult men, reinforcing the secrecy that surrounded the operation.

The belief that menstruation ruins the smelt derives from a different principle. Menstruation is the visible evidence of failure to conceive, of provisional sterility. It is therefore inimical to any activity which assimilates itself to fertility, that is, which involves an act of transformation seen analogically as a form of reproduction.

In both cases we should be wary of accepting uncritically such terms as

---

15. This caused no small problem for Dittmer in filming Senufo smelting, since it meant even the camera had to be kept at a distance!

16. When my colleague Kanimba inadvertently stepped over a creeper attached to the plug used in the tuyere of the Lopanzo furnace, he was warned not to do it because it would cause impotence.

17. It also should not include lactating women, since they are supposed to avoid sexual activity and pregnancy until the baby is weaned, but there is virtually no information on this.

pollution, filth, and *uncleanness* in connection with sexual activity or menstruation, or *purity* in connection with abstinence. There is simply not the dichotomizing of body and spirit in African thought that figures so prominently in the Judaeo-Christian and Hellenistic traditions that still inform our view of the world and that have been exported now to Africa. If menstruation is to be feared, it is because it represents anticonception and the barrenness of witches. Indeed, the situation may be even more complex since menstrual blood also goes to form the fetus and hence is an ambivalent force, partaking of both sterility and fertility. In this sense it, too, can be seen as a metaphor for iron itself.

These taboos, then, are best understood, I would argue, in terms of the social control of sexuality and reproduction. They are aimed not only at maximizing reproduction but at doing so within the boundaries of an ordered society, just as the production of iron should occur within a socially acceptable order. Like medicines and sacrifices, they are all part of the arsenal of empowerment and protection, skeins of a web of metonymically interrelated means of controlling the processes to which they are applied. Not all can be directly tied to the reproductive paradigm, but some may be in ways not yet apparent. Thus, the spatial coordinates of some of the rituals (e.g., Echard 1965:360–61; 1983:216ff.; Smith and Dale 1920:203ff.) may, for example, invoke the gender connotations of space (see below, Chapter 9).

FOUR

The Smith and the Forge

[The hammer] is the mother-thing for the world.
Babungo smith, Cameroon

It is not my intent to examine smithing in as much detail as smelting, and yet the two cannot be totally divorced. Sometimes the personnel were one and the same, and even where they were not, each depended on the other. Both accomplished works of profound transformation that required long experience and mastery of a substantial repertoire of knowledge, technical and occult. I have argued, however, that smelting took precedence over smithing as the supreme embodiment of the metallurgist's skill and control of supernatural forces. Patrick McNaughton, the author of one of the few detailed studies of a particular smithing tradition, makes the same point: "Smelting, when still practiced, was even more fundamental to the essence of the blacksmith's professional identity. And, while forging is contemplated by the Mande as an extraordinary activity as well as a technical one, iron smelting was held to be exceedingly awesome and mysterious" (1988:148).

The greater ritualization of smelting would seem to bear this out—the greater the labor of transformation and accompanying risk of failure, the greater the need to invoke all available forces by all available means. Ian Fowler is one of the few researchers who has explored the ideological separation of smelter and smith. While his data may be unique to the Cameroon Grassfields with its high degree of specialization, they may serve to stimulate other scholars to look for echoes in comparable areas. During the nineteenth century, Babungo smelting and smithing were distinct from each other with different mythical origins:

The smelting founders of the chiefdom emerge from a cave behind a waterfall which denotes associations with the ancestors who live beneath the earth and who reach there by passing through water. The founders emerge from this enclosure within the earth through the water bearing 'medicines' which will enable them to extract fecundity from the earth to produce bloom and children, i.e., the wealth of the chiefdom. The 'medicines' and sorcery that facilitate this are socially controlled through cooperation, patronage and sharing of the products. In contrast, the ancestor of the smiths falls from the sky, the world of powerful combative mythical beings. In some versions he may descend on a spider's web or the iron hammer he bears may be wrapped in such a web. Fragments from the 'original' hammer are incorporated into each new one made by smiths and embody continuity with the world of powerful sky spirits that is expressed in the power to issue mortal oaths. This hammer is the 'mother-thing' for the world; with it the smith can make and unmake and he is associated with powerful 'medicines' that serve as defence against the predations of hostile witches. (1990:232)

The spider's web, linking the world of the ancestors below and the sky spirits above is the conceptual link between smelter and smith. This opposition of earth/fertility/peace/water with sky/sorcery/combativeness, it may be noted in passing, has intriguing parallels with Kongo cosmology as explicated by Hilton (1985).

Smithing was attended with much less ritualization than smelting and used far fewer medicines. Those that it did use were of a different order from smelting medicines, concerned primarily with protecting the chiefdom against foreign witches and removing pollution. "It is important to set this notion of smiths possessing powerful medicines to prevent the extraction of wealth and life essences by external sorcerers against the notion that senior smelters possess medicines to do exactly the reverse, i.e., to extract wealth and fecundate the bloom in the furnace" (Fowler 1990:197).

The contrast with the neighboring chiefdom of Oku is instructive. Oku relied entirely on recycling slag from smelting operations elsewhere to produce the iron that was forged. The whole process was the work of a single set of personnel using an open bowl furnace and was almost entirely devoid of ritualization and the sexual proscriptions associated with other forms of smelting. Demoted to an insignificant political role at Babungo, the Oku smith enjoyed a position of authority second only to the Fon. Fowler hypothesizes that this situation represents the end stage of a collapsing of earlier systems, "leaving only smithing as the organizing principle behind production" (Fowler 1990:226). In other words, because it was assimilated to smithing rather than smelting, the process invoked a different conceptual paradigm, one that required none of the magical paraphernalia of the latter—a striking illustration of how technology, political ideology, and cosmology accommodate to one another with historical change without undermining fundamental beliefs.

HAMMERS AND ANVILS

The most exhaustive smelting rituals, as I have noted, coincide with the construction of a new furnace and the first smelt in it or with the beginning of a smelting campaign. When a furnace is used over and over, rituals are pared down considerably. The same thing appears true for forging. That is, the rituals that provide the most important clues to understanding how the process is conceptualized may be those surrounding the manufacture of the basic tools and the consecration of a new forge, rather than the everyday practice of the craft. This hypothesis must be tested by more information, especially from West and Central Africa. For now, a look at existing documentation may suggest areas for further inquiry as well as points of convergence between smithing and smelting.

The rituals surrounding the forge are commonly open, in contrast to those surrounding the furnace. Thus, Labouret (1931:68) describes the consecration of a Lobi forge as a *fête familiale* to which clients as well as family are invited and everyone partakes of the sacrifices offered. In the elaborate ceremonies involved in setting up a new Mafa forge, both the father and the wife of a young smith take part. Once it is built, the smith does not settle in with his family until after a small boy or girl has spent the night there with his wife (Podlewski 1965:22), reminiscent of the smelting furnace rituals that incorporate young children but also emphasizing the reproductive motif within the family context rather than outside of it, that is, socially sanctioned sexuality.

Indeed, it is in the personifications of the hammer and the anvil that we find the most intriguing parallels with smelting as far as the reproductive paradigm is concerned. "They are our parents. The anvil is our mother, the hammer our father. They have nourished all of our family," according to a Tuareg smith (Echard forthcoming:19; cf. Robert 1949:245). Or, as Ogotemmêli explained to Griaule (1966:80), "The hammer is also the entire body of the *génie de l'eau*, of the great male Nommo of the sky. . . . As to the anvil . . . it is the female form of the hammer and represents the great female Nommo." The wood in which the anvil is embedded is in fact the "bed" of these two génies, and "when the hammer strikes the iron, the couple unite."

The making of a new hammer and anvil, especially the first ones of a fledgling smith, is often highly ritualized, conferring legitimacy on the new smith and underscoring the sacral as well as the utilitarian importance of his work. Among the Ekonda (Zaïre) the interdictions, sacrifices, and medicines associated with the manufacture of the hammer and anvil are very close to those associated with smelting. No sexual relations are allowed the night before, and a smith whose wife is menstruating may not come near the forge. The same interdiction holds for those attending the feast when these tools are publicly given to the young smith by his master (Célis 1987:112, 122–23).

Hammer and anvil rituals are even more elaborate among the Nyoro and neighboring peoples in East Africa. For Nyoro smiths, sexual and other taboos cover the whole operation from building the smithy to making the charcoal and bellows as well as the hammer and anvil. But, according to Roscoe (1923a), when the clay bellows pots were ready, the smith was *obliged* to have sexual intercourse with his wife "to make them sound and ensure their working well." The anvil was, in fact, a stone, either found whole or split to suitable size.[1] It

---

1. It is surprising to note how commonly anvils and even hammers—unhafted masses—continued to be made of stone in many regions of sub-Saharan Africa well into the twentieth century.

was put down just short of the smith's house, while he went to inform his wife of its arrival. "The stone was called a bride and the man and his wife, each dressed in two bark-cloths, came out to meet it. The smith took a bark-cloth to cover it as a bride was veiled and his wife carried a basket containing millet, and a bunch of purificatory herbs, that it might bear many children. The men who had carried the stone were then regaled with a plentiful meal of meat, vegetables, and beer." The stone remained in seclusion in the house for two days before being installed in the smithy. The first piece of work turned out on it was a knife that could not be sold in the market but had to be exchanged for millet, which the smith gave to his wife so that she could grind it for porridge. This they ate together "as a sacred meal." Thereafter the anvil could be put to ordinary use.

The hammer involved a slightly different sequence. The smith bought two lumps of iron from the "pig-iron worker" (refiner) but could not make it himself: He called in two smiths for help and his parents also had to be present. Work had to begin in the early morning hours, and while it was being made he could not wash himself or approach his wife. When it had been properly shaped, it was handed to the smith's father, who plunged it in a pot of water to harden it. The smith himself was not allowed to touch it until it was finished. Once ready, a feast was given and the smiths who made it were compensated with four hundred cowries. "That night the smith had sexual relations with his wife and the hammer was treated like a bride and secluded in the house for two days." Again he had to make a knife, this time trading it for goods that he gave to his parents (Roscoe 1923a:223–25).

Ankole anvil and hammer rituals are close variations on the same theme. When a new hammer was being made, however, a smith prepared a large feast and invited some twenty fellow-craftsmen to assist. The iron for it had already been smelted but not cleaned of the fiber in which it had been transported to the forge. The men worked through the night and finished the hammer about 8 A.M. They then dug a pit, filled it with water, and summoned the smith's wife, father, mother, and grandparents from the hut in which they had been waiting. The father and grandfather dipped the still-hot hammer in the water to cool it, and passed medicinal herbs over it in the water to purify and bless it. It was then carried to the house where another feast was prepared and eaten. Any fiber still adhering was put at the head of the man's bed, while the hammer was placed at the foot. The smith and his wife completed the work by "laying" on the bed, presumably having sexual relations. Finally, several days later, a bit of the remaining iron from which the hammer was manufactured was forged into a knife or hoe and given to a member of the family to show that the hammer was good (Roscoe 1923b:106–7).

Nyoro pig-iron workers, intermediate between smelters and smiths, followed comparable rituals in preparing the stones that served as both anvils and hammers in their trade, offering sacrifices of grain (millet, semsem, and beans) and meat (sheep and fowl) to the stones and abstaining from sexual relations beforehand. In this case, the hammer was smaller than the anvil and was referred to as the child of the anvil. Both were carried home slung on poles with the bearers singing as if they were bringing home a new bride. Here, too, the wife came out to greet "her," dressed in barkcloth and carrying a basket of millet, beans, and semsem, which she sprinkled over the anvil. A sumptuous feast followed, then the seclusion of the stones and their integration into the smithy (Roscoe 1923a:221–22).

The genderization of these objects, then, is just the beginning: they must be given a social as well as a sexual identity, inserted into the family structure with all the rituals appropriate to a second wife. The prescription of abstinence followed by obligatory sexual contact underscores the extent to which the work of the forge is equated with human sexuality and fertility, with all the vulnerability that this implies. These accounts also suggest the possibility of fluid identities: not only that the first wife serves as surrogate for the second—that intercourse with her ensures the fertility of the anvil—but also that the hammer is not inalterably adult male. In the case of the Nyoro pig-iron workers, the hammer seems to be regarded as the child of the anvil, evidence already of her fertility. Or, in the Ankole account, both anvil and hammer seem to become wives of the smith.

In some areas of Rwanda, the sexualization associated with the manufacture of the large iron hammers echoes that found in Uganda. Since this hammer is the symbol of the smith's knowledge, as Célis emphasizes, its fabrication is an event for rejoicing and demands a rather elaborate ritual of consecration. It is made in an ordinary forge, then dunked while still hot in a mortar that usually contains plants which are supposed to impart their virtues to the tool. Next it should spend at least one night in the house of the smith during which sexual intercourse is obligatory for the smith and his wife *and* for the *muse*, the head of the nonsmithing clan with which smiths have a special relationship. And, reminiscent of ceremonies in Uganda, the hammer is often subsequently paraded in the environs of the smith's house, receiving gifts and contributions to the celebration (Célis 1989:32–33; cf. idem 1988:179). How widespread a custom this is, Célis was not able to ascertain since he only became aware of it in the course of his survey and therefore had no data from the areas first researched where it could well have been overlooked.

In Burundi, on the other hand, the fabrication of hammers does not involve prescriptive sexual intercourse but does takes place with the same rituals and taboos as smelting. Three hammers must be made at a time on successive days. The first is impressively large and takes two men to wield; it is considered male. The second is smaller and considered female. The third is still smaller. Is it the child? Célis and Nzikobanyanka forget to tell us (1976:95, 100).[2] The Ewe smith in Togo refers to his tools as the "hammer and his

2. In a footnote on forging in neighboring Rwanda, Lestrade notes that to keep the handle of an implement from burning while a blade is being forged, it is covered with an aspersion derived from the same plant as that used to induce abortion. Unfortunately, he offers no comments from smiths themselves to explain this intriguing analogy (Lestrade 1972:37n.1).

family" (Forbes 1950:83). If the Bayaranké master smith (Senegal) has no daughter to give his apprentice, he gives him an anvil (Simmons 1971:80).

In some cases the equation of forging a hammer and the birth of a child may be explicit. Among the Ondulu (Mbundu, Angola) the rituals surrounding the manufacture of the first hammer for a novice smith suggest that, like the Nyoro pig-iron workers, they regard it as a child rather than a wife. It is made by experts, and when it is finished women brew large amounts of beer for a feast. The hammer is sprinkled with the blood of a chicken, then tied onto the back of a young girl in a cloth, just like a baby on its mother's back. So it is carried to the owner's village, accompanied by the chief blacksmith, his assistants, their relatives, and all the inhabitants of the village where it was made, all of them singing special songs (Read 1902:48).

A more veiled reference to childbirth may be implicit in the ritual surrounding the fabrication of the hammer among the Yira or Nande of northern Kivu. Here it is made by four or five master smiths in an aura of great secrecy. Animal sacrifices are offered before the work, which extends over a day and a night during which the workers may neither eat nor drink; all women are excluded except the first wife of the smith. When it is finished, the hammer is heated, then plunged into a bowl of water by the wife of the smith (E. Maquet 1965:57). The fact that it is the smith's wife who performs this last act, rather than the father or grandfather as in the Nyoro and Ankole cases, suggests a surrogate birth. It also reminds us that metalworking and birth are intensely concerned with notions of hot and cold (cf. Cline 1937:115–16).

Above and beyond these rituals, which concern the making of new tools and the creation of a new forge, there is further evidence for the genderization of the forge, although this is neither as extensive nor as securely documented as that for the smelting apparatus. The most sweeping claims for such a genderization are found in Germaine Dieterlen's *Essai sur la religion bambara* (1951), and the rather similar description of Dogon forging is found in her "Contribution à l'étude des forgerons en Afrique occidentale" (1965–66), which she sets in the context of the Dogon creation myth. Dieterlen asserts, for example, that the Bambara (Bamana) forge replicates the body of the artisan: "The furnace is his body, the bellows his testicles, the tuyere his penis, the fire his head. When the red iron is struck by the hammer, a replica of the *gosilande* [the primordial hammer in wood that is the repository of all human technologies] which symbolises the universe, the sparks are thunder and lightning" (1951:119).[3] The altar within the forge contains the blackened handles of old tools and fragments of ash enmeshed in clay that are the legacy of earlier proprietors, while the ax called "mother of the altar" is the model of ancestral axes, the first implement that was forged and an object of veneration in various agrarian and other rites. The altar is thus a "living" genealogy, but

---

3. There is a similar equation of the smith's testicles and bellows, penis and tuyeres in Dogon belief, but these beliefs are at the same time embedded in a complex genesis myth (Griaule and Dieterlen 1965:377).

at the same time it receives offerings to Faro and other divinities who taught the arts of metalworking to man.

In addition to these attributes of individual forges, Bambara smiths hold a number of ritual objects in common that are brought out for religious ceremonies. These include a rounded blade of iron whose name (in an archaic language) translates literally as "mother of the iron" and which the patriarch engraves with small bands representing the ancestral heads of the primordial smithing family as well as those of other smithing lineages: "The ensemble symbolises the totality of the smiths of the village." Once this blade has been fashioned, it is deposited in the sanctuary containing the ancestral tools. Here it remains for two or three months to be impregnated with the power of the ancestors, a process that is abetted by the blood of animals sacrificed at night. Finally it takes its place with a bell adorned with the same motifs and known as the "son of iron" in the house of the patriarch. Every year the smiths of the village march in procession to the river to invoke the aid of Faro to cool their iron as one of the assistants strikes this bell to the "rhythm of the sons of the testicles."

Because it is a living being "pourvu de force vitale et d'une âme," the forge is surrounded with taboos, seven in all, intended to protect its material and spiritual integrity. They concern not only the smith but also his clients and anyone who passes by. Among them is a ban on sexual relations near the forge, as well as injunctions against curses, ill will, or jealousy—any evil sentiments, discord, or violence. All of these impede the proper functioning of the work: "To break the prohibitions of the smithy fire is to harm the virility of the smith, for the bellows are his testicles." Therefore, the smiths present themselves nude before anyone who is guilty of such a trespass and force him to undergo a rite of purification on the anvil before the forge is reconstructed and reconsecrated (Dieterlen 1951:119–24).

Pâques (1956:387) shows still another dimension of the anthropomorphism of the forge in her study of the Samake, a Bambara subgroup. The forge is divided into masculine (right) and feminine (left) halves. In the latter is a small pile of fresh clay used in welding, referred to as the breast of the forge. There are then both male and female elements, testicles and breast, that compositely make up the smithy, although they would seem to refer to noncomparable aspects of masculinity and femininity.

Dieterlen's work has been challenged by other investigators who have not found corroborating evidence in their own fieldwork. How do we evaluate such discrepancies? Dieterlen's research was carried out within the context of the Missions Griaule, and Griaule's approach and conclusions have come under increasing scrutiny, indeed sometimes under heavy fire (vid., e.g., Clifford 1983; Ezra 1988; van Beek 1991; and McNaughton, pers. comm. 1991; but vid. also de Heusch 1991). In fact, it has become the Africanists' version of the Freeman-Mead debate. Critics charge that he, and to some extent his students, relied too heavily on a few overly imaginative informants; con-

sciously or unconsciously, they tended to fit indigenous thought into an idealized Procrustean bed more Gallic than African and characterized by an almost
baroque symbolic elaboration. Under Griaule's influence French ethnography
listed heavily toward a preoccupation with symbols, as his introduction to
Dieterlen's book makes emphatically clear. It endorses the "total ethnology"
of Dieterlen and her team as the only way to do justice to the richness of
African thought and the relevance of even the most minor detail of life. "By
the play of assimilation applied to a considerable number of symbols and thanks
to a power of abstraction of which we have only begun to glimpse the grandeur, these men have systematized the universe. . . . [N]o image, no spiritual action, no technical or religious gesture are unrelated to this ensemble of
classifications" (Dieterlen 1951: vi–vii).

The minute description of the forge and its paraphernalia are thus understandable as part of a larger agenda, although one may find it troubling that
she does not include anyone identified as a smith among her primary informants (one who is referred to as a chief of the *kòmò* society would presumably
have been a smith). As a woman, it is highly unlikely that she would have
been able to apprentice herself to a smith as McNaughton was later to do—
in any event this sort of participatory approach was not part of the Griaule
method.

And yet for several reasons I am hesitant to dismiss out of hand Dieterlen's
explication of the Bambara forge. First of all, she and her colleagues carried
out their field researches some three decades before McNaughton. It is a
truism that rapid change in Africa has led to the loss of a great deal of information in the face of modernization, the spread of Islam, and the impatience—even embarrassment—of younger people with old ways. In addition,
Dieterlen probably benefited from her quasi-official status under the colonial
regime, which assured the cooperation of local officials. I would suggest, too,
that as industrially produced hammers and anvils have replaced locally forged
ones (or stone anvils) in recent years, the rituals associated with the latter that
Dieterlen studied have diminished or been dropped altogether. Also, while
Dieterlen's areas of Bambara research overlapped with McNaughton's, they
were not identical, so one would expect some differences both in practice and
in what different informants know and are willing to divulge, to say nothing
of the impact of differing personalities and research styles.

But the main reason for accepting, albeit with caution, the main outline of
Dieterlen's schema, if not necessarily all the details, is that it is not inherently
improbable. Much of the discomfort with Griaule's presentation of Dogon
cosmology stems not only from the inability of other researchers to duplicate
the information but also from the anomaly of this mythology and astronomy
within the corpus of African thought; the welter of correspondences do not
add up, in the eyes of some critics, to a veritable myth and are not replicated
in the myths of other West African peoples. In contrast, the key elements of
Dieterlen's description of the forge and associated rituals *do* find parallels in

other ironworking traditions: the attribution of personhood, with both gender and familial position, to the forge; the emphasis on genealogy and the ancestral continuity; the taboos against sexual relations, violence, and ill will; the distancing of active sexuality; and even the prescriptive nudity of the smith during the purificatory rites.

Jean Lombard's study of the Bariba forge in present-day Benin, for example, while by no means as detailed as Dieterlen's, confirms the sexual and generative elements. According to Lombard, the Bariba forge "has spirit and life." Once, no one could touch a smith's tool without becoming ill with fevers, abcesses, and the like, which were held to be the vengeance of the crab to whom God first entrusted the knowledge of smithing and who then transmitted it to man. The crab continues to live in the stone anvil of the forge and receives the sacrifice of goats. Further, the forge is sexualized: the right-hand bellows is male; the left, female. "In alternately pumping each of the bellows, the smith symbolizes copulation, the fruit of which is the air that is expelled." The ensemble of the Bariba forge, however, is male, characterized by an *antinomie totale* between it and the feminine (Lombard 1957:16).[4]

McNaughton's own work on Mande smiths and smithing brings in gender in a different way (1988: ch. 1). His focus is on the smith, rather than on his tools and workplace, and here he draws on the Mande concepts of *fadenya*, "father-childness," and *badenya*, "mother-childness," to elucidate the nature of the smith and what he does. These concepts are modeled, in fact, not so much on male and female as on the sibling relationship. Thus, fadenya stresses the "competition for honor and resources that invariably occurs between siblings who have the same father but different mothers," while badenya reflects the affection, loyalty, and gentleness assumed to exist between children of the same mother and father. These complementary ideas become the poles around which all behavior is structured, but they do not refer solely to male and female—women can manifest fadenya behavior and men badenya—nor is one valued more than the other. Both are admired, for the Mande value aggressiveness as much as they fear its consequences. Smiths, along with other endogamous specialists such as griots and leatherworkers, are strongly associated with "father-childness" because of the power they wield and their access to occult knowledge, not only of metallurgy but of healing, divination, circumcision, and sorcery. These concepts are also extrapolated to define space: the protective space of badenya, the dangerous space of fadenya.

This model, then, projects onto a larger canvas the stereotypes of behavior that are as basic to relational experiences in polygamous societies as gender and age. But it does not necessarily exclude or supersede the latter catego-

---

4. The prudery of observers may be as relevant here as in the discussion of gynecomorphic furnaces. Paul Gebauer's description of the Kwadja (Cameroon) smithy, for example, conspicuously omits any description of the furnace. The collection of his photographs in the Metropolitan Museum, Ian Fowler observes, explains why: the tuyere is adorned with a sculpted male figurine with an erect phallus (pers. comm.).

ries. And, as we have seen, they too are best understood relationally rather than essentially: mother, father, wife, child—and ancestor.

Griaule and Dieterlen tend to emphasize the genealogical elements of Mande smithing by reference to the Dogon genesis myth in which the blacksmith figures as the twin of Nommo, carrying with him the sacrificial blood from Nommo's umbilical cord and sex organs, or, in the case of the Bambara, by reference to the myth of Faro and Pemba. These myths they see reenacted in the symbolism of the forge and the actions of the smith. McNaughton's informants did not make these connections. Nevertheless, they did confirm the centrality of the ancestral smiths to their work. When asked why they hammered in rhythmic patterns, then tapped the anvil lightly every time they stopped, they replied that it was so they could examine their work. "But they also say the anvil symbolizes their fathers, and so the gesture could also be a ritual of respect and continuity." Sometimes they pour water on the anvils to cool them *and* the spirits of their fathers. The water basins, they say, symbolize their mothers. In addition, they offer sacrifices of kola nuts and chickens to the anvils just before the farming season begins, the busiest time of the year, to protect themselves from injury (McNaughton 1988:30, 65, 203n.6).

In this respect Okoro's (1990) research on the centrality of the stone anvil in northeastern Ghana suggests an important line of investigation that may have been neglected in the past. Okoro studied smithing families in Mamprugu, near the Togo border, but all of them were immigrants from outside, primarily Hausa. The smiths, although not endogamous in principle, tend to be so in practice. They believe that the smith inherits his skills from his ancestors, who are, in fact, the source of his power. "This power is renewed and refreshed and, in fact, embodied in the form of an important piece of equipment—the stone anvil." The anvil is the most sacred part of the workshop and is passed down as an heirloom from father to son so that there was no information about making or installing a new one. It serves as the link between the smith and his ancestors and has both a practical and a mystical side. It is the focus of sacrifices and rituals to the ancestors to solicit their aid both in matters relating to the forge and in family problems as well. The sacrifices include chicken, guinea fowl, goats, and dogs. The dog was believed to be the most powerful of domestic animals: "Its . . . vigilance, clairvoyance and alertness are regarded . . . as attributes which rejuvenate the power inherent in the stone anvil: it revives the 'soul' of the anvils."

Dogs are, of course, the preferred sacrifice of Ogun, the Yoruba deity of metalworking. But reverence accorded the anvil in northern Ghana also parallels that of the Maguzawa, the non-Muslim ironworkers in rural Hausaland, who have assimilated ritual aspects of their craft to the bori cult. Three of the bori spirits are associated with ironworking: Makera ("anvil"); Batoyi, her son; and Randa, Batoyi's wife. Sacrifices are performed to Makera whenever a new anvil is set up and before other metallurgical activities are begun, but there is no mention of a dog (Rogers 1990:90–91).

SMITHING TABOOS AND PRESCRIPTIVE BEHAVIOR

As we have noted, smithing is an exclusively male occupation,[5] subject to many of the same prescriptions and proscriptions as smelting. Women are commonly—but not universally—barred from the forge. This is especially true of menstruating women but sometimes includes pregnant women as well (e.g., interviews Kuandi Mammam 1985 and Boukari Saley 1985, Banjeli, Togo; Ardouin 1978:16; Garrard: pers. comm.). A Rwandan informant explained that if a smith tried to forge the large hammer that plays so prominent a part in practice and ritual while his wife was menstruating, the hoes he later fashioned from it would not fuse properly (Célis 1988:194)—a displacement of the analogy from the hammer to the hoe. In the past, smiths frequently worked naked or wore skin clothing, identifying themselves situationally at least with nature and the wild (P. Gebauer 1979:102; C. Gebauer: pers. comm.; Jeffreys 1962:152; Cornevin 1962:88; Martinelli 1982:64; Haberland in Jensen 1959:231; Killick 1983:D:12 and pers. comm.; H. Kuper [1947]1961:143).

Lestrade (1972:40) explains the exclusion of women from forges in Rwanda in terms of the incompatibility between the principle of fecundity that she represents and the destructiveness of iron implements made by the smith: while exception is made for hoes and tools used in the household, a woman is not supposed to use an ax or handle arms or even to see them manufactured. In this case, at least, the danger may be as much to her as to the work of the forge.[6] It underscores the ambivalence of the smith's role: he makes instruments of both production and destruction and, especially in West Africa, serves as mediator. Indeed, the smithy is often a place of asylum.

In some areas, too, sexual relations are forbidden the night before forging (e.g., Martinelli 1982:64; Podlewski 1965:22; Célis and Nzikobanyanka 1976:188; Jeffreys 1962:152 and 1971:74). Dusseljé (1910:66–67) reports the belief among the Tégué of the Alima (Congo Republic) that if a man had sexual relations within the previous twenty-four hours, a fire would not catch if he approached nor would iron redden in the forge. A smith even claimed that it botched his work if he merely received a visit from one of his numerous wives. Usually such interdictions are simply stated as matters of fact, but Nyakyusa informants explained that "when a smith forges a spear he does not sleep with his wife because, we say, when a woman conceives, the fire blazes within her to forge a person, and the woman's fire and the smith's fire fight. When a smith comes with the fire of his smithy on his body and lies with a woman, the woman has a miscarriage." The pregnant woman was felt equally to be a dan-

---

5. It is intriguing to compare the Babungo myth that the iron hammer was introduced by a smith who fell from the sky (Fowler 1990:174, 194) with the Hausa myth from Mogar, which centers on a woman who fell from the sky with the hammer in her hand (Echard 1965:354).

6. And yet there is an interesting exception: a recalcitrant young wife is discreetly led to the forge to make her more tractable and sensible (ibid.)!

ger to the forge. For the Nyakyusa, the opposition between procreation and smithing (they do not smelt) was part of the larger opposition of like and like (Wilson 1957:141). By extension, the injunction against stepping over a smith's hearth, noted by Weeks (1913:90) elsewhere in the Congo Basin, probably parallels the same taboo for smelting, mentioned above, and is likewise an allusion to the sex act. The prohibition against sexual relations must have been adapted to circumstances, however; it could not really be observed where smiths were full-time craftsmen.

FERTILITY AND THE ANCESTORS

To the extent that the forge is sexualized and forging is analogized with reproduction—in this case, the reproduction of tools and ornaments—it is comparable to the smelting furnace. A major difference derives, however, from the fact that the forge is generally a public, "urban" place, in contrast to the isolation and secrecy of the smelting furnace, often located in the bush or at least shielded from public traffic. If the Tégué smith tended to work in solitude (consistent with the strictures against sexual contact), this is not true of most smiths. More often the smithy plays a central role in the community, not only as a gathering place for men to exchange the news but as a refuge from violence, a place of purification, even a place of healing. In the forge judicial disputes are settled, oaths are sworn, asylum is granted.

But here, too, a woman can seek a cure for sterility (Dieterlen 1951:122) or surcease from a difficult labor (Pole: pers. comm.; Bourgeois 1956:123), both functions obviously related by association with the fertility of the forge. Indeed, the Minyanka "attribute to the smith the occult power of favoring fecund unions, metamorphoses, births, successful gestation." Furthermore, if a woman gives birth to a child after her previous ones have died, she confides the newborn to the smith. He sacrifices two hens to the anvil and prays that it will protect the child. He then presents the baby to his wife, who symbolically puts it to her breast. Once weaned, the child is temporarily adopted by the smith, who puts on its ankle an iron ring made on his anvil to protect it from evil influences by virtue of the beneficent power (*nyama*) of the smith. The child then receives a name indicating its close connection to the smith. Once grown, he or she must undergo a special ceremony before marrying, called "cutting the bracelet," that involves a symbolic death and rebirth, followed by a feast attended by all the bards and musicians of the region.

Jonckers explains the rationale of this practice by appeal to Minyanka ideas of personhood. Every individual is believed to come into the world as a result of being called by one of numerous Minyanka spirits (*yapere*). The name a baby is given indicates the particular spirit under whose auspices it has been born. When a woman loses her children at or soon after birth, the diviner explains that several spirits have disputed the breath of the child. The only way to resolve the problem is to solicit the aid of the eldest of the smiths, the "priest of the anvil," a spirit who takes unchallenged precedence over the rest. If the sacrifices offered to him are accepted, the breath of the child will be in the custody of the sacred anvil (1979:118–19).

The explanation for the role of Bogaba smiths in curing barrenness is somewhat different. Like the Earth priests, they are believed to predate the Mossi invasion of Yatenga (Burkina Faso). As autochthones as well as metalworkers, both smelters and smiths, they share with the Earth priests an especially close relationship with the Earth. Their assistance in helping barren women to conceive is therefore of a piece with their ritual responsibility for maintaining proper relations with the deity believed to ensure plant growth and agricultural prosperity (Hammond 1966:171).

The Kongo smith was also closely identified with fecundity through his intimate association with the local simbi spirits, who were responsible for the fertility of crops and women. In some areas he was the principal simbi priest, a logical connection, as MacGaffey points out, in view of the dependence of agriculturists on iron tools (1986:178–79).[7] Smithing seems to have been linked with terrestrial water. The initiation of a smith demanded that a large stone be brought from the river and placed in the smithy; according to one informant, smithing itself "comes from the water simbi." But the smith seems to mediate between the two divisions of Kongo cosmology, on the one hand intimately joined to the world of "below"—women's activities, river waters, healing, and fertility—and on the other to the world of "above"—men's affairs, fire, and destruction (ibid.).

Among the Soninke, Malinke, Bamana, Fulani, and Dogon in the western Sudan and in other areas such as eastern Nigeria and western Cameroon south of the Benue (Tamari 1991:230; Wente-Lukas 1972:136), the smith commonly oversees circumcision. Among the Bamana, his wife performs the excision of girls. Dieterlen refers to circumcision as a form of sacrifice (1973:53), but it seems most immediately analogous to the smith's action in manufacturing an implement from an amorphous, unusable chunk of raw iron: the smith provides both an identity and a social utility. "Like iron working," as McNaughton observes, "circumcising effects a transformation of monumental proportions" (1988:67; cf. Zahan 1960).[8] It is much more than a physical operation, removing what are considered the physical characteristics of the opposite sex; without it, people cannot marry or have socially sanctioned sexual activities, nor can they have access to the knowledge that enables them to function as adults. "Circumcision is a rite of passage that confers sexuality on sexually undifferentiated children" (Simmons 1971:79). It is also extremely dangerous, requiring all the surgical skill and supernatural energy (*nyama*) the smith can muster to protect both the patient and himself. Even though smelt-

---

7. It is intriguing that these *bisimbi* are pictured as phallic: large, red-headed dwarves who have trouble standing up.

8. McNaughton makes an interesting comparison between circumcision and wood carving, which is also the domain of the Mande smith. Both, he notes, involve cutting away to bring out "a core that is socially malleable" (ibid.:103).

ing has long since ceased in most areas, most of the spears used in Bamana circumcision have been forged from traditionally smelted iron to harness its nyama. After the operation, boys are called "children of the circumcision," a term that underscores the belief that they have been born again through the agency of the smith.

On the other hand, as McNaughton acknowledges, circumcision and its attendant rituals are in some ways more analogous to smelting than to smithing since they take place in secrecy in the bush. The Mande smith also leads the kòmò society, which young men usually enter right after circumcision and which continues the process of socialization.[9] Significantly, he retreats to the bush to carve the animal masks used by the society (McNaughton 1988:68, 103, 114, 130ff.). In these multifaceted roles he is both the embodiment of "mother-childness" and of "father-childness," suggesting somewhat the same mediating position between worlds as the Kongo smith or as Ogun, the Yoruba deity of ironworking who also has dominion over circumcision and conception and represents polar opposites of procreativity, healing, and civilization on the one hand and violence and destructiveness on the other (S. T. Barnes 1989; Roache-Selk 1978).

Two other aspects of the smith's role are relevant: rainmaking, with its obvious associations of fertility, and participation in ancestral cults. It is intriguing that two regions where the separateness of the smithing groups is most pronounced see the smith's relationship to rainmaking in diametrically opposed ways. Bamana blacksmiths claim to be able to produce rain through a combination of the power they are born with and the secret knowledge they acquire during their training (McNaughton 1988:50–51). The Dogon also attribute rainmaking powers to smiths by virtue of their close "twinness" with Nommo, the "primordial being who brought order, purity, and fertility to the universe and who is manifested in life-giving water" (Ezra 1988:81). In stark contrast, smiths among the Mafa and Dowayo of the Mandara mountains of Cameroon are anathema to rainmaking and rainmakers: the Dowayo even ban them from rainmakers' villages because they represent fire as opposed to water (Barley 1983:14; Podlewski 1966:34).

The rituals of setting up a new forge and manufacturing hammers and anvils highlight the links between smiths and their ancestors, as we have already pointed out. The same is true in the explicit genealogy of the Dogon smith, whose eponymous forebearer descended to earth to bring mankind fire, iron, and seeds—the raw materials of civilization.[10] Dogon smiths also make the sculptures used in family ancestral altars and in the sanctuaries devoted to the cult of clan and individual ancestors. Further, they carve the *sigi*, the "mother of masks" in the form of a snake that represents the dead ancestor, which is the center of the cycle of dances that take place throughout the Dogon region

---

9. *Kòmò* is believed to have a female counterpart, but little is known about it. Girls had to undergo excision before they could participate (McNaughton 1975; idem 1988:130).

10. Apparently, the Dogon do not see a fundamental incompatibility between the blacksmith's association with fire and with water.

every sixty years. The sigi commemorates both the first appearance of death and the renewal of life (Dieterlen 1973; Ezra 1988:23–25). It is still very much the case among the Shona of Zimbabwe that the ancestors call upon men to become smiths so that they may continue to make ceremonial objects such as the knives and axes used in ancestral veneration, divination, healing, and possession (Dewey 1990).

CONCLUSION

Smithing invokes the reproductive and ancestral paradigms at certain key junctures, especially those involving the "birth" of a new forge and its primary tools. There are hints of this, too, in menstrual taboos and the role of the forge in facilitating birth. The paradigm is attentuated, however, for several reasons. Although the smith is primarily known through his working of metals, he commonly plays a variety of other roles such as healer, diviner, amulet maker, even, in the Mandara mountains, gravedigger and burier of the dead. These seem to derive more generally from his access to unusual amounts of power and may in some cases be directly connected to the model when they relate to enhancing fertility or mediating ancestral intervention, but this does not always seem to be the case.

Second, the smith and his forge are far more integrated into the life of the community than the smelting furnace; what goes on there is open to public view, and the smithy becomes simultaneously a place of asylum and an adjunct to political power. While not the chief or king himself, the smith is intimately involved in the creation as well as the maintenance of political power, so the reproductive model takes a different twist.

Finally, whereas smelting stopped rather abruptly, frozen at a moment in history, smithing has continued, adapting to the modern world. We do not know, and probably cannot know, how the beliefs enveloping its practice have changed as well.

CODA

"From Thence Came Our Mothers"

IRONMAKING AND BRIDEWEALTH

Bamama banso bazwami awa.
The mothers originate here.

Elders, Lopanzo, Zaïre

In a discussion with my colleague Kanimba Misago, some of the elders of Lopanzo (Zaïre) pointed out the nearby pits from which iron ore was extracted and declared that it was the source of the mothers of the village. Their statement confirmed the role once played by iron in bridewealth payments among the Ekonda, a crucial extension of its association with fertility. It sums up the equation of iron with the power to appropriate the fertility of women.

The zone of iron bridewealth currencies extends over large areas of Central Africa. Indeed, Guyer suggests that a "perhaps quite substantial proportion" of the iron output was used in these vast regions to "create marriages." In a detailed study of the iron currencies of southern Cameroon, she documents the great variety of forms and denominations used. All were based on the template of the spearhead, but they differed widely in size and in the care of fabrication (fig. 28). While they could theoretically be converted to utilitarian objects, most would have remained in the exchange sphere. The amounts involved were often quite large—some Ewondo payments totaled eighty to one hundred pounds (1985:4).

Socially, this had several important implications. Among the Beti, for example, more people may have been mobilized for iron production than for agriculture or hunting. "Their work was not just devoted to expanded production, in the narrow sense of tools, but, in significant proportions, to expanded reproduction through the promotion of accumulative polygynous marriage." If the original form of marriage here as elsewhere was sister exchange, the introduction or substitution of iron currencies for this purpose would have increased the possibilities for some men to acquire more wives through their control of more of the currencies. The wealthy could become wealthier by using one form of wealth—iron—to gain another—wives. Unlike sister exchange, access to wealth in iron would be more difficult for elders to control in gerontocratic societies: men could claim a share of iron by working for smelters and smiths or by learning these trades themselves, or they could earn it through other skills. The use of iron currencies was therefore associated in Beti society "with a competitive struggle to accumulate" (ibid.:16).

Iron bridewealth currencies took many forms and were not necessarily different from other forms of iron currencies. While the Beti, Azande, and Ngombe (Wolfe 1961:57) used spearheads or knives, the Thonga of southern Africa used hoes (Junod 1913:121), as did peoples on the Bamenda Plateau in the Cameroon Grassfields (Warnier and Fowler 1979:337), in parts of northern Nigeria (Smith and Smith 1990:248), and in northern Malawi (Davison and Mosley 1988:71; Killick 1990:257), as well as the Hutu agriculturists in Rwanda (Célis 1988:204–5). Iron bars were the standard form among the Marghi and Sukur (Nigeria), in some areas "the only acceptable bridewealth" (Vaughan 1973:176; cf. Wente-Lukas 1977:115).

Far to the south and some seventy years earlier, Mary Kingsley also found that bundles of small iron ax heads, *bikei*, were the only currency that the Fang of Gabon would accept for bride payments ([1898] 1987:139). In the Zaïre Valley above the confluence with the Ubangi, "couteaux monnaies" were forged especially for bridewealth transactions by specialist smiths (Mumbanza mwa Bawale 1980:125).

In many of these areas, however, the situation changed during the nineteenth century. If the Sukur of northeastern Nigeria still occasionally demanded iron bars for bridewealth in the 1960s (Vaughan 1973:176), many peoples of the Zaïre Basin and other areas such as the Cameroon Grassfields had long since shifted to copper and brass currencies. Exactly when the change occurred in different parts of this vast area is difficult to reconstruct. In Lopanzo, for example, informants gave a range of replies when queried about bridewealth. Some had apparently forgotten that iron was ever used. Others referred to payment in iron blooms or bars or some combination of iron and copper currencies, as well as slaves (cf. Célis 1987:131) and were able to produce iron and brass rods and a blade that looks somewhat like the iron currency Bruël illustrates from the Irebu region, well to the west (1918: fig. 25). The etymology of the words for copper and brass reflects their foreign sources: Lokongo and Tio, respectively. In any event, with the expansion of commerce in the nineteenth century, the sequence at Lopanzo seems to have replicated that in other regions of the Zaïre Basin: from iron to copper to brass and finally, in recent times, to money—from iron smelted locally to copper produced in Lower Zaïre, to brass imported from Europe (Harms 1981:86ff.; Herbert 1984a:197–200).

Interestingly enough, the changeover from iron to copper and brass bridewealth currencies need not have meant a radical revision on the symbolic level. As I have argued elsewhere (Herbert 1984:266 et seq.), copper and brass carried profound connotations of fertility in precolonial Africa. Looking at material culture as a language, one might be tempted to view the two metals as synonyms, at least in the context of bridewealth, certainly as complementary rather than opposed where they coexisted within the same value system.

The impact of iron and copper was particularly great in the equatorial forests and savannas of Africa. The practical uses of iron, especially, are so obvious that they tend to have been exaggerated and to have distracted attention from the social and political implications. In this vast area, these metals were virtually the only material goods that were both scarce and durable, capable of accumulation and storage as wealth; their availability "made it possible to create a patrimony which could be converted into the acquisition of people" (Vansina 1990:60). As with cattle in eastern and southern Africa, chiefs and big men, by controlling stores of metal, could enlarge their following through polygynous marriage, clientage, and the imposition of fees and fines. Small wonder that this is the area par excellence where chief and metallurgist are closely associated—even fused—on the level of myth and ritual.

FIVE

Ironmaking and Belief

De fait, le travail forgeron incorpore, sans disso-
ciation possible, pratique technique et pratique
symbolique.

Nicole Echard

In the preceding chapters we have broken down the processes of ironworking
and analyzed them, as it were, under the microscope. We have looked at the
allocation of work roles, at the physical objects used in the technological processes, at accompanying rituals, and at behavioral prescriptions. Now it is
time to put these pieces back together to see if they do indeed form a "semantic web" (de Heusch 1980). Can we look at a technological complex and
read a system of beliefs from it, using the combination of actions and objects
as texts? Do these intricate dance/dramas and the fragmentary exegesis offered by the participants reveal any homogeneity of underlying beliefs? Given
the tremendous variations in social, political, and cultural systems across sub-
Saharan Africa, and the presumption that technologies as a whole mirror these
systems, is there any reason to expect that a paradigm that fits one complex
will fit another?

First of all, let us try to summarize, to the extent that is possible, the
similarities and differences between smelting and smithing, an endeavor made
difficult by the fact that smelting has virtually disappeared while smithing
continues. Inevitably, a certain amount of telescoping and forgetting has confused some of the relevant issues. Since in the past the smelter and smith
may have been the same person or different people, it is clearest to focus on
the *activities* to bring out key distinctions.

Both smelting and smithing employ fire to effect transformation. Both are
the work of male specialists. Beyond that, the differences are often great:

Smelting	*Smithing*
Generally isolated and secret	Public
Highly ritualized	Rituals mainly limited to new forge and implements
Process and/or artifacts commonly genderized	Genderization exists but extent uncertain

Smelting	*Smithing*
Women usually excluded	Women may or may not be excluded
Sexual relations taboo	Sexual taboos exceptional
Menstrual women taboo	Same
Music, dance, song common	Bellows rhythms; sometimes other music
Results may be highly variable	Less risk of failure
Perceived to be dangerous	Less dangerous
Not asylum: isolated	Smithy often an asylum; taboo against violence

Several hypotheses can be proposed on the basis of this schematization. First of all, smelting is more extensively ritualized because it involves a more fundamental act of transformation than smithing. It also demands a different sort of skill, "the kind . . . required is the ability to carry on a complex process with incomplete technological understanding and limited information on the progress of events within the furnace" (Killick and Gordon 1990:120). Inevitably it is much more prone to failure, and that failure represents a considerable loss, given the expenditure of work in preparing charcoal and ore. From the smelter's viewpoint, he is charging and operating the furnace the same way each time, and yet the results may differ wildly. African systems of thought do not allow for chance and assume that the world is theoretically knowable and controllable. Therefore, though he may acknowledge technical errors and make adjustments accordingly, the smelter is more likely to look for the ultimate explanation and solution in the "supernatural" sphere, the interlocking network of agents that ultimately determine the outcome: ancestors, spirits, witches (cf. Killick 1990:125ff.). He will also invoke the intricate system of correspondences, analogies, and oppositions that influence the process negatively or positively and inhere in human sexuality, menstruation, and animal and vegetable medicines—recall that the two most common reasons cited for failure were violation of sexual taboos and witchcraft.

To successfully maneuver in such an extraordinarily complex cosmological field requires a great deal of knowledge: technical, ritual, herbal. The knowledge itself provides access to "supernatural" power, but this may be augmented by inherited power in the case of endogamous craftsmen—what Bird and Kendall refer to in the Mande case as the "initial set of means provided by birth" (1980:16).

Smelting takes place away from human habitation because the most powerful actions take place in secret (cf. Cole 1989:28–29) and because it is easier to enforce the ban on sexual activity and to exclude menstruating women in secluded sites. There the smelter orchestrates the full panoply of rituals—medicines, sacrifices, movements, and prescriptive behavior—centering on the artifact that is created by the smelters and in a real sense brought to life and made fecund by their actions. Each part of the ritual complex has its function. Sacrifices, medicines, libations, words, and music all mobilize the assistance of spirits and ancestors to favor the enterprise and to ward off malevolent forces. But the reciprocal to this mobilization of power is that it is accomplished at great risk to the smelter and his work: he is literally playing with fire.

The closest counterpart to smelting, as we have seen, is the construction of a new smithy or, more specifically, the manufacture of a new hammer or anvil that, like bloomery iron, has the potential for unlimited creation. Just as in areas where smelting was carried out over long periods in permanent furnaces the most extensive rituals were concentrated on the construction and first smelt, so with forges that are generally in constant use it is not surprising that ritualization seems to be most intense when it is first created. Once its fertility is ensured, it can continue with more modest levels of protection and empowerment.

The use of sacrifices, invocations, and offerings demonstrates the alliance between the smelter and the spirit world: he has the secret knowledge to invoke their aid, but he cannot operate without them. Most commonly he establishes his claims to their assistance genealogically, through his hereditary links with a line of ironworkers, either biological or social. The smelter is a mediator between the human and spiritual world, but it is likely that the ancestors mediate within the spirit world.

The web of sexual and menstrual taboos reiterates the social dimension of the transformative process. Smelting is not simply "like" gestation and birth; it *is* gestation and birth. As we have seen, the furnace is given a human, then a genderized, identity in many if not most cases, but it is the analogy with the *process* that is important, so the constituent elements do not have to resemble their human counterparts (Rowlands and Warnier 1988:16). The iron produced is equated with fertility and the wealth symbolized by children, especially twins. The process is as important and as precarious as human procreation—and the product as dangerous as twins—and must therefore be socially regulated to ensure a happy outcome.

Beliefs about hot and cold are so basic to transformative processes, including both smelting and human reproduction, that they are worth looking at more closely than has been possible in earlier sections, particularly to provide an exegesis about just how unsanctioned sexuality and menstruation are understood to work. These beliefs are either most common or have simply been most carefully studied in Central Africa. While the details differ in particular societies, Marwick's discussion of the Chewa (Malawi) *mdulo* complex offers one template (1965:66–68, 232–33). "Hot" and "cold" do not have absolute values; what matters is the context. Thus, when a person is supposed to be "cold," contact with someone who is "hot" is dangerous. For example, a pregnant woman and her unborn child are considered cold. Therefore, if her husband commits adultery during the pregnancy, it will make him hot and he will kill the fetus as soon as he enters the doorway of her hut. He may also kill his wife. A newborn child remains cold until its parents perform a ritual known as "taking the child" when the child smiles for the first time at four or five months. The ritual consists of coitus interruptus while the mother holds the baby to her chest; then the baby is "warmed" by rubbing it with mixed semen and vaginal fluid and passing it over the fire. The baby is now properly hot.

A woman committing adultery becomes dangerously "hot" and can endanger her husband and his work anytime he must undertake a hazardous activity such as iron smelting, hunting, or working in the mines. A menstruating woman is also "hot" and avoids seasoning food with salt, which is sure to "cut" (i.e., cause illness to) anyone eating it. People in a liminal stage are "cold" as well: boys and girls undergoing puberty rites, headmen and chiefs during their installation, initiates into the secret society, and mourners. Special taboos are therefore imposed on those around them to avoid *mdulo*, "getting cut in the chest"; intercourse is then obligatory when it is time for a boy being initiated into the secret society to reenter village life (ibid.).

As Marwick emphasizes, this idiom of belief is firmly anchored in the social system. Its purpose is "the preservation of the social relationships conducive to effective human reproduction. Their ultimate reference, through the obscurer channels of symbolism and mystical belief, is to the fertility of the soil and the fecundity of animals and men." These form an interconnected system: "A woman who has died in childbirth should be cut open to release the harmful tension . . . , and her corpse either thrown into a deep pool or tied in the branches of a tree lest its 'heat' should destroy the fertility of the soil" (ibid.:68).

Among the Bemba to the west of the Chewa, "the dogma relating sex and fire is the *idée maîtresse* behind most of the ritual behaviour" (Richards [1956]1982:30ff.). Sexual activity makes a couple "hot," a state in which it would be perilous to approach the ancestral spirits in any prayer or sacrifice. If a chief were to perform ceremonies while hot from sexual relations or to approach his ancestors without purification, there would be a grave risk of disaster in the land. As with the Chewa, this concept has permutations throughout Bemba social life. Thus, menstruating women are cold, as are corpses.

The Thonga of southern Mozambique, on the other hand, see menstrual blood, along with the blood of birth, as hot. It provides the heat necessary to fire the embryo in the womb. In this code it is dangerous because it is linked to solar heat and fire but is also indispensable to gestation; it is not equated solely with infertility. It must, however, be controlled, as it is in the cooling rituals following childbirth and the successive stages of growth, rituals which are coordinated with the phases of the moon to invoke its cooling action (de Heusch 1980).

Jacobson-Widding (1991b) offers an intricate reading of Manyika Shona (Zimbabwe) conceptions of heat and cold, and relates them explicitly to the model of ironworking: that is, ironworking provides a paradigm for human fertility and vice versa. She notes that the hearth in the center of the gynecomorphic smelting furnace is known as *chido*, which has multiple meanings but most basically connotes love, longing, desire. Fertility depends on the oneness of male potency, equated with rain/semen, and female fire. But in all processes of transformation the essential fusion demands a temporary suspension of order or "coolness"; the oppositions and hierarchies of everyday life must be reversed for the moment in favor of nonstructure, equality, formlessness, and darkness. Where women are normally lower than men (a status reduplicated symbolically throughout Shona culture), "in lovemaking, total equality prevails" to achieve fecundity, and women must be hot—women are thought to catalyze men so that together they make a fertilizing fire (ibid.:69).

In all of these belief systems, then, impurity and pollution are relative, not absolute. They refer precisely to states of being that are inimical and therefore dangerous to others at any given moment, and they carry with them injunctions about how to resolve the danger by purification or removal of pollution. But it is clear that sexual activity in and of itself cannot be equated with pollution, only sexuality out of place—heat where it does not belong; in fact, prescriptive and ritualized sexual activity may remove the pollution. The same is true of menstruation, although it is most often seen as the negation of fertility so that it must be excluded any time that fertility is the object.

While these notions are most clearly articulated in Central Africa, it is likely that ideas of hot and cold in some form are common throughout the continent as organizing metaphors and that they are closely associated with sexual intercourse and menstruation. The avoidance of "adultery" by iron smelters and the exclusion of menstruating women who represent infertility are therefore part of the same metaphorical system as, for example, the use of medicines associated with fertility, conception, and delivery.

I would argue, in fact, that *any* process where these exclusions and taboos are operative implies that the process is seen within a reproductive paradigm. If sexuality and barrenness are inimical to an enterprise—or if sexual activity is prescriptive—it must be because it is conceptualized at some level as analogous to procreation and therefore incorporated into the same power field: what is harmful or beneficial to one is harmful or beneficial to the other. Where Rowlands and Warnier have maintained that "iron production stands at the intersection of two independent lines of thought: (a) it is a fertility process, and (b) iron is potentially very dangerous" (1988:23), I would suggest that these are two aspects of a single line of thought. Iron and iron production are quintessential metaphors for sexuality with all its potential for creativity and abundance but also for violence, danger, and destruction.

The Yoruba have caught this tension superbly in the characterization of Ogun, the *orisa* of ironworking. Ogun is a violent warrior, impetuous and hotheaded, who killed his own people in a fit of short temper, but he is also a leader known for his sexual prowess who nurtures and protects and provides (Barnes 1989:2). His "many faces" are the faces of iron and the faces of human sexuality.

NEGATIVE EVIDENCE AND THE PROBLEM
OF CHANGE

Having proposed this paradigm, we must also confront negative evidence. While the sexualization of metalworking, especially smelting, is a leitmotiv to be found in a multiplicity of cultures throughout sub-Saharan Africa, it is by no means universal to judge from the available evidence. What does this mean? Should we assume that the process was not given a sexual or procreative dimension by certain peoples? That it once was, but that contemporary informants have forgotten about it? That many observers simply missed it? That this is a part of ritual knowledge that is being held back for reasons of secrecy?

Here the Bassari reconstruction may be illuminating. Although our informants freely used human anatomical terms to refer to parts of the furnace, they volunteered nothing to suggest that the furnace was female or that the process was seen as the gestation of iron. We were also unable to obtain literal translations of the invocations at the time, either because our translators did not understand their importance or because they were instructed to hold back by the chief (who had definite ideas about what we should do and know). Only later when other Bassari, unconnected with the enterprise and unrelated to the participants, listened to the sound track of the film and translated it for us did parallels between smelting and reproduction become explicit.

In our experience at Lopanzo as well, no one overtly referred to smelting in terms of gestation, and obviously we refrained from questions that might prompt the answer. Since we do not yet have a full translation of all the invocations, our hypothesis that it fitted the reproductive paradigm is based on a combination of factors: the insistence on sexual and menstrual taboos, the use of medicines known to promote fertility and ease birth, the terminology employed for the tuyere assemblage, dietary parallels with the birth of twins, and the pelvic thrusts of the workers during certain rituals. It is altogether possible that none of those involved would have subscribed to my interpretation, just as van Beek's Kapsiki informants were unaware of the symbolic dimensions he extrapolated from smiths' eating habits: the reality is so self-evident that it does not call for theorizing (1982). Or, to put it simply, one does what one does because that is the way it is done—the common answer to most questions in most societies.

This may help to explain why Killick's Chewa and Tumbuka informants did not volunteer any evidence that the furnace was seen as female or that the formation of the bloom was equated with gestation, although some of them referred to the interior of the tall furnace as "stomach" and to the slag as "feces," while one of the words for the constriction in the middle was "belt," reminding us of the belts on Shona and other furnaces. Is it, in fact, possible to have a furnace that is generically human without a more precise social identity, given the framework of African thinking about personhood? Furthermore, Chewa and Tumbuka smelting was characterized by the same prohibition against sexual relations and the same exclusion of fertile and menstruating women as we have seen elsewhere, reflecting the belief that violation of these rules would anger the ancestors and cause the work to fail. As I have argued, it is hard to account for these taboos if the smelting process is not understood at some level in sexual and reproductive terms—to say nothing of the smelters' joke, referred to earlier, about going home to make "ng'anjo" [furnace] with their wives (Killick 1990:124ff.; idem 1983:6).

Nevertheless, it is good to be reminded of Chinua Achebe's comment that "nothing is totally anything in Igbo thinking" (1976:137), a caution that can probably be extended throughout Africa. Thus, when one smelter informant in Rwanda insisted that there were no taboos concerning women and that in the past the smelter and his aides slept freely with their wives the night before a smelt (Célis 1988:116),[1] we can consider the possibility that he meant just that, even though it runs counter to the evidence of neighboring parts of the country, to say nothing of Africa as a whole. We should probably be more suspicious of information that is *too* consistent than of that containing anomalies.

More and more, we have to allow for change. Accounts of smelting in an area at different periods quite naturally reflect changes, especially when smelting has ceased to be practiced on a regular basis. Thus, when Chisinga smelting was revived during World War II after a hiatus of several decades, Brelsford wondered quite appropriately whether the medicines and rituals he observed represented all the usages and customs that had accompanied smelting a generation earlier, and he noted in particular that the exclusion of women was no longer as strict as it had been (1949:29). Similarly, in those areas where there is a record over time, for example, among the Fipa, Mafa, and Bassari, differences are obvious: rituals are dropped or modified, procedures varied. But there are also essential continuities.

At the same time, there are tantalizing hints of fundamental changes in the organization of ironworking resulting from dynamics internal to the craft and from regional borrowings well before the intrusion of the colonial economy and westernization. A major problem in a study such as this is the misleading synchronicity that results from most of the sources—as if processes were frozen in time until they collapsed in the face of irreversible and modernizing forces from abroad. And yet we know that change was a constant in precolonial Africa just as it was everywhere else. The view that African technologies were inherently conservative and that innovation was stifled by ritual and taboo has been increasingly refuted; as Ian Fowler has observed, the tremendous diversity of metalworking apparatus and techniques alone would undermine this characterization (1990:12–13).

Nevertheless, there are only a few cases where we can document such change in any detail, particularly in several areas that have attracted attention be-

---

1. One of Killick's Chewa informants also denied that menstruating women were kept away from the smelting furnace, in clear contradiction to the testimony of others (1990:129n.)

cause they saw a large increase in scale during the nineteenth century, before European imports were a factor. One of these was at Babungo on the Ndop Plain of western Cameroon where Fowler (1990) has so magnificently reconstructed the evolution of the industry. Here the earlier small furnaces were replaced by large clump furnaces. In its heyday the industry may have engaged as much as a third of the male population in one capacity or another, with some sixty smelting furnaces in almost constant operation on a year-round basis, suspended only at such moments as the death ceremonies of a Fon (chief) or the annual celebrations for the chief's ancestors. Anyone who could supply the raw materials could smelt iron on payment in kind to the owner of the furnace; no kinship ties were necessary nor any ritual knowledge. In other words, economies of scale seemed to go hand in hand with a diminution of ritualization.

But, in fact, the ritualization was adapted—one might say concentrated—rather than abandoned. It centered on the initial construction of the foundry and on the technician who oversaw its operation. The Babungo clump furnace required a considerable initial investment in labor and time, but once built it could continue to operate indefinitely with only minor repairs (even fifty years after smelting ceased they are remarkably well preserved). The owner, the *tunaa*, not only had to be able to mobilize the resources to build the furnace but he was also the keeper of medicinal knowledge, responsible for the medicines placed on the posts that held up the roof above the furnace and in the two pots buried below the base of the furnace. He played no further role except to replace the medicines if they seemed to be losing their efficacy. The actual smelting was delegated to the celibate specialist who supervised the foundry (Fowler 1990:151), usually a son or male slave of the owner. In other words, the sexual taboos were consolidated in his person as a very rational response to the economic takeoff. In addition, others using the foundry had to observe sexual taboos on the eve of smelting and while preparing the ore and the wood chips and raffia stem charcoal used as fuel, but the fact that only the *woenfiibuu*, the celibate smelter, was allowed to touch the interior of the furnace indicates his particular ritual status vis-à-vis the more transient work force.

Just as interesting is the industrial strategy of Njanja ironworkers in Zimbabwe. If the industry of the Cameroon Grassfields has been likened to the Ruhr, that around Mount Wedza was described by an English missionary in 1893 as "the Wolverhampton of Mashonaland" (Shimmin 1893:51, 55). To take full advantage of the highly productive ores of the region, Njanja smelters, like their Babungo counterparts, needed to mobilize manpower on an unprecedented scale, but they chose a different tack. They encouraged neighboring peoples to join them, apprentice themselves, and learn ironmaking skills, and they utilized female labor to the hilt. At the peak of the industry in the second half of the nineteenth century, it was estimated that ten to twenty *viras* (furnaces) might be working at the same time, and from forty to eighty men plus women employed, "all under the supervision of one expert headman smelter."

A successful smelter would use his wealth to acquire ever more wives, while the resulting daughters would attract apprentices, building up his economic and political power by classic means. MacKenzie (1975) claims that whatever taboos may have existed excluding women or regulating sexual relations during smelting were no longer in force, implying that they would have been an impediment to the growth of the industry, but some ten years after MacKenzie's fieldwork Dewey found considerable evidence for the preservation of sexual taboos during smelting (Dewey 1990; Childs 1991:349). The Babungo case makes us wonder, too, if these taboos might not have devolved on the headman smelter and been overlooked in MacKenzie's account.

Be that as it may, Dewey and MacKenzie concur that the Njanja did not cease emphasizing the sexual symbolism of the smelting operation: furnaces were invariably decorated with female breasts, with traditional patterns on the "stomach" and the waistbelt traditionally worn by fertile women. "The bellows and the tuyere were seen as the male genitals inserted into the female torso of the *vira*, and the removal of the metal was like a birth from the womb of the furnace" (MacKenzie 1975:214; cf. Dewey 1990).

The Bassari (Togo) iron industry also expanded greatly during the nineteenth century using rather similar methods. In a wave of nostalgia, one German visitor described a village where "the whole night through fire leaps in the small huts and the rhythmic sound of hammers reverberates"; it reminded him very much of "die Heimat," his homeland (Klose 1899:497). At the turn of the century, an official estimate put the number of working furnaces in the region of Banjeli alone at close to five hundred (Cornevin 1962:87). Annual output at this time reached between 150 and 200 tons (de Barros 1986:168). The Bassari accomplished this remarkable production through the maximum use of female, child, and probably slave labor, but they did so without abandoning sexual restrictions or the ritualization of the smelting process and without opening up the craft to nonsmelting lineages.[2]

The labor-intensive part of the operation was not the smelting itself (which relied on natural draft rather than bellows) but the mining and preparation of ores, the production of charcoal, and the hauling of ores and fuel to the ovens. All of this could be, and apparently was, done by women and children (Gehrts 1915:227–48; Schomburgk 1914; Martinelli 1982:39ff.; Goucher 1984; Herbert and Goucher 1987). Since furnaces were used again and again with only seasonal repairs, their supervision required skill rather than hard labor. This made it possible for the typical three-man smelting teams, drawn from the same family, to operate several furnaces at once (Martinelli 1982:47–48). The wealth gained from the sale of iron blooms could be used, in turn, to acquire not only wives but also slaves and agricultural produce. What we do not know, however, is whether smelting crews rotated at the furnaces to mitigate the demands of sexual abstinence. The natural draft furnaces required only one

---

2. While there is excellent technical information from the 1890s, early accounts say little about the ritual aspects of Bassari ironworking. Most of them were written by people who did not actually watch a smelt, and none observed furnace construction.

master smelter to adjust the plugs and tap slag when necessary. Hence the sexual taboos would not have represented the same sort of impediment to large-scale or continuous production as with furnaces relying on bellows. As Killick has noted, these furnaces were far less fuel efficient, so their use must have been dictated by other factors, such as conserving male labor (1990:151).

While not on a scale comparable to these examples, Angebauer (1927:111) refers to the bustle of a Kwanyama (Angola) metalworking village in similar terms: "The many small bellows caused the noise that first struck me and that echoed across the whole yard like the hum of a large factory." Does this expansion of the local industry also explain the involvement of the whole family and of San in Kwanywama metallurgy?

One of the last groups to cease smelting iron was the Senufo smelters of Koni, Ivory Coast. According to Eckert (1974:174), these ironworkers observed no rituals or taboos at any point in the smelting, mining, or charcoal making process, not even during the construction of a furnace. Once a year at the beginning of the rainy season, a bull or ram and fifty chickens were sacrificed to the spirit of the mines by chief of the smiths and two other notables; that was all. It is possible that the choice of time for the sacrifice suggests a link between iron and fertility, but no such explanation was offered. And yet Senufo smelters filmed in 1955 in neighboring Burkina Faso followed rituals much closer to those we have documented in West Africa and elsewhere, and they were bound to observe strict sexual taboos during both mining and smelting (Dittmer 1962:8–9). The same is true of Senufo smiths of the Ciranba subgroup in Burkina Faso (Dacher 1984:167n.6). Is this simply a case of variation among the same specialist group living in different areas, or has the desacralization occurred as part of a more general secularization? Have the Koni come to divorce their technology from an all-encompassing system of belief, or was it never part of such a system? It may in fact be an example of what Warnier and Rowlands (1988:40) refer to, "in Weberian terms," as "a disenchantment of the symbolism of iron production"—indeed, an apter example than that of Babungo.

At the other end of the time spectrum, however, are the Early Iron Age sites in Zambia and one in central Malawi where the evidence is equally hard to interpret. Here it appears that smelting was carried out within the confines of the village, in contrast to the nineteenth- and twentieth-century insistence on isolation. Does this mean that a thousand years ago smelters were not yet concerned that the presence of fertile and menstruating women could cause the process to fail or that they did not fear the evil intentions of witches and sorcerers? As Killick (1990:76–77) observes, either the inhabitants of these regions did not share these beliefs or they had other strategies to protect their furnaces, such as the wall "decorations" or the small holes in their bowls, found in some Early Iron Age furnaces in northwestern Tanzania (Schmidt and Childs 1985).

Based on more recent ethnographic evidence from other parts of the continent, a few writers have suggested that there may be a correlation between the antiquity of metalworking in an area and the strength of associated taboos (and perhaps ancient sites situated in inhabited areas compensated for their lack of isolation by enforcing taboos to control access—this is something archaeology cannot tell us). Hombert, for example, contrasts the extremely strict sexual taboos in the central area of the Cameroon Grasslands with their almost total absence in the western Mono River area, and he attributes this to the likelihood that metalworking was probably introduced into the latter area much more recently (1981; cf. Fowler 1990:22). Pole (1975:34) offers a similar explanation for the Busanga of northern Ghana who, he believes, were latecomers to the area east of the White Volta and were much more productive than their predecessors because they were bound by none of the common taboos against women's participation in smelting and smithing. Unfortunately, we do not have information about other aspects of ritual and belief in these areas.

In any event, these examples refer to the introduction of ironworking to areas where it had not existed previously. What effect did technological innovation have on belief systems *within* an existing metallurgical tradition? Célis maintains that each type of technology would have had beliefs adapted to it; therefore, technological change would have been accompanied by changes in belief. As an illustration, he argues that in Rwanda the "fours à paroi tronconique" (low-shaft furnaces) were the most recently introduced of the various types of smelting furnaces and that the proof of this is not only their demonstrably greater efficiency but the uniformity of beliefs associated with them— the longer ago a furnace type had been in use, the more one would expect to find variations in design and in belief (1988:272, 280). But he does not really spell out the evidence for this hypothesis nor whether he is referring to details of belief or more fundamental tenets.

In fact, the Babungo example suggests a more likely model. Here the adoption of the large, long-standing clump furnace may have led to a sharper division between the owner as master of medicinal knowledge and the smelter as technologist and observer of sexual taboos. Further, it is undoubtedly significant that only he could touch the interior wall of the furnace. And yet, just as Fowler sees a continuity in the development of the full-blown clump furnace from earlier types (even though it is presented in the traditions as an innovation from elsewhere), so he postulates a continuity in basic beliefs. The developed furnaces were not built on the same sites as the earlier ones because of their association with misfortune, but "it seems plausible," Fowler asserts, "that there should have been a notion of continuity in terms of relations with the mystical force of 'Nywi,' or spirit, associated with the successful transformation of ore to bloom in the smelting process. This force was focused on the pot of leaf medicines buried deep beneath the furnace hearth. The conceptual basis of this is that through the activating function of the leaf medicine life and fertility are extracted by this force from the earth and transformed into bloom. When neglected, i.e., when regular libations cease, this mystical force is thought to turn against those living close by and extract life from them so that sickness and other misfortunes ensue"—as evidenced by the association of misfortune with the older furnace type (1990:111–12).

In other words, the rationalization of the industry did not eliminate the need for medicines, libations, and the observance of sexual taboos because the belief system that explained and controlled the smelting process did not change, nor did it need to change. The model of fertility was still applicable, as was the understanding of the role of Nwyi, the spiritual force that guaranteed fertility, protected against witches, and responded to traditional rituals: the new furnace type, as we have seen, was indeed more fertile than its predecessors, offering twins in place of a single bloom/birth. Long after smelting had ceased, Babungo furnaces were still believed to be so powerful that they were offered annual libations of oil, wine, and camwood, and Fowler was not allowed to excavate any of them (1990:76).

Unfortunately, the evolution of metallurgical beliefs over time is even harder to document than the evolution of furnace forms and smelting technologies, and it is one of the areas where oral tradition may be least reliable. Nevertheless, the study of African religions, of which these beliefs are an integral part, is increasingly demonstrating their resilience. One suspects, therefore, that in broad outline the conceptualization of ironworking could accommodate a large measure of change. After all, Ogun still has meaning for mechanics and bus drivers.

TOWARD SYNTHESIS

We began this chapter with a quotation from Nicole Echard about the inseparability of symbolic and technical practices. This seems a better way to frame the discussion than the old juxtaposition of science and magic. Or, one can note Smets's (1937:60) shrewd observation a half-century ago: "We are too tempted to believe that for the primitive, everything is magic. It would be truer perhaps to say that for him everything is technique." The smelter manipulates earth, fire, and air according to "laws" that he has learned through his apprenticeship and by virtue of "means" that may be hereditary, acquired, or a combination of the two.

All devolve from an understanding of power, in this case the power to transform useless stone into supremely useful raw material. The details of each belief system may differ from culture to culture, but one may hypothesize from the evidence that the system is comprehensive enough to accommodate change. There is a bedrock empiricism: if the process does not work, it is adjusted—witness the infinite variety in everything from furnace design to rituals. Such adjustments are possible within the framework of belief and at the same time do not invalidate it in any way since they do not challenge the underlying assumptions about how transformation is accomplished.

Further, the power to smelt and work iron is not qualitatively different from other forms of power. They all have their ultimate source in the under-lying forces that govern the cosmos, forces that in theory are knowable and accessible for human enterprises. What has struck students of African cosmol-ogies is their down-to-earthness; what is not of direct relevance to human life is of little interest. Conversely, human experience is projected onto the cos-mos as a way of bringing order out of chaos. As Fowler says, beliefs underpin-ning iron production "appear to be very closely associated with core beliefs about the nature of things and the role of human, mystical and other material agencies in providing for the satisfactory reproduction of human society" (1990:344). But where he sees the "notion of mystical powers" as a more fun-damental metaphor than the procreational paradigm, it seems to me that they are inseparable, the latter being invoked to explain *what* is happening, the former, *how* or through what ultimate agency it happens since the world is assumed to be orderly. Just as human fertility depends on mobilizing ances-tral and other spiritual forces, so the fertility of furnace and forge depends on the same mobilization: both are fully possible for those humans who possess the requisite knowledge and the power to use it with impunity.

What I will propose in Part II is that the procreational paradigm and the understanding of power associated with it can be invoked to illuminate other transformational activities. Like smelting, they reveal an imposition of the human model of fertility on the world but, at the same time, an exclusively male control of that fertility.

PART TWO

Symmetries and Asymmetries
Power and Fertility

SIX

Le Roi-Forgeron

We smiths are indeed the *ba mama* of the consecrated chiefs. Without us, no chiefs.

Kongo blacksmiths

The king sets up a forge
In Cyirima's rear courtyard
And pumps the bellows four times. . . .
He instructs the descendant of Muhinda
To beat the iron four times.

Sacred text, Rwanda

Homage to Ogun, the Iron-Smelter of the World
Homage to Ogun, the Iron-Smelter of Heaven
Homage to the three patriarchs, iron-smelters
when existence began!

Praise song to Ogun (Yoruba)

Les deux sur la terre qui mangent, le forgeron
et le roi.

Moundang proverb

In 1687 Padre Giovanni Antonio Cavazzi da Montecuccolo, a Capuchin friar
who had spent seventeen years in Kongo, published a history of the kingdoms
of Kongo, Angola, and Matamba. One of the best-known illustrations from
this work is the drawing of the Ndongo king at the forge with musicians playing in the background. An unpublished manuscript version of the work contains beautifully hand-colored variations on this theme (fig. 28). Cavazzi's illustrations are, incidentally, the earliest known firsthand representations of
African life by a European and are surprisingly accurate in many details (Cavazzi 1687; Bassani 1987).

As Pierre de Maret (1985) has pointed out, historians have often interpreted
Central African traditions of royal blacksmiths literally. They have seen them
either as proof that the polities were founded by smiths or that control of iron

deposits was the stepping-stone to political and economic domination of an area. More recently, however, anthropologists and archaeologists in particular have called attention to the symbolic dimensions of the pairing of smith and chief and proposed a rethinking of the historical components of the association.

I will argue that metallurgy and kingship share a common understanding of the nature, sources, and control of power. The paradigmatic elements that I have surveyed in discussing the conceptualization of the smelter/smith's power are equally applicable in many cases to the political leader—and to the hunter as well, as we will see in the next chapter. These are all male-dominated activities that invoke paradigms of fertility and age for their accomplishment and that are interdependent but also potentially competitive. Attempts to anchor these linkages in history, however, are extremely difficult. Just as the imprecision of terminology in indigenous languages and foreign sources often beclouds the distinction between metallurgy proper (smelting) and smithing, so the disappearance of the former and greater reliance on internal and external trade for raw iron has undoubtedly affected memory and practice (cf. Dupré 1981–82).

The interrelations between political and metallurgical power are immediately apparent. I will use de Maret's stimulating 1985 essay, "The Smith's Myth and the Origin of Leadership in Central Africa," as my starting point, then expand on some of his theses and extend the discussion beyond Bantu Africa. Clearly, one would expect to find the highest correlations in societies where metalworking and chiefs both played an important role, the lowest in areas where metalworking was least developed and authority decentralized, and this does, in fact, seem to be the case. Nevertheless, in view of the unevenness of the evidence, some of my findings must be seen as both speculative and incomplete, to be confirmed, refuted, or revised by other scholars.

It is a vast topic, but three closely interconnected themes are germane to the interpretation: the identity, real or structural, of smith and chief; the appropriation of the paraphernalia of metalworking as insignia of political office; and the role of smiths in chiefly investiture and funerals.

SMITH AND KING IN CENTRAL AFRICA

Traditions linking metallurgy and political leadership are especially widespread in the interlacustrine region of eastern Africa, throughout the Congo Basin, and in northern Angola, that is to say, over a huge area stretching some two thousand kilometers from the Atlantic coast to the western Rift Valley (de Maret 1985). Scholars have argued for a basic cultural unity over much of this region, at least for the Congo basin broadly defined, as well as for the antiquity of the beliefs informing these cultures (e.g., MacGaffey 1986:23; cf. Vansina 1973:444, 467; 1990:5ff.). In this area centralized authority was often highly developed and smithing (like kingship) was generally hereditary, but the smith was free to marry women from nonsmithing lineages, in contrast to the western Sudan and parts of northeastern Nigeria and northwestern Cameroon.

But were kings themselves smiths or vice versa? The early, unpublished draft of Cavazzi's manuscript accompanies the illustration of the king of Ndongo at the forge with the following inscription:

> A black by the name of Angolla Mussuri, who was a relative of the King of Kongo, came from the Kingdom of Kongo, and practiced the art of ironworking, which with the art and industry of his hands and the sweat of his brow have brought great wealth not only to the population called Dongo but also to others. (Bassani 1987:77; translation mine)

In the published edition, Cavazzi claims that according to indigenous traditions, it was an ancient king of Kongo who, in fact, invented ironworking and was the first practitioner (Obenga 1974:15). Kuba traditions also link smithing with kingship, from the epic confrontation with the hammers and anvils (to be discussed below) in proto-historic times, to the affirmation that since the early days of the kingdom, all men of royal lineage had to be acquainted with the art of smithing. One king is remembered for his improvement on the razor blade, his successor as an excellent smith: a "portrait" figure identified with this ruler supposedly shows him with an anvil (fig. 29). Myeel, an unsuccessful contender to the throne, is nevertheless remembered as "the best smith there ever was" (Vansina 1978:67, 70–71, 182, 213).

The pendulum has swung back and forth about whether to take this and other traditions of blacksmith-kings literally or metaphorically. One can never rule out the possibility that kings may really have taken a turn at the anvil— Livingstone, after all, noted matter-of-factly that a Manyuema chief in eastern Congo paid smiths to teach his sons to work in copper and iron (1874:2, 71), and Barbot, writing in the seventeenth century, declared that the "king of Gabon follows the trade of a black-smith, to get his living, being like his subjects very poor" (1732:5, 393). During his seven years as missionary with the Lamba in extreme northwestern Zambia (1914–1921), Doke found "a great number of chiefs" who were eager to learn the profession (1931:351). Some years later Redinha (1953:129) encountered a chiefly lineage who were also smelters in southern Lunda: the chief had taught his son, who in turn carried out the smelt that Redinha documented. An old photo of a similar furnace in action shows the master smelter wearing a leopard skin, the attribute of chiefs (fig. 30) (J. Maquet 1962:102).

Consequently, one cannot dismiss Kuba traditions out of hand. Since they have obviously discarded a great deal of what was not considered worth remembering, why would they have retained details about razors if there were no foundation? In any event, whether true or not, these traditions do indicate, as Vansina points out (1978:67), the high status of the craft among the

Kuba and the equivalence, on some level at least, of smith and king or chief. Nor is this view limited to the Kuba. Because the Pende smith forges the chief's bracelet of office, he, too, "is considered equivalent symbolically to a chief. One honors the visit of a blacksmith in the village like that of a chief with a day of rest" (Strother 1989:31).

But the king had also to assert his ultimate dominion over the smith and his ability to appropriate his power, both tangible and intangible. This is presumably the statement being made by the hammer/anvils that serve as chiefly insignia throughout Central Africa. Shaped like a large spike, the head could be wielded as a hammer, or the pointed end could be fixed in a log or in the ground so that it could serve as an anvil. Until quite recently Kongo chiefs had miniature versions of these, which they alone could strike against each other in ceremonies to announce their coming (Mertens 1942:81). One of the titles of the Tio king was "owner of anvils," and he had anvils in the kitchen of the palace (Vansina 1973:379, 442; cf. Nooter 1991:143–44).

The hammer/anvil was also the quintessential emblem of royal power in Rwanda and Burundi. "If it is a symbol of the knowledge of the smiths, it was equally a symbol of power for the former *bami* [kings] of these countries who were never separated from them" (Célis 1989:26). Thus, the tomb of Mwami Cyirima Rujugira (ca. early seventeenth century) contained two of these forged hammers serving as headrests. With each new "cycle" of kingship, the hammers were ritually reforged, signifying renewal of the dynasty (d'Hertefelt and Coupez 1964:52). As a member of the Tutsi aristocracy, the king of Rwanda could not actually have been a metallurgist, a trade reserved for the Hutu or Twa, but as king-elect he participated symbolically in the rituals in which the royal hoe was forged, striking it with a reed rather than a hammer (ibid.:xvii, 85–101). This act recalled the myths that attributed the introduction of iron-working to the founder of the dynasty. By extension, the royal hammers were very closely associated with both fertility and ancestral protection (ibid.: passim).

In the "noble language" of Rwanda, the word for hammer also designated the legs of the king (Célis 1988:19, 170). This concordance finds an echo in the Luba ceremony of "striking the anvil" in which the knees of the king are struck as a blacksmith strikes an anvil to remind the king that it was his ancestor Kalala Ilunga who introduced iron technology into the area (Reefe 1981:82); the ritual serves to transform the candidate into a sacral king just as the smith forges raw metal into the finished objects of civilization (Nooter 1991:151).

During the secret rites of Nyanga investiture in eastern Zaïre, the smith beats two hammers during the prescriptive act of copulation while pronouncing these words: "If you are not a true chief, may you die on this woman, may your strength become weak" (Biebuyck 1956:328)—a striking illustration of the convergence of sexual, metallurgical, and royal power!

Kuba legends of the hammers and anvils provide what Vansina (1978:49–52, 121) terms "a genuine political charter of kingship." However much individual versions vary, they agree that at the site where contending claimants threw hammers and anvils into the water at Iyool to see which would float, Kuba kingship was born, confirming Bushoong dominion over related peoples. To commemorate this event, miniature anvils were later sewn onto caps, and the anvil remained one of the central emblems of both royalty and lesser chiefs among the Kuba (fig. 31).

Smiths also fabricated other indispensable items of regalia: not only the bracelets of Pende chiefs but also those of Kongo rulers (fig. 32) (Mertens 1942; ill. Dapper 1668:583), the single and double bells (Vansina 1969) and ceremonial axes found over huge areas of West and Central Africa, as well as spears, knives, and collars. Among the Chokwe, Lunda, and Ovimbundu virtually all the objects signifying prestige and status were made of iron (Mesquitela Lima 1977:349). These emblems of leadership go back centuries—in some cases perhaps a millennium or more (vid., e.g., Herbert 1984a, 1984b; de Maret 1985:84ff.; Childs et al. 1989:57; Biebuyck 1985–86:2, 256; Miller 1976:63).

Objects are static, however. To find clues to the historical relationship between metallurgy and leadership, we need to look more closely at how they are used, at the dramas of power represented by royal investiture, and at the legends and myths that often underpin them. Royal investiture, like all forms of initiation, involves a period of seclusion in which the candidate is removed from normal everyday life, often to a special enclosure in the bush where he spends a prescribed period of time with prescribed initiators and companions carrying out a set range of activities that aim at the destruction of his former identity and the creation of a new one. He must literally be reborn as king in order to carry out duties of the office he is about to fill. During this seclusion the candidate is usually brought into close contact with his ancestors/predecessors. His reentry into society is the occasion of a further set of rituals to establish and express the legitimacy of his new persona. Since van Gennep (1909), we are accustomed to viewing these initiations as enactments of ritual death and rebirth, but they also have a great deal to say about the social construction of gender as it relates to power. Commentators have been so fascinated with the role of real or putative incest in rituals of royal investiture in Africa that they have accorded insufficient attention to the more general relevance of prescriptive sexuality itself in this context and its implications for the definition of power. Nor have they taken full account of the part of smiths in these rituals in Central African societies where iron production is of major importance.

Because of the ultra secrecy that has surrounded investiture rituals, we have, unfortunately, very few full descriptions—and it may be misleading to have less than a full description, no matter how overwhelming the welter of minutiae may be.[1] Nevertheless, accounts of Kongo, Tio, and Bashu investiture suggest models that receive confirmation from other sources as well.

---

1. This becomes resoundingly clear, for example, in the case of the Pende (Zaïre) investiture, which Zoë Strother was allowed to witness and which is surely one of the most completely recorded (pers. comm.).

INVESTITURE

Mertens's account (1942) of chiefly investiture among the eastern Bakongo is based on oral information obtained during the 1930s. At this time every village had its chief and *femme-chef*, so we are talking about power dispersed on a local level. Although this is a far cry from the institution—or at least the ideology—of kingship as it existed in the late fifteenth and sixteenth centuries, it nevertheless retains the essential links between smith and leader that are referred to by Cavazzi and other earlier writers so that, for all the change that must be assumed, one can argue for a persistence of core beliefs.

In these societies, a chief cannot become a smith, but it is possible for a smith to become a chief, in which case he gives up smithing. It is no exaggeration to say that the smith orchestrates the entire initiation of a new chief and femme-chef: Mertens refers to him as the "forgeron consécrateur." He leads the candidate into the enclosure where he remains secluded and then back into society at the conclusion. In between he forges the bracelets that are the special emblems of power. One of these, however, is not forged anew but is extracted by the smith from the *corbeille des ancêtres*, the basket of ancestral relics that confers legitimacy. The new chief generally takes the name of the ancestor whose bracelet it is, so the smith is responsible in effect for naming the chief. In other chiefly rituals, too, the smith is the only one who can open the basket and offer blood sacrifice to it. During the period of seclusion he and the *besi kanda*, the clan leaders, teach the candidate the names of his predecessors.

Unlike most investiture rituals for which information is available, no women are allowed in the initiation hut; the new chief is forbidden to have any sexual relations whatsoever during his seclusion, although he is initiated with a female counterpart, the *ndona* (about whom very little is said). A curious ritual marks the end of the period of seclusion. The smith and chief join fingers through the door of the enclosure, and the former tries to draw the latter out. The chief exposes his head, then withdraws inside. This is repeated three times before the chief finally emerges. Then the smith leads him around behind the enclosure where he washes him with water that he (the smith) has drawn. At this point the chief climbs onto his stone forge and the smith slips the bracelets onto his upper left arm. The chief then recites the names of the ancestral *bisimbi bi nsi* and all the rivers that the ancestors had to cross before reaching the present locality. Before leaving the initiation site, the smith traces the outline of a cross in the sand, then repeats it with a cross about a meter high made of horizontal and vertical branches on the spot and waters it. The cross is, in fact, a cosmogram of the universe, joining the worlds of the living and the dead (Fu-Kiau 1969; Thompson 1981), and it will later take its place in the house of the chief. Finally, smith and chief wash in a river deep in the forest before setting out for the village and the public aspects of the ritual.

On the way back to the village, the party is accosted by a "wild man" figure, usually a slave, who must run out to meet them in the forest with one leg painted white, the other black, and dance before the chief and his female counterpart. He then takes his place with the chiefs, occasionally dancing and ringing his bell while everyone comes to pay respect to the new chief. These "coming out" ceremonies in the village involve a great deal of reciprocal gift · giving and represent a considerable expense to the chief; apparently it is only the smith who gives no gift in return for what he receives.

The smith is in charge of one last ceremony, which takes place during the reentry of the chief but also at other times of crisis when witchcraft is suspected. He makes a paste of the blood of oxen sacrificed for the occasion, of palm oil and of red powder *(nkula)*. This he offers first to the ancestors, then smears on the body of the new chief and the ndona so that death will not touch them.

The importance of the smith at the death of a chief parallels that at his initiation. He sprinkles the clotted blood of an ox on the new burial mound, then on those of all the chiefs and femmes-chefs previously buried in the cemetery. He also rubs some of this sacrificial blood on the bracelets removed from the corpse, which will be kept in the *corbeille des ancêtres* and on the *bilwi*, part of this basket to which have been added bits of skin from the late chief. When all the mortuary rituals are over, he returns the basket to its place of safekeeping. His role at the death of a femme-chef is more concise: her husband takes off his clothes in the forge, where they are burned in a fire built specifically for this purpose, whereupon the widower is free to remarry.

Others have confirmed or added to Mertens's description but without altering the general outline. How do we interpret it? First of all, the symbolism of birth is obvious in the actions surrounding the exit from the enclosure: the head presented to the hand of the smith, the repeated attempts to draw out the chief, the washing. Small wonder that Kongo smiths refer to themselves as the *ba mama* of the chiefs; they might equally be seen as their midwives!

To go farther in understanding how this relationship may have come about, we need to turn to Kongo oral traditions and ethnography, particularly the work of de Heusch (1975a) and Wyatt MacGaffey (1986). Over the large area of Kongo-related cultures, there are many myths of an autochthonous people who were either incomplete (only one side of the body) or dwarfs. What is intriguing is how commonly they are associated with the working of iron and with the prestige and power that it confers. Later immigrants into the region, the ancestors of the present Bakongo, settled on the lands of these people. This could be a distant memory of the movement of Bantu populations into regions previously inhabited only by Twa (Pygmies), but it is anachronistic in that the Twa were not metalworkers before the arrival of the Bantu. However, they would have used fire, so there is probably a conflation of fire and metalworking: throughout the forest the Twa are generally acknowledged as the masters of fire (Vansina 1990:56).

In fact, what has happened seems to be a telescoping of historical sequences that becomes clearer through an examination of the earliest European accounts relating to Kongo kingship. These concur that the king of Kongo could only be installed by the *mani Vunda*, even after the conversion of the rulers to Christianity in the very early sixteenth century. The mani Vunda, who represented the earliest inhabitants of the land, belonged to a different clan from that which supplied the kings and was believed to descend from the autochthonous priest who cured the conqueror, Lukeni, eponymous hero of the Bakongo. The *nsaku* clan to which the first mani Vunda belonged was supposed to go back, in turn, to the ancestral dwarfs or Pygmies.

It may or may not be true that the peoples south of the Congo River practiced metallurgy earlier than those from the north; in any case, the invasion of those who were to found the kingdom of Kongo in the fifteenth century is alleged to have come from the north and to have spread into the area that is now northern Angola. While some traditions might claim that Lukeni and the immigrant Bakongo introduced ironworking, the ritual dependence of the kings on the mani Vunda implies the opposite: an acknowledgment of the ancient claims to political and religious authority of the indigenous metallurgists with which the alien dynasty had to come to terms. Thus, the king needed the legitimation of the corporation of smiths to make good his claims to suzerainty over the land. Far from being a "blacksmith-king" in his own right, he owed this title only to the initiation conferred on him by the mani Vunda as representative of the corporation and to possession of the emblems of the trade that came with it.

Unraveling this complex story, de Heusch (1975a:174–75) sums up its essential features: the Bakongo attribute the symbols of power associated with the forge to a mythical people with whom the autochthonous chiefs they have defeated are in direct contact. The dominant nsaku clan claims descent from these mythical mbaka and therefore imposes its religious authority on the Bakongo by ancestral right. Modern chiefs, dependent on the smiths for their investiture, reenact the "historical" position of the founder of the new dynasty vis-à-vis the elder of the nsaku clan.

But there is a second strand of Kongo tradition that links autochthonous smiths in some Bakongo areas with the local spirits that control the fertility of crops and of women. De Heusch (1975a:175–77) found echoes of this in Mbata traditions. MacGaffey (1986:65–68, 179) equates smiths with the ancestral spirits who are held to be responsible for both technology and fertility, the *bisimbi*. The bisimbi lie at the fuzzy intersection of ancestors and local nature spirits: some informants suggest that the older an ancestor is, the more likely he is to blend into nature spirit, a belief consistent with de Heusch's traditions concerning autochthonous peoples. These spirits are strongly phallic in form, often pictured as large-headed red dwarfs who have trouble standing up (!), and are remembered as technicians and manufacturers—especially expert in metalworking and weaving. They are believed to control the fertility of women and crops. MacGaffey is more skeptical than de Heusch of traditions that identify the Kongo aristocracy as an immigrant group, leaning more toward an urban/rural distinction than one opposing immigrant and indigene: "If the

Mani Kavunga [mani Vunda], rainmaker, fertility priest, and 'owner of the earth' was the chief priest of the simbi cult, no distinct ethnic identity and no temporal priority need be accorded him" (1986:194).

In some areas the smith was the principal simbi priest because of the association of iron tools with agricultural fertility and because smithing, according to some informants, comes from the water simbi. His own initiation reinforced this linkage in requiring that a large stone be brought from the river to serve as anvil: usually such stones are considered simbi objects, the abode of a nature spirit or even a "fossilized" ancestor. So strongly localized were they that if a smith moved, he could not take his stone anvil with him but had to acquire and consecrate a new one. The smith was also a healer: he healed by using his bellows to blow on the sick (ibid.:68, 76, 196).

It was as simbi priest, then, that the smith acted as consecrator of chiefs. But as MacGaffey points out, "The smiths were sufficiently like the chiefs, in Kongo eyes, that it was necessary to impose ritual distinctions" (1986:67). They might be from the same clan, share food taboos, and both wear bracelets, but the smith was forbidden to wear some of the other emblems of chiefship. The chief was essentially the head of a cult of the dead, tied by mystical links with his predecessors in office, "ancestors" who might be fictive as much as actual kin. He was the only one who could communicate directly with them, so his role was primarily to mediate between living and dead, to propitiate the ancestors and prevent them from harming his people. MacGaffey makes the interesting observation that the Kongo chief was "as much sacred object [*nkisi*] as he was priest" (ibid.:66). His investiture paralleled the ritual followed to create a charm, establishing communion between the living and the dead as the source of power that could then be "constrained to produce extraordinary effects, good or bad" (ibid.:148ff.).

Often, too, chieftaincy was associated with violence, at least on a symbolic level: violent acquisition of power or the destructive power wielded by the chief. In some areas, the investiture process itself was violent. According to Kongo belief, ancestors themselves might be violent and require preventive measures to forestall legitimate but unpleasant and capricious intervention. Simbi spirits, on the other hand, were anchored in localities, not lineages, and were associated with benevolent actions, prosperity, and well-being. There is, of course, overlap; the boundaries are never sharply defined—note that the smith must often be an auxiliary in ancestral rituals—but the fundamental dualism of the politico-religious system is reflected in the interdependence of chief and priest, a dualism that seems to extend back to the era of the old kingdom of Kongo, that is, at least to the seventeenth century (ibid.:17, 66–73, 195–97).

The Kongo model of the relationship of chief and smith is valuable because these institutions were carefully studied before change made it impossible to reconstruct their earlier forms and also because the oral data can be checked against European written sources from the period of intense contact, beginning in the late fifteenth century. Both types of sources help to elucidate and substantiate each other, and, as MacGaffey observes, there is a remarkable continuity between the two (1986:196ff.). A comparison of the Kongo material with other areas in the Congo basin then tests the hypothesis that we are indeed dealing with a uniformity of core beliefs and at the same time may help us to understand them better.

In Tio investiture, the royal smith did not direct the ritual as in eastern Kongo, but he was responsible for lighting the new fire when the candidate went into seclusion and for forging the great collar with twelve points that was the emblem of kingship. Each day that the king was in seclusion, the royal smith steeped his iron tools in water and sprinkled the water over the king. He also put a red blanket over the fire and blew on it so that the smoke fumigated the king. Both the water and the fire were intended to strengthen the king. The cooking fire in the kitchen built for the new ruler was placed between three anvils (Vansina 1973:375–87).

During the king's seclusion, the contents of the basket of royal charms were revealed to him day by day, progressing from the most innocuous to the most potent. Although its contents were secret, it is known to have contained nine anvils. If the charms did not kill him by the third day, it meant that the ancestors and the nature spirit, Nkwe Mbali, had accepted him. On the sixth day he received the great brass collar of kingship for which, it was alleged, he had to condemn to death by witchcraft twelve of his kin (one for each point on the collar). The same day he was also exposed to the *ano* rings, which definitively destroyed his virility. It is not known what metal they were made of: iron, copper, and lead would all have been available. On the eighth day he had to eat human flesh (ibid.:375–81, 386n.22).

Finally, on the ninth day (nine being a sacred number), he left his seclusion with his first wife, who had shared the initiation with him and also wore a brass collar, and accompanied by a small child. Because the king was rendered impotent by his initiation, this wife was an older woman who should be beyond childbearing. Nevertheless, her title was "master of cereals" and she was supposed to ensure agricultural fertility. So important was her position as alter ego of the king that if she died first, he was killed because he could not rule without her. If he predeceased her, however, she had only to go through a reverse initiation to undo her royal identity, and then she was free to remarry (ibid.:379, 384–86).

The separation of ritual power in this case is apparent from the fact that although the smith was a major actor, he was neither the head initiator nor the priest of the most important cult that legitimized the king, Nkwe Mbali. Among the many nature spirits linked with prosperity and with fecundity in all its forms, Nkwe Mbali was preeminent; it was considered the national spirit of the Tio kingdom, and the king was sovereign because he was "master" of it. The spirit was lodged in the Lefini River just opposite the Falls at Mbā, a flat rock in which six anvils were stuck. The two middle ones represented the king and the priest of the spirit, while the four on the sides represented the two dominant lords of the kingdom. The anvils were metonyms not just of power but of life itself: according to Vansina's information, each morning the priest visited the site, "and if he saw an anvil loosened, he would know that the lord, king, or himself whom it represented would die" (ibid.:374). Interestingly enough, the priest of Nkwe Mbali plays no part in the investiture of the king.

This account immediately suggests some provocative points of convergence and divergence with Kongo belief.[2] Both Kongo and Tio kings need the approval of the ancestors whose presence is made concrete in the basket of relics and power objects. Both also need the acceptance of nature spirits: in the case of the Kongo these seem to be mediated by the smith, but the Tio royal smith must share ritual authority with the priest of Nkwe Mbali and others. Both rulers must go through their initiatory seclusion with a female counterpart. In these two cases, however, sexuality is negated. The Kongo chief-elect is forbidden to have sexual relations during the initiation and, in any case, the ndona does not seem to have been in any sense a wife. The Tio king becomes permanently impotent while his wife, who symbolizes earthly fecundity, is beyond childbearing. This asexuality can be construed as just as "abnormal" in societies that put a premium on socially regulated fertility as the prescriptive incest in other investiture rituals, especially since in the Tio case it is combined with the killing of kin and the consumption of human flesh.

But what is its purpose? As I have discussed earlier, I would not agree with Vansina that sex is antithetical to the sacred in the usual sense of pollution. The very fact that the chief must have a female counterpart and that his sexual behavior is central to the ritual would seem to mean, more basically, that this process invokes the paradigm of human reproductivity and that the allocation and regulation of procreative powers are very much at the heart of it. Sexuality must be carefully controlled to ensure that transformative processes succeed, but it seems to be integral to chiefly initiation—in eastern Zaïre, Nyanga investiture even demands public copulation with one partner, private and secret copulation with a second under the watchful eye of the smith (Biebuyck 1956:315, 328). Whether the end result of transformation is a chief or raw iron or a forged hammer, all are closely identified with fertility. The temporary celibacy of the Kongo candidate, however, may simply represent protection during a period of liminality (when he might be especially vulnerable to witchcraft, for example).[3] It is unfortunate that we do not have more information about the ndona and the femme-chef. The permanent celibacy (impotence) of the Tio king must have a different meaning. Since his (older) wife is

---

2. Marie-Claude Dupré (1981–82) contrasts the Tio and Kongo political ideologies in relation to the control of metallurgy in ways that are extremely provocative but still very tentative in my estimation.

3. Zoë Strother offers several reasons for the celibacy imposed on Pende chiefs during their investiture: the conservation of energy for the work to come; the vulnerability to witchcraft by jealous rivals, which has a higher risk of "taking" during sexual activity; and asceticism as a test of character (1989:20).

The chief was joined in his prescriptive celibacy and seclusion by the blacksmith during the period that he was forging the bracelet of chiefship (ibid.:32).

also a key player, it may symbolize a double fusion of masculine and feminine, or possibly a transfer of their fertility to the nation as a whole (see below). The impotence of the ruler does not affect succession as it might in societies that insist on more literal descent because an heir is usually chosen from the lineage but not necessarily from the actual sons of the king.

To some extent, then, the initiator, smith or others, is analogous to the smelter who symbolically oversees the gestation and birth of iron, this time with human actors (male *and* female) who must, however, be transformed as dramatically as the products of the earth. This interpretation gains credence not only from the Kongo data but also from Randall Packard's description of Bashu investiture in extreme eastern Zaïre. At the climax of the very complex Bashu investiture ritual, the mwami rises from the "grave" while an official known as "blacksmith to the mwami" holds a hammer in each hand and beats them together. The ritual leaders respond by asking, "Whom have we forged?" The smith strikes the hammers a second time and says the name of the new mwami. "The mwami is thus compared to a piece of forged iron. Like a piece of iron, he has undergone a transition from one state to another." Moreover, as Packard observes, "like a piece of iron, the mwami is still 'hot,' still ritually dangerous" and must be cooled by a series of rituals over the next seven days. The danger, in fact, is generalized to a prohibition against the use of all iron tools during this period as well as a prohibition against sexual activity among the entire populace. The explanation given is that the mwami is a newborn infant at this time, "born" of the queen mother, and that he and the land itself are highly vulnerable to both iron and sex: iron because it comes from under the earth, that is, the world of the ancestors, and sex because it could abort the birth (Packard 1981:38–39, 45, 208n.20)—presumably referring to the taboos against sex immediately after birth. In other words, both sex and iron are dangerous because of the ambiguity inherent in their power, necessary for human and social reproduction but carrying multiple valences by virtue of their associations with gender and with the ancestral dead. This same ambiguity is by definition inherent in political power, perhaps a further reason for a necessary separation while that power is still a "nursling."

The fertility of iron and of political leadership can be explored further in the traditions linking anvils/water spirits/chiefs. Nkwe Mbali is identified with both water and with the ancestors, like the Kongo bisimbi, and both Tio nature spirits and bisimbi are associated with fecundity. Indeed, Vansina (1973:237) points out the apparent paradox that in the dualism underlying Tio belief, fertility and fecundity belong to the female sphere (as symbolized by the king's first wife), but the nature spirits are located in the male domain. Does this explain the presence of the anvils with their connotations of *male* fertility, a parallel to the male chief as guarantor of fertility to his people? Is it possible that the lost fertility of the Tio king is simply transferred to his realm? After becoming king of the Kuba, Shyaam's magic became so powerful that it absorbed all his reproductive power, making him unable to procreate. To compensate, his people designated the capital as his wife and named all their children after him (Vansina 1978:60–64).

Against this backdrop of watery anvils, the Kuba story about throwing hammers and anvils into the lake also seems less bizarre. These insignia of the Bushoong chief were "miraculously" accepted by the nature spirit of the area while those of his competitors were rejected, legitimizing him as sovereign over other chiefs. Subsequently, King Shyaam came to be considered a nature spirit in his own right, elevating Kuba kingship to a level of spiritual power: kings were called "God on earth." Where Kongo cosmology was hazy about the line demarcating ancestor and nature spirit, Kuba belief was unusual in ignoring ancestors altogether so that kings did not need to invoke dual sources of power. The only relic of ancestor worship may have been the practice of putting the "portrait" statue of a deceased king close to the bed of his successor so that he could absorb its "life force" (Vansina 1972:44f.; idem 1978:113, 122, 129, 207f.).

Kuba traditions further reinforce the identification of kingship with fertility in the form of twins, a theme we have also encountered in connection with metallurgy. Although ultimately unable to procreate himself, the civilizing hero Shyaam demonstrated his qualifications for kingship by causing twins to be born as soon as he had left the capital. And when he visited a pregnant woman on his return, she, too, bore twins. Twins, as Vansina (1978:60) says, are a "symbol of overpowering fertility," and in memory of Shyaam's prodigious power, by the nineteenth century male twins had their own quarters in the king's palace. Their leader was the spokesman for the king (ibid.:138). In Kongo belief, twins represented exceptional fertility but also the danger associated with unusual power. Of the several sets of names given to the three bracelets of Kongo chiefship, one designates the first two with the names given to twins, the third with a name meaning guardian—to look after the others (Mertens 1942:69). The Tabwa in extreme southeastern Zaïre make analogous associations between twins and chiefs: at the rising of the new moon after the birth of twins, their parents dance at home and then visit neighboring villages to dance and receive gifts. These gifts are called "gifts in honor of chiefs" since "twins are like chiefs." The parallels are based on the duality of twins:chief:moon, the links with both prosperity and misfortune (Roberts and Maurer 1985:30).

These examples suggest just how complex are the layers of correspondences between metalworking and political power. Thus, the hammer of the Ondulu (Angola) blacksmith is on one level a "child," on another, a "chief." "This tool is called osoma, the name given to the chiefs of the country, the idea being that it is the provider of the food, for without it there would be no hoes, no cultivation, and consequently no food. The sledgehammer (onjundo) 'feeds' the people, or is their 'mother.'" Read (1902:48) goes on to explain that this correspondence dictates that the hammer, when it is taken from one part of the country to another, never passes the night in the village but sleeps with its owner in the woods. If a chief stays overnight as the guest of a village, the women do not work in the fields the next day, however busy they may be; likewise, if the hammer were to "sleep" in the village, they would have to pay it the same deference as the chief and no work would get done—hence the "honorable compromise."

While we have thus far treated hammer and anvils together, they are not always identical. The anvils taken from the water by Kongo smiths, for example, would have been flat stones. Smiths also used rounded stones for rough forging. The double-duty hammer/anvils in the shape of a spike or cylinder, on the other hand, were solid pieces of forged metal, often viewed as explicitly phallic. The Lega see this type of hammer as "creator," something that makes things that last. Indeed, there is an identity between hammers and the masks that are the insignia of high ranks of the Lega Bwami society: these masks are compared to hammers left by dead ancestors, which symbolize "the creative energy of high initiates, living and dead." Just as the sound of hammers communicates what is happening in the sacred precincts of the forge, so the maskettes alert the initiated to the wisdom of their predecessors and their continuing duties (Biebuyck 1986:2, 130, 137, 187). Similarly, during Lega initiation rites, the preceptor beats two pegs together, imitating the sound of hammers, and sings, "In the forge the hammer sounds" (ibid.:191), again linking the hammer with the procreativity that is the ultimate object of circumcision. Bushoong (Zaïre) initiation does not involve circumcision, but it does invoke the culture hero and first king, Woot, who is incarnated in the smith "hammering out new men" in the tunnel-vagina through which novices pass (Vansina 1955:148)—a comparable association of smithing, procreation, and political authority.

COMPETITION, CONFLICT, AND INTERDEPENDENCE

Analogic and symbolic thinking have their counterpart in down-to-earth politics. The need to establish structural boundaries between smith and chief to which MacGaffey refers was matched by the practical need of a central authority to establish political control over metal resources and production—to take what was symbolically identical or at least similar and bifurcate it. Iron was immensely important to the African economy, crucial to the subsistence sector of farming, fishing, and hunting. Vansina (1978:175) calls iron smelting and smithing "the most significant craft of all" in the precolonial Kuba kingdom. With salt and copper, it was the most widely traded commodity on a regional and subregional level (Gray and Birmingham 1970), and it was not only unevenly distributed but always scarce and expensive (in terms of labor and resource inputs): indigenous production never seems to have outstripped or probably even to have met demand.

With the introduction of metals, Goody (1971:46) maintains, "kingdoms are in the cards" precisely because metals were scarce and valuable commodities whose production and technology could be controlled, in contrast to stone, wood, and bone. Such a sweeping claim runs counter to the historical evidence for Africa, where ironworking also thrived in acephalous societies (as Goody acknowledges), and in any case the relationship between metalworker and king was not predetermined; it had to be negotiated (cf. Dupré 1981–82).

The image of smith-king is then a shorthand representation of one adaptation but only one among many possibilities. As we have seen, Kongo traditions can be read as an assertion of the primacy of the king over iron production. Whether the dynasty founded by Lukéni was actually foreign to the region or whether its foreignness lay in its efforts to impose kingship over what had been fragmented, clan-based, and locally legitimated polities, it was clearly important to subordinate metalworking and bring it within an economy that was more and more dominated by the capital: hence the report of a quarter devoted to metalworking within the royal city, Mbanza Kongo (de Heusch 1975a:172).

A similar process is reflected in the Luba myths that ascribe to Kalala Ilunga the introduction of iron and ironworking, myths that also have their counterpart north of the Congo River (Dupré 1981–82). According to Luba traditions, Nkongolo and his followers did not know how to smelt iron and were therefore forced to acquire iron tools and weapons from others. Kalala Ilunga's use of a magic iron ball to defeat Nkongolo in the game of *masoko* hints at this technological superiority. When the hero then proclaims himself lord of Munza, it may reflect the historical process by which this iron-rich province was incorporated into the proto-Luba state. One of his first acts was to send for a master-smith/smelter from his father's land east of the Congo River, who came to Munza and showed the Luba how to smelt iron. As we have seen, this smelter, Kapasa Kansengo, was the first to make furnaces in human form with the mouth at the top. He also carried the technology north to the Songye, and, in fact, his name is still frequently given to slag heaps in these regions of Central Africa. Kalala Ilunga subsequently bestowed the technology and its accompanying paraphernalia, forges and bellows, on subordinate lineages throughout the land. In earlier times, the final act of Luba investiture symbolically reenacted the ties with Munza: the victor journeyed to Munza where the guardian of the sacred spear and copper ax of Kalala Ilunga handed them over to him, and he went through the ceremony of "striking the anvil" as a reminder of his ancestor's role. The tradition and the ritual, like those of other iron-producing areas and smiths' villages within the kingdom, mirror the transformation of the state whereby the royal control of iron production was affirmed (Reefe 1981:81–83, 89–90).

In fact, the genesis myth probably inverts history, in that ironworking undoubtedly preceded kingship in the Luba heartland as in Kongo and in the area that became the chiefdom and then kingdom of the Kuba. These regions, like others north and south of the Congo River, attracted settlement because of their metal resources (Dupré 1981–82:197f.). An explicit goal of Kuba rule then was to assert royal control over production of iron and iron wares. A government official was specifically in charge of overseeing and taxing iron mining. Indeed, major wars were fought between Luba and Kuba over possession of excellent iron ores near the Mwabe River during the eighteenth and nineteenth centuries (Vansina 1978:56, 93, 141, 163–64, 182).

Peter Schmidt has offered one of the most ambitious attempts to put the various pieces of the puzzle together in his reconstruction of the interwoven strands of ideology and political economy in two Haya kingdoms west of Lake Victoria.[4] Integrating both archaeology and oral traditions, he recapitulates the process by which intrusive dynasties of kings were able not only to gain control of iron production but also to control the "associated symbolic and ritual meaning in order to maintain political legitimacy." He sees iron goods as mediating the "relationship between agricultural productivity and human reproduction" so that it was imperative for the rulers to gain ascendancy over the industry and its "ideological superstructure": myth, ritual, symbolism.

What Schmidt argues is that the iron industry in this region was very productive because of its highly efficient iron smelting technology. Not only did it supply the tools essential to agriculture but it also fed trade networks encompassing a wide area of what is now western and southern Uganda and Rwanda. As elsewhere, iron was vital to the state system of redistribution, the circuit by which it was channeled to the ruler and then to his followers to maintain their allegiance. The Haya iron industry may be one of the oldest in sub-Saharan Africa, dating back to the first millennium B.C. According to oral traditions, in ancient times local rulers were the heads of ironworking clans. Babito and Bahinda dynasties imposed themselves on the area in the second half of the seventeenth century, presumably attracted by the wealth in iron. They faced intense opposition from the leaders of the indigenous ironworking clans and from the Bacwezi spirit mediums. Myths of the Bacwezi are widespread in the interlacustrine region and the subject of much dispute as to their historical meaning. In this case, traditions identify social groups claiming Bacwezi descent with ironworking as well as with spirit mediumship and rainmaking, and they associate iron and fertility with the sacred sites revered by these groups and attributed to Bacwezi gods "and/or aetiological events."

In one of the kingdoms, Kiziba, the process by which the new dynasty achieved control over these groups is encapsulated in the investiture ritual. An important stage of this was the visit of the new king to a hut built specially by the smith in the palace compound. Here the new king would work the bellows of the forge, thereby signaling that this was something any man could do, even the king. But, as Schmidt observes, the symbolism is more layered. Certainly the rite marks the special relationship of king and ironworkers and can be compared with the practice of bringing the smith's youngest son to the forge to operate the bellows "so the child will not fear the forging process." Working the bellows, unlike forging itself, requires no skill at all and is often

---

4. Schmidt has presented this interpretation in a number of publications. This summary is based on those of 1978, 1983, and 1990 and on O'Neill et al.'s film *Tree of Iron* (1988).

done by children and apprentices, so it could be read as confirmation of the king's subordinate role. At the same time, the location of this forge within the royal compound confirms the control of the king over ironworking and a denial of monopoly rights by any one clan. Overall, then, this ritual marks the end of the industrial independence on the part of metalworking clans but in a form that "creates the illusion of parity" (1983:175–76).

In the kindom of Kiamutwara a parallel evolution took place. Here the evidence comes not from the investiture ritual but from the identification of a huge shrine tree named Kaiija ("place of the iron forge") with an ancient forge, which Schmidt was able to excavate and which is dated to ca. 500–300 B.C. Oral traditions linked the tree to an iron tower built by Rugomora Mahe, the Bahinda king, who would have reigned from about 1650 to 1675. As de Heusch (1982b) has pointed out, towers joining heaven and earth are a very common mytheme in Bantu traditions, to say nothing of the Tower of Babel, but what is relevant here is that the tower was built of iron and that it fell down. Schmidt identifies the tower with a human phallus and evokes the process of intercourse through an analysis of place names associated with its collapse. He sees the occupation of this ancient shrine as marking the turning point by which the Bahinda dynasty gained control over both the "symbolic space" and the productive economy hitherto dominated by the Bacwezi clans, as well as a reiteration of the close association of ironworking with fertility.

Schmidt's deciphering of these parallel "histories" is ingenious. While it does not fill in the almost two-thousand-year void between the earliest evidence of metallurgy and the dynastic takeover during which it is inconceivable that productive relationships and belief systems would have remained static, it does confirm the importance of the link between ironworking and political leadership. It tells us *what* may have happened but not *how*, for oral traditions impose meaning on the past from the vantage point of the present.

Incidentally, we should not assume that the evolution always ended with the unconditional subordination of the smith to the chief. Among the Fipa, the ironsmith was accorded the respect and submission due to a chief and even the title of *umwaami*. The foundry or forge became a "sovereign enclave" for the period of his activity that neither the king nor his family could approach. His work was recognized as uniquely important to both the subsistence and the trading economy. As Willis notes, however, this sovereignty was "transient and relative": the first hoe made from each smelt was presented to the king as tribute, although both parties regarded it rather as payment for the scrub that provided fuel for the furnace. In other words, the relationship was one of mutual interdependence (Willis 1981:150; Wise 1958:233; cf. MacKenzie 1975; Childs: pers. comm.).

SMITH AND KING IN THE NON-BANTU WORLD

In the non-Bantu cultures of West Africa and the Sudanic regions, models run the gamut from identification of king and metallurgist to total separation, but there is virtually no use of metalworking tools as insignia of leadership (cf. de Maret 1985:85)—staffs, bracelets, swords, and axes aplenty but no hammers and anvils with the notable exceptions of Benin and Ife. Here we will offer a brief overview of available information, then focus on the figures of Sundjata and Ogun in more detail to explore the understandings of transformative power in Mande and Yoruba culture.

Close associations of metalworking and political authority are common (and not only in the person of the Sosso king, whom we will discuss below). Moundang (Chad) identification of king and smith is repeated in multiple contexts, referring both to the role the smith plays in supplying royal emblems and his equivalent ability to exercise supernatural power (Adler 1982:126ff.), but the king himself is not considered a smith. Similarly, the Asante goldsmith was the only one besides the king, his wife, and the greater chiefs who could wear gold jewelry, and the ancestral bellows at Bekwai became the center of an important shrine (Rattray 1923:301). This mirrors the exceptional importance of gold in the establishment of political power in Asante, in contrast to the role of iron (and copper) elsewhere.

Where Bashu investiture in eastern Zaïre uses the metaphor of forging the new chief, some Chadic cultures "smelt" their rulers. According to Nicholas David (comment 10/29/1988), the king as part of his initiation goes through a ritual symbolizing the process from ore to finished iron. He is also an actual smelter. The chief in Banjeli, too, belonged to a smelting lineage and supervised the reconstructions from behind the scenes. In addition, he had rainmaking powers, as the following story illustrates. Earlier in his incumbency the chief, Sertchi Magnibo, had been banished to Bassar some twenty-five miles away. A successor was installed, but the region suffered more and more intense drought. Finally, the powers that be gave in and recalled the deposed chief. He had barely left Bassar when the rain began to fall.

Nevertheless, the smith-king, as reality or mytheme, is much rarer in West Africa. An exception is the tradition reported by Pâques (1967:188–90) from Baguirmi, a region subject paradoxically to considerable Arab and Muslim influence. This concerns the descendants of the hero Dala Birni who are smith-kings of Barma. As a result, the anvil is taboo to any of their subjects except the king, so they rely on a group of Muslim outsiders, the Choa, for this work. There are echoes in Baguirmi traditions of the more widespread belief that the first anvil fell from heaven at the time of the primordial sacrifice and is tied therefore to the replication of human society on the celestial model, as in Dogon cosmology. The king is compared to iron in the saying "He is hard like iron," and, like the mythical smith, he is part of a triad with two female figures, his ritual wives. This is rendered schematically $\\underset{}{\\parallel}\\!\\!\\!-$, symbolizing the "parallel" wife and the "transverse" wife. The former is seen as the king's twin, equated with his right arm, which is ritually killed during investiture; the other is the image of fertility.

Relationships between smith and chief are mirrored in both Hausa traditions and ritual. Iron ores are widely distributed in Hausaland, and the blacksmiths of Gaya, in particular, figure in the founding legends of the core Hausa states as the suppliers of Bayejida's magic knife. In the Ader region, the two groups may intermarry, in spite of the prescriptive endogamy of metalworkers. Here, too, several rituals still enact the alliances of smith and chief, emphasizing, on the one hand, agricultural prosperity through the tribute in hoes and, on the other, military supremacy through the provision of arms. On the eve of the installation of a new *chef des forgerons* and each year thereafter on the eve of the Muslim festival of Tabaski, the political chief abdicates his authority from sunset until midnight in favor of the chief of the smiths. He seats himself below the smith, symbolizing his dependence, and his entourage remove their shoes as a sign of respect. The two leaders recall past glories won with the arms forged by ancestors of the current master smith and exchange jokes about the temporary reversal of their positions. On leaving, both chief and company bow to the smith, and that same night the chief gives him lavish gifts, including the clothes he wore for the annual ceremonies and the horse he rode, complete with its trappings. "The temporary reversal of hierarchical relationships," as Echard points out, "takes place as a function of what the smith represents as practitioner of metallurgical technology, and this symbolic event, whose carnival-like appearance is attenuated by the value of the final gift, serves to maintain the difficult equilibrium in the relations between the political power and the only real technical power in this society" (1965:366–67). Further, the chief-smith takes part in other ceremonies associated with life, but never with those related to death, unlike the smiths of the Cameroon Highlands.

Echard's comments sum up very nicely what could be said about the relations between smith and chief over much of Africa. Where the smith ranks situationally with the chief, even when he is a member of a casted group, it may be because he monopolizes a primary technology and also because he represents an autochthonous group, analogous to the earth-priest. This is the explanation offered by Bariba traditions for the high status of smiths and their symbolic equivalence to kings: they were settled in the area near Nikki (northeastern Benin) before the arrival of the first kings, who then gave them their daughters to cement the bonds. Smiths continued to be revered. At circumcision their sons took precedence even over the sons of princes and were the first to be operated on, "an iron anvil in their hand." Like princes, they have the right to hear their praises sung on the royal trumpets: "The handsome smith strikes the iron. . . . He is the mother of the world, the protector of the king" (Lombard 1957:16).

Traditions of several Marghi kingdoms in northeastern Nigeria make the same point to explain why Marghi kings are *required* to marry women from the smith caste and why smiths and kings are equivalent on a symbolic level. The installation of kings in these societies is a complex and long-drawn-out affair. While there is much local variation, the consistent element is the role of the *enkyagu*, the smiths. In Sukur, for example, the oldest of these kingdoms, the elders of the smiths shave the new king's head and leave only a single lock of hair, the symbol of royalty. They receive gifts of meat, and although they play no part in selecting the king, it is commonly said that they "make" him. The head of all the smiths in another of the kingdoms is the only one besides the ruler who bears the title of king and wears the royal hairlock and bracelet of iron. Only kings and smiths do not farm (or did not do so in the past). Finally, the Marghi king is buried as if he were a smith: upright, seated on an iron stool surrounded by charcoal.[5] Incidentally and unusually, ordinary Marghi can smelt iron, but only smiths can forge it (Vaughan 1973:168–70; Wente-Lukas 1972:133–34; cf. Kirk-Greene 1960:71, 92).[6]

The existence of metalworking castes as they are found widely across the savanna regions south of the Sahara, then, does not necessarily preclude symbolic identification of smith and ruler. Even in the Mande heartland, it was the practice for certain Malinke chiefs to marry women from the smithing caste shortly after their accession to power (Tamari 1991:230). It has been argued, however, that social and belief systems that rigidly separated smith from the rest of society facilitated control of their production by centralized authority (Haaland 1985:71). The Sundjata epic itself has been marshaled to support a recent formulation of this view (Tamari 1991), although, as far as I know, the case of Ogun has been ignored in this respect.

SUNDJATA AND OGUN

When the child Sundjata (or Son-Jara) belatedly rose to his feet to begin the fulfillment of his destiny, he did so by leaning on an iron staff that he commanded of the blacksmith when his mother rebuked him for refusing to walk like other children. The royal forges were located beyond the walls of the royal compound, and more than a hundred smiths worked there. It took six apprentices to carry the great bar that had long been waiting for the hero. When they put it down before the door of the hut, the crash made his mother jump with fright. Smith and bard watched as Sundjata

> crept on all fours and came to the iron bar. Supporting himself on his knees and on one hand, with the other hand he raised the iron bar without any effort and stood it up vertically. Resting only on his knees, he held the bar with both his hands. A deathly silence had gripped those present. Sogolon Djata closed his eyes . . . the muscles in his arms tensed. With a violent jerk he braced himself, and his knees left the ground. Sogolon Kedjou was all eyes and watched her son's legs, which were trembling as if from an electric shock. Djata was sweating and the sweat ran from his brow. With a final effort he straightened up and was

---

5. The Sar king of Bédaya in extreme southeastern Chad is also buried on a bed of charcoal (Fortier 1982:120).

6. Unusual as this distinction is, it has also been documented by Félix Yandia in the area north of Bocaranga (Central African Republic), where the ordinary population may mine and smelt iron but where smiths form a group apart (1985: pers. comm.).

on his feet at one go—but the great bar of iron had buckled and taken the shape of a bow. (Niane 1960:46–47. Translation mine)[7]

The epic of Sundjata, the Mande hero, offers one lens for looking at the relationship of smith and king in West Africa, the cult of Yoruba Ogun another. Both anticipate the subject of the hunter (to be dealt with in the next chapter). Together they suggest a range of possibilities which, in the end, is not altogether dissimilar to what we have seen in Central Africa.

Sundjata and Ogun are eponymous heroes presented as historical figures. But there is a major difference: although the memory of Sundjata is still very much alive in oral traditions throughout the Mande world, he is revered rather than worshipped. Ogun, on the other hand, is actively worshipped in present-day Nigeria and in Afro-American cultures of the New World. Ironically, his association with ironworking is probably more responsible for his longevity than his kingly status.

Sundjata was the magician-king of Manden. He was not a smith but relied on clans of smiths as his allies in the wars that created the empire of Mali, above all in the struggle against his nemesis, Sumanguru, the king of Sosso. In the traditions, Mande society already reflects the division into the endogamous occupational groups of bard (griot) and blacksmith, separate but indispensable to kingship. Sundjata inherits his occult powers (*nyama*) from his mother, but they are still unequal to those of Sumanguru, who is king *and* blacksmith. The hero is only able to defeat his enemy because his sister discovers Sumanguru's Achilles' heel: his vulnerability to the arrow made of the cock's spur. Sundjata's power is thus presented as great but finite: from his father he inherits his claim to the throne, a claim that would have availed not at all against his rivals had he not possessed superior magical powers through his mother's line and the loyalty of his sister, Sumanguru's wife, who had drawn the secret from her lord and then fled to her brother. He also depends on the bard who empowers him through the recitation of history and stirring words and the music that transcends words—the bard who, indeed, offers him immortality. Finally, he needs the blacksmiths who supply his armies and, in the epic, join in the fray themselves.

While recognizing that oral tradition cannot be confused with history, Tamari (1991:235–41) uses the Sundjata epic to throw light on the origins of the Mande caste system and the relationship of smith and king. She argues for the historicity of the Malinke-Sosso wars from documentary sources in Arabic that date them to the first half of the thirteenth century. Sumanguru, the Sosso king, was not a blacksmith in the literal and casted sense, she maintains, but "formed an alliance with divinities associated with ironworking, and thus iron, ironworking and certain iron objects were for him both symbols of—and means to—mystical and political power," as was the magic xylophone

---

7. In the version translated and annotated by John Johnson (1986), the iron staff is not sufficient and Son-Jara must use a staff from the apple custard tree to stand fully erect, uniting a second source of occult power to that of iron.

that he kept in his most secret chamber. After his defeat this special relationship with both metallurgy and music was gradually reinterpreted in the direction of craft specialization so that smiths and bards could no longer pose a
threat to Mande power.

They could not, however, be entirely dispossessed of their power. As we
have seen in interpretations of Kongo traditions, even when groups are con-
quered politically, they are considered to retain certain rights and powers.
Earth priests are a common example of this in West Africa. Tamari argues
that the bards and blacksmiths are another, so in the aftermath of the Malinke-Sosso wars Malinke rulers had to placate and even form alliances with
the defeated Sosso leaders: "Only by this means could they preserve themselves from their potentially dangerous magical powers and even turn them
to their own advantage" (ibid.:240). She marshals an impressive array of evidence to support her contention that castes do date roughly from the period
in which these wars would have taken place and that the Mande area was one
of the primary centers from which caste institutions diffused throughout West
Africa.

The gist of this argument is not new (e.g., Haaland 1985), although previous scholars have not made the same exhaustive use of linguistic as well as
oral and documentary sources. As we have seen, the problem is well-nigh
universal in polities encompassing an important iron industry and aspirants to
centralized authority. The question is, Why have "castes" when other states
such as Kongo and the Haya achieved this *modus vivendi* without them? And,
how would one explain the extension of castes to such distant regions as Darfur and the highlands of northeastern Nigeria and neighboring Cameroon as a
result of events far to the west, especially if it is granted that ironworking
technology "preceded the emergence of a well-developed caste system among
most West African peoples" (Tamari 1991:241)? Even in the core Mande areas,
the separation between smith and chief may not be as rigid as the term *caste*
suggests. McNaughton (1988:9) cites reports of the nineteenth-century ex-
plorer Raffenel that smiths served as chiefs in some Kaarta towns and his own
experience in the early 1970s that Bamana chiefs were expected to seek ad-
vice from senior blacksmiths. In sum, the relationship remains an ambiguous
one.

At the same time this type of institution did not spread into the forest
kingdoms of West Africa, which were much closer. Nevertheless, Meyerowitz
(1951:35–36) reports two rituals from Takyiman in which the *omanhene* (local
ruler) or the Tano high priest "battles" with blacksmiths armed with tongs; in
both cases the ceremonies are said to commemorate the fact that the smiths
were the first inhabitants of the land and "opened" it for the *omanhene* and
the priest. This would suggest that here, too, smiths had prior claims and
probably powers that needed to be reconciled with those of the political and
religious leadership. Metalworking is believed to have reached the Akan areas
from the Mande to the north, but the Akan and Fante states early became

dependent on imported iron so that memories have faded (Reindorf 1895:264–65; Goody 1971:52n.10).

As to Benin, scholarly interest in the origins of its brass casting traditions has far overshadowed attention to ironworking. Nonetheless, the *oba* of Benin is the only ruler in West Africa, to my knowledge, who is linked directly to smithing paraphernalia. Several plaques and statues portray the king or his messenger holding a blacksmith's finishing hammer *(avalaka)*. The standing figure from the Metropolitan Museum (fig. 33) may, like its counterpart in the University of Pennsylvania Museum, represent the priest of Osanobua, the creator god. The cross on his chest, of the type that so misled early Europeans in their quest for the Christian king Prester John, is, in fact, a "cosmological symbol referring to the creation of the world" (Ben-Amos 1980: fig. 40). In other words, hammer and cosmogram—and whatever might have been in the figure's other hand—are making statements about the creation of the universe and of ordered society, that is, of civilization. A nineteenth-century statue now in the Smithsonian Institution depicts the oba carrying an Ogun staff, its hammer blades projecting at right angles from the vertical column and surmounted by a figure holding a smith's hammer (fig. 34). The Ogun staff still plays a protective role in royal ritual (Nevadomsky 1984b: fig. 10; Freyer 1987: fig. 4).

This is even clearer in the iconography of the cast brass stool said to have been commissioned by Oba Eresonyen in the mid-eighteenth century (fig. 35) Ben-Amos 1980: figs. 30–31). On the slightly concave surface are blacksmith's tools with the anvil in the very center, flanked on either side by two different types of hammers and tongs and ceremonial swords. Above, another sword is balanced by the bellows, and between them are moon and sun and the maltese cross and square, symbols of the cosmos. Below are the monkey's head and two elephant trunk/arms terminating in hands holding sheafs of medicinal plants. The animals on the surface and around the base are symbols of the bush and water: monkeys, frogs, and snakes, interwoven with the hands that are common on altars to the hand and signify human achievement and control. The snake not only encircles the rim but also joins base and top. According to Ben-Amos (1980: fig. 32), the python is the king of snakes and acts as messenger for the ruler of the great waters, Olokun, who is also the senior son of the creator god. On brass plaques they are shown protecting the palace of Olokun's counterpart, the oba, who is seen as the king of dry land. The frog also moves between water and land. What is intriguing, incidentally, is the incorporation of incised Portuguese heads (the Portuguese also came from the water) interspersed between the reliefs of animal forms, the quatrefoil cosmograms, and the guilloche patterns. What this stool does, then, is to put metalworking at center stage in the drama of civilization, the imposition of kingship on the dry lands of the earth: without the smith, there are no emblems of kingship and no separation of bush and civilized space.

In some Benin traditions Ogun is identified with the great fifteenth-century king Ewuare (Nevadomsky 1984b:49–50). In more recent times, Ogun has simply been the patron deity of ironworkers in Benin who are organized in a guild with a chief and have their own wards in the city, separate from those of the brass casters. Some of the blacksmiths are believed to be indigenous, others highly valued captives of war. When the oba wanted the services of the blacksmiths, he would send a goat to be sacrificed or kola nuts to be offered at the shrine to Ogun as well as presents to the smiths themselves (Dark 1973:53–55). In this arrangement, therefore, the king recognizes the importance of the smiths, but they are clearly subordinate to him and perhaps even to the brass casters, who work exclusively for the king. A hint of a different historical relationship occurs during the annual festival honoring Ogun that is said to date from the semimythical first dynasty of Benin rulers. The oba participates in sacrifices to the deity and in mock battles, emphasizing Ogun's warlike character. Then the king receives medicines from the Ine Ogun, the chief of the smiths, who holds his ceremonial sword upright while the oba holds his downward "to show the power of Ogun" (S. T. Barnes and P. Ben-Amos 1989:59). Nevertheless, the symbolic equivalence of king and smith that one might expect from the artistic evidence is clearly much attenuated—at best a distant historical memory—nor do smiths play any part in the installation of a new king, at least in the public rituals documented by Nevadomsky in 1979.

The image of Ogun, "progenitor of iron and warrior king," is prevalent in many of the Yoruba and Yoruba-related kingdoms of the Guinea Coast. Although Ogun takes various local forms, the "Ogun concept encapsulated the progression from hunting to agriculture and the mastery of metallurgy, to urbanization and, ultimately, in these peoples' own view, to the development of empire" (Barnes and Ben-Amos 1989:39,59). Ogun summed up all the benefits and losses of this evolution, the blessings of civilization on the one hand, the attendant violence of the state on the other—all expressed through the metonym of iron. Yoruba traditions identify him as the king of Irè, a descendant of the royal line of Ife (Babalola 1989:167), but, in fact, he is credited with founding many communities and dynasties in his wanderings.

Reminiscent of the Benin stool, the Ogun Laadin shrine in Ife symbolized the relationship of smith and king. It consisted of a blacksmith's hammer, two stone anvils (*okuta Ogun*), and a stone fish and crocodile to guard them near the entrance.[8] The shrine was named for the mythical ancestor blacksmith and served as a meeting place for chiefs to debate judicial matters and to swear oaths (ibid.:58; Palau Marti 1964:164; Willett 1967:101). This use reflects the mediating role of the smith that is often found in West Africa: the smithy as a neutral place or even an asylum. And yet John Pemberton, in a brilliant analysis of the Ogun festival in Ila-Orangun, sees an essential conflict

---

8. Palau-Marti, who visited the shrine in 1956, gives a slightly different description from Willett and Ben-Amos, identifying their "lump of iron" as a tear-shaped iron hammer, evidently of the type usually referred to in French as *masse-enclume*. The illustration opposite page 33 in her book *Le Roi-dieu au Bénin* makes this quite convincing.

between kingship and the god of iron. The ritual is a meditation on the "problem of violence and culture." The "pathos of Ogun" is that "he cannot provide political order," and hence a higher authority must be found in the institution of kingship (1989:131). If metallurgy was the sine qua non of urbanization and state building, the smith, nevertheless, could not be allowed to monopolize political, technical, and ritual power. Rituals of Ogun act out the negotiations between smith and king, reaffirming the ultimate assertion of royal supremacy.

KINGSHIP, FERTILITY, AND FEMALE POWER

Kings and smiths are intimately associated with fertility. The "fecundity of power," in de Maret's (1985:79) words, is the principle that unites ironworking, sacred kingship, and rainmaking as well. He draws on de Heusch's (1982:15) description of sacred kingship as "a symbolic machinery made to render more efficient the productive and reproductive forces, fecundity in general." A small caution is in order, however. While widespread, the correlation of ironworking and rainmaking is not unequivocal; in some cultures, as we have seen, the two are antithetical.[9]

Be that as it may, one can express the equation with fertility:

$$\text{king:smith::human fertility:agriculture:wealth:expansion}$$
$$[\text{rain}]$$

In a continent that was largely underpopulated until the present century, a state was defined in terms of ruler and people, not territory—whether it be ancient Ghana or Moshoeshoe's Lesotho. The interests of kingship and the ancestors coincided in maximizing reproductive capacity. More people meant greater production, reproduction, and prestige. Iron contributed to this in multiple ways: providing the implements of agriculture and war, the emblems of authority, as well as many of the goods and currencies with which one acquired both wives and subjects. But since ironworkers often had prior claims to the power sources of a region, identified with local spirits and autochthonous ancestors, rulers always needed to find ways to come to terms with them, a historical process that is telescoped and masked in surviving oral traditions and rituals.

Both ruler and smith must fuse male and female power. The political chief

---

9. How hard it is to make generalizations without qualification is apparent when one looks at the Bashu of extreme eastern Zaïre. Not only are Bashu rainchiefs distinct from other types of chiefs in their specialized ritual power (versus the more generic power of later chiefs), but iron implements are to be avoided at all costs during rituals of accession of both types of chiefs. Packard (1981:39, 70, 208n.) explains this in terms of iron's origins under the earth, that is, in the land of the ancestors rather than of the living. Thus, the avoidance at moments of ritual danger such as death or investiture—even though the investiture of the *mwami* is explicitly compared to forging iron!

and the smith "escape dualist categories. They combine, in effect, masculinity and femininity." Devisch (1984:28) is referring specifically to the northern Yaka of Zaïre and includes the sculptor, whom we have not discussed (but who is often the blacksmith), but I believe that this observation applies equally well to many states of tropical Africa. The ways in which this combinant power is acquired, conceptualized, and expressed, however, are extremely different. It may be graphic, as in the Luba royal staff surmounted by the king in the form of a female figure (Nooter 1990:42), or it may be more veiled, hidden in the iconography of chameleons and birds.

In kingship we see this fusion taking place in two phases: first in the creation of the ruler himself, his death and rebirth through the ritual of enthronement, which always seems to involve a female presence and a sexual component, and then in his exercise power. I will limit myself here to examples from three cultural areas: the Yaka; a cluster of small states in southeastern Chad (Moundang, Sar and Baguirimi); and the Yoruba of southwestern Nigeria.

Yaka investiture transforms the chief into the "supreme mediator of the (re)generative processes in and between the cosmos, the land, the society and man." Indeed his solemn title is the bridge. He personifies the "overcoming of death" and "secures fertility and well-being in his territory." The initiation process itself symbolizes this on multiple levels, invoking the metaphors common to Yaka thinking and climaxing in the collective rebirth of the candidate and his fellow dignitaries from the "womb" of the chief's first wife through an act of "autofecundation." The ruler thus created is ideally "male and virile" but at the same time "female and fertile." He is qualitatively different from and superior to his people because of this integration of opposites. But Devisch offers the interesting, and I think insightful, comment that we are dealing not so much with dialectical opposites of male and female as a "ternary logic" that mediates and connects the differences without obliterating them, a higher order principle of fertility that encompasses "three terms and two generations: genitor, genitrix and ancestor or child." Even though the rebirth of the chief through the first wife might be seen as an act of incest, parallel to others found in investiture rituals, Devisch prefers to interpret the enthronement more fundamentally as "a continuous process of boundary crossing" but one whose transformative and innovative capability does not depend on a monstrous transgression (Devisch 1988:261–63).

In the shorthand of the Moundang of Léré (Chad), the king is also female: "le roi est femme." He, too, is responsible for the well-being of his people, especially through his rainmaking power in this sahelian region. But his female potential is anticipated even before his investiture: as a prince and potential king he does not go through ordinary male initiation rites, which would remove all traces of femininity through the action of the great masks. At the time of his investiture, he cuts himself off from wives and children acquired before this, and henceforth does not pay any brideprice for the wives whom he takes from the group of "maîtres de la terre." The fact that he does not pay bridewealth makes him the equivalent of a woman. At the same time, he gives wives to another group of young men. The wives he receives are the foundation of the palace economy, a *"ferme gigantesque"* (Adler 1982:307), which supplies the goods that sustain the public obligations of kingship; the wives he gives reproduce the cadre of men devoted to his service. He is at once debtor and creditor, woman and father. In these multiple roles and in his ritual function as rainmaker he reenacts the founding myth of the hunter king who was both male and female. He is also, be it noted, equated with twins who simultaneously exaggerate and negate the forces of fecundity, bringing life at the risk of death (Adler 1982; idem 1969).

The Sar of Bédaya also hold their king, or *mbang*, responsible for the fertility of the kingdom, but the source of his power is outside his person. The ritual cycle culminates in an annual festival that extends over several months, at the end of which the rain is supposed to fall and the king sows the first seeds. At the center of the entire ritual is the most sacred emblem of kingship, the magic throwing knife. Though always referred to in the singular, there are actually two of these, one male, shaped like an F, and one female, its end curved in a spiral. They are kept in a small straw hut adjoining the royal palace, lying side by side, the female knife turned to the left, the male to the right, just as man and wife used to be laid out at burial. They leave the hut only once a year for the sowing festival (Fortier 1982:126–27).

While the pairing might seem to be a metaphor for the complementarity of male and female in the agricultural and human cycle, this would be an oversimplification, for the female knife is much more important. It is considered the wife of the king, a beautiful woman, capable of taking on human form in the night and going to find other lovers if she is not content with her royal husband. The power of the king derives explicitly from these objects, above all from the mystical marriage with the knife. His ritual effectiveness depends on the knife *(miya-bo)*, not on any intrinsic quality of his own (ibid.:142). On a political level, the knife symbolizes the alliance of the king with the autochthonous clans of smiths, which enabled him to impose his authority over the *chefs de terre* with their own local control over fertility (ibid.:165).

In this context we can carry the exegesis of Baguirmi investiture one step further. Not only is the king, *mbag*, equated with the smith and the stars, but he must have two ritual wives: one who is his twin and is symbolically put to death, the other who represents female fertility (Pâques 1967:190). The trinity seems almost to beg for an application of Devisch's "ternary logic" to explicate it in all its subtlety, especially the allusions to twins and female duality.

Yoruba rituals of enthronement and the replenishment of royal powers also play out interwoven notions of masculine and feminine power. Nowhere is this clearer than in the symbol of the royal crown itself, which is a "visual metaphor of the authority and power of the oba," uniting the two kinds of creative power, biological and political. The crown and he who wears it "are linked to both the powers of Obatala, which are also associated with 'the mothers,' and the powers of Oduduwa—the power of procreating and the power of establishing and preserving the body politic" (Pemberton 1989:124–25). The iconography of the crown is a coded reference to its multiple sources of power, *ase*. The king may look at the bird perched on top of the crown, which symbolizes the "mothers," but he may not look at the medicinal powers hidden inside. The crown becomes itself an *orisa*, a deity. When the king wears it, it must be placed on his head by his senior wife, standing behind him, "by one who possesses the *ase* of 'the mothers.' " In its structure and iconography, the crown "refers to a power that relies upon and transcends the contrastive powers of male and female. It links, bridges, relates opposites" (ibid.:125).

Assimilation of female power takes a different form in the annual Yemoja festival of the Ekiti Yoruba town of Ayede. This ritual enlists the aid of the *orisa* to revitalize the king: "to replenish the body politic with fertile women, abundant crops, and a strong, healthy king" (Apter 1992:98). The power of the *orisa* is mediated by cult priestesses, above all the priestess of Yemoja. At the climax of the ceremony, she becomes, in effect, the king. The sacred calabash of Yemoja, which she carries balanced on her head, contains "the concentrated powers *(ase)* of kingship, conceived of as a 'hot,' explosive, and polluting force" that can only be controlled by esoteric incantations and medicines. It is praised as a crown, but a crown that is the embodiment of female power through its identification with Yemoja as an orisa of female power and fecundity, the "owner of the breasts of honey" and of "innumerable children." She approaches the king, but turns toward and then away from him three times. Finally, he places his hands on her and at that moment absorbs the female power of the calabash and is "recharged" with ase for the coming year (ibid.:104–6).

But the ambivalence of female power becomes emblematic of kingship as well, for the "mothers" confer both life and death. Yemoja's calabash, as Apter observes, "contains antithetical powers. As a delicate womb, it contains witchcraft and fertility; as a female crown, it deposes and regenerates the king; as a unified town, it contains the contested violence of deposition and fission; as cosmos, it contains earth and sky." While the "official discourse" openly acknowledges the positive aspects of the ritual—that the calabash empowers the king, transfers the "coolness" of female power, promotes fertility, subdues witchcraft, and generally fortifies political hierarchy—it suppresses the more disturbing countertext of the king's deposition and mortality as the prelude to regeneration, the price of fertility. "When the king receives Yemoja's calabash, he embodies the paradoxical condition of his own reproduction—the hidden power to break the rules and structures which establish his authority" (ibid.:114).

The choreography and paraphernalia of other Yoruba rituals also invoke this need to underpin political with reproductive power, for example, the Odun Agemo of Ijebu-Ode. Here the male Alagemo chiefs carry sacred loads on their heads that women must never look upon or come in contact with, for they contain the secret power of this group of foreign but politically indispensable chiefs. John Pemberton reads the power that they carry on their heads as "perhaps the power that women possess in their wombs—the power of reproduction upon which men are dependent." In a patrilineal society such as the Yoruba, the wife comes to the patrilineage as a stranger, like the Alagemo to the Ijebu polity; the polity cannot exist without them, just as the patrilineage cannot exist without women. The Alagemo's power is thus a metaphor for the power of women. But the loads are vulnerable to the power of menstruating women and hence must be kept away from them. If a menstruating woman were to see the loads, it would make them too heavy to carry (Pemberton 1988:62).

This and other Yoruba rituals also involve cross-dressing to make the point about fusion of male and female in the construction of kingly power (ibid.; idem 1989). There is also a fusion along the axis of time, for the king "belongs to the past, present and future" (Apter 1992:116). He must replicate the "multiple identities" of Ogun himself, creator and destroyer.

CONCLUSION

We began this chapter with the image of the king of Ndongo at the forge and ended with an evocation of Ogun, founder of royal dynasties and deity of iron. In the series of correspondences that order thinking about power, metallurgist and ruler must be paired because they both have the means to manipulate the forces that undergird the cultural and natural worlds. Another way of putting it is that they mediate not only between male and female fields of power but also between the ecological, technical, and social divisions of the cosmos (Newbury 1981:91)—a process beautifully captured in the images on the Benin royal stool. They gain the power to do so partly through a "genetic" filiation with ancestral smiths and kings, partly through actions of their own that augment it.

Even the mastery of fire, which would seem peculiar to smiths (and potters), was symbolically associated with kingship, since fire was so often identified with the force of life itself and with prosperity. The method of making fire by friction has commonly had explicit sexual overtones, paralleling those of iron smelting: the Tabwa cultural hero Kyomba was credited with introducing the whole triad—fire-making, iron smelting, and chiefship (Roberts and Maurer 1986:25); the same was true of the mythical dynastic ancestor of Rwandan kings (d'Hertefelt and Coupez 1964:111, 291).

Fire, however, could be viewed as both beneficent and malefic: "fire, feared and dangerous, which can only be manipulated without risk by those who command the sorcerer's art" (Echard 1965:365). Accordingly, the power acquired by kings through their initiation was uncomfortably close to sorcery—kingly power, frighteningly hot as in the destructive figure of Shango, who brought the lightning down on his own people. Death and other moments of crisis were often accompanied by elaborate prescriptions about extinguishing fires and relighting them, prescriptions that were magnified at the death of kings and chiefs and the installation of their successors (e.g., Nevadomsky 1984a:46; Abrahams 1966:139–40). These are all conceptualized within the larger framework of the necessary cosmic balance between hot and cold. Just as Ogun, the hot warrior king, could also perform the "cooling" work of healing through his knowledge of the plants of the bush, so, too, smiths as healers were associated with the cool as well as the hot. Or, in a tour de force, they might display their power to reverse domains by using slag as well as herbs to heal (e.g., Okoro 1990:8).

The symmetrical relationship between smith and king holds whether smiths are organized as endogamous occupational groups or more fully integrated into a society. Paradoxically, even in regions such as Darfur (Sudan) where smiths are a particularly stigmatized group, rigorously set apart from the rest of society, they are still "assigned an important ideological role in maintaining the moral order of the community" comparable to their contributions to the economy (Haaland 1985:57). Only when the smith is totally dissociated from the procreative paradigm, it would appear, does the correspondence break down. Thus, among a few Ethiopian peoples such as the Gurage, smiths are forbidden to cultivate the soil or herd cattle in the belief that they will contaminate the fertility of the soil and domestic animals (ibid.:60). Access to agriculture and pastoralism may, in fact, be the crucial factor in regard to the status of metalworkers, more important than the presence of endogamous castes per se.[10]

Thus far, I have side-stepped the thorny question about whether a distinction should or can be made between smelter and smith in discussing their links, symbolic and actual, with political leadership. De Maret (1985:77–78) draws attention to the fact that although smelting was the "metallurgical work *par excellence,*" it is seldom evoked in rituals associated with political power. These are much more likely to feature the forge with its hammer/anvil. He explains this by pointing out the parallel between smelting and parturition. Neither is a public event; both take place in private or in the seclusion of the bush. In contrast, the forge is a public place where men meet to discuss the affairs of state. "The smelting process is superseded on the level of symbolic sexual dichotomy between male and female by the forging process." This may not be sufficient explanation. For one thing, most kingship rituals have both a private and a public aspect, and there is obviously little information about what goes on in the former. Secondly, the language of both African and European sources is often so imprecise that we can't be sure what aspects of metallurgy are being referred to, especially as memory of smelting has dimmed in so many parts of Africa. Modern Teke, for example, use the same word for low furnace and forge (Dupré 1981–82:196). As Dupré comments (ibid.), "Even the celebrated expression smith-king [roi-forgeron] applied to numerous chiefs

---

10. But like all generalizations about Africa, this also needs to be qualified since the connection between king and smith in Marghi society was underlined by the fact that neither farmed (Vaughan 1973:170).

of Central Africa may be false since one discovers in reading the texts carefully that they are really metallurgists," by which she means smelters and refiners. Finally, it is hard to imagine what *objects* could serve as symbols of smelting in royal insignia in the same way as hammers and anvils do for forging. To be sure, forging is much more widespread and fixed than smelting, as it no doubt was in the past, so it lends itself readily to incorporation in kingly ritual.

Nevertheless, fragmentary evidence does make an explicit link between king and smelter. Not only do Luba legends refer to the introduction of iron smelting technology by the founding hero, Kalala Ilunga, but the very name *ilunga* or *lungulungu* is the term for furnace (Roberts and Maurer 1985:pl. 66b). In some areas, too, locally smelted iron was preserved for use in ritual contexts even after smelting on a regular basis ceased (Pole 1982:511). This was the case in Bas-Congo where, according to Ramona Austin (pers. comm.), some locally smelted iron had to be included in the bracelets fashioned for Kongo chiefs. Something of the same mystique may continue to adhere to slag heaps in eastern Nigeria, which no one is allowed to touch, on pain of death (Clara Ellis, pers. comm.) [11]

Given the frustrating lack of distinction between smelting and smithing in so many sources dealing with metallurgy and kingship, Ian Fowler's work is particularly valuable—all the more so as it concerns a transitional area between the cultures of West and Central Africa. As we saw in Chapter 4, Fowler's researches in Babungo in the Cameroon Grasslands document "an ideological separation of smith and smelter" and a corresponding separation in their relationship with political authority. As owner of the massive clump smelting furnace and keeper of the medicinal secrets that were the key to its success, the *tunaa* was closely identified with the *fon*, or ruler. The iron bloom itself is seen as a metonym for the fon as mediator with Nywi, the supreme spirit or breath. Thus, when the bloom was extracted from the furnace and broken free from the surrounding slag, it was placed on a stone facing the mouth of the furnace, the same stone on which the medicines buried underneath it had been prepared. The foundry workers bowed and clapped their hands to the bloom, invoking the praise names of Nywi. Only then could the bloom be sold or worked. This ritual exactly replicated rituals of respect to the fon because "fonship" also is considered to be sacred and to embody the fertility and prosperity of the chiefdom (Fowler 1990:160).

Foundation myths reiterate the identification of chief and smelter: the descendants of the first fon and his followers were all smelters. Smiths only enter the story later, arriving at the invitation of a later fon. Both fon and smelter are intimately associated with the fertility of the earth, the one through agriculture, the other through his transformation of a product of the earth into

---

11. It is intriguing to speculate that the small pieces of iron known as *jingola*, which became fundamental symbols of authority among the Mbundu (Angola), may have started out simply as bits of raw iron. These *jingola* were believed to give their guardians "access to special spiritual forces useful for regulating the affairs of men" (Miller 1976:62–63).

blooms that represent wealth for the kingdom. Small wonder that Fowler (ibid.:166) speaks of the "almost genetic ties between fon and tunaa and the earth." Large twin blooms as the "gift of Nywi" rightfully belonged to the chief and were included in his grave goods at burial.

Babungo smiths, on the other hand, have an entirely different social, political, and cosmological status. On an ideological level, smiths were believed to possess powerful medicines to "lock the roads" against the intrusion of foreign witches at planting time and to remove pollution. Fowler sees a dichotomy between the role of smith in preventing the "extraction of wealth and life essences by external sorcerers" and that of the smelter whose medicines aimed to accomplish "exactly the reverse, that is, to extract wealth and fecundate the bloom in the furnace."

Where smelters were identified with the fon and with senior ranks of *tif-wan*, the regulatory association, smiths were largely excluded from political power. As a result, they added a turbulent presence to the political scene, implicitly challenging their exclusion from power. This is still acted out in ritual form during major palace celebrations in which members of the smiths' association *dance* their hammers and appear to threaten to kill the tifwan: since their iron hammers "delivered" tifwan, that is, manufactured its sacred insignia, now the "mother of the child is coming to kill it"—again the language of reproductive and family relationships. At that point red and black maskers appear, red representing the camwood-smeared legs of the smelters, black, the smiths with their legs covered with the ash of the hearth. Interestingly enough, the black maskers are considered more powerful than the red because of the identification with the sacra of tifwan, and the ritual ends with the retreat of the smelters. Like other rituals of rebellion, this both dramatizes and partially diffuses the dangers inherent in the relationship of smith and political authority. And yet underlying the conceptual duality that opposes fon and tifwan, smelter and smith, royal and commoner, even peace and war, the complementarity of their relationships is symbolized by other elements in the ritual, such as the inclusion of a smith among the two servants of the red maskers (ibid.:192–200).

In fact, as we have seen across the spectrum of African societies, there is an obvious interdependence of smelter and smith where they are not one and the same person, just as there is an interdependence of king and metallurgist. Ideally, rulers would like to monopolize all forms of power, including ritual and technological power. Since that is impossible, accommodations are reached that are translated into ritual and myth.

Is the Babungo case in any way paradigmatic for what might have happened in other societies with specialized smelting and smithing industries and centralized power, or is it unique, just as the massive furnaces and organization of foundry labor appear to be unique? The question is impossible to answer, but it does suggest the complexity of a history that must have been played out in many parts of the continent and whose memory, alas, has been lost.

The smelter or smith, then, depending on the culture, shares his exceptionality with the chief or king. He also shares it with the hunter. Before synthesizing the notions of power behind these forms of exceptionality, we must look at the hunter and the ways he both resembles and differs radically from metallurgist and ruler.

SEVEN

Of Forests and Furnaces, Anvils and Antelopes

The hunter has killed,
And tears are very near his eyes.

Asante hunters' song

Ogun, here is your festival dog.
Do us no harm.
Keep us safe from death.
Do not let the elderly suffer disease.
Do not let pregnant women have miscarriages.
Do not let the hunter be killed.
Let us have peace.

Prayer to Ogun (Yoruba)

When Sundjata pulled himself upright by means of the giant rod of iron, it bent into the shape of a bow. His bard immediately broke into the *Hymn to the Bow*—"Take your bow, Simbon, Take your bow and let us go"—and shortly thereafter the "young lion" went hunting. While still a youth he received the title of "Simbon," or Master Hunter, and on the day of the fateful battle of Krina against Sumanguru, he appeared dressed as a hunter-king in tight-fitting trousers and tunic bedecked with charms. Sumanguru himself was blacksmith, king, and hunter all rolled into one, as were his legendary counterparts in Baguirmi, far to the east (Pâques 1967:188).

The Yoruba deity Ogun is blacksmith, king, farmer, circumciser, warrior, civilization bearer—and hunter. He embodies the paradox that still fascinates some and perplexes others: Why after millennia of settled, urban life does the hunt continue to hold men everywhere in its thrall? From English royalty to Chinese emperors, from Theodore Roosevelt to the ordinary citizens portrayed in the film *The Deer Hunter*, hunting has been and continues to be an activity surrounded by a special mystique, an activity that refuses to admit its anachronism. Ogun "lived half his life in the wild and disorderly state of nature . . . and the other half in the orderly state of human existence," but Ogun loved best his solitary life in the forest (Ajuwon 1989:180). Human history is telescoped in Ogun, but does he, at the same time, express mankind's regret for the price that civilization has exacted?

Ironically, high-status, large animal hunting by men has probably never contributed anywhere near as much to mankind's diet as the low-prestige, small animal hunting and trapping by women and children (Roger Inskeep 1978: pers. comm.)—and certainly not as much as farming. When women kill small animals or children snare birds, it usually isn't even defined as hunting (La Fontaine 1978:10; Turner 1967:280). As Vansina (1973:124–29) points out a propos of the Tio (Congo Republic): "Trapping achieved two things which hunting did not, in that it caught all sorts of animals which hunters did not get and it gave a much more regular supply with less expenditure of energy than hunting. Like agriculture it was not an esteemed occupation, but nevertheless a profitable one." In fact, Vansina makes a direct connection between Tio men's love of hunting and the overwork and undernourishment of Tio women who are left with almost the entire burden of productive work. Excitement and fun explain more about the appeal of hunting than theories of protein deficiency (cf. ibid.:128; idem 1990:91).

The hunter king is as much a cliché of African myth as the blacksmith king; he is the immigrant stranger, bringing civilization and new technologies. Such myths are most familiar from Central and East Africa but may be more prevalent in other areas than has been generally recognized (cf. Baumann and Westermann 1957:414); they are certainly common in the Chad Basin. Oral traditions link hunters with chiefs and even with smiths, presumably because they are perceived as to some degree analogous or complementary. Oral traditions are not history, but together with ethnographic data they help us explore the way hunting is conceptualized in different African cultures and how this in turn relates to metallurgy and kingship, the two other quintessentially male-dominated activities. Oddly enough, however, hunting has been much less studied, so there is far less material available for comparison. It is even harder to factor in change given the paucity of relevant documentary and archaeological evidence. Vansina (1990) is virtually the only historian who has even tried to address its evolution over a long period of time, in the vast area of equatorial Africa, drawing primarily on linguistics and technology. In the contemporary world, in spite of its persistent mystique, hunting has more and more gone the way of smelting and sacred kingship, albeit for different reasons.

With kings, smiths, and hunters we are clearly dealing with a tripartite representation of male power whether separated or concentrated in the same person. All three manifestly embody and exercise the power of life and death, creativity and destruction, and they accomplish this by their ability to appropriate feminine as well as masculine forces. This makes them by definition deviant, as does their excessive individualism, in constant tension with the needs of the collectivity. The linkage between them is made visible in the artifacts that the smith supplies to both king and hunter: insignia of office in the one case, tools of the trade in the other. It is also a recurrent theme of mythology. Kalala Ilunga, according to some Luba traditions, introduced a new technology of the hunt in the form of bows and hunting charms, as well as superior iron smelting methods and sacred kingship (Mesquitela Lima 1977:349).

There are other points of convergence. If hunters do not catch one of three specific types of antelope during the investiture of a new Kongo chief, it is taken as a sign that the ancestors do not accept the candidate, and he has to leave the enclosure and allow a new chief to be chosen (Mertens 1942:58). Conversely, when hunters come up empty-handed at a time when the clan has a properly installed chief and femme-chef, it means that a new blacksmith should be consecrated immediately (ibid.:444). The investiture rites of a Batembo chief in eastern Zaïre bring all of these elements together: the chief-elect forges some of his insignia on a new anvil, then takes part in a symbolic hunt with his counterpart Pygmy chief (Biebuyck 1986:2, 256).

The most striking difference within the triumvirate of culture heroes, one that sets hunting apart, is that men are not born hunters. Kings must be chosen from royal lineages (although they need not be sons of a past king), and smiths commonly come from smithing families, but hunting is essentially egalitarian except for the gender requirement. Only men may be true hunters, whether kings or commoners. In this sense hunting cuts across the social if not the gender hierarchy and across ethnic boundaries—to the extent that these actually existed in the precolonial past. Among the Malinke of the western Sudan, even slaves might be initiated hunters (Cissé 1964:179). However, this generalization must be qualified somewhat, since in some areas of equatorial Africa hunters formed increasingly specialized, quasi-professional groups, separate from the rest of the population (Vansina 1990:143; cf. Turner 1967:281), while in the southeastern Sahara and central Ethiopia their status was similar (in some cases identical) to casted smiths (Cline 1937:123; Carl and Petit 1955:73; Haberland 1962; Haaland 1985:60).

HUNTING: FERTILITY AND DEATH

Like metallurgy and kingship, hunting is a locus of belief. Bush and forest are cosmological as well as geographical constructs. Even where it is a significant source of food, as among the Lele of Kasai (Zaïre), the forest seems more important for its religious function than for its contribution to nutrition (Douglas 1954; cf. Biebuyck 1973). Hunting becomes a microcosm in which, I will argue, the same beliefs are acted out as in ironworking. The rituals and traditions of hunting also reveal a world where power is structured along the axes of gender and age, between the poles of fertility and sterility, projecting onto the natural world the image of the human. It is, in fact, the realm of male fertility par excellence.

While hunting takes many shapes, we will be concerned primarily with that carried out by those perceived from within as true hunters because it is here that these ideas seem to be expressed most clearly, just as the ideas embedded in metallurgy are thrown into sharpest relief by the rituals of smelting. This focus excludes peoples who have lived exclusively by hunting and gathering such as the Twa (Pygmies) and Basarwa or San (Bushmen) and who have historically not practiced metalworking nor developed hierarchical forms of social organization, as well as pure pastoralists such as the Masai and Nuer for parallel reasons.

More than sixty years ago, the ethnographer-missionary C. M. Doke observed perceptively that the "profession of hunting . . . is held in very considerable esteem among the Lambas, and is akin to that of the blacksmith." Like the witch and the diviner, he noted, hunting and metalworking were matters of choice and initiation and "inseparably connected with the use of *ubwanga* (charm) and the derivation of dynamistic power"—they could not be understood without reference to the spiritual world. The Lamba, like the Tio, made "an absolute distinction between the professional hunter . . . and the trapper or fisher, who gets probably as big results, but has no status in the community" (1931:321).

Almost all detailed accounts of hunting rituals bring out a series of rather uniform features that are immediately reminiscent of smelting rituals: the use of a truly impressive array of charms and medicines; sacrifices; invocations to nature spirits or ancestral hunters; taboos concerning sex, pregnancy, and menstruation, but sometimes also relating to food or washing or to the maintenance of domestic and communal peace; and the proper division of the animals killed, according to social and gender hierarchies. Often hunting has its own body of music and chants. All this must be learned by the novice, along with the practicalities of the art. The ritual panoply has two purposes: to achieve success and to protect. Like iron smelting, hunting is both uncertain in outcome and dangerous to the participant. Just as iron smelting rituals take place in secret, away from village and compound, and exclude women, so hunting takes place deep in bush or forest. But does hunting ultimately invoke a procreative paradigm to make sense of these components? Is hunting understood as a transformative activity that can be equated with human reproduction? In some cultures, the evidence is strong that this is so. In others, the evidence is unclear or simply inadequate; in still others, such an interpretation demands wrestling with apparent paradox.

The Lele of Kasai and the Ndembu of northwestern Zambia fall into the first category. Lele hunting is a communal activity but exclusively male. It occurs in the forest, which is seen as a male sphere even though both men's and women's pursuits take them there. The forest holds immense prestige as the source of virtually all the things the Lele value, both necessities and pleasures: food, drink, clothing, building materials, sacred medicines, and a cool refuge from the heat of the open savannas. At the same time, it is a place of danger for both men and women, and yet it also provides the medicines that protect and heal. Women are forbidden to enter the forest on so many occasions that it actually makes daily life a bit difficult: every third day, during menstruation and childbirth, during mourning, at the birth of twins, at the departure of a chief, and at the appearance of the new moon—that is, at any moment of individual and collective vulnerability. The night before a hunt, all adult villagers must abstain from sexual activity (Douglas 1954).

Not only does the hunt carry inordinate prestige for the Lele but it serves as "a kind of spiritual barometer of village well-being" (ibid.:13; cf. Vansina 1978:200). And this well-being is directly compared with female childbearing "as if they were equivalent male and female functions." Bad hunts are believed to coincide with barrenness and death, and both are under the direct control of nature spirits. When things go badly, diviners prescribe remedies that are distinct for the two spheres but lumped together by the populace. Incidentally, the only time a Lele woman is allowed to hold ritual office is when she bears twins. In this case both she and her husband become diviners on an equal footing, and both perform special rites concerning hunting and fertility. The ultimate purpose of the hunt (aside from the excitement it provides) is to furnish meat for the feasts of village cult groups. These groups reinforce the social solidarity of a village. Hence one begins to see the logic in the pairing of male hunting with female childbearing: both are crucial, but hunting is seen as even more vital to general prosperity, by implication because it is associated with social, not simply biological, reproduction (Douglas 1954; idem 1963:206–12).

But the Lele extend the association of hunting with fertility one step further. At the new moon sexual relations are forbidden, women are not allowed to pound grain or to enter the forest, and no one may make loud noises in the forest. The next day the men go hunting and must shed blood, even if it is only that of an insignificant animal. This lifts the restrictions, and normal life resumes. The object of the ritual, however, is specific: to prosper the maize crop, the most important staple of the Lele diet (ibid. 1954:11).

Douglas glosses the segregation and exclusion of the women from the forest in terms of the "full ritual pattern," and her comments undoubtedly deserve wider application:

> It is not merely that sexual intercourse and menstruation were thought to be dangerous to men, but that in their most vital function, child-bearing, women themselves were highly vulnerable. On the one hand, they were liable to frustration of their function in barrenness, miscarriage and stillbirth. On the other, they were liable to die in labour. Child-birth was a matter of fear, and for all the more anxiety since every man's career depended on his becoming a father and grandfather and on the increase of his matrilineal clan—a triplicated focus on child-bearing. Hence the emphasis on fertility in Lele ritual. The spirits in the forest controlled both child-bearing and hunting. They could make all women or individual women barren, all the men or individual hunters fail, as punishment for individual or collective transgressions. (1963:207)

Although the context is somewhat different, Victor Turner finds essentially the same equivalence at the bottom of Ndembu hunting rituals: "In all this an important analogy is made by Ndembu between what they consider is woman's dominant role, the bearing of children, and the man's, which is the bringing home of carcasses from the hunt. In hunters' and women's rites of affliction the same symbols stand respectively for a multiplicity of kills and a multiplicity of children" (1967:284; cf. Devisch 1984:104). True, women do not possess the particular "ripeness" of the greatest hunters, and indeed their reproductive powers are endangered by close contact with "the things of huntsmanship," but the parallel still holds. As with the Lele, big game hunting "epitomizes masculinity in a society jurally dominated by the principle of matrilineal descent" (Turner 1967:280). In Ndembu belief, however, ancestor shades rather than nature spirits are responsible for the fortunes of the hunt and of reproduction, and therefore must be wooed assiduously.

What are the symbols that manifest the correspondence between successful hunting and successful childbearing? They are the three components of the temporary shrine hunters erect to the hunter-ancestor in every kind of hunting rite, whether it be a ritual of affliction, aimed at undoing the neglect that brought down the rebuke of the ancestor, or a ritual of propitiation for bounty already provided. They consist of a forked branch, a small piece of termite earth, and a braid of grass. These materials and the ways in which they are manipulated invoke and evoke gynecological rituals, phallic symbolism, and the power of ancestral hunters; they are variations on the theme of fertility and virility as it is played out in the hunt (ibid.:282ff.). The effect of sweeping with the "medicine broom" is even believed to make the hunter irresistibly attractive to animals, with the sexual overtones that this implies (idem 1953:40–41).

Conversely, a woman who is suffering from excessive menstrual flow and concomitant barrenness will take part in the Nkula cult that incorporates hunting symbolism and ritual—here the blood spilled by the hunter is equated with both the "wasted" blood of menstruation and the desirable blood of childbirth. In fact, the symbols of Nkula represent just about every kind of blood to make the ultimate point that the patient, "in wasting her menstrual blood and in failing to bear children, is actively renouncing her expected role as a mature married female. She is behaving like a male killer" (Turner 1967:42). This seems a rather strong statement on the basis of the evidence given, and in fact it implicitly contradicts the argument presented above, which draws on another of Turner's essays: could it not be that just as hunting rituals invoke gynecological rituals to ensure the fecundity of the hunt, barren women invoke the rituals of the hunt to remedy their own infertility? For, if the hunt is to be located in the same semantic field as human childbearing, the emphasis cannot be so much on the act of killing per se as on the provision of meat and its role in social relations and reproduction, as Douglas so rightly suggests.

Luc de Heusch, in turn, draws on Turner to support his structural analysis of Luba and Lunda myths of origin as they concern the "blood of women and the blood of beasts" since the Ndembu are closely related to the Lunda (1982a).

Hunting, in Ndembu eyes, is a form of sexual activity, and the fecundity brought by the hunter is analogous to that of women; the blood of the hunt is analogous then to the blood not of menstruation—which is sterility—but of childbirth and even of circumcision. Both de Heusch and Turner underscore the ambivalence of blood and the necessity of distinguishing its different forms and changing meanings, although de Heusch's tendency to scoop up everything into his cosmogonic net must serve as a caution to those of us inclined to generalize too broadly (cf. Vansina 1983).

In a study of Rwandan traditions of Gihanga, the mythic ancestor of the royal dynasty who is supposed to have introduced not only kingship but metalworking, hunting, fire, cattle, woodworking, and pottery into the land, de Heusch ([1972] 1982b:182) examines the "subtle dialectic" between hunting, metallurgy, kingship, and fecundity. Gihanga's name, in fact, has become synonymous with the ancestral spirit that has dissolved into the cosmogonic force of *imaana*, responsible for creation and fecundity (d'Hertefelt and Coupez 1964: sec. III, 66: commentary). De Heusch's argument is rather difficult to follow because at one moment he seems clearly to recognize the important distinction between forge and foundry, but then he blurs it. His point seems to be that there is a homology between smelting and hunting but that both have a double valence, the one associated with fecundity, the other with death. Immediately, however, he switches to the forge in asserting that metalworking and hunting intersect with women at only two points, the sexual act and birth, while gestation itself—pregnancy—is inimical to both. As a result, he reads the myth of Gihanga to mean that "the hunt and the work of the smith constitute two successive and complementary overtures to fecundity, but these two activities are incompatible with pregnancy" (de Heusch [1972]1982b:185).

The research of other scholars (Célis and Nzikobanyanka 1976:35; Bourgeois 1956:539–40) does indeed bear out the belief in Rwanda that pregnancy is harmful to smelting and hunting,[1] but, then, so are sexual activity and menstruation. The commonsense explanation would seem to lie in the maxim that processes that are both like and unlike can be seen as mutually harmful, as we have argued earlier, and that one can operate comfortably in both dimensions without worrying about contradictions. Thus, the Rwandan king goes on the hunt, is presented with the royal hammers and fire tools, but does not actually take part in the killing; he is expected, however, to accomplish a ritual copulation with one of his wives (d'Hertefelt and Coupez 1964:VI, 81), a parallel, incidentally, to the ritual copulation in the Rwandan sorghum ritual (ibid.: VIII, 84). Surely all of this suffices to convey the idea of hunting (and agriculture) as analogous to both sexuality and potential reproductivity (and symbolically to metalworking), for how can the two be separated?

Nevertheless, the readiness to see hunting only as killing may have led some scholars to miss its more complex, even paradoxical symbolism. Mac-

---

1. One suspects that the danger is reciprocal. Barley, for example, points out the danger the hunter poses to women and pregnant women in particular (1983:18).

Gaffey, for example, reports the Kongo belief that a hunter whose wife is pregnant will not be able to kill game unless he wears around his wrist a strip of his wife's perineal rag; if he does, however, his success is assured.[2] "The idea is that the strip forms a barrier . . . separating his gun from the life-giving function of his wife, just as the rag itself protects her from forces hostile to her fertility; thereafter, the notion of life giving in the village evokes its opposite, death healing [dealing?] in the forest" (1986:49). He then cites Turner in support of his oppositional pairing of

man, gun	: woman, rag
death	: life
forest	: village

By emphasizing only the "destructive capacity of men as hunters," however, he ignores Turner's (and Douglas's) equal emphasis on hunting and fecundity. Pemberton's comment that rites of Ogun, the deity of hunting, iron, and king-ship, force the Yoruba to recognize the irony of cultural existence, namely, that death is essential to life may be apt here: like ironworking and kingship, hunting "symbolizes the reality and ambiguity of violence in human experi-ence" and the intricate interplay of violence and creativity (1989:107). These characteristics often function as a series of correspondences that mediate op-positions.

Feierman's exegesis of Shambaa myths of origin may help to clarify more generally the ambiguous nature of the hunter (1974: ch. 2). Mbegha was the quintessential outsider—the man driven out by his kin because he was an abnormal child (he cut his upper teeth first) and therefore brought death to those around him. He wandered in the wild living solely on game and contin-uing to indulge his insatiable and illicit sexuality. And yet after he exchanged meat for starch and helped the Shambaa rid themselves of wild animals who were destroying their farms, they made him their king, symbolically giving him the entire wealth of their land, including their daughters without pay-ment of bridewealth.

Shambaa traditions make it clear that Mbegha was welcomed because of his life-giving qualities. Rain magic, the key to fertility, began with him, as did the healing medicines of the wild: "His magical powers, which were also the powers to kill, and which derived from his wildness, were also the powers to bring fertility to Shambaai" (ibid.:61). It is axiomatic, as Feierman points out, that such power can be used to help or harm, to cure or injure, that all power is Janus-faced. "Mbegha had the power to destroy and the power to bring

---

2. According to an Ngombe (Zaïre) variant, the husband of a pregnant woman may not join a collective hunt for fear that animals would flee the net, but he may hunt on his own. He may not do any hunting at all while his wife is menstruating, lest the angry animals try to kill him. Finally, he is sure to come up empty-handed if he has sexual intercourse the night before a hunt (Wolfe 1961:89). It is hard to interpret the distinction between collective and individual hunting here, but otherwise the general proscriptions seem consistent with the association of the hunt with fertility, which is jeopardized by both human fertility and sterility.

fertility" (ibid.:62). The myth records the transformation of the hero from death bringer to life giver as he moves from a solitary existence in the wilderness, subsisting on meat, to the social life of the village with its proper exchange of meat and starch:

> dispossessed person > owner of the country
> bringer of death > bringer of fertility and life (ibid.:61).

The Shambaa express the eventual relationship of Mbegha and his people in terms of masculine and feminine: Mbegha was masculine while the Shambaa were feminine. In other words, they genderize the power relationship (ibid.:54–55).

This finds corroboration in another myth, common among the Shambaa and their neighbors, which is strikingly similar to that of Mbegha. Sheuta, too, is a hunter living alone in the wild who is distinguished by prodigious sexuality—in one version an elephant gives the hero a magical charm for making his penis longer or shorter at will—and Sheuta becomes chief by overpowering women. In one case he vanquishes the female scourge of the land thanks to his magic charm, in another by subduing the chieftainness of a "land of women" (ibid.:66ff.).

Feierman is concerned with the grains of history as well as ideology to be winnowed from these myths. Our interest is somewhat different. These traditions, like others dealing with hunters, date from a very distant past, and yet they still make sense to their preservers, at least in their current forms, as statements about human interactions between wild and settled space. They do this by analyzing the fundamental duality of power in terms not of good and evil but of socially restrained and unrestrained. The parallel with kingship and metallurgy is obvious: both kings and smiths have quintessentially masculine powers that are potentially destructive and creative; they are by definition sorcerers. But they are indispensable to civilized life.

Small wonder, then, that sexual taboos run as a leitmotiv through hunting rituals, just as they do through those of metalworking and kingship. In some sense animals are identified with women, so a violation of the prohibition against sexual relations before and during the hunt becomes tantamount to adultery, causing an unsuccessful hunt and injury or even death to the hunter (e.g., Carvalho 1890:454; Weeks 1913:232–33; Korse 1989:19; Jackson 1977:90; Barley 1983:18; Felix Yandia: pers. comm.), just as adultery causes a difficult labor or stillborn child. And yet, as we have seen, the rules may be reversed in the case of the Rwandan king who is required to copulate ritually with one of his wives during the hunt to ensure its success. For ordinary Rwandans, a hunter who has just killed a large animal must abstain from sexual relations with his wife *after* the hunt as well, while he undergoes a ceremony analogous to mourning because, "like a newly charged battery," he has accumulated so much deadly power from the animal. The dominant Tutsi, however, dissipate this dangerous energy by having intercourse with a servant and then drinking a purifying liquid (Bourgeois 1956:50)—note that they do not expose their wives to this transfer of danger!

Regulation of sexual relations before or during the hunt is aimed at maximizing power over the fecundity of the animal world but also raises more general issues of the compatibility of sexuality and the bush or forest. Sex in the wild is almost universally prohibited under any circumstances. The reasons may be numerous—fear of capricious spirits or malevolent *djinns,* for example—but they also involve conceptualizations of the earth and how it is delimited. Gottlieb (1982) provides a cogent analysis of such thinking in the case of the Beng of the Ivory Coast. It should be pointed out that Forest and Earth are not opposed concepts in Beng cosmology and that cultivation of crops such as yams takes place in the forest. Formerly, too, hunting was a more important male activity than it is now.

The Beng consider intercourse outside the village a heinous offense against the Earth that has grave consequences: death, drought, difficulties in childbirth. The explanation is that "sex in the forest is forbidden because no kapok tree has been *ritually* planted there which would legitimate sexual activity." The village kapok tree is the "beginning of all things in the village," so a forest camp only becomes a place "where sexual activity may take place and thus the members may reproduce themselves" when a Master of the Earth plants a kapok tree there (Gottlieb 1982:38–39). There are also strict regulations about bathing to "wash off" sex before entering the forest/fields and to wash off the forest before "entering" into sexual activity. Menstruation is equally inimical to the forest if the woman is initiated, married, or has previously been married.

In the case of both types of pollution, the consequences are associated with aborted fertility. "To the extent that human fertility and forest/field fertility are seen as parallel . . . to the same extent they must be separated. If they are inappropriately combined, the mediating force which makes each possible becomes in its own way aborted: the rain stops, the delivery of the child is impeded" (ibid.:41). This is not, Gottlieb argues, emblematic of any "universal" culture/nature dichotomy, because the Beng do not see such a distinction: for them the forest/fields are orderly space intimately tied to village life and all under the unitary control of the Earth, which, be it noted, is *male.* The incompatibility with sex and menstruation in turn derives not from gender opposition but from their common denominator. Conceptually and spatially the two realms of fertility must first be separated before they can be joined: "The actual creation of human life—the act of sex—and the symbolic principle representing human fertility—menstrual blood—must be separated from the creation of the Earth's fertility in the forest/fields" (ibid.:42).[3]

---

3. The Beng are unusual in allowing sex during menstruation for reasons consistent with the analogic thinking summarized here, but they forbid a husband to eat food cooked by his menstruating wife. As a result, they firmly believe that women cook the most delicious food during their periods, which is probably true since they have much more time to devote to it (Gottlieb 1982:43f.).

Gottlieb's formulation is specific to the Beng and certainly does not hold in all regards for other cultures, although it does, for example, find striking echoes in areas of Lele belief—this in spite of the fact that the cultures are thousands of miles apart and otherwise very dissimilar. More generally, it offers, I believe, a well-supported model for exploring beliefs that lie behind sexual and menstrual taboos, a model that can be tested more generally and one that rejects too facile an acceptance of terms such as pollution, nature, and culture.

HUNTING, AGE, AND THE CULT OF ANCESTORS

The goodwill of ancestors is a key factor in a successful hunt, but whose ancestors? The answer is not self-evident. Among the mainly patrilineal Nso of Cameroon, for example, it is the maternal ancestors who determine success in hunting (Kaberry [1969] 1971:190). Unfortunately, the literature abounds in references to generic ancestors that tell us little. While hunting, like other activities, is usually embedded in a matrix of kinship, the relevant kin group must be defined in each case. An excellent demonstration of this is Roulon's (1981) study of the 'Bodoe, a subgroup of the Gbaya Kara (Central African Republic), which inserts hunting into the full spectrum of manual activities and shows how all are related to concepts of female fecundity and to the cult of ancestors.

The Gbaya Kara Bodoe are a patrilineal, patrilocal people who now live primarily from agriculture, but hunting, fishing, and gathering loom much larger in their ritual lives. Roulon speculates that this may be because agriculture is a relatively late arrival in this society, but since the same tendencies exist in other societies that privilege men's hunting more than women's productive activities, it need not be the case (cf. Turner 1953:25; Devisch 1984:35). Needless to say, the products of the hunt are appreciated more than the products of gathering, as the elaborate ritualization accompanying them attests.

Hunting is broken down according to means—hunting by spear, trap, net, dog, etc.—and in each case the first catch by a novice is eaten by a prescribed group, while succeeding catches are eaten by the whole lineage with the exception of certain parts of the animal. Both the first catch and these key parts are believed to contain the essence of fecundity, the *koyo*, and those who are allowed to eat them are believed, in effect, to control the future fecundity of the hunter. For example, in the case of hunting with a spear, the first animal of significant size killed by a young hunter is designated as "the fecundity of his hand" and can only be eaten by his "fathers" (i.e., all the men and women on the paternal side and of that generation). A piece of charcoal symbolizes the koyo and circulates from hand to hand among this group until it is ritually applied to the forehead of the novice and to the handle of his spear. Subsequently, a member of this same group will be the custodian of the koyo. If the hunt goes badly, it is passed to another member; in more serious cases, the hunter undergoes a ritual to renew the "fecundity of his hand." Similarly, other types of hunting ensure optimum results by maintaining the koyo through proper division of meat and performance of relevant rituals.

Three points are worth emphasizing. One is that the woman who kills a small animal with her hoe during the fire-drive at the end of the dry season is seen as one category of hunter among the many others and allots the crucial animal parts according to whether or not she is married. Another is that the individual considered the author of the kill never eats those parts of the animal believed to contain the germ of fertility. And finally, the group that does consume them is essentially male since paternal aunts have the status of males in Gbaya society. Hence it is only "males" who ritually consume koyo and by so doing participate in its protection.

Not surprisingly, the same notions are adapted to women's fecundity. A woman's koyo is believed to be inborn, but she loses it to the first man with whom she has sexual relations: she only regains it if she becomes pregnant, but once this occurs she is believed to have total control over her fertility. Obviously there can be complications if a woman has relations with a man that do not lead to pregnancy and then marries someone else, but there are various means to deal with this. Incidentally, much as Roulon emphasizes the Gbaya obsession with ensuring fertility, she is one of the few researchers to note that women may also on occasion want to postpone or prevent further pregnancies. In such cases they practice contraception by performing a ritual that transfers their fertility temporarily or permanently to a termite hill.

While these rituals reinforce the dominance of the patrilineal group, other Gbaya ceremonies expand that definition to include its ancestors. In former times, an annual rite at the end of the dry season sanctioned the last fire-drive of the year. It was organized by an elderly man who addressed himself to the lineage ancestors. A central actor, however, was a young boy who was given a chicken to eat, containing the koyo of the hunt, and then was believed to die and become one with the ancestors, dictating to them their conduct toward the living. Not until the following day was he "revived" and the fortified koyo restored to the hunters. Other rites to the ancestors consisted of sacrifices, prayers, and songs and dances exalting the dead.

Roulon points out that the rituals concerning the protection of the koyo have an ideological unity in that they distinguish those areas of Gbaya life deemed most important and over which they wish most keenly to "neutralize chance": "Every hunter should kill game, every snare should capture them, every trap catch fish, every woman be able to give birth" (Roulon 1981:357). The rituals that accomplish this do so by bringing women and young men tightly under the control of the older men of the patrilineage. As outsiders, women do not participate in the system that they reproduce except as a function of their relationship to males. Finally, the exhortations addressed to the "ancestors of my grandparents, ancestors of my fathers, ancestors of my elders" emphasize the importance of age and the social bonds linking past and present. Of all members of the lineage, the ancestors are, ironically, the most difficult to control.

Lineage ancestors, then, intervene in hunting as in other affairs of life. But where access to hunting skills and magic requires formal initiation, the active ancestors are more likely to be those of the hunting association rather than of an individual's own kin group. Mande hunters' societies from West Africa and Fipa from East Africa illustrate this. Societies of the Mande type are found, in fact, across the western Sudan and are truly supra-ethnic. They rest on variations of the myth of Sanin and Kontron, the pantheon to whom hunters owe their primary allegiance. Cissé (1964) and Cashion (1982), who provide the most detailed studies of Mande hunters, present them as mother and son. Sanin conceived Kontron without ever having known a man; Kontron in turn became the exemplar of the devoted and dutiful son. Together they wandered without kin or country, but so great was Kontron's skill as a hunter and his knowledge of the bush that he attracted ever more followers. Through the initiation ritual, each of these followers became the "son" of Sanin and "brother" of Kontron, a process repeated today. According to Travelé's version (1928), which seems less widely diffused, Kondoro (Kontron?) was the wife of Sanéné (Sanin?) and is reputed to be a much greater hunter.

The initiation takes place in the bush and may last two to three years during which the initiate attaches himself to an established hunter as mentor. He learns not only the techniques of stalking, tracking, cutting up meat, and smoking it but also the rituals encapsulated in the cult of Sanin and Kontron. Cashion (1982:207–9) argues that all Mande hunters' ceremonies are structured around the two points of birth and death: the birth of the new hunter as a child of Sanin and younger brother of Kontron at the conclusion of the initiation and the annual rebirth of each new hunting season after the rains. In addition, if the former chief of the hunters' society has died since the last season, a new one is installed. He is the "oldest," but according to the structure of the society this means the one initiated earlier than all the others because the age hierarchy—the only hierarchy in the hunters' guild—is based not on chronology but on when one was initiated. Thus, a younger man can actually be considered "older" than his senior.

Initiation rituals take place at the crossroads, the symbolic boundary between village and bush; formerly they were held in the sacred grove of the hunters. They consist of sacrifices and prayers to the presiding deities and interrogation of the initiate, who must demonstrate not only skills but also character and knowledge. If the sacrifices are accepted, he becomes a member of the family of Sanin and Kontron for life, renouncing his former kinship affiliations: "Kontron alone replaces his ancestors" (Cissé 1964:179). Both the candidate and his gun undergo a ritual bath that marks his new status and endows both with some of the magic power they will need to withstand the dangers they will encounter. The hunters then depart, usually in small bands, on a long journey to gain fame and honor.

Mande hunters rely heavily on the protection of their ancestral sponsors—deceased hunters as well as Sanin and Kontron—and on the amulets that they learn to fashion. These amulets incorporate a range of powerful medicines: leaves, bark, metals, celts, knots, even bits of paper with excerpts from the Qu'ran. Hunters' tunics are literally covered with them (fig. 36). Together with the ritual baths, sacrifices, and observance of sexual taboos, they are intended to attract game and to protect the hunter against the animal's *nyama*, the force or energy inherent in all matter, animate and inanimate, sometimes also equated with intense heat (Zahan 1963:147). *Nyamakala*, endogamous Mande occupational groups (smiths, bards, leatherworkers), are born with the unusual amounts of nyama that enable them to perform their work of transformation. Very old people become "hot" with nyama simply by virtue of their age and knowledge. Hunters must acquire theirs through the secrets imparted during the initiation process and by appropriation from animal victims. Killing animals (like working with metals) releases dangerous forces, forces that could be fatal to the hunter were he not fortified with his own superior force. This enables him not simply to survive his encounter with the nyama of the animal he kills but to add it to his own store (Bird and Kendall 1980:16; McNaughton 1988:15ff. and passim). Hunters, like smiths, are "associated with concepts of heat in the sense of staggering accumulations of power and the imbalance of aggressive action." When great hunters die, the world is said to have "cooled off" (McNaughton 1988:71).

Thus, both hunters and smiths "play with fire" and both operate perilously close to the divide that separates socially beneficial action from sorcery, the cosmological spaces identified by the terms *fadenya*, lit. "father-childness," and *badenya*, "mother-childness," which we encountered earlier. The former evokes the aggressive, competitive behavior expected of siblings having the same father but different mothers, while the latter exemplifies the warm, affectionate bonds between children of the same mother.[4] The Mande see an interplay of both as necessary for a dynamic society because an excess of either could be disastrous. Nevertheless, the unbridled individualism of fadenya behavior, whether in warrior, hunter, smith, or sorcerer (all those who possess exceptional amounts of nyama), is much to be feared. The hunter operates very much in the aggressively individualist fadenya sphere, constantly demonstrating his superior force in the pursuit of lasting renown. Sanin and Kontron, however, epitomize the ideal of badenya, the perfect bonding of mother and son with no father in the picture at all. Paradoxically, then, each new hunter joins this fatherless family and emulates Kontron's behavior within the group as a means to success (Cissé 1964).

Both Cissé and Travelé stress the importance of sexual purity on the part of both a hunter and his wife. According to Travelé, almost all hunting accidents are blamed on faithless wives. To remedy her adultery, a wife must

---

4. Adler (1982:161–62) draws attention to a comparable distinction as fundamental to Moundang thinking and comments on how underappreciated it has been by ethnographers.

make a sacrifice to her husband's gun at the crossroads; otherwise, he is in danger of being attacked by wild animals. The myth of Kontron's chastity is used to explain the emphasis on sexual purity and danger of adultery. Cissé adds that sex diminishes one's nyama and that the hunter needs every bit he can muster to deal with the nyama of his victims. But implicitly there seems to be a further dimension, for he also notes that great hunters are not only in danger of madness or paralysis but are very likely to be sterile or to beget abnormal children—one thinks immediately of the impotence of the Tio king. In other words, their own fertility has in some way been transferred or sacrificed to their animal counterparts. They thus risk the extinction of their line— the ultimate cost of supernatural power.

Scholars such as Cissé and McNaughton have drawn attention to the parallels of hunting and smithing in Mande conceptualizations of power, including ancestral power. These parallels are also to be found among the Fipa. In what may well be a unique association, Fipa hunters even collaborate with smelters and smiths in preparing the charcoal used at all stages of metalworking and take part in smelting rituals (Wyckaert 1914). However, the focus here will be on the death and initiation of the hunter.

When a great hunter dies, he is believed to become even more powerful than other ancestors. His hunter-heir preserves his skull and makes it the focus of a cult, honoring it constantly with sacrifices so that the ancestor will bless his fellow hunters with good fortune. In case the hunter died while harboring ill will against any of his kin or the initiates, they perform purification rites by washing with a decoction of strong medicines. Then the hunters alone perform further rites to protect themselves and their guns in the seclusion of the bush (Robert 1949:230–31).

The initiation of a new hunter is directed by the *mwami*, the hunter in charge of the ancestral cult, who is considered a powerful magician and whom the novice must obey and respect as a father. The novice must also hand over to him stipulated parts of each animal killed. In return the mwami teaches the initiate how to propitiate the hunter ancestors and how to manufacture the medicines that protect him and bring success in the hunt. Such medicines are vital to hunting everywhere, as they are to smelting, and are customarily matters of the utmost secrecy, so it is remarkable that Father Robert was able to obtain a list of key ingredients—and a very revealing list it is.

The ingredients are used to make a powder, one portion of which is actually inoculated into the skin of the hunter, while the rest is used to purify the hunter's gun and to make two cylindrical amulets. The medicines, collectively known as *mashina*, are gathered from three types of trees: one that bears thorns, one that antelopes like to rub against, and one that bears abundant fruit. In each case bark must be gathered from both the east and the west sides of the trees. The second set of medicines consists of

1. something shameful from one's mother-in-law (piece of loin cloth, excrement, etc.);

2. a piece of afterbirth from a mother of twins;
3. a piece of the corpse of one who has died by hanging;
4. a piece of flesh from the root of an elephant's tusk;
5. a piece of the corpse of a pregnant woman;
6. a piece of the skull of the deceased hunter. (ibid.:231–32)

These materials obviously make a powerful statement about death and fertility. Given the rigidly circumspect behavior demanded everywhere between son-in-law and mother-in-law, the first is especially shocking—in its own way perhaps as shocking as the incest required in some royal investiture rituals. It suggests the violation of a primary kinship taboo and perhaps the augmentation of power that such a violation confers (cf. Jacobson-Widding 1991).

In the ritual purification of the gun with these medicines, the ancestral hunters are invoked as the liquid is sprinkled three times to east and to west, then the remainder is actually poured down the barrel of the gun. The novice hunter should avoid sexual relations until he has killed his first animal. As to the amulets, whenever he is not hunting, he must make sure that they never come in contact with a menstruating woman, who could destroy their efficacy (Robert 1949:232–33).

The detailed evidence about Mande hunting rituals and beliefs unfortunately is not matched by direct evidence of smelting practices to complement those of smithing. Nevertheless, Cissé (1964:179) declares that the ardent attachment of hunters to the "powerful pantheon of Sanin and Kontron" has no equal except perhaps that of smiths, "the men of fire who, in the secret of the sanctuary that the forge represents, *numou so*, the most venerable of all sanctuaries, reenact to the accompaniment of the rhythm of bellows and hammers the mystery of creation." The transformation of iron ore into bloom would have given off even more enormous amounts of nyama against which the smelter would have had to protect himself, both by endogamy and by marshaling an array of charms and medicines (McNaughton 1988:4, 16).

For the Fipa and Gbaya we are in a better position to compare smelting and hunting directly. In the case of the Fipa, not only do metalworkers and hunters cooperate but there is also a predictable ritual and symbolic overlap. Both the head smelter and the master hunter have the title mwami or mwene and are seen as veritable magicians whose power is objectified in the basket of medicines, the *ntangala*, or the amulets made from the medicines. Both these mwami enforce sexual and other taboos and preside over ancestral rituals. Consistent with Fipa belief, hunting and smelting rituals are explicitly oriented to east and west. But while the furnace itself personifies a nubile and fertile female, the fertility dimensions of hunting are suggested rather by the choice of medicines.

As for the Gbaya, both Roulon and Moñino, the one focusing initially on hunting, the other on smelting, underscore these parallels, which do not occur in any other productive activities (except, of course, human procreation). "Only hunting . . . displays types of rituals comparable to those of metallurgy": rituals to protect against "the dangers linked to the creation of a new matter and the harmful emanations" given off by iron and animals. They are accompanied by medicines, prescriptive behavior, and rites of fertility and purification that acknowledge the power of the lineage ancestors (Moñino 1983:288). Indeed, the smelting process itself is explicitly compared to the hunt: "The bellows operators are the dogs that track the game, the smelter is the master hunter who encourages them, the game in this case being, of course, the iron" (ibid.:305). As with the hunt, there is a symbolic sacrifice of a child to the ancestors. Both are directly equated with human fecundity as a necessity for survival. Even the division of output is dictated in both cases by customary ritual. And both, for all their danger and symbolic baggage, display "un aspect ludique"—they not only invoke a sexual model, they also share its pleasures (ibid.:307).

EXCURSUS: ANTELOPES

Hunting conjures up images of elephants, leopards, lions. But there is tantalizing evidence that antelopes and duikers occupy a special symbolic space as well, mediating between the bush or forest and the village. It may be no accident that the majestic huntsman, vaguely ascribed to the "Lower Niger Bronze Industry," is depicted with an antelope slung over his shoulders (fig. 37). To my knowledge, Suzanne Blier (1984, 1987) is the only scholar to have looked at this subject in any detail. She has demonstrated fascinating links between antelopes, ironworking, and domestic architecture among the western Tamberma (Batammaliba) of northern Togo.

According to Tamberma traditions, smithing originated with antelopes, specifically with the tiny duiker believed to be the most powerful member of the antelope family (cf. McNaughton 1988:16). The name *antelope* is also used by extension to embrace all wild animals that are the object of the hunt (cf. Siroto 1977). In one version, God, "the sun," made humans out of clay but antelopes out of iron ore or the material originally used to make the Earth. Antelopes owned the first forges, and iron was their exclusive gift and prerogative. They are able to light the fire of the forge with sparks given off when their hooves strike stony ledges. Red antelopes in particular serve as smiths to the forest game, using the forge to make their own jewelry along with weapons and the protective medicines that render them virtually impossible to kill unless they choose their own death. Growing tired of life in the forest, they are sometimes ready for the comforts of home life. Undigested iron ore is said to be found in their stomachs and becomes part of antelope shrines (Blier 1984).

The spirits of these antelopes killed in the hunt take up residence in hunters' houses where they often request that forges be built so that they can continue to work as in the wild. Sometimes this request is made through dreams; more commonly it is conveyed through misfortune or "heat" afflicting a member of the hunter's family—especially in the form of burns. This is treated by the blacksmith. If it is successful, the hunter buys forging rights from him, and a member of the family actually apprentices himself to learn the trade. The antelope is then viewed as the sponsor of the new forge and smith, the being that brings the knowledge of forging to the family. Simultaneously, the antelope actively sponsors and protects new children in the home. They wear iron jewelry to symbolize the fact that at least one antelope sponsor has been brought into the family by an ancestor: iron pendants, a hunter's thumb guard, the twisted iron and copper python bracelet. The motifs on the jewelry invoke both the game and its gifts (ibid.).

At the same time, forge-bearing antelopes are reflected in smithing symbolism and ritual. The smithy is, in effect, a religious sanctuary dedicated to the antelope sponsor (fig. 38). It is circular in form with a mound-shaped earthen shrine that shelters the antelope spirit of the forge; branches of its favorite trees are "planted" close by. Other parts of the forge replicate the antelope's body: the pelt is represented by incised designs on the interior wall, the lungs and breath by the pot-bellows, the nose by the hole where the forge is lit. Penis, testicles, and tail are all included. In hot weather smithing is said to cool off the house-dwelling antelope because the fire leaves her and enters into the forge. The offerings made to the forge also invoke the game trapped by antelopes in the forest, including a bird whose name means "bird of the forge." Antelope and forge share water taboos: since water quenches the heat of the forge, both the sponsoring antelope and the forge detest anything to do with water, preferring land animals to creatures of the water. The crab is especially unwelcome, and anyone who has eaten crabs risks being burned if he enters the forge (ibid.).

As long as antelope spirits are properly propitiated, they willingly aid smiths in making equipment for the hunt. They also assist in another area that brings smith and hunter together: the treatment of illness. Men are called to be smiths by serious illness, which is cured by learning to forge. They then treat other illnesses associated with the forge with plants and roots believed to have been part of the antelope pharmacopeia in the forest—and with iron jewelry. Iron bracelets, for example, may be boiled with herbal remedies and then removed before they are administered; such jewelry is the symbol of the vital link between medicine and the forge and helps to explain why Tamberma smiths see themselves preeminently as makers of jewelry.

It is somewhat paradoxical, in fact, that among an agricultural people such as the Tamberma smithing traditions are linked primarily with hunting and that smiths make jewelry rather than hoes (which are imported from outside). Blier argues that the dominance of art over "utility" is found in the symbolism and functions of Tamberma iron arts themselves, that is, in the "variety of factors drawn from hunting traditions, medicinal practices, ideas of human regeneration, views of political governance, and historical circumstance" (1984:58). The etymology of the terms for iron smith and forging supports the common belief that smiths create new objects from the iron of the Earth in the same way that ancestors create new children. The forge corresponds to the ancestral "village of forging" where deceased elders go to forge new children. Iron jewelry is often a metaphor for ideas of human fertility and birth, the circular shapes of bracelets representing protective encirclement and continuity. Thus, the most sacred object in men's initiation ceremonies is the bracelet of twisted strands of iron and copper, symbolizing the python and the chain of life, the same bracelet that children wear to commemorate an ancestral antelope sponsor (ibid.).

Antelopes run through the fabric of Tamberma life. Some are believed to own rights in fertility shrines, others to cure with "medicine pots." Still others take part in associations linked to death and war (ibid.). Game mounds adorn many houses, honoring the animals that bring game and other gifts to the family. They are arranged according to a precise order, reflecting the gender and status of the person who killed the animal: although women do not participate in the hunt, they do kill animals while farming and guarding the crops (Blier 1987:274–75n.35). Houses themselves are identified with antelopes in their generic sense through spatial orientation. They face the western sky and the village of the ancestors (the village of forging) where the spirits of animals killed in the hunt also live. During the final phases of a funeral for a dead elder, young people, together with the men carrying the bier, perform a dance imitating the graceful movements of the duiker (ibid.:274n.31).

Tamberma place antelope horns on the facades of their houses because animal horns are believed to be the repository of their spirit. In so doing, they not only honor the deities of creation and hunting but also allow the antelope to view the forest from its new home in the hope that if it is pleased, it will attract more game and more power to the hunter's house. Although both horns are identified with the game, it is the female horn, on the north side, that serves as the particular resting place of the house antelope. An explicit analogy is made with the new wife who comes as an outsider to her husband's house following her initiation. Her husband feigns killing her with a lance while she is still wearing the horned headdress of the initiation rite, and like an animal killed in the hunt she is brought to her new home. In an elaborately symbolic fugue on the themes of hunting and human fertility, the game mounds of wild animals are sometimes decorated with the waistbands associated with women, just as hunters wrap the red and white cords worn by young girls around their hunting bows to make them more effective, and men who excel in courting women are said to have a good marriage bow (ibid.:261n.25, 273n.30).

Are the Tamberma unique in the richness of their beliefs surrounding the antelope and its synedochic use to represent the repertoire of game animals? Probably not. One thinks immediately of the *tyi wara* headdresses of the Bamana (Mali) cultivators' society with their graceful representations of various kinds of antelopes, male and female, closely tied to the fertility of the fields. It was tyi wara who first taught people how to hoe, using his hooves to scratch the ground and his penis to penetrate it. Tyi wara links humans with the cosmic forces of earth and sky, plants and animals, through farming and tangentially through smithing, since the blacksmith makes the masks and the basic farming implement, the hoe. In fact, Zahan (1980:65–66) even proposes that the profile of the ancient Bamana hoe is incorporated into a primary type of male antelope headdress along with the head of the serpent. McNaughton (1988:39) tells the story of a Bamana woman who brought her elegantly shaped, beautifully patinated hoe to the forge to be sharpened. Its name, she said, was ci wara (tyi wara). As to the masks danced by the association, the male represents the sun, symbolized in the roan antelope, the female the earth in the form of the waterbuck. But both may incorporate motifs of snakes, pangolins, and other animals associated with the complex myths of tyi wara (Zahan 1980; Imperato 1970; Brain 1980:82–87). The antelope mask is also among the most important Dogon masks and is danced during the final phase of the funeral (Ezra 1988:73), linking death with rebirth as in the case of the Tamberma.[5] The Jukun attribute unusual power to the "soul-substance" of the roan antelope (Meek [1931]1950b:418–19). Finally, the bongo holds a unique position in Asante phenomenology and ontology, thanks to both its behavior and its physical characteristics: the bongo not only flaunts the color spectrum of red, white, and black but even appears to "bleed" when it rains. The animal "positively resonanted in crucial areas of Asante thinking and belief" (McCaskie 1992:233).

We have also noted the importance of the antelope in Kongo investiture rites. If hunters do not catch one of three species during the seclusion, the candidate is considered to have been rejected by the ancestors. At the death of a chief or femme-chef, bits of their hair, nails, and skin are guarded in an antelope horn wrapped in red cloth (Mertens 1942:22, 57–58). Mertens does not identify the type of antelope, but de Heusch (1975a:167) believes it is almost certainly the dwarf antelope to which the Kongo attribute extraordinary intelligence. It is, in fact, common to store medicines in animal horns (e.g., Willis 1974:48) as well as to use them as parts representing the whole. Feierman explains (1974:47) that the most powerful and therefore the most dangerous medicines come from the forest or bush, medicines that would be too strong to keep in the horns of domestic animals; they are stored in the horns of wild animals or kept in a patch of wild land preserved among tilled fields. Horns of the mangala antelope were a major emblem of Bolia kingship in the Lake Mai Ndombe region of Zaïre (Vansina 1990:120).

Let us return to the association of antelopes with metalworking. Since Kongo smiths are consecrated to remedy poor hunting, it is not surprising that during this ceremony the anvil rests on antelope skins and thereafter the smith must not eat certain antelopes (Mertens 1942:441–42). In Gbaya smelting, the skin covering of the bellows is seen as a female red antelope, the stick that operates it as a male who pursues her (Moñino 1983:304). Among the Chokwe, great hunters and great metallurgists, the term for the smelting furnace, *lu-*

---

5. Dieterlen notes that the Dogon associate the roan antelope with mythical aspects of the blacksmith, but she does not provide details (1973:47n.11).

tengo, is closely related to that for the large antelope, *ntengo*, which is the "dream of Chokwe hunters" (Mesquitela Lima 1977:349n.15).[6] Perhaps in keeping with this, Redinha's Chokwe smelter donned an antelope skin for the operation (1953:130). If Martins's information is correct, *lutengo* also means vulva (1966:40). Clearly, this is a fertile field for further investigation.

CONCLUSION

Hunting invokes an understanding of power set in a wider context of belief about space, agency, and transformation. As we have seen, hunting involves the same constellation of rituals as metalworking to tap into the power necessary for success and protection. The hunter is acting out a drama of fecundity in the bush or forest and must invoke the rituals particular to human fecundity to succeed: propitiation of ancestral and nature spirits through sacrifice, prayer, and observance of taboos. Like the smith he is a specialist in medicines found in the wild. Plants, animals, and even minerals are all endowed with quotients of nyama or its equivalent that can be activated to protect him against the forces that his activity releases. Like the metalworker, this ability makes him valued as a healer but feared as a sorcerer. The hunter often has his own songs. Mande hunters even have their own uncasted bards, and Yoruba hunters have their corpus of ijala chants, because music, as we have seen, is an integral part of rites of transformation.

But where the smith deals out death indirectly, through the weapons he produces, the hunter confronts the paradox of life through death directly: "Hunting is associated simultaneously with procreative male virility, fundamental to social life, and with violence" (Devisch 1984:35). A paradox indeed, and yet surely that is the meaning behind the ubiquitous traditions of hunters as founders of towns and states—the claim that social reproductivity through male agency ranks higher than the biological reproductivity of women.

Earlier we raised the question of why the hunter maintains his special status even in settled agricultural societies. An essay by Susan Kent (1989) proposes a provocative hypothesis. Kent surveys the literature on hunting in sedentary societies cross-culturally, although her data from Africa are limited to Basarwa (San) and Twa (Pygmies) and their Bantu patrons. She concurs that the contribution of hunters to the diet and to the economy of most sedentary societies is insufficient to account for their prestige. It is particularly hard to understand why their status is so much higher than those concerned with planting and gathering in view of the more significant contribution of these activities. Even the risk factor may be exaggerated: those who work in the fields, gather wood, fetch water, and fish are constantly exposed to danger, while for the hunter the danger is real but episodic. One cannot even make the case that hunting is by its nature more exciting than those other pursuits

---

6. Baumann gives the form *tengu* for roan antelope (1935:43).

since much of the time absolutely nothing is happening—the hunter treks on and on without finding any game. Kent therefore argues that

> *cross-culturally* hunting is differentiated from gathering-farming *not* because hunting is seen as fundamentally more dangerous, exciting, socially important, and so on; but because animals are intellectual beings grouped with humans. This is in contrast to nonintellectual plants that compose a separate and distinct category. . . . [T]hey are then perceived on the culture-specific level as more dangerous, exciting, economically, and/or socially important than plants. (Ibid.:16)

Domesticated animals, incidentally, are placed in a separate nonhuman category in her schema, and, in fact, it appears that purely pastoral peoples have a rather different attitude toward hunting and wild animals than do settled agriculturalists (e.g., Barley 1983:18).

This is obviously a hypothesis that needs more thorough testing by those familiar with African classificatory systems. Impressionistic evidence seems to bear it out in many cases: the associations of rulers with leopards, lions, or elephants, ordinary humans with animal totems and doubles, the mythic role of antelopes, pythons, jackals, lizards, chameleons, spiders, and the like—all of these may be more than simply metaphoric linkages. Speaking of Moundang clans that bear animal names, for example, Adler (1982:100–105) postulates not an identity between man and the animal whose name he bears but a transfer of qualities between human and animal species and a signifier of immortality in the passage of the "soul" of the dead to the world of ancestors. Humans may even learn basic skills from animals: the monkey clan introduced into human society the techniques of circumcision, childbirth, and childrearing they had acquired from their animal alter egos.

Such correspondences may be situational as well as generic. In Nyakyusa belief, because a pregnant woman is often angry, animals hunted by her husband will also be angry and try to kill him (Wilson 1957:140–41). Ideas of intercommunication between the two are, indeed, common. Accounts of the sexual taboos associated with hunting often assert that if a hunter's wife is unfaithful while he is away, the animals being hunted are clairvoyant and will tell him in time to protect him from its consequences, sometimes by mating themselves as a signal (e.g., Doke 1931:329–30). Cardinall's hunting tales from Togo, collected in the 1920s, are full of this same sort of sentient intelligence and clairvoyance attributed to animals: they warn the hunter of a wife's infidelity or attack him in a fury if they smell the blood of menstruation (1931:110 and passim). It was an elephant, too, who gave Sheuta the charm that enabled him to lengthen his penis at will and thereby bring a new patrilineal and patriarchal order to the Shambaa. Like Androcles and the lion, humans and animals often seem able, in these traditions, to interact on some level of reciprocity. Animals are not simply anthropomorphized; humans are zoomorphized. The Asante relationship with animals (and all nature), McCaskie (1992:235) points out, "was dialogical or conversational (in however fraught a manner)," and the same is probably true of many other societies. Thus, antelopes were supposed by the Tamberma to be vulnerable to the hunter only when they acquiesced in their own death.

But caution is in order since nonanimal substances balance the role of animals—in power if not in the quality of the relationship with humans. Plants are just as crucial in the makeup of medicines, for example, as are animal parts. In sacrifices, the main distinction seems to be a matter of where blood is appropriate and where it is not. It is difficult, then, to know how literally to read the connections between humans and animals—whether we are talking about classification systems or simply thinking in terms of homologies and correspondences.

Nevertheless, the equivalence of hunting and human fecundity becomes more understandable in the context of such beliefs. The Tamberma identification of the new wife with the game animal finds its echo in the hunting symbolism of *chisungu*, the girls' initiation rituals of the Bemba; here, the future bridegroom even pretends to bring down his wife with a bow and arrow (Richards [1956]1982:73–74, 106–7). Similarly, the carryover of the rituals of fertility in the one sphere to the other makes sense if the killing of animals corresponds to the procreativity of women, both ultimately under the control of ancestors but mediated by adult males with the requisite technical and ritual skills.

Still, it would be an oversimplification to leap to the conclusion that game animals and wives are simply trophies to be bagged by the male hunter. Semantically there is an association—indeed, a series of associations—where the wife comes from "outside" (Hultin 1991:155–56), but in both cases there is an interdependence and reciprocity. The power is not all on one side: both the animal and the wife have the power to elude and to harm, to give or to withhold. In the end the hunter is dependent on their fecundity. While he projects the image of lonely self-sufficiency in the bush, the activity itself betrays his dependency.

Hunter. Chief. Smith. Each seems to keep intruding into the domain of the other. Wandering hunters become founders of chiefdoms, chiefs are metallurgists, and antelopes teach humans to cultivate or to forge. When Sundjata goes hunting or to war, he dons his hunter's tunic; when he returns to his capital, he reassumes the robes of peace and statesmanship. (In modern versions of the epic, he puts on Muslim garb, symbolizing still another alternative source of ritual power.) Ogun, too, has "many faces"—hunter, warrior, healer, sponsor of agriculture. How do we put the personae together?

All three of these masculine activities oscillate between life and death, procreativity and killing: the use of iron in the arts of civilization and war; the power of the ruler to give and to take life and his "ownership" of the human, animal, and agricultural fertility of his realm; the fecundity of the hunter/ warrior manifested in killing animals and men. Whether power is conceptualized as *nyama*, its Yoruba counterpart *ase*, or the Rwandan variant of *imaana*, any person who makes exceptional claims on the earth or the forest must have great quantities of it to succeed and to survive: the smelter or smith who transforms ore into workable metal and metal into objects of use, the candidate who is transformed through initiation into a sacred ruler, the hunter or warrior who negotiates with the spirits of animals. In many societies one might add the bard/musician to this select group, for he, too, accomplishes transformation through the power of the word and of music. There is, as it were, a common repository of force, dynamic energy, power—any translations are certainly inadequate—but each group draws on it through its own body of arcane knowledge and ritual so that they are ultimately interdependent; no single group has a total monopoly of power sources, much as they may try, like Sumanguru, to corner the power market.

Further, these groups are almost exclusively male. A comparable female group who should exhibit the same relationship to ancestral and reproductive power by virtue of their technologies of transformation are the potters. Whether they do, in fact, rank with these culture heroes is the subject of the next chapter.

Fig. 28. The first king of Ndongo forging arms and implements. *Manuscritti Araldi* of Cavazzi, *Istorica Descrizione* (Bassani 1987, pl. 7). Courtesy of Associazione Poro.

Fig. 29. Wooden figure *(ndop)* commemorating the Kuba ruler Mbop Pelyeeng. British Museum 1909.5–13.1. H. 55 cm.

Fig. 30. Chokwe smelter wearing leopard skin (J. Maquet 1962:102).
Photo Thomas Jacob.

Fig. 31. Bushoong hat pin in the form of a miniature anvil.
L. 3.6 cm. Private coll. Photo Thomas Jacob.

Fig. 32. Royal bracelets of the king of Kongo (Dapper 1668:583).

Fig. 33. Royal messenger with hammer. Benin. Brass. The Metropolitan Museum of Art, Gift of Mr. and Mrs. Klaus Perls, 1991.

Fig. 34. Figure of an *oba*. Benin. Cast copper alloy. H. 41 cm. Gift of Joseph H. Hirshhorn to the Smithsonian Institution in 1966, NMAFA, 85-19-12. Photograph by Jeffrey Ploskonka. National Museum of African Art.

Fig. 35. Brass stool believed to have been commissioned
by Oba Eresonyen, mid-eighteenth century. Benin.
D. 39.5 cm. Museum für Völkerkunde, Berlin.

Fig. 36. Hunter's tunic, Maninka, Korhogo, Ivory
Coast. Coll. Charles and Joan Bird. Photo Thomas
Jacob.

Fig. 37. Huntsman carrying an antelope. "Lower Niger Bronze Industry."
H. 36.8 cm. British Museum.

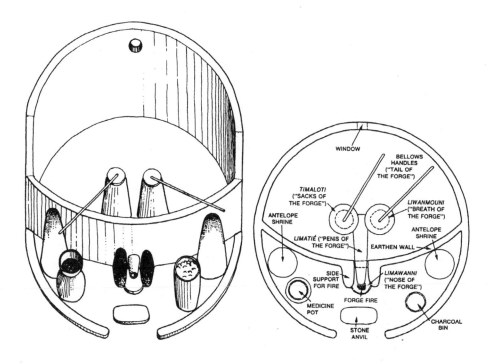

Fig. 38. Diagram of antelope forge (Blier 1984).

Fig. 39. Potter at work, northern Ivory Coast (Senufo). Photo Carol Spindel.

Fig. 40. Women carrying pots to be fired, northern Ivory Coast (Senufo).
Photo Carol Spindel.

Fig. 41. *Awo ota eyinle* by the Yoruba potter, Abátàn. Note iron
chain necklace (Thompson 1969, pl. 93). Photo Thomas Jacob.

Fig. 42. Ngum-Ngumi
pot. Ga'anda. Photo
Marla C. Berns.

Fig. 43. Ngum-Ngumi (close-up). Photo
Marla C. Berns.

Fig. 44. Yoruba *edan òsùgbó (edan ògbóni)*. Brass and iron. British Museum.

Fig. 45. Half of an *edan* pair, showing androgynous figures. Brass. The Metropolitan Museum of Art. Michael C. Rockefeller Collection, Purchase, Nelson A. Rockefeller Gift, 1962.

Figs. 46–47. Royal pair from Ita Yemoo. Brass. H. 28.57 cm. The face of the *oni* has subsequently been restored. Museum of Ife Antiquities, Nigeria. National Commission for Museums and Monuments (Willett 1967, fig. 10, pl. III). Photo Thomas Jacob.

EIGHT

Potters and Pots

We cannot cook. Who will teach us to make
pots?

Tetela myth (Zaïre)

The women of Kafongon, the potters. Like flowers, they came in clusters.

In the Shadow of the Sacred Grove

Carol Spindel

Both the blacksmith's ores and the potter's clays are products of the earth,
and both are transformed by fire into objects of the most basic use. It is not
a perfect fit, since metallurgy requires two interventions of the smith, smelting and forging, to produce finished artifacts while the potter accomplishes
this by modeling and firing. Most commonly, too, pots are fired in the open,
without using a kiln. Nevertheless, the close analogue in processes is reflected
in the fact that the potter in Africa is frequently the wife of the smith.

Both ceramics and metals have served as defining milestones in human
history, and prehistorians have hypothesized that experimentations in firing
pottery may have led to the discovery of true metallurgy. Skills acquired in
making pottery would also have been transferred to lost-wax casting of metals,
which employs a clay investment. Pottery in its own right and in its various
forms is at least as central to African ritual and religious observance as metalwork and the wood carving that is also often the province of the smith; it is
certainly as significant a medium of art as these and older than both.

If metalworking and pottery go hand in hand and are equally fundamental
to the evolution and replication of complex societies, one might reasonably
expect that ceramic industries would be the mirror image of metallurgical
ones, similarly conceptualized and similarly ritualized but with the dominant
roles played by women. As Stössel (1984:54) emphasizes, potting has its roots
"deep in the microcosm of society," deriving its social and ritual prescriptions
from the larger culture but also acting on it. The striking fact, however, is
that in spite of all the compelling reasons—practical and ideological—why the
potter should stand on a par with the smelter/smith as culture hero, peer of
kings, and master of the bush, she does not. In discussing his decision to

study the ancient metallurgist in order to understand how "primitive" societies understood the properties of matter, Mircea Eliade ([1956]1962:7) explained: "It would perhaps have been more worthwhile to study the demiurgic experiences of the primeval potter, since it was he [*sic*] who was the first to modify the state of matter; these experiences have, however, left little or no trace in the mythological record."

The same asymmetry has carried over into the ethnographic literature. Nigel Barley (1984:93) charges that "smiths constitute an ongoing obsession of social anthropology while potters appear only in footnotes." In this chapter we will summarize the history and organization of the industry and its integration into social and ritual life but leave speculation about its asymmetrical relationship to metallurgy, kingship, and hunting for the final chapter.

HISTORY AND TECHNIQUE

Saharan peoples may have begun making pots as early as 8000 B.C. (Berns 1989a:32). The technology presumably spread southward in the following millennia, although it may have had other sources as well. Pottery fragments are by far the most abundant manufactured remains uncovered by archaeologists in Africa as elsewhere, and consequently they serve to define prehistoric cultural traditions and their diffusion and interactions throughout broad areas more securely than any other form of material evidence.

Figurative terra-cottas from the Nok region of central Nigeria constitute the earliest known corpus of sub-Saharan African art if one accepts the dubious distinction between art and artifact.[1] Since a tin miner accidentally unearthed the first one in 1943, more than fifteen hundred terra-cottas have been found, all sufficiently homogeneous in style to be ascribed to the same tradition and all dating from the second half of the first millennium B.C. to the early centuries of the Christian era. It is intriguing that the earliest iron smelting site south of Sahara lies within the Nok culture area and is roughly contemporary with the oldest pottery there. In fact, iron objects have been found in association with terra-cottas (B. Fagg 1984).

The terra-cottas of Ife, the Inland Niger Delta, and Igbo Ukwu illustrate the development of regional styles elsewhere in West Africa and demonstrate brilliant mastery of the potter's art in these centers by 1000 A.D. and the centuries immediately thereafter. To indicate something of the scale of these early industries, twenty thousand pottery fragments were found in the three very small sites at Igbo Ukwu in southeastern Nigeria excavated by Thurstan Shaw and dated to about the ninth or tenth century A.D. (Shaw 1984). How many whole pots this translates into is impossible to say, but it is a lot. Referring to the hill country around the Asante gold-mining town of Obuasi in later times, Rattray wrote, " It is no exaggeration to state that there is hardly a

---

1. Somewhat arbitrarily, the term *terra-cotta* is generally used to refer to pottery sculpture as opposed to pottery pure and simple (vid. Fagg and Picton 1970:7).

square foot of ground on the tops of some of these hills which does not contain fragments of pottery" (1923:325). Traditions from other parts of tropical Africa are less well known but equally prolific and imaginative, as recent exhibitions in London, Munich, New York, and Washington attest (e.g., Fagg and Picton 1978; Stössel 1984; Schildkrout and Keim 1990; National Museum of African Art 1992). For all the evidence aboveground, there must be countless tons below (cf. Eggert 1980; Kanimba 1988; Berns 1989a:36).

As with all other African art forms, techniques vary. However, two generalizations hold: African potters use neither wheels nor enclosed kilns. The potter's wheel is of recent introduction, and most pottery is still shaped and turned by hand. Smaller jars are simply rotated on a base, but for larger ones, the potter herself becomes a wheel, walking around the stationary pot. This method is more difficult to learn than throwing on a wheel, but it produces just as fine a pot when done by a skilled artist; moreover, it is better suited to African clays and the purposes for which the ceramics are intended (Simmonds 1984; Stössel 1984:54ff.). Clay is mixed with appropriate materials such as sand and pulverized shards of old pottery, then pounded or kneaded to the requisite plasticity before being modeled. The base is often molded over an old pot and built up with sausagelike coils of additional clay, with constant scraping and smoothing both inside and out. Usually it will be dried in the sun at progressive stages until it is leather-hard. Once completed, it may be covered with a wash and other forms of decoration: relief, incisions, dimpling, rouletting, and so forth (fig. 39).

When a number of pots are ready, they are commonly piled up and fired in the open, using grasses, cornstalks, wood, or other combustible material, sometimes after a preliminary preheating. Carol Spindel has provided splendid descriptions of firing by Kpeenbele Senufo (Ivory Coast) potters who may amass as many as 350 pots at a time (fig. 40). The operation was overseen by older women who directed how pots should be placed with stones or shards to stabilize the larger ones and prevent them from rolling (1989a:70). They were covered with sticks, then bundles of thatch, so that the mound finally resembled a large haystack:

> Salimata chose a long bunch of thatch, held it to the coals, and fanned it until it burst into flames. Then she divided the flaming torch, giving half to Nafini. Standing side by side, they touched their torches to the giant haystack. It was a race between the two young women and the fire! Quickly, they ran around the mound, touching their torches as they ran, so that a chain of flames encircled the mound, for they wanted the haystack to catch evenly. When they reached their starting point, they ran away quickly because at that moment the mound of hay and pots broke into one glorious mountain of flames. We all stood, our arms folded, a short distance away, enjoying the excitement. All potters have a red-hot streak of pyromania in their blood (idem 1989b:206)

An hour later, the smaller pots were extracted one by one with long wooden poles that had iron hooks at the end and plunged into basins of water and pounded bark to color them, sending up clouds of steam. As Spindel comments, everything she had learned in four years of art school told her the pots should have exploded from thermal shock, but very few did, during either the firing or the basting (Spindel 1989b:206–7).

This type of firing obviously produces a lower temperature (usually about 600–800°C) than would be achieved in an enclosed kiln, but there is a trade-off: while pots so fired are more fragile than ones fired at a higher temperature, they have the advantage of being more porous so that water stored in them remains cooler (Priddy 1974:49; Gosselain 1992; Childs: pers. comm.). Furthermore, they are better able than less porous ceramics to contract and expand according to the uneven distribution of heat in open cooking fires. In some areas, pots are fired in trenches or in enclosures formed by low mud walls with holes to provide a natural draft. More rarely, as among the Yombe of Lower Zaïre, bellows may be used to attain higher temperatures. After firing, potters often add a final burnish or basting, as in the Senufo case, to enhance objects aesthetically or to make them watertight (Stössel 1984:55–65; Fagg and Picton 1978:13–16; Wahlman 1972:327; Lafranchi 1991).

WHO MAKES POTS?

The equation potters = women as smiths = men is virtually a given in Africa. Once upon a time, according to Bariba (Repub. Benin) traditions, men made pots, but they all died from massive swelling, attributed to the vengeance of the earth spirit. Women, however, were not affected (Lombard 1957:17).

In broad regions of the Sudanic belt and Cameroon Highlands where smiths belong to endogamous occupational groups, their wives also have a near monopoly on making pottery.[2] Even in areas where such "castes" do not exist, potters tend to be wives of smiths, or at least to be women, and to hand down the craft from mother to daughter. And yet in spite of this preponderance of women, there are more exceptions in the case of pottery than in metallurgy. Men make pots or share the work with women in parts of Niger and northern Nigeria, in the lower Congo, among the Chokwe of Angola, in Bunyoro and Buganda, among some Voltaic peoples such as the Mossi, and in parts of Ethiopia (Stössel 1984:66–67; Etienne-Nugue 1982:98; Roy 1989:253–54; cf. Haaland 1985:60). In Rwanda and Burundi, potters are primarily Twa (Pygmies), either male or female (d'Hertefelt 1962:32, 34, 127).

It is conceivable that Portuguese influence may have affected the division of labor in pottery in the Lower Congo. Portuguese contact in this area dates back to the late fifteenth century and was more intense and of longer duration than in most other parts of sub-Saharan Africa before the colonial period. Just as the Portuguese tried to "industrialize" metal production by bringing German miners and smelters into northern Angola in the sixteenth century (Her-

2. It is somewhat paradoxical therefore that among the Hausa Ader, only the wives of smiths are *excluded* from making pottery (Dupuis and Echard 1971:32).

bert 1984a:20), they also tried to introduce European-type kilns and potter's wheels to intensify ceramic production (anticipating Belgian efforts in the early twentieth century). It is impossible to say whether this went hand in hand with a shift to male potting, but there are conspicuous enclaves of male potters precisely in this area, and apparently they have been there since at least the very end of the seventeenth century (Stössel 1984:67), while among neighboring peoples potting is still women's work (cf. Volavka 1977:63; J. MacGaffey 1975; Lafranchi 1991).

The imposition of stricter forms of Islam in Hausaland following the establishment of the Sokoto Caliphate early in the nineteenth century may have had a comparable impact on the sexual division of labor, accounting for the prevalence of male potters in some parts of northern Nigeria and Niger (Fagg and Picton 1978:13; Stössel 1984:67). This would be especially likely where potters were itinerant (Simmonds 1984). Islam seems even to have affected male and female pottery production among the Dogon, where women potters still make vessels used in smithing rituals but men make other types (Stössel 1984:102).

Sometimes the designation of work roles depends on what is being made. We have already seen that men may make clay tuyeres for metalworking where under normal circumstances they are not potters. In societies where both men and women do make pots, they may not make the same objects and may not even use the same techniques (Fagg and Picton 1978:13; Baumann 1935:77; Priddy 1974:49; Kreamer 1989:3ff.). Among the 'Bena (Nigeria), for example, men make sacred vessels while women make domestic ones (Berns 1989b:54). The case of Mangbetu anthropomorphic pottery reflects a comparable split but raises additional questions about change and cultural borrowing. Mangbetu women make, and apparently have long made, utilitarian pots of very high quality. Anthropomorphic pots, on the other hand, were the work of men but probably date only from the early colonial period and the stimulus of giftgiving offered by the complex political and diplomatic relationships of the time since they were explicitly prestige items. One source explains that men made "artistic" pottery in contrast to women's pottery, a suspiciously Western-sounding formulation. To compound the problem, it is not clear whether the male potters were even Mangbetu rather than artists from surrounding peoples, patronized by Mangbetu rulers. Since Zande potters were evidently male, they may have been commissioned to make these pots, or Mangbetu smiths and carvers may have adopted the medium of clay and expanded their repertoire to meet new demands (Schildkrout et al. 1989).

Photographs from 1949 raise still another possibility. They show a Mangbetu woman building up an ordinary pot with coils of clay until she reaches the neck; a man then adds the sculpted head. By the late 1940s, however, the art was in decline, so it is not certain how general this particular arrangement may have been; in addition, there were always considerable differences from region to region (ibid.:45–46). In Benin, (male) metalworkers—specifically brass casters—may have extended their art to clay in order to make the terra-cotta heads for their personal shrines (Dark 1973:34, 63–64; cf. Fagg and Picton 1978:10–11).

The Asante, however, offer the best-known example of gender distinctions based on the type of object. Although women produce most types of pottery, they are forbidden to make pots or pipes in anthropomorphic or zoomorphic form (Rattray 1927:301). McLeod (1984) comments that most of these representational forms of pottery were pipe bowls: not only were the pipes likely to have been smoked by men but they were viewed as a form of carving, in contrast to ordinary pots that women "wove." It is intriguing that Doke (1931:117) found the same prohibition against women modeling pipe bowls among the Lamba of Zambia, and Meek discovered it among the Jukun (1950a:434). According to Rattray (1927:301), the reason given by the Asante was that these forms required greater skill than ordinary pots and that only males had these skills—not a very convincing explanation, considering the generations of experience women potters have to draw on—but his informants also cited a tradition linking the prohibition to a famous woman potter who became sterile after modeling pots with human figures on them.

These and other examples have led some scholars to propose a dichotomy: women produce utilitarian ceramics, men produce objects associated with art and ritual. Like most neat distinctions made about Africa, this amply describes some cases (e.g., Berns 1989b) but ultimately crumbles under the weight of contrary evidence. As Kreamer (1989:2) notes, there are case studies demonstrating the whole gamut of roles: women producing ritual as well as ordinary objects, men and women both making utilitarian pots, men as primary producers of all forms of pottery. McLeod (1984) goes even further, demolishing the misleading distinction between ritual and everyday or utilitarian pottery. Like many other things, a pot may move from one domain to the other as circumstances dictate. Thus, when an Asante woman's husband dies, she carries her small cooking pot to the edge of the village and smashes it, marking the end of her relationship with her deceased husband; the pot has thus been transformed from a cooking vessel into a "widow pot." Broken crockery is, in fact, a symbol of death in many African cultures (cf. Thompson 1981; Berns 1989b:n.11; F. T. Smith 1989:61); in areas of Tanzania it could even be a means of suicide (Moreau 1941). One could cite many other examples of ordinary vessels being used during rites of passage, in the preparation of medicines, or to hold offerings in a shrine. Often, as Spindel (1989a:66) observes, "a sacred pot taken out of belief-context looks exactly like any other." In fact, to divide experience into secular and sacred ignores the fact that the two are "inextricably interwoven in African life and thought."

The category of "woman" is equally problematic, as we have seen earlier, since postmenopausal women may be allowed to make objects forbidden to younger women such as the Asante anthropomorphic and zoomorphic pottery

(McLeod 1984).[3] The Senufo medicine pot, *tolorokodoli,* also can only be made by postmenopausal women (Spindel 1989a:72). In other regions of West Africa, potting is, in fact, the domain of older women (e.g., Nicholson 1931; Middleton 1973; Johnson 1984; Hardin 1988; Anquandah 1988), but the reasons may be practical as much as cosmological: younger women have less time and less experience and, conversely, it is something that older women can still do well (Rivallain 1985–86; Wahlman 1972:315; Thompson 1969). Still, younger women do make pottery—and must if they are to learn the craft well—and in many regions making pottery is a dry-season occupation when women have more time.

But what is the conceptual thinking underlying pottery that dictates what is produced, by whom, and under what conditions? Does potting in sub-Saharan Africa invoke the paradigm of human reproductivity as one might justifiably expect? McLeod (1984) insists that it does as far as the Asante are concerned. Their division of labor on the basis of representational/nonrepresentational has no apparent technological basis. Rather, it is justified in terms of the equation of such potting with childbearing. If women made anthropomorphic images while they were still able to bear children, it would be an offense to the ancestors, jeopardizing not only their fertility but also that of other women and even of the earth itself. Sometimes a younger woman making even nonrepresentational pottery will, like her ancestress, be afflicted with problems of infertility; in that case she will give up the craft (Anquandah: pers. comm.).

Asante belief is explicit. Elsewhere we must look to the rituals accompanying pottery and then to the forms and uses of the objects themselves for clues to the cosmological understanding of pots and potting.

POTTERY RITUALS

Like smelting iron, pottery involves the transformation of inchoate masses of earth into objects indispensable to civilization; like smelting, too, firing pots offers a serious risk of failure and even some danger to life and limb. One would therefore expect that the entire process would be intensely ritualized, at least at some key points, in order to mobilize protective and beneficent forces and thereby maximize success. This is certainly true in certain cases, but all in all the rituals of potting seem distinctly impoverished compared with those of iron smelting. Is this merely a reflection of less extensive and less thorough research, as Drost argues (1964:103), of the lower status ac-

---

3. This does not seem to be true for the Kwahu, a people closely related to the Asante. Here, according to Sieber (1972:179), both men and women may be commissioned to make funerary pottery. Among the Aowin, also an Akan group, some traditions refer to women making funerary pottery but do not specify whether they would have been postmenopausal. Some of these terracottas portray female chiefs (Coronel 1979). Preston (1990:71) asserts that with rare exceptions women were makers of all forms of pottery, including figurative terra-cottas, among the Akan because working with earth was a female prerogative.

corded to potting vis-à-vis metalworking, or of rapid change that has led to the disappearance of both the technology and its rituals? These are questions I will try to answer after looking first at the picture that does emerge from the documentation available.

The Shai potters of southeastern Ghana are the subject of one of the most meticulously researched studies of a major potting industry with deep historical roots. Quarcoo and Johnson (1968:48) estimate that annual production was still roughly a half-million pots in the 1960s, every one of which they were able to sell without difficulty—this in spite of forced relocation from the hills to the plain early in the colonial period and the competition of imported metal and enamelwares. Potting was exclusively a woman's art, one which girls learned during puberty rites that lasted two or three years. Potters made some thirty-five different kinds of pots, but each woman tended to specialize in a particular type. This meant that production was largely geared to the market, not to domestic consumption, and operated with a high level of efficiency— one might almost say cost-effectiveness. The most active Shai potters were thus able to earn a good income from their work, and even older women had an unusual access to the cash economy through continued production (ibid.).

Even in the 1960s, however, potters continued to observe a series of rituals and prescriptions that mirror some of those found in iron smelting but with specifically Akan elements. Each of the pits providing the clay was under the control of a priestess responsible for the "health" of the pit. She performed the rites to keep them free from danger and enforced the taboos of the pits. Disputes, quarrels, or any manifestations of ill will were absolutely forbidden because they were thought to cause the pots to crack and break in the presence of fire. No digging was allowed on Thursdays and Fridays, and on Sundays the soul of the pits had to be invoked and propitiated. There were other ritual cycles that had to be observed by priestess and potters. Special songs and dances were also part of the clay-pit rituals. This notion of propitious and tabooed days carried over to firing as well. The rounded, saucerlike disk on which all other pots were made was passed down from mother to daughter. It was treated almost as a deity in its own right and was never sold or given away. So powerful was it that if food was accidentally spilled on it, the disk would swell up and die, taking other family members with it unless the priestess performed special rites (ibid.:69–70).

Men were rigidly excluded from the pits and from pottery in general: it was believed that any man who tried would immediately lose his sexual potency.[4] In fact, no one was allowed near the pits except initiated women. When women changed from digging with older fire-hardened sticks or stone axes, they adopted iron hoes that are different from those used by men for farming. Menstruating

---

4. A male potter of a different ethnic group was working in the area at the time of Quarcoo and Johnson's study. He was English-trained and used a potter's wheel and kiln, making a limited number of forms adapted to the wheel. Apparently because he was an outsider in every sense, he was tolerated and did not fear for his sexual potency. It is not clear how he obtained his clay.

women were also forbidden to go to the pits because it would harm the clay and cause premature menopause. There were also taboos against selling or eating from the baked clay saucer on which a pot was built up. Finally, young potters were not allowed to decorate their pots with designs; only old and experienced potters could do this. Quarcoo and Johnson speculate that this may have been because the designs are largely proverbial and symbolic and young potters might get them wrong or because, since the designs have ritual associations, it was dangerous for the young to make them (ibid.:68–70). Probably both explanations are relevant.

Asante women are forbidden to dig clay or make pottery while menstruating. Such women are considered "hot" and dangerous and therefore must retire to huts on the edge of the village to avoid contact with the ancestors through contact with shrines or chiefly stools or with male creative forces through cooking or approaching male craftsmen. There are further taboos against counting unfinished or unfired pots, removing them from the village, or making pottery at all while the Asante armies are in the field. Furthermore, pottery cannot be made on Fridays, a "male" day (McLeod 1984).

Non-Akan cultures rarely have as ritualized a sense of time as the Akan and their neighbors, so propitious and unpropitious days play a less important role in pottery rituals, but phases of the moon do occasionally figure. Some Bantu peoples avoid firing—the most vulnerable operation—during the waning moon. This seems to be rarer in West Africa, although the Kurumba (Burkina Faso) potter specifically chooses dusk on the third day after the sighting of the new moon for firing (Sayce 1933:5; Stössel 1984:69).

In general, however, the Shai case is paradigmatic, judging by the available evidence. The exclusion of men from all or some of the operations seems especially widespread (cf. Drost 1964; Stössel 1984). Just as men blame unfaithful women for failures in smelting and hunting, Kikuyu women "always suspect that some ill-behaved man has crept to the spot [where women make pottery] during the night and has spoiled their work" when some of the pots break on the fire—as they usually do (Kenyatta 1938:84). If men were to be present when Manyika (Zimbabwe) women gather clay for pottery, women believe they would be unable to produce children (Jacobson-Widding and van Beek 1991:25).

Also, there are prohibitions against sexual activity for varying lengths of time. Thus, Mandja potters must abstain from sexual relations during the entire process or their pots will crack during firing (Vergiat 1937:107). One suspects that Shai potters do not observe sexual interdictions because of the regularity of their work—like smiths who work day in and day out.

Pregnant women may be taboo in some cultures: forbidden to visit clay pits, to make pots, or have contacts with other potters. Among the Nyoro (Uganda) a pregnant woman should not even look at an unfinished pot. In all these cases, violation of the taboo would result in pots breaking during firing (Roscoe 1923a:228; Drost 1964:105). According to Dieterlen (1951:126), pregnant Bamana (Mali) women cannot approach clay pits by the water's edge without simultaneously causing the death of her child and compromising the solidity of any pottery that would be made from the clay.

Bamana potters also have village altars, presided over by elders. Their principal function is to receive the spirit of dead members. Girls do not become full-fledged potters until after excision, when they go through a ceremony on the field where pots are cooked. The ceremony includes a check of their virginity. If they fail, they are not allowed to become potters. Like other forms of initiation, they learn the history, techniques, and proper behavior associated with the craft. Every year, they make an offering to Faro, the divinity of the water. In addition they make annual offerings to their altars on the same day as their smith husbands sacrifice to their forges. On this occasion they first crouch in front of the forge, then move on to their own altar where they take off their clothes and present their sexual parts, front and back, to mark their submission to the spirits of pottery, which are the same as those of the forge. They also cultivate a common field in which a girl twin sows white peas. The harvest is partly consumed communally, partly sacrificed to the potters' altar and tools (ibid.:125–27). Senufo apprenticeship also functions somewhat as an initiation society, firmly in control of older women, but much of the ritualization seems to have been discontinued with conversion to Islam (Spindel 1989a:73; idem 1989b:201–4).

In the far fewer cases where men are potters, the rituals seem simply to have been reversed, as one would expect, with women excluded. Exceptionally, women collect firewood or even clay, but mostly they are prohibited from any contact with the unfinished work (Drost 1964:105).

To sum up, exclusions of the opposite sex (sometimes of any stranger) appear to be relatively common, together with menstrual, sexual, and pregnancy taboos. As Hardin points out, the importance of older, postmenopausal women in the profession may well be a function of these prohibitions (1988; cf. Stössel 1984:106). An analogous situation occurs in indigo dyeing among the Bunu Yoruba, for example, where the indigo itself is closely identified with fertility. The dye pot can enhance or endanger human fertility and vice versa so that ideally the industry is in the hands of older women who also have the knowledge to control these forces (Renne 1990:174–79).

Sacrifices, offerings, and propitiation of spirits occur mostly in connection with digging clay, if they occur at all, but seem to involve very little explicit invocation of ancestors except in the Bamana case. Compared with metallurgy, the use of medicines is surprisingly minimal. The ritual apparatus is overwhelmingly directed toward controlling the firing process, where losses can be substantial (Stössel 1984). In accounts that make no mention of rituals of any sort, we are left to wonder whether they do not exist or whether they have disappeared in the face of revolutionary social change. Certainly the impact of Islam has been profound in much of the Sudan. Nevertheless, Wahlmann (1972:328) points to Yoruba women potters in a village near Ife who call themselves Muslim but still follow the taboos while making ritual pottery and decorate these pots according to the directions given by cult priests.

POTS AS PEOPLE

Speaking of pottery among a Bamana (Mali) subgroup, Viviana Pâques (1956:385) writes: "The fabrication of pottery . . . derives from technological rules as much as spiritual values which are indissolubly linked in the mind of the potters." Brief as is her description of the process, she makes clear that technique and ritual are inseparable from the conceptualization of pottery itself. The actions of the potter, like those of other technologists, are regulated by a belief system that leaves nothing to chance. In this schema, as in other realms of Bamana thought, gender and age are dominant categories and have spatial and numerical correspondences.

In forming the pots, the woman potter moves around them, always following the direction believed to be taken by the stars. She makes two types of pots: masculine, with neck, for cooking food, and feminine, without neck, for holding water. These are modeled differently, not only because of their different uses but because of their different "personalities." For the feminine pots, she presses a tightly woven net around the lower part to make a losange pattern in the still moist clay, while on the upper portion she makes a chevron design with a twisted cord. These are the symbols of earth and water, both feminine elements in Bamana thought. Then, to complete the identification, she adds a representation of breast and navel, surrounded with the same scarifications that potters incise on women. The scarifications vary according to the "age" of the pot, which will influence not only its eventual use but also the method of firing.

Firing takes place in a cleared field to the west of the village, and men are forbidden to come near. The pots are arranged according to their gender and age. Thus, two female pots are inverted on four stones (four is the female number), the "older" one to the north, the "younger" to the south; two male pots are inverted on three stones (the male number), placed west and east. Small pots surrounding them (children?) are inverted on two or four stones "according to their character." The embers to start the fire should be brought from the village by two twin girls who have not yet been excised (ibid.).

This attribution of personhood to pottery forms is not unique to the Bamana. It is part and parcel of Asante thought and has also been particularly well documented among peoples of northeastern Nigeria and the adjacent Mandara Mountains of Cameroon. Thus, for example, Yungur anthropomorphic vessels are not passive portraits of ancestral leaders but active agents continuing to maintain the world in which the Yungur live: "The reality of their ancestors is inseparable from the reality of the ceramic symbols in which they dwell and with which they become inextricably linked" (Berns 1990:50). Following the analogy of smelting furnaces, we can suggest that this personhood takes both explicit and implicit shape; that is, some pots are created with visibly anthropomorphic traits while others have humanity thrust upon them. Some become "vessels of the spirits" (cf. David 1990), the abode of

ancestral and other divinities. The personhood is idealized rather than indi-
vidualized in that it serves to communicate and reinforce socially desirable
norms of behavior. Further, it is probably safe to say that all pottery which
serves spiritual ends must be made sacred through ritual; as in the case of
smelting furnaces, form is not sufficient, just as anatomy alone does not create
the whole person.

Perhaps all peoples have used human terminology to refer to pots—mouths,
necks, shoulder, body, arms, feet—and pottery terms to refer to humans (crock,
potty, cracked, weaker vessel) (David et al. 1988). This seems the most natural thing in the world, but Westerners, while still using the terminology, have
lost the sense of literalness they probably once had. Further, African potters
are apt to go beyond pure anatomy to the adornments that are seen as intrinsic to full humanity: surface decoration, scarification, jewelry—even tooth
chipping and earpiercing (Berns 1990:54; cf. Barley 1983:23, 28). These may
be modeled directly onto the clay with or without overt anatomical allusions.
Luba potters, for example, see pots as human bodies and would not think of
leaving them unscarified any more than a human body would be' allowed to
remain blank (Nooter 1990:44). There is also no hesitation about mixing me-
dia: as with other forms of sculpture, potters may add on beads, feathers,
metals, and the like.

David, Sterner, and Gavua (1988:370) argue that "pots share with persons
the characteristic of owing their existence to having been irreversibly transformed, by fire and by enculturation, respectively, from a state of nature into
cultural entities." Among the Mafa and Bulahay of northern Cameroon, pots
and people often share a common vocabulary of adornment, and various pottery forms play a profound part in ritual life: funerals, ancestral veneration,
the worship of the creator god, Zhikile, iron smelting, and the birth of twins.
They are, in fact, the primary form of communication with the spirit world
because they are believed literally to contain the essence of these spirits (ibid.;
David 1990; Sterner 1989).

The gender of a pot may be conveyed by its type, that is, what it is used
for. Thus, the Bamana distinguish between male pots used for cooking and
female pots used for storing water. In northern Cameroon a beer jug may
even be carried on a woman's back like a baby; burnished black pots with legs
are male, used for meat, which only men can dispense (David 1990). Sexual
attributes may be more overt as well. Mafa and Bulahay ancestral pots may
have stylized penises on the male ones, breasts and vulva on the female (David, Sterner, and Gavua 1988).

In northern Cameroon, as in other parts of Africa, pots accompany people
from the cradle to the grave, from the pot in which the placenta is buried to
the vessel containing the spirit of the ancestral dead. Like people, pots identified with individuals change status over the life cycle. A pot used by Bulahay
children has no decoration at all because children are powerless, that is, not
fully human. Adults, however, have personal spirit pots with appropriate decoration. In the course of a Mafa funeral, the pot of the deceased man or

woman is reddened with an ochre wash and renamed to represent its owner in the period between burial and the manufacture of the new pot that will receive sacrifices from his or her children. The red color protects against the dangers in the passage to the spirit world, just as the living, especially women (who are seen as particularly vulnerable), ward off sorcery with red body paint; women and the newly dead need all the protection they can get (David, Sterner, and Gavua 1988:371–72). Among the neighboring Sirak Bulahay, the combination of eating bowl and flour storage pot is used to mark the tomb of a woman who has borne many living children. And just as domestic pots can become sacralized at death, "sacred" personal soul pots may become desacralized when the owner dies and be recycled for other uses, sacred or profane (Sterner 1989:458). All of this supports McLeod's (1984) contention that the boundary between ordinary and ritual pottery is a very fluid one.

Pottery may also be associated with especially powerful individuals, such as Yungur male ancestors. Spikes on Mafa pots symbolize the horns/penises that appear only in male contexts, especially wealthy and successful males. They are found on pots representing male ancestors and on pots for the god Zhikile, including those used by iron masters in smelting where they replicate the spikes on the roof of the furnace. In their own way, too, twins must be acknowledged as powerful and potentially dangerous, and therefore they have their own pottery. Among the Mafa, it is a pot with two bodies joined with a single mouth, since twins' souls are believed to be indissolubly linked; the Bulahay make two identical sets of bowls and small jars. During sacrifices to the twin spirits, both parents and pots wear necklaces of Bermuda grass and strips of Borassus palm leaves—plant metaphors for exponential growth. The idea is to co-opt their power as well as to protect the parents and community. The twin motifs are picked up in spirals and roulettes on bracelets as well as pottery that symbolize the force of nature's sometimes wild and elemental fecundity and offer protection against it (David, Sterner, and Gavua 1988; Sterner 1989).

Eyinle pottery from Nigeria offers a further example of how much can be encoded in a single vessel (Thompson 1969). These are relatively large pots made by older women for the worship of Eyinle, one of the major gods of the Oyo Yoruba (fig. 41). The lid of the rounded pot is modeled in the form of the half-figure of a woman (rarely, a male) with coiffure and ethnic scarification. Small bosses encircle the base, which is also decorated with ram's head and thunder god ax as well as more abstract designs. After firing, the pot is polished with indigo and decked out with gold earrings, iron or gold chain necklaces, and miniature head ties and wrappers of sumptuous cloth.

Eyinle is king under the water, but he is also closely related to Ogun, the god of iron, and to Oshoosi, like Ogun a patron deity of the hunt; with them he shares emblems of hunting and ironworking. Even closer, however, is the concordance with the cults of Oshun and Yemoja, identified with herbalism and watery coolness. All three of these *orisa*, one male and two female, use earthenware vessels filled with fluvial stones and water. Each initiate into the cult of Eyinle receives two stones that are believed to bear children, multiplying under water. The bosses on the bulge of the vessel refer to the stones of Eyinle within, with their reference to initiation and promise of increase. Although his informants did not mention this explicitly, Thompson (1969:142) sees the vessel as "a kind of womb, harboring the fertile stones." The sculptress Abatan, in fact, called the stones the children of Eyinle and declared that each had a name.[5] Further, the left hand on the swelling belly and the right hand on the breast are motifs of fertility and continuity. Thompson carries the exegesis still farther, but the point should be clear. The pottery encodes a complex message of the interaction of humans and spirits, reiterating primary social and spiritual values through its material substance, technology, form, and use but at the same time situating these in a culturally specific context.

One needs to invoke a concept such as transsubstantiation, however, to fully convey the role of pottery in rituals such as these. The pot is much more than a symbol, for the spirit, whether *orisa, vodun,* or ancestor, actually comes to reside in it permanently or at appropriate moments. Small wonder, therefore, that Abatan was a senior member of the cult of Osun and Eyinle or that priests would dictate the decoration of other Yoruba ritual vessels to the potters (Wahlmann 1972:330; cf. Ben-Amos 1980:47).

One could extend the examples and variations almost indefinitely. What we have already said should be sufficient to suggest that we need to refine the initial equation of pots with people. First of all, they are not generically human; like people they require a social identity with its multiple connotations of status, ascribed and achieved: gender, age, differing degrees of power and vulnerability. There are any number of ways that these facets of identity can be conveyed: through direct representation of anthropomorphic elements, through scarification and coiffure, through culturally recognizable attributes, even through color—one can find the whole gamut, from synedoche to metonymy to metaphor. In discussing Shona iron smelting furnaces, we noted that the waistband was just as important an indicator of female procreativity as the sculpted breasts; for pottery, too, socially and culturally constructed markers may be as important as anatomical ones. In other words, pottery does not have to be anthropomorphic in the literal sense to represent human beings. Second, the definition of "people" must expand to include ancestors, nature spirits, and other divinities, the whole *dramatis personae* with whom humans share their ceramic world.

If pots have the potential for becoming people, it seems natural that women should produce them. Pottery can be seen as a transformation analogous to that of gestation. De Heusch (1980), in fact, devotes a detailed analysis to Thonga rituals of birth, which see the child "as the product of successful firing," a utensil that has been fired and has not cracked. Premature babies are

---

5. Stones are associated with water, rainmaking, and fertility over surprisingly wide areas of Africa, but the reasons for this continue to baffle me.

the result of insufficient firing; twins, of excessive firing. Rituals in the days after birth carry through this metaphor by subjecting the child to medicinal smoke and using potsherds. He sets these rituals, in turn, in a more elaborate structural framework that invokes the entire "cosmogonic code." Others have called attention to the resemblance between pots with their rounded "bellies" and pregnant women or the metonymic association with women's nurturing roles generally: cooking, brewing beer, fetching water (e.g., McLeod 1984; Berns 1988:68; Spindel 1989a:73).

They also underscore the common association of the clay that is the raw material of the potter with the deified Earth and its life-giving qualities (F. T. Smith 1989). *Oriki* (praise poems) to Iya Napa, the divinity who is supposed to have introduced pottery to the Yoruba and still serves as patron saint of potters, refers to her as

> Mother of potters
> Mother of mothers
> Silent mother of the hushed earth (Stössel 1984:82)

Among the Kurumba and Lobi (Burkina Faso), women potters also make offerings to the Earth deity (ibid.:83). Writing of the Fali of northern Cameroon, noted for the elegance of their ceramics, Gauthier (1969:70) asserts that women have a monopoly on the craft because of its connection with the earth: "The earth is . . . not only the female element par excellence but also the mother of humanity. Pottery which is a 'womb' [*ventre*] is equally female." He notes that Fali women make pots at the beginning of the rainy season, and he likens them to "wombs which are ready to receive their content, as the earth is to receive seeds and rain" (ibid.:71).

In myths of origin among the Dogon, Jukun, and Mafa, for example, clay was the primordial material out of which the earth or the first humans were created. Meek (1950a:189–90) recorded a Jukun tradition that Ama, the second ranking god, created people and things "just as a wife sits making pots while her husband looks on seated in his chair." She builds up their bodies as a potter builds up a pot, coil on coil. But Ama is not unequivocally female. Meek speculates that s/he may be a fusion of two more gods since s/he is regarded sometimes as male, sometimes as female, sometimes as Creator, sometimes as Earth-goddess or World-Mother. This may well be the case, but Ama may also reflect the gender ambiguity one finds in other divinities in Africa (cf. Berns 1990:53).

In any case, s/he should make us cautious about accepting the "naturalness" of the association of women:female earth:potting unreservedly. For one thing, men do make pottery, and sometimes they make the most powerful pottery. Among the Ga'anda of northeastern Nigeria, for example, they make the spirit-pot named Ngum-Ngumi, which embodies their culture hero and the ultimate spiritual authority in Ga'anda life (figs. 42–43). In profile, it closely resembles the basic water pots made by women, but these do not have overtly anthro-

earth mother

pomorphic characteristics. Similarly, among neighboring 'Bena, men make the pots that contain the spirits of deceased male elders and priests. These are also domestic pottery translated into ritual form by the addition of anthropomorphic features and other decorative motifs (Berns 1989b but cf. Berns 1990:53). When we put these cases together with the somewhat ambiguous Asante material—where women were in some areas forbidden to make anthropomorphic terra-cottas—we find male potters in some instances claiming the prerogative of producing vessels that incarnate powerful beings who continue to influence human destiny.

This replication of procreativity is not, then, unique to women, even in the domain of ceramics, nor is the Earth universally female: it may be somewhat androgynous, as in the Jukun case, or male as with the Beng (Gottlieb 1982) and Wan (Ravenhill 1978), both of the Ivory Coast. Among the LoWiili (northern Ghana), iron smelting and smithing are just as closely tied as pottery to Earth shrines with their connotations of fertility of the soil. Furthermore, these shrines can be ascribed both male and female identities (Goody 1967:91, 96). At the same time, potting is not always compatible with female childbearing; it can, in fact, be viewed as inimical to women's fecundity. We have seen examples of this in proscriptions against fertile women making certain types of pottery or decoration and the prominence of older, postmenopausal women in some cultures. In Ede (Yoruba) it was explicitly only "bloodless" old women who could make ritual pottery because of the danger it would pose to younger, still menstruating women (Stössel 1984:114)—old women who are quasi males in status.

The location of potting within the nexus of sexual, menstrual, and pregnancy taboos emphasizes its analogy with human reproduction but at the same time invokes the danger of like to like: human reproductivity may imperil potting and vice versa. The relation between the two is therefore ambivalent, just as the relation between nubile women and the Earth may be ambivalent. While the evidence makes it clear that pottery is predominantly a female craft in sub-Saharan Africa, it is not so "natural" that the terms of participation do not have to be negotiated. In other words, the understanding of the relationship must be worked out in the context of belief systems particular to a given culture, particularly those regarding reproductivity and activities seen as analogous or identical to it.

CONCLUSION

Nigel Barley has argued that the " 'smithing obsession' has deformed the literature on the West African ritual implications of potting" (1984:99). The Dowayo (Cameroon) circumcision ritual, he maintains, corresponds more closely to a "potting model" than a "smithing model" of transformative change. While some of the prohibitions associate change in the boys' status with heat and dryness, parallel with smithing, other parts of the ritual mimic the piling up and firing of pots. Even the process used to make dry sesame adhere to the balls of millet that the newly circumcised boys eat corresponds to the process of making "potters' sesame," the grog of ground-up broken shards mixed with clay to form the potting mixture. In fact, "all processes that a human undergoes in the course of birth, sexual maturation and ultimate conversion into an ancestor are phrased in terms of two parallel processes—circumcision/threshing and drying/baking of pots" (ibid.:97).

Smiths and potters form an endogamous group among the Dowayo and are closely associated ritually as well as socially. With rainchiefs they are the most sensitive to pollution, and the two groups must never come together. While the smith makes the knife that is used in circumcision, there is nothing special about it otherwise, whereas pottery is ubiquitous in ritual activity, including rainmaking. More important, Barley notes, "All Dowayo ritual activities associate heads and bellies with pots, especially water pots, and use them in a generalised idiom of change" (ibid.:98).

Barley's intent was to be provocative, and he succeeded amply. But his own evidence from the Dowayo suggests some of the weaknesses of his argument. First of all, the "potting model" may provide a better way to think about transformative change in humans than the "smithing model" within many cultures, but it does not necessarily provide a better way than a "smelting model," which Barley does not even consider since the Dowayo do not smelt. Obviously, cultures are going to invoke the technologies they are familiar with. A more interesting question would therefore be, What happens in cultures that practice both potting and smelting? Are the two models elided, or is one subsumed within the other? After all, the smelting furnace is often seen as a type of pot:womb and makes use of pottery tuyeres.

Second, Barley himself acknowledges that although the potter makes objects that are indispensable to everyday life, including its religious dimensions, "she is excluded doubly by her caste and sex from most important rituals. Her real importance lies in her role as an instrument of social thought" (ibid.:97). Exactly. What she does and how she does it are vital. She provides the pots in which water is stored for drinking and for rainmaking, she transforms raw food into meals and raw clay into finished forms through the medium of heat, and in so doing she provides a way of thinking about the most central aspects of human life. But the actual woman potter has no public function and no acknowledged status. In fact, the parallel with childbearing is complete. Here, too, her indispensable role in the survival of the group is acknowledged but does not translate into any form of recognized authority. The paradox applies to both functions. Although women produce the pottery used in most rituals, they rarely officiate at them, just as they produce children but usually do not take charge of rituals associated with them until the women are postmenopausal. Much as they mediate transformative processes, they do not have ultimate control over them.

This, I think, is the crux of the matter. The problem is not with scholars, although we surely need much more research into potting. Since most investigators in the field have been men, they undoubtedly have concentrated on male activities—and would not have had access to women's activities, in any case—but this does not necessarily mean that they have created the asymmetry between pottery and metallurgy. Now that more women are researching these areas, they are filling out the picture, and both men and women are looking more closely at issues of gender and technology. But I see their findings as refining power relationships rather than undermining previous models. While it would be salutary to reverse things and refer to the smith as the potter's husband in order to jolt us into questioning conventional formulations,[6] it would probably not alter the fact that in most societies where they are paired, the smith has a far greater public role.

It seems to me, too, that the lesser ritualization of potting itself—as distinct from the ritual uses of pots—bears out this interpretation. The rituals that exist are similar to those in other transformative activities, but they are simply less common. Generally, the more ritualized an activity is, the more power is assumed to be involved in accomplishing it successfully. There may be both underreporting and an abandonment of rituals in some areas, but this seems unlikely to account for the fact that potting involves so much less ritual than smelting, even though the transformations accomplished and the importance of the end product are comparable. As we have seen, what rituals there are mostly concern digging clay, even though they may ultimately affect firing. It could be argued that metallurgical rituals are concentrated in the building and first use of a smelting furnace and the establishment of a forge and that potting involves no comparable structure or apparatus. Still, most potters use something to knead or pound clay in and to form pots in or over, as well as implements to scrape and decorate, which could be the object of ritual. The Shai *zene*, the "pottery disk" in which pots are modeled and which is passed down in the maternal line, is a rare example of a pottery tool that is sacralized (Quarcoo and Johnson 1968:70).

Speaking of the Abuluyia of Kenya, Wagner (1954:39) equates prestige and power with the possession of secret knowledge. In this society, rainmakers, diviners, and smiths all have prestige because of a long ancestry of secret knowledge. Basket makers, wood and leather workers, and potters do not because they are not "owned" by particular families or clans; they do not therefore possess magic and arcane knowledge. In fact, pottery is "owned" by the "casted" groups in much of the Sudan and Cameroon Highlands, and in some of these cases, at least, potters are considered to have special powers analogous to those of their smith husbands and fathers (Smith 1989:64–65; Spindel 1989a:68). But these seem to be exceptional cases; there is little evidence that this is a generalized belief. If potters were held to have secret

---

6. Spindel (1989a:71) comments that this now makes sense as far as the Kpeenbele Senufo potters are concerned: fewer and fewer of their brass caster husbands practice their trade, but potting continues to be important.

knowledge and the power that it implies, they would, like smiths and kings and successful hunters, be feared as well as respected, but we do not hear of potters being feared.

Wagner's observation also raises the wider issue of ancestral power. I have noted that ancestors figure very little in what rituals there are in pottery, although the craft is very much a mother-daughter affair and older women often dominate its organization. Perhaps the question is, which ancestors would the potters invoke? Are female ancestors powerful enough to be remembered and to intervene actively? Are male ancestors relevant? Does it make any difference whether descent is matrilineal or patrilineal? Udvardy (1991) addresses a related question in her study of pots that play a central role in ensuring the fertility of Giriama (Kenya) clans. Her concern is not with the inheritance of the craft but with the inheritance of custodianship over the pots, an important ritual role. This passes from mother to daughter or grandmother to granddaughter, that is, matrilineally. But since women move to their husbands' homesteads at marriage, the pots leave the patriclan whose health and fertility they are intended to safeguard. This dilemma was only occasionally resolved by introducing a male link into the succession. Unfortunately, there is very little information on these matters.

Pottery is occasionally associated with myths of creation or traditions of origin, as we have seen. The large ritual vessel of the thunder god, the *hampi*, is found in every Songhay village and symbolizes the mass of red earth from whence came the first humans. Its upper part represents the world, on its rim are the genies of earth, and within are the water and thunderstones of Dongo. According to myth, it originated with Faran Maka, ancestor of the Sorko fishermen (Rouch 1960:157–68). Similarly, the spirit-pot Ngum-Ngumi embodies the culture hero of the Ga'anda (figs. 42 and 43). Moving on its own, the pot led them from their earlier home in the Mandara Highlands of Cameroon to their present location in the Gongola Valley of northeastern Nigeria (Berns 1989b:51–52). But though Ngum-Ngumi was a pot, he was not a potter. Nor do we find traditions of *roi-potiers* or *reines-potières*.

We have to make careful distinctions, then, between pots, the potting process, and the potter. In spite of the undeniable social, economic, and religious importance of the pots themselves and the model that potting technology provides for conceptualizing human transformation, we must confront the fact that the potter simply does not rank with the smith or hunter. She does not participate in kingly investiture nor make the emblems of royal or chiefly authority. Powerful as a "female" pot may be, and Coquilhat (1888:292) describes an Ngala "pot femme," for example, that is very powerful indeed since she speaks and is indestructible, it does not appear that this power carries over to the potter or even to the technology she employs. It is hard to explain a negative—why something doesn't happen—but that is part of the agenda of the concluding chapter.

CONCLUSION

Anthropomorphism and the Genderization of Power

Le fils de l'homme d'où vient-il, d'où sort-il?

Moundang funeral chant

How many people are there in our village? Two, man and woman.

Bushoong initiation riddle

People still alive have no power; only the dead have real power.

Bassari informant

Man never dies in the woman's portal—like the iron, like the iron and the fire.

Fang circumcision invocation

Early in her fieldwork among the Senufo of the northern Ivory Coast, Anita Glaze was talking with the head of the principal blacksmiths' Poro society and hoping to obtain detailed information about divination sculpture or the standing male and female statues displayed in funeral rites for Poro elders. She asked him, "Why is it that figures are always carved as a pair, male and female?" He looked at this strange young woman with incredulous pity and responded gently, as if to a child, "Why, haven't you noticed? The cock and the hen, the dog and its mate, the billy goat and the she goat, people—everything was made to be 'two,' male and female—everything!" He was saying, in effect, that male-female complementarity is so fundamental that it hardly requires comment or explanation (Glaze 1986:31).

But Glaze's question was not really so foolish, for the meaning of gender is not as obvious as it might appear, above all not in African contexts. Like the hidden image in Poe's "Goldbug," we may need to put it over the fire (literally as well as figuratively) to make it materialize. As we have already seen, gender is a highly fluid concept. On the one hand, African societies go to great pains to establish separate gender identities and domains, while at the same time they accept more readily than Western cultures that gender can be situational, that one can change gender at different points in the life cycle, and even that one can be simultaneously male and female. Paternal aunts, for example, can have the status of males in some circumstances, as we have seen in the case of Gbaya hunting. Women of wealth in certain societies can function as "female husbands" by sponsoring marriages. The same ability to conciliate opposites exists on the life/death continuum. A phenomenon or activity can be simultaneously life-giving and death-dealing, and for all the energy expended to keep the two domains apart, there is a recognition that the boundaries are ineluctably—and necessarily—permeable. Ironworker, king, and hunter all cross the domains separating the genders in dealing with life and death.

Indeed, it is precisely in such "technologies" of transformation that these fundamental tenets of belief become clearest because they are structured along the twin axes of male/female and life/death. These axes intersect crucially with each other, and both represent not only primary explanatory paradigms but power fields through which certain humans claim control over the social and natural world. Three of the technologies we have looked at—metallurgy, the creation of chiefs and kings, and hunting—are preeminently male domains; only the fourth, pottery, is primarily a woman's task. All four invoke the explanatory model of human reproductivity not simply as a symbolic system but as an active force that is integrally related to success or failure of the operation. Human fecundity in its various phases interacts reciprocally with each of these activities and is intimately connected with ancestral intervention and regeneration. Within this quadrivirate, however, pottery is anomalous: it is not as intensively ritualized and neither the technology nor the product secures for the producer the same status as the other three.

Using metallurgy as a template for transformative processes, we have isolated three defining characteristics. Despite the tremendous variability in apparatus and in technical and ritual practices, these elements recur so frequently that they justifiably characterize the complex as a whole:

> designation of work roles by gender, age, and other social criteria, based on possession of both learned skills and esoteric knowledge, resulting in the exclusion of significant numbers of people
>
> anthropomorphism of paraphernalia, process, and product, including genderization
>
> ritual and prescriptive behavior by the participants
> sacrifices and medicines
> invocation of ancestors and other spirits
> songs/dances
> taboos: sexual
> > menstrual
> > other

This model is by no means unique to metallurgy. It is equally relevant to the areas we have looked at and, I would suggest, to still others that aim to control and transform the natural world but whose outcome is uncertain, for example, agriculture, initiation, divination, healing, and warfare (which is close to hunting). These processes demand unusual powers and often bring danger as well as failure; even success may be achieved at the cost of the envy of fellow humans, the suspicion of witchcraft, and the hostility of the spirit world.

Just as the same repertoire of decorative motifs tends to turn up across the range of arts within a culture, the same metaphorical complex dominates its rituals, serving as a code for a common set of beliefs. But I am also arguing that the transformative model has wider applicability; for all the stylistic variations, so to speak, there are certain constants in the cosmologies of sub-Saharan Africa: recurrent clusters of belief that suggest a more general, albeit tentative, hypothesis about technology and power, one that involves both the assertion and the blurring of distinctions of gender and of life and death.

The difficulty with any analytical framework is that it separates concepts that are, in fact, closely interrelated. This becomes readily apparent as we examine the schema proposed above, for work roles and rituals are predicated on anthropomorphized and interactive conceptions of the world.

A GENDERED UNIVERSE

Work roles are gender-specific across the whole gamut of activities; rarely are they interchangeable or left open. Even within an activity such as agriculture, tasks and individual crops are broken down by gender. The same is true with crafts. Some are solely the work of a single sex; others, such as the preparation of raphia cloth, involve both, but the constituent parts are gender-specific, as we have seen in the various activities of ironworking.

Nor is gender the only criterion. Other functions may be limited to free men or to members of certain lineages or hereditary occupation groups. In many cultures of the western Sudan, bards and leather workers are "casted," just as smiths are. More generally, only members of certain families are eligible for political office or priestly roles. In equatorial Africa, the different spheres of Bantu and Batwa (Pygmy) are analogous in many ways to those of free and nonfree in other areas. Age plays an equally important part in defining eligibility and exclusion: "La division du travail se fonde sur le sexe, et sa qualité sur l'âge" (Patokideou 1970:37). As we have seen, age criteria apply particularly to women who are viewed very differently according to whether they are potentially fertile or nonfertile, but they also define male roles in many societies.

This rigid categorization of work roles has a number of implications. Clearly, it tends to preserve power relationships based on access to goods, technologies, and ritual skills and on control of labor. But it could not survive without an ideological basis, and this basis is rooted in both cosmology and history.

Cosmology, or more precisely cosmogony, is invoked to explain the origins of things, including male and female, senior and junior, casted and noncasted, and the proper interactions of the various spheres. Remote history is often telescoped into cosmology as historical experience is absorbed into beliefs about the "natural" order of things: who were the first inhabitants, the eponymous heroes, and the later arrivals, and what their relationship is to the environment. With the passage of time the division of work roles takes on a timeless authority, valid because this is the way things have always been.

And yet, this realm is as subject to change as any other. Because it confers legitimacy and power, history itself—"tradition"—may be contested by competing social groups or by men and women, as Renne (1990) has shown so skillfully in her study of the *gbe obitan* ritual among the Bunu Yoruba and its relation to the weaving of certain types of cloth by women and men. Even work roles may change. Thus, the women weavers of Akwete village in southeastern Nigeria have built up a profitable monopoly of their craft only over the past century, effectively excluding men and non-Akwete artisans (Aronson 1989:47). As New World crops such as manioc, particular types of yams, maize, and peanuts spread to all parts of the continent, the sexual division of labor had to adapt, as it did to the later imposition of cash cropping under colonialism. Unless or until it became impossible, however, change was accommodated to preexisting belief rather than undermining it. In a classic example, Etienne (1980) has documented how the evolution of textile production among the Baule during the colonial period was shaped by preexisting ideas about work roles and gender relations.

The coherence of the system and the series of correspondences in which concepts of male and female are embedded come out beautifully in Guyer's description of gender roles among the Beti (Cameroon):

> Male activities were thought of in terms of warfare, hunting and tree-felling, however much or little time was spent in each. The male tools were iron and wood: the spear . . . , the hatchet . . . and the long planter. . . . The male activities carried explicit military and phallic symbolism, involving cutting down and building up, as with yam stakes and house poles. Men worked upright, climbed palm trees to tap the wine or cut the fruit, prepared the tree-trunk barriers around the newly cut fields . . . , and the picket storehouses for yams. . . . The male milieu was the forest . . . , the source of the wood for tools and the most prestigious meat for the diet, the site of the hunt, the terrain to be conquered to open up a new field or prepare a new village site. The crops associated with male labor and male ownership were tree crops, crops of the forest fields, and crops which could be grown with the *nton*, the long-handled digging stick.
>
> Women's milieu was, by contrast, the earth itself, the open clearings or the savanna. . . . A woman worked the fields, bending over the earth with her short-handled hoe. . . . She cooked in earthenware pots, bending over the fire, fished by building earth dams across streams, bending into the water to trap the fish, and she 'cooked' babies in her womb. Bending over the earth to tend to it,

shape it, and coax it to produce was woman's attitude. Her crops were the savanna crops, planted with the woman's tool, the hoe. (1984:18–19)[1]

This series of oppositions united the social and spatial realms: "The oppositions of forest and savanna, digging stick and hoe, wood and earth, upright and bending, dominant stance and submissive shaping, gave the opposition of male and female both enormous power and concrete content. The sexuality and fertility of marriage brought the sets of oppositions together, conceptually but also organizationally" (ibid.).

As the quotation from Guyer suggests, it is not just a question of what people do but how, when, and where they do it. Thus gender is commonly extended by a whole series of equivalences—right/left, up/down, forest/village or savanna, sunrise/sunset, hot/cold, earth/sky, light/dark, and so forth—all of which may come into play in confirming male and female roles. The designation of objects as belonging to male or female domains theoretically follows from these defining characteristics. For example, men and women may use different hoes and axes, baskets, pots, clothing materials, and the like. Among the Guidar of northern Cameroon women cultivate with a curved hoe, men with a straight one (Schaller 1973:139). In Ufipa (Tanzania), the distinction is a matter of size, with men using larger hoes to heap up the compost mounds (Willis 1981:147).

Gender opposition runs through the whole repertoire of Bambala material culture, but Kazadi points out the contradictions between theory and practice. The hoe, for example, is an object firmly in the female domain, the axe and the machete in the male, but in reality, both sexes often use both objects without altering the conceptual scheme of gender oppositions. Ironically, Bambala women make certain pots which they are then forbidden to use or even touch—especially pots associated with elders and political leadership (1988:7).

On a more abstract level, gender categories may be extended to materials, such as the female medicines used by the Thonga to protect male objects such as weapons, the male medicines used to treat illness (Junod 1936:2, 408), or to male and female *maléfices* against which the Mafa make pottery charms (Podlewski 1965:27n.1) and the male and female fortune that attends the Badjoué (Cameroon) hunter (Koch 1968:15). The Dowayo alternate male and female years (Barley 1983:80), while the Shambaa even distinguish between male and female farming seasons, not according to what is planted but according to whether it is successful or not (Feierman 1990:7, 82).

Space, architecture, music—all are subject to similar structuring. The Fang are not alone in extending "the body microcosm . . . to organize macrocosmic space" (Fernandez 1982:105). The "primary experience of body and

---

1. Or, as Elenore Smith Bowen (Laura Bohannan) summed up the Tiv division of labor in *Return to Laughter:* "Like everything else that can be done while attending court sessions and other important meetings, knitting is man's work. Woman's proper occupation is weeding and cooking" (1964:17).

body image" that determines Fang spatial architectonics is equally common elsewhere. Space mirrors male and female, senior and junior at the same time that it makes correspondences with right/left, east/west, front/back, and so forth (e.g., Huffman 1981; Dupire 1960; H. Moore 1986; Griaule 1966). Houses, like furnaces, may become "people" with a life cycle and gendered parts (e.g., Blier 1987; F. T. Smith 1986).

As for music, drums alone could serve as the quintessential exemplar of the anthropomorphized and gendered universe. The sacred drum of Rwandan royalty is a personification of the king himself with its entourage of lesser drums (d'Hertefelt 1962:70). Its counterpart is the female drum manufactured for the ritual of investiture (d'Hertefelt and Coupez 1964:482). Talking drums are commonly male and female (e.g., Perrot 1982:11). Yoruba musicians still play hourglass-shaped *bata* drums in groups of three, with the rhythm given by the largest, the "mother," and defined in cross-rhythms by the two smaller drums: "When the mother speaks, the children listen" (Pareles 1987). The drum that announces the death of a king of Nkansi (Ufipa, Tanzania) is also known as "mother" (Willis 1981:32), as are the principal drums of Akan ensembles with their prominent breasts (Nketia 1990:26). And yet, like ironworking, there are only a very few exceptions to the rule that drums are played by men alone. ———————————— —organising strategy

This propensity to genderize the world—as part and parcel of an even more fundamental and pervasive anthropomorphism—serves a number of ends. It provides a coded statement of what men and women do, an ideal representation of the interlocking but separate worlds of men's and women's work. It also alludes to when in the course of the life cycle they do it. As Henrietta Moore (1986:106) points out, the model always refers to the moment of full adulthood of the household. As an organizing principle, it makes visible fundamental beliefs about male and female, elder and junior, living and dead. Further, the model is not normatively male; that is, females are not seen as incomplete or defective males, in contrast to the models that have dominated Western thinking. With the emphasis on dualism, they may lack qualities attributed to males, but males lack female qualities as well; the fusion of both is seen as indispensable to the proper functioning of the world—as with the Mande model of *fadenya* and *badenya*. The dualistic model derives its authority from myths of origin, the stories of how things came to be. But in ostensibly giving historical form to these distinctions, myth also demonstrates their flexibility. In Fipa myths of origin, for example, the wild, wandering, and powerful stranger women reverse roles (and character) when they encounter the wild Nyika hunters and sire the founders of the ruling Twa dynasty (Willis 1981).

There is a paradox, however, in the use of male and female as basic categories of classification in that it seems to partake of both essentialism—the recognition of essential, biological differences between male and female—and of the view that gender is socially constructed and relational. Most African societies offer a detailed description of female and male character traits that are intimately related to parts of the body and presumed therefore to be both universal and inborn. The strict segregation of roles and activities then follows "naturally" from these distinctions (vid., e.g., Jackson 1977:87ff., 220; Douglas 1954:2; Devisch 1984: ch. 2). And yet most societies also devote a great deal of attention to transforming the amorphous, asexual, and uncivilized child into the fully human adult, assuming that it doesn't just happen. As Claude Meillassoux (1980:354) has observed, the categories female and male are by no means as all-embracing as they appear since in practice they asymmetrically oppose adult men to women during menarche *("femmes pubères")*; even the category of adult male as idealized type may be further limited to senior men, that is, men of senior lineages as well as older men. Women during their reproductive years are identified totally with their sexuality and reproductivity, while older women fall into a Janus-faced niche in which one visage is benevolent mother and the other is witch.

Since these cosmologies of gender are articulated almost exclusively by male informants, they would seem to offer a male's eye view of the world—often, in fact, a senior male view. Women's experience is unquestionably validated but largely in men's translation. Whether African women genderize their world differently is thus far impossible to say, just as it is impossible to determine how the male view should have come to dominate. While women are no longer in quite the same position as the "Nuer's cows, who were observed but . . . did not speak" (Ardener 1977:4), there are few studies that elicit women's constructs of the world. And yet Edwin Ardener's provocative "Belief and the Problem of Women" forced researchers to recognize that women may genderize the "wild" and the "settled" quite differently from men of the same culture. Renne has found the same differences between male and female perspectives on gender in her study of the Bunu Yoruba *gbe obitan*, a ritual associated with marriage and procreativity. When Renne asked a Bunu woman whether it was true, as some insisted, that only women were witches, she responded provocatively, "If men are talking, they will say it is women. But you have to decide for yourself" (1990:319). Further, Renne has demonstrated that female belief and practice have adapted to accommodate religious and legal change in Nigeria.

If there were, in fact, more information on how women genderize the world, it would be interesting to see if it reflects the same ambivalence as men's beliefs. Would women's constructions reveal, for example, anything corresponding to the dichotomization of femininity—the devouring witch versus the nurturing mother, sexuality versus maternity, wife versus sister—the one a source of fear, the other a refuge and a comfort, that seems to underlie so many cosmologies? Is there any ambivalence at all in the way women perceive men and maleness? Is the ambivalence at all affected by matrilineality, exogamy, or residential patterns after marriage? The ambivalent attitudes engendered by power itself, whether it be the power of the smith/smelter, of the king, or of the hunter, may in fact partake of the ambivalence toward the feminine.

Ritual practice follows largely from the ideology of anthropomorphism. Anthropomorphizing the world is part of the attempt to bring it under control by naming its parts and equating them with the human, that is, by making it rationally comprehensible in the light of human experience, above all the experience of male/female opposition and complementarity as they play themselves out in sexuality and procreativity. A corollary of this process is that there is constant transfer between realms; fertility is a "closed circuit" within the natural world (Bourgeois 1956:149). Procreative power and its antithesis, sterility, are especially transferable from one order to another within the order of animate objects: human, animal, and vegetable (Dupire 1960:53). Hence the reiteration of this theme in the use of medicines—the multiple reinforcements offered by magical substances that analogically promote fertility and protect against infertility, as well as the behavioral codes that have the same effect.

Menstrual taboos are among the most common of all. They apply not only to cooking for and sexual relations with male humans but to the whole gamut of activities that are perceived to be in some sense equivalent such as ironworking, hunting, cattle tending, farming, warfare, even forms of "magical" practice. Among the Asante, menstrual taboos extend to anything concerned with the gods, ancestors, and senior chiefs and even to some fetishes and medicines. If a menstruating woman entered a stool room, her state would drive away the spirit of the ancestors. But she is also forbidden to "touch or handle any tools used to make things or to change one sort of thing into another" (McLeod 1981:35), a clear statement of the incompatibility of menstruation as failed conception with activities that are construed as transformative, that is to say, "procreative." Rattray (1927:75) explains: "Contact with her, directly or indirectly, is held to negative [sic] and render useless all supernatural or magico-protective powers possessed by either persons or spirits or objects (i.e., *suman* [charms, "fetishes"])"—testimony, indeed, to the power of menstrual blood. Small wonder that the Asante locate their menstrual huts on the margin between village and bush, along with the middens and the burial place of babies and prepubescent children, witches, criminals, and victims of inauspicious deaths, all of them "damaged or incomplete beings" (McLeod 1981:36–37). The fiber used by a menstruating woman is also used to make the greatest suman of all in the form of a broom that sweeps away "every kind of filth" (Rattray 1927:13). In Rwanda, menstrual blood is used in the composition of the most harmful charms (d'Hertefelt and Coupez 1964:VIII:61).

Indeed, menstruation becomes a metaphor for the ambivalent qualities of women since it is also thoroughly recognized by all cultures I am familiar with that menstruation is indispensable for conception, that it simultaneously represents sterility and the potential for fertility, and that it purifies as well as "pollutes" (cf. Kuper [1947] 1961:107). In this it shares the dual character of blood itself; as with the blood of sacrifice, for example, death bestows life. It is the aim of much ritual activity, therefore, to keep the various kinds of blood in their proper domains, not to mix them up where they do not belong.

At the same time, women's periodicity is often equated with the periodicity of the moon with its double valence of waxing and waning, growth and death, order and disorder (cf. Tessmann 1913,2:16). In Lozi (Zambia) belief, the High God communicated with man through the cycles of nature, including those of the sun, the moon and the menstrual cycles. Menstrual taboos therefore served to dramatize "the dangers inherent in the procreative power of Nature, while attention to the phases of the moon in particular could release their potentialities." Female procreativity was thus analogized with natural procreativity, both of them tenuous and uncertain (Prins 1980:146). It may be no accident that an Asante girl is supposed to have her first period at night and will pretend that she did even if she didn't (McLeod 1981:36).

Sexual taboos are also quasi universal in Africa. The interdictions against sexual relations, marital or otherwise, so characteristic of iron smelting apply before and during almost all major undertakings that involve danger or uncertain outcome. Nowadays that can even mean football players will abstain from sex the night before a game (just as Christian women will often not go to church during their periods). But such taboos do not reflect a revulsion against the body or sexuality such as one finds in other traditions—celibacy as an ideal is incomprehensible in societies where people are the source of prestige and tangible power, where "production and reproduction of human beings takes precedence over that of material goods" (Meillassoux 1980:357). To die without living progeny is the greatest misfortune imaginable, and most strategies in the past have been focused on preventing this. One does not want to be cast on the middens or left in the bush at death, with no hope of continued existence as an ancestor or reincarnation in a descendant. Ancestors, in fact, have just as much stake in human procreativity as the living because they die definitively only when a lineage comes to an end.

Why, then, interdict sexual activity at all? Because sexuality is too powerful a force, socially and cosmologically, to leave unregulated. On the sociopolitical level, it is hemmed in with restrictions to benefit not reproductive strategies in the abstract but specifically those of senior males, chiefs, and kings. On the level of cosmology, however, sexuality epitomizes the fusion of the most powerful oppositions to create new life and must be equally directed in ways agreeable to ancestral and other supernatural forces in order to succeed. This means that while all sexual relations are forbidden before certain activities, they will be obligatory between man and wife at other times, as in the Fipa examples drawn from both smelting and agriculture. In both smelting and agriculture, Fipa insist on strict prohibitions against adulterers entering the smelting site or the fields (Robert 1949:214).

It is often hard, in fact, for an outsider to understand the logic of tabooed versus obligatory sex. Douglas (1954:6–7) notes that for the Lele most activities which custom allocates entirely to one sex or the other are protected by sexual, and usually menstrual, taboos and that this is particularly true of male activities—in fact, disproportionately true of male activities in most societies. In general sexual relations are suspended at times of danger and the exercise of power. They resume with the return to normalcy and order, as at the conclusion of mourning, smelting, hunting, and so forth, and, in fact, are thought necessary to make things normal.

The larger issue seems to be the assumption that both likes and opposites have a mutual influence on each other, whether dangerous or beneficent, and that appropriate behavior depends on the entire web of beliefs, since no single aspect of ritual behavior can be understood separate from the whole (cf. Wilson 1957:4ff.). But I would argue that transformative processes in which men mobilize female as well as male power are the most vulnerable of all and hence subject to the strictest regulation, for it is precisely when domains must be fused or crossed that danger as well as potential are the greatest.

POWER, GENDER, AND AGE

The iron smelter constructing his furnace and summoning all the forces at his command to make it bear iron demonstrates his control of both sides of the procreative equation, male and female, father and mother. When Yves Moñino's Gbaya companions congratulated him after the successful smelt with the words "Tu as accouché du fer" (Moñino 1983:301), they were recognizing this male usurpation of a quintessential female act. But an understanding of the power field is, in fact, much more complex. In Gbaya thinking, while the smelters may "assume the procreative role of women," the true fathers are ancestral, the dead smelters of the past (ibid.:307). However, their role is mediated—and presumably can only be mediated—by male smelters.

This conceptualization brings together precisely the interplay of genders and of ancestors and living that are at the heart, I believe, of African notions of power generally. Female power is not denied; it is appropriated or assimilated because male power alone would be inadequate to the idiom of reproductive and regenerative power encapsulated in ironworking. The same notions inhere in the exercise of political power where the chief or king is held to be responsible for the fertility of his people in the widest sense. "Le roi est femme," say the Moundang of Léré, but he is simultaneously father (Adler 1982). He may combine masculinity and femininity within himself; he may depend on his "marriage" to a female emblem, like the Sar king of Bédaya (Fortier 1982); or he may require female agency like the Yoruba king, crowned by the queen mother (Pemberton 1989). Nooter argues that Luba kingship was perceived as feminine since kings "believed that the source of their authority resided in the deepest recesses of a woman's body" (1991:276). Like smiths, kings and hunters must be able to move back and forth between the domains of gender and age that hem in ordinary people; it is necessary to the exercise of their power and at the same time evidence of that power.

One could cite other male activities that follow the same model. In the initiation of boys, for example, the community of older men orchestrate the entire process of ritual death and rebirth, often enacted quite graphically (e.g., De Boeck 1991b). At the height of the Masai ceremony that transforms circumcised men into warriors, the candidates enter the warrior house naked. The officiant performs the act of ritual coitus whereby the junior warriors are symbolically conceived as senior warriors, to be reborn into their new state through its single opening, replicating precisely the birth of children in the women's houses (Arhem 1991:71).

Similarly, with rare exceptions, men manufacture and dance both male and female figures in masquerades that are intimately associated with human and natural fertility. There is no better instance of this than the Dogon *sigi*, the cycle of dance rituals held every sixty years. The cycle follows a prescribed temporal and geographical sequence. In essence it is a reenactment of the drama of birth, gestation, death, and ancestorhood, with men playing all the parts (Dieterlen 1973; Stoller 1992: ch. 11). The red fiber costumes associated with Dogon masks, on the other hand, represent the murderous power of female menstruation, which men have appropriated to themselves (Michel-Jones 1978:125–26).

But what happens when women exercise power? Does this also require gender crossover and the combining of masculine and feminine elements? Fragmentary as the evidence is, I suspect it does. Unfortunately, the abundant oral traditions about past women who ruled in their own right tell us little about the ideology of power except to verify that, in theory at least, it could be held by women (Lebeuf 1960). But there is modest documentation on this subject from more recent times. Women who are chiefs in their own right or women who hold ritual power within the context of marriage to a chief or king are often expected to act in ways that run counter to normal behavior. Princesses who are appointed subchiefs in certain districts of Mashonaland (Zimbabwe), for example, are not allowed to marry but are expected to have sexual relations with as many men as possible to enhance the fertility of the land; in this as in many other ways, they are both sexes in one (Jacobson-Widding 1991:55–56). A recent reexamination of the apparently monstrous actions of Nzinga, the seventeenth-century queen of Angola, suggests that they were also part of this need to demonstrate both male and female power. On the one hand, she was intimately associated with the *kimpassi* cult, which promoted fertility; on the other, she killed her rival and slaughtered a host of children (Skidmore 1992). The "Rain Queen" of the Lovedu (Transvaal) is structurally male, married to numerous "wives" and yet allowed to take lovers as well (Krige and Krige 1956).

Certain wives of chiefs or kings may also be singled out for particular ritual roles that involve a denial of female sexuality. Among the Moundang (Chad), the wife in charge of the royal regalia is the only legitimate wife of the king since he pays no bridewealth for any of the others and yet, paradoxically, she must remain sterile. While there may be political considerations involved, it is also as if her fertility would be incompatible with the sacred power of which she is the custodian and priestess (Adler 1982:317ff.; cf. Roscoe 1923a; Nooter 1991:271–72). The entourage of the Nyanga (Zaïre) chief is replete with gender crossover. During the investiture ceremony, the candidate must have a public and a private sexual union. In the first case, which is considered incestuous, the woman (who should not be a virgin at the time) acquires the status of a man: she constructs her own village with dignitaries and clients, marries female serfs, has a wife to prepare food, and no longer has sexual relations with her husband, the chief. When he dies, she even inherits some of his wives. But the wife with whom he has sex in the secret part of the ritual actually plays the more important role as the counterpart of the chief. Further, two men function as *femmes mâles* of the chief (Biebuyck 1956).

Rattray may have exaggerated when he referred to the Asante queen mother as "perhaps the most powerful person in the kingdom" (1927:108), but clearly queen mothers represent another group of women who exercise considerable power. Among the Luba, not only the queen mother but a host of other royal women play major roles (Nooter 1991:264 ff.). Often, indeed, they are part of a political structure paralleling and complementing or reinforcing that of the king. One of Nooter's Luba informants asserted that "Men are chiefs in the daytime, but women become chiefs at night," perhaps alluding to women as the ultimate source of secrets (ibid.:236). In less centralized societies, women play prominent roles in women's secret societies and in religious cults, but these are usually segregated and do not exercise authority over the whole society. Among the Fang, women have their own hierarchies and even their own chiefs. Nevertheless they "do not participate truly in the life of the *cité*, or, more precisely, they form among themselves a *cité* distinct from that of men" (Alexandre and Binet 1958:81). In such cases, then, we would not expect the same sort of concentration of both male and female powers, but these institutions have been so little studied that we cannot be sure.

We have noted that men dance both male and female masks in almost all African cultures. There are, however, a few occasions when women adopt not male masks but male clothing to perform rituals. One of the most interesting is the *imitation des maris*, danced by Moundang (Chad) women at the funeral of an old woman who has left behind a numerous progeny. On this occasion women not only don men's attire, they also mimic male gestures and behavior. Even old women will imitate a mason at work or a schoolmaster beating his students or a Muslim trader armed with his tattered plastic document case. The representation may be both hilarious and pitiless. According to one tradition, the dance goes back to an old woman who always instructed her daughters that God had created men and women to be different and that women must respect their husbands as the equals of the gods. When she died, the daughters decided to prove the contrary and, as part of the funeral celebration, appropriated the clothes and weapons of their husbands, disguised themselves as men, and proceeded to demonstrate "que ce n'était pas grand-chose qui faisait la différence entre les sexes" (Adler 1982:330).

At first glance this might seem like a classic ritual of rebellion in the Gluckman sense. Adler acknowledges the element of social critique, but he stresses much more that nullification of sexual differences is the key, for this ritual is performed not only at the death of old women but also at times of drought when the king's power to bring rain has failed. The king then turns to the women of Léré for help. They are led by an old woman dressed in a boubou, a turban on her head: "She is the king, robed in his ceremonial costume" and followed by an army of women dressed as nobles, warriors—the whole male populace. Nature is constrained by pushing difference to the limits of no difference at all. In Adler's view, the act of subversion is directed not against the social but against the cosmic order (ibid.:329–31). One might add, however, that in a society that sees its king as *femme*, it is a logical extension that women, too, might *in extremis* need to cross gender boundaries to maximize power over nature.

A leitmotiv of this book has been the ambiguous gender of postmenopausal women, particularly older women who have successfully borne and raised children. Older women become "like men." In northern Ghana, old women may even be buried dressed in men's clothes: Rattray saw the corpse of an old woman "complete with trousers, cap, and gown" (1932:2, 419, 506). In such cases, women's status as quasi male seems to derive on the one hand from their proven fertility, on the other from their asexuality and amenorrhea. They no longer threaten transformative activities that depend both on an actual separation of genders and a symbolic fusion of them under male control. But they also represent positive accumulations of power, allowing them a public role denied to younger women: one does not reach a ripe old age and bear living children by chance. Not only are they allowed, therefore, to participate where younger women are excluded but their presence may be indispensable, as for example in the case of men's Poro societies among the Senufo (Ivory Coast). In fact, on an ideological level, the woman is considered the true chief, or head, of Poro (Glaze 1981:50–51).

These ideas about gender, age, and power converge elegantly in the ritual and paraphernalia of the Ijebu (Yoruba) Osugbo society, sometimes known as Ogboni. The Osugbo society brings together older men and women and has long played an important political and judicial role in Yoruba life. Osugbo sculpture takes two forms: the small *edan* and the larger *onile*. Both are paired male and female forms cast in brass. Through the rituals of their manufacture, both are endowed with *ase*, or vital force, but the onile have much more because they represent the cumulative power of generations of members, past and present. Together the edan and onile symbolize the bonding of male and female, often accentuated by a chain that links them (fig. 44). In the words of a Yoruba diviner: "They have joined them together to make one couple . . . because the two together have only one power. . . . It's for oneness." The casting process itself reiterates the joining of male and female by including iron within the brass: the Yoruba associate iron with men and male divinities and brass with women and female divinities (Drewal 1989:160–62).[2]

The edan and onile usually have pronounced male and female sexual characteristics, but they may also mix male and female genitalia and other attributes such as hats, beards, and coiffures (fig. 45). "The clear definition of either femaleness or maleness in many castings is deliberately blurred in others, while symmetricality is maintained." This bisexual imagery Drewal explains by reference to the membership of Osugbo itself: the elders, both male and female. Old age, in Yoruba belief, "confers increased spiritual power, wisdom, and impartiality." Osugbo female title holders no longer need to observe the rules of separation that apply to men and women during their reproductive years because they are no longer menstruating. Edan and onile imagery thus "articulates Yoruba conceptions of the sexes: Firstly, it proclaims the absolute necessity of both for the efficacy of Osugbo and the maintenance of society and, secondly, the essential oneness and coevalness of its aged female and male membership" (ibid.:162–64). To invoke Devisch's formulation apropos of Yaka conceptions of male-female dualism, there is a "ternary logic" that mediates and connects the differences without obliterating them (1988:261–63). But this becomes most apparent in older age when relationships can be expressed generationally as well as sexually.

The bronze sculptures excavated at Ita Yemoo and assumed to represent the *oni* of Ife and his consort may provide historical depth for these ideas (figs. 46 and 47). They are part of the corpus of Ife brass sculptures tentatively dated to the fourteenth and fifteenth centuries A.D. Although partially damaged, the pair are exquisitely intertwined (in ways that defy anatomy) to express rhythmically the dance of gender and perhaps of seniority as well, for they do not appear to share the pronounced youthfulness of the portrait heads but to depict rulers in the fullness of maturity. But even here, interlaced and equal in the elaboration of their adornment, the male figure is slightly larger than the female.

At this point we may finally hazard a guess as to why women potters do not have the same status as male smiths. The fact that pottery is more ephemeral than objects of iron, like much of what women produce, seems hardly sufficient, for in fact both are durable but not eternal. One looks ultimately to cosmology for an answer. Could it be that potting technology can be contained entirely within the female domain? That making and firing pots is too close to gestating a child, the pot too easily assimilated to the womb? Both suggest cooking and the domestic sphere. True, there is some uneasiness, probably stemming from the recognition that the activities are *too* similar, in which case some types of pots will be left to older women or infertile women

---

2. The strips of iron on the foreheads and in the pupils of cast brass Benin heads may carry the same male-female connotations (Herbert 1984a:290).

will abandon the craft. Conversely, there is no violence, no life-negating mirror image in the work or product of the potter comparable to that of the smith, king, and hunter. The technology, then, does not invoke the same fusion of masculine and feminine power; without the Promethean element, it is less dangerous and less impressive. The same might be said, indeed, about girls' initiation, which as a rebirth into adult womanhood, orchestrated by women, falls entirely within their "natural" domain.

SINGULARITY AND UNIVERSALITY

Anyone familiar with Africa should greet with considerable skepticism any hypothesis proposed for large areas of the continent. When I began this study, I had no idea whether the gynecomorphic furnaces I had heard hints of were a purely local or a more widespread phenomenon. One might logically expect that a unitary cosmology might underlie a range of ritual activities within a given culture and that it might express itself in a common repertoire of visual motifs: witness the scarification pattern and breasts that Theodore Bent found not only on Shona smelting furnaces but also on granaries and drums (figs. 7a–c) (Bent 1893:46, 76, 308; Childs 1991:352–53). (If he had looked closely he would also have found them on pots symbolizing marriage [Goodall 1946].) They represent what Huffman (1989:156) refers to as "the repetitive code of cultural symbols." But even within a more or less homogeneous group they are not identical. There is such a range of physical environments and historical experiences in Africa that we are constantly fighting against generalizations that deny this multiplicity and heterogeneity.

In fact, the languages of belief and expression do vary widely. The area of explicitly gynecomorphic furnaces is primarily limited to a sweep of Central Africa, as are myths of blacksmith kings narrowly defined (map 4). But the genderization of the ironworking process and the association of ironworking with political authority can be found from the Niger to the Limpopo, if not farther south. Perhaps an assemblage of beliefs spread with the technology itself, but since we are talking about a time period of some two millennia, it is impossible that belief systems have not undergone profound change just as the technology is not practiced in exactly the same way in any two places (sometimes even in the same region). With rare exceptions (Schmidt and Childs 1985) the archaeological record does not allow us to plot subtle technological change, much less change in belief and practice. And yet, as two of the outstanding young archaeologists of West Africa have commented, "We believe it will be impossible . . . to understand the emergence of smiths without giving as much research weight to their occult knowledge as to their social standing or sources of ore and fuel" (McIntosh and McIntosh 1988:159).

The technological model may, however, provide a paradigm that allows for unity within diversity. No matter what the design of the furnace, the types of ore or fuel or the draft system, certain things have to happen to carry out reduction in a bloomery furnace or it won't work. These are the irreducible minima that ultimately limit variation. The same may be true of beliefs and the rituals in which they are played out: there is an irreducible core that ties the technology to the closest analogue in human experience—the drama of procreativity, or more correctly, regeneration, through sexual reproduction. Over this are laid layer upon layer of culturally specific symbols that not only articulate the process but are believed to act homeopathically to make it happen.

Consequently, it is not surprising that although the choreography and props may vary, the key elements of African ritual are broadly similar: the use of sacrifices, medicines, invocations of ancestors and other spirits, music, and the observance of behavioral prescriptions and proscriptions. Further, within the rituals of a given culture the same dominant symbols will recur and are likely to have the same significance (Wilson 1957:4–5). They constitute a core vocabulary, as it were, based on perceived homologies and interactions between animals, plants, foods—the whole repertoire of power substances—and the object of the ritual. Just as the boy in the Banjeli smelting ritual was supposed to eat the mudfish in one piece so that the bloom would come out in one piece, so a pregnant woman will observe all manner of taboos of foods, actions, sights, etc., that are deemed to be "like" what she wants to avoid: miscarriage, prolonged or difficult birth, or an ugly or deformed baby. A pregnant Sakata woman will not eat the *capitaine* fish, for example, because it bleeds a great deal and would therefore cause her to hemorrhage during birth, nor will she sit in the doorway of her house because it would "bar the way" for her unborn child (Bolakonga 1989). The substances will differ, but the principle and signification will be the same.

Nevertheless, I did expect to find major differences not only between Bantu Africa and West Africa, for example, but even between western and eastern Bantu. Similarly, one would postulate differences between patrilineal and matrilineal societies, although these hard and fast categories are themselves becoming somewhat doubtful. The differences may well be there. I have, in fact, noted some between Bantu and non-Bantu in Chapter 6 with regard to the conceptualization of political authority, but even here they are not as great as I expected. I am reminded of Youssouf Cissé's remark after hearing Luc de Heusch's presentation on king and smith in the early kingdom of Kongo: "What strikes me . . . is the extraordinary similarity of Kongo and Bambara myths. It might be said that one is dealing with the same material, worked differently" (de Heusch 1975a:179).

Nonetheless, there are limitations to the proposed model. It must be apparent that it is derived above all from cultures of West Africa and the Sudanic belt, from Bantu areas as far south as the Limpopo in the east and the Kunene in the west. The model is relevant primarily to settled agricultural cultures or to those based on a mixed economy of farming and cattle keeping; it does not fit purely pastoral societies that have different ideologies of both metalworking and hunting and possibly political authority as well. The lion's share of the material is drawn from centralized or semicentralized societies because of the interest in the cosmology of power as it is writ large in kingship or chiefship, but, of course, less centralized societies also have structures of power and also work metal.

I am sure that scholars working from deep inside individual cultures will challenge the model I have presented, perhaps proposing modifications, perhaps questioning its fundamental validity. The fading of ancestral shades from Kuba and Lele belief in favor of nature spirits is a case in point: it is they who control fertility, especially the fertility of the hunt as emblematic of the whole (Vansina 1978:200). Nonetheless, in other ways, much of Kuba belief seems consistent with patterns I have disengaged.

Not only are we faced with a mostly blank screen when we try to plot the historical evolution of beliefs and rituals, we are also confronted with just as troubling questions of terminology. Throughout the book I have used words like *analogy, metaphor, metonym, equivalence* in an attempt to suggest ways of thinking about how things relate to each other and interact reciprocally. They are inadequate terms to convey ideas of causality that are at variance with those of the post-Newtonian west. Diana Wylie once suggested to me that I needed to consider whether there comes a moment when something becomes a metaphor for something else instead of identical to it. Does this happen when people are confronted with alternative belief systems instead of a single one with variant expressions or when a technical practice and its accompanying beliefs become obsolete? I wish I could answer these questions.

There is also the question of the uniqueness of the African experience and African cosmologies. Ancient and medieval alchemy offers one of the most obvious parallels to the model we have presented for African metallurgy. As Eliade ([1956] 1962) was one of the first to point out, ideas about the birth of ores and the sexual union of minerals to produce higher forms seem to have attended metallurgy wherever it existed: from Central and South America to the Mediterranean to India and China. Alchemy persisted in Europe in the work of the Renaissance Hermetic, Agricola, and Paracelsus. Even Newton was obsessed with its secrets. In the twentieth century, Jung revived interest in alchemical symbolism and its emphasis on the union of opposites as keys to the study of the unconscious. Eliade's own approach to the historical study of alchemy may have been overly general, but there can be no doubting his contribution in calling attention to the pervasiveness of "cosmological conceptions [reinforcing] the homology between man and universe" (ibid.: 33).

The penchant for anthropomorphizing the world and for using the body as the referent for social structure also is not peculiar to Africa. "The human body," Mary Douglas (1970:70) observes, "is always treated as an image of society and . . . there can be no natural way of considering the body that does not involve at the same time a social dimension." We cannot think purely socially about society nor purely physically about the body. Deities, too, have almost universally been anthropomorphized throughout the world. While they may be sharply defined as male or female, they may also be represented as androgynous. In an exhaustive study of preindustrial societies around the world, Baumann (1955) has demonstrated just how common notions of androgyny and bisexuality are. Clearly, many societies have wrestled with the necessity of setting clear boundaries between the sexes for the sake of order but also of recognizing that creativity can only come from fusion—with all its attendant risks of danger and disorder (cf. Douglas 1966). Medieval Cistercians, for example, felt the need to soften the authoritarianism of God the Father with the counterimage of Jesus as Mother (Bynum 1982). When Kongolese artists depicted the crucified Christ as both male and female or with a child on his hip (John Thornton: pers. comm.), however, they were probably not familiar with medieval European traditions but simply translating the power of Christianity into an idiom comprehensible in their own culture.

Gender, as Iris Young insists, "is not merely a phenomenon of individual psychology and experience. In most cultures it is a basic metaphysical category by which the whole universe is organized. . . . . The integrating mythologies of most cultures rely heavily on gender symbols, as do most legitimating ideologies" (1984:135). Until we start listening closely, however, we often do not realize how much our own vocabulary and traditions are infused with gender imagery. Sometimes it is purely physical—for example, references to male and female plugs and similar components. Other times it may blend the sexual with the metaphysical, as in the artist's relation to his (female) muse as the source of creativity—which poses problems for the female artist. Indeed, painters and estheticians have long schematized art in gender terms with drawing as the masculine, color as the feminine element (Robert Herbert: pers. comm.).

The difference is that for contemporary Westerners symbols of the body and gender images have indeed become metaphors, a way of seeing something in terms of something else. We no longer believe in an active homology where like and opposite actually affect outcomes across the boundaries we have erected between humans and the natural world. And yet our own ideas of gender are, if anything, much more problematic than they have been in other societies; we find ourselves still troubled by the notion that masculine and feminine are not fixed categories but vary according to context (cf. Scott 1988:39).

We have already referred to Ngum-Ngumi, the culture hero of the Ga'anda of northeastern Nigeria, who is personified in a clay pot (figs. 42 and 43). The pot is anthropomorphic in form, with round body, narrow neck, and open mouth to which are added sculptural details such as arms, navel, breasts, and male genitalia as well as male tools and weapons. But characteristically, Ngum-Ngumi has a bib pattern down the center of the body—"a graphic, and textural reference to female scarification." The pot encodes both history and cosmology to reinforce "norms of male and female social responsibility and the spirits' role and authority in Ga'anda life" (Berns 1989b:52). But I believe that the gender ambiguity of the figure conveys a further statement about power in its multiple referents to physiological and social identity. In this case, too, the pot is made by male potters.

It provides a visual summary of the principle we have been tracking: the coeval realms of male and female power and at the same time their ultimate control by men, especially senior men who have the technical, ritual, and historical knowledge within a society. Claude Meillassoux has argued that "the great historical enterprise of man (male) has been to gain control of the reproductive functions of women and at the same time to contain the power that they draw from them. To this end they have employed every means: violence, war, education, slavery, law, ideology and myth" (1980:365). Nonetheless, it remains impossible to explain satisfactorily how this has come about. That it has been a source of some bafflement to many societies besides our own is evident in the many myths that evoke an age when things were not always thus—when androgyny prevailed or when women ruled the world and even when there was no death. But usually Eve in some form or another violated a taboo or through carelessness destroyed the pristine order—or women were just too despotic to put up with.

Echoes persist, however, in the numerous traditions of women's secret knowledge and power. Through the transformations of their body, Luba women become vessels which capture the most potent energies and most profound secrets; hence their role as "stewardesses" of royal interdictions, spirit mediums, and custodians of sacred sites and insignia (Nooter 1991: chapter 5). The Wan of Ivory Coast believe that women once stole the most beautiful mask of all from them and through it continue to exercise power over life and death (Ravenhill 1978). The secrets of the "mothers"—significantly a euphemism for witches—are a potent force in Yoruba belief. Men counter women's secrets with their own, sometimes going to amazing lengths to do so, as in the Chagga (Tanzania) case where women are supposed to believe that during initiation boys have their anuses sewed up and do not defecate for the rest of their lives (S. Moore 1976), or Kuba initiation where women are told that boys undergo terrifying ordeals to prove their manhood (Vansina 1955; cf. Barley 1983).

Official beliefs may assert that the male is the active agent of reproduction, the female only a passive recipient. But that does not do away with the view from the male perspective that women's reproductive powers are mysterious in their periodicity and that women's sexuality is both seductive and frightening. Some of these male myths may be an attempt to counter mystery with mystery. And yet, I strongly suspect that women go along with men's "secrets" rather than really believing them, while men are not so sure they understand women's secrets. Just as the slave knows everything about the master and the master knows very little about the slave, women know more about men than men know about women because women's survival depends on it.

Ultimately, social systems endure because of ideological consensus. Power, to be translated into authority, requires a cosmology, and cosmologies cannot be created by force and coercion. But how, then, do African cosmologies that rest so firmly on a bedrock of essential gender complementarity underpin social structures of manifest inequality between men and women? I would venture two thoughts. First, because reproductivity is literally a matter of life and death, it must be controlled to the *n*th degree to maximize success, and this means the control of the means of production: fertile women. The same strategy applies to all processes analogized to reproductivity—virtually the gamut of transformative activities—but includes in its sway the labor of younger men and dependents as well. Those groups that exercise this control are able to do so because they can legitimately claim to benefit the larger society. When they fail, they face both human and supernatural retribution.

But there is a second aspect that I think makes the African situation different from the Western, and that is the role of older women, one might almost say the collusion of older women, in the maintenance of the social and cosmological order. Observe almost any ritual and you will see older women clustered together, watching hawk-eyed, knowing how things should be done, fearsome in the power of their age and knowledge. Older women who have successfully played their role in the drama of regeneration are as much involved in the control process as their male peers and have as much at stake in the status quo. One penetrates the glass ceiling by living long enough; gender is not a stable category but one that transforms itself through the life cycle, so much so that the power relationships between men and women must take into account age as well as the usual qualifiers of class and race/ethnicity or occupational group. Indeed, it is in old age that the axes of life and death, male and female, intersect: at the point of intersection, gender differences tend to dissolve.

Early in the chapter I alluded to the hidden image in Poe's "Goldbug." The image, of course, was of a skull. It is impossible, as we have seen, to dissociate ideas of gender and reproductivity from those of life and death. There are many compass points and plumb lines by which humans order their world and thereby gain a sense of mastery. Many scholars have treated gender and age simply as two of many categories within the systems of dual classification so common in Africa. Certainly all of them together form a totality, but I believe with Sally Falk Moore (1976:368) that the dichotomies of male/female and life/death are the most fundamental, not only as human concerns but also as "dominant cultural categories." They are the primary markers that align the others.

A banal object such as a hoe sums up all these potentialities: "La houe qui creuse la tombe [est] irréfléchie; elle a desséché notre coeur" (Zahan 1963:96). The hoe that provides nourishment through agriculture is also used to dig the tomb. Just so the pot that cooks the food lies smashed on the grave. African technologists of transformation deny not so much death as the role of chance in human affairs. Faced with the omnipresent experience of disorder, they assert order through controlling the interplay of male and female, living and dead. But only the potter resolves the riddle of regeneration without violence.

APPENDIX
Reconstructions of Iron Smelting in Africa

Date	Place	Researcher	Film: distributor
[1927	Ethiopia: Dime	Eike Haberland	Göttingen I. W. F.]
1930	Johannesburg: Shona	J. W. Posselt, G. Stanley	
[1930	Angola: Chokwe	Heinrich Baumann	Berlin Staatliches Museum]
[1937	Angola: Kwanyama	D. and A. Powell-Cotton	Birchington, Kent Powell-Cotton Museum]
1937	Cameroon: Yaoundé		
1944	Rhodesia: Njanja	F. W. McCosh	
1946	Angola: So. Lunda	Jose Redinha	
1953	Cameroon: Matakam	René Gardi	Göttingen I. W. F.
1955	Burkina Faso: Senufo	Karl Dittmer	Göttingen I. W. F.
1956	Tanganyika: Fipa	R. Wise	
1956	Angola: Chokwe	M.-L. Bastin	
1957	Gabon: Kota	Peter Telfair	
1958	Zambia: Luchazi	Reid Ray, Murray Armor	American Machine Tool Association
1960	Zambia: Kaonde	J. H. Chaplin	Central African Film Unit
1962	Nigeria: Zamfara	Kurt Krieger	
1962	Angola: Chokwe	J. V. Martins	
1963	Libya: Bäle	B. Fuchs	Göttingen I. W. F.
1964	Nigeria: Isúndùnrin	Denis Williams	U. Ibadan Photo Unit
c. 1964	Nigeria: Sukur	Hamo Sassoon	BBC TV
[1965, 1967	Niger: Hausa	Nicole Echard	Paris: CNRS]
1965	Cameroon: Kirdi		
1967	Tanzania: Fipa	J. Wembah-Rashid	Dar-es Salaam
1969–72	Burundi: 5 foundries	G. Célis, E. Nzikobanyanka	
1971–73	No. Ghana	Len Pole	Ghana Broadcasting
1973	So. Ghana	Len Pole	
1972	C. A. R.: Gbaya	P. Vidal	
1973	Ethiopia: Dimi	J. Todd	
1973, 1974	Zaïre: Ekonda	G. Célis	
c. 1973	South Africa: Buisport	M. E. Dingle et al.	
1974	C. A. R.: Gbaya	P. Vidal, J. M. Chauvy	

1974?	Togo: Bassar	Dovi Kuevi	
1970s	Zaïre: Amadi	F. Van Noten	
1975	Rwanda: 5 foundries	G. Célis	
1976	Tanzania: Buhaya	Schmidt et al.	U. Florida
1977	C. A. R.: Gbaya	Moñino	
1977	Rwanda: Rukara	G. Célis	
1978, 1980	Rwanda: Muganza	F. Van Noten	
1981	Burundi: Kangozi	J.-P. Chrétien et al.	
1982–83	Malawi: Chewa	N. van der Merwe,	
		D. Avery	
1984	Zaïre: Kivu	K. M. Kita	
1985	Togo: Bassar	C. Goucher,	D. E. R.
		E. Herbert,	
		C. Saltman	
1986, 1989	Cameroon: Mafa	N. David,	U. Calgary
		Y. Le Bléis	
1986	Niger: Djerma	G. Célis	
1988	Zimbabwe: Shona	W. Dewey	U. Iowa
1988	Togo: Bassar	Hans Hahn	
1989	Cameroon: Mora	N. David et al.	
1989	Ivory Coast: Senufo	G. Célis	
1989	Zaïre: Mangbetu	C. Keim et al.	American Museum of Natural History
1989	Zaïre: Ekonda	E. Herbert et al.	Unedited
1991?	Nigeria: Isúndùnrin	D. Aremu	U. Ibadan

The [] indicates uncertainty about whether the smelting was a reconstruction or is still regularly practiced.

Abbreviations:

I. W. F.: Institut für den wissenschaftlichen Film

D. E. R.: Documentary Educational Resources

BIBLIOGRAPHY

Abbreviations Used:

Afr. Arch. Rev.	*African Archaeological Review*
Afr. Econ. Hist.	*African Economic History*
Afr. Hist. Stud.	*African Historical Studies*
Afr. Stud. Rev.	*African Studies Review*
Amer. Anth.	*American Anthropologist*
Arch. f. Völkerkunde	*Archiv für Völkerkunde*
BIFAN	*Bulletin de l'Institut Français d'Afrique Noire*
Bull. Soc. Neuchatel Géog.	*Bulletin de la Société de Neuchâtel de Géographie*
Bull. Com. Et. AOF	*Bulletin du Comité d'Etudes de l'A.O.F.*
Bull. Inst. Et. Centr.	*Bulletin de l'Institut d'Etudes Centrafricaines*
CA	*Current Anthropology*
Cah. Cong. Anth. & Hist.	*Cahiers Congolais d'Anthropologie et d'Histoire*
CEA	*Cahiers d'Etudes Africaines*
Cah. ORSTOM	*Cahiers de l'O.R.S.T.O.M.*
Encycl. Cin.	*Encyclopaedia Cinematographica*
Et. Cam.	*Etudes Camérounaises*
Et. Dah.	*Etudes Dahoméennes*
Et. Maliennes	*Etudes Maliennes*
Et. Tog.	*Etudes Togolaises*
Eth. Zeitschr.	*Ethnographische Zeitschrift*
Geog. J.	*Geographical Journal*
Geog. Rev.	*Geographical Review*
HA	*History in Africa*
IJAHS	*International Journal of African Historical Studies*
J. Arch. Anth.	*Journal of Archaeological Anthropology*
J. Field Arch.	*Journal of Field Archaeology*
J. Hist. Met. Soc.	*Journal of the Historical Metallurgy Society*
J. Iron & Steel Inst.	*Journal of the Iron and Steel Institute*
J. Manchester Geog.	*Journal of the Manchester Geographical Society*
J. Roy. Anth. Inst.	*Journal of the Royal Anthropological Institute*
J. Roy. Geog. Soc.	*Journal of the Royal Geographical Society*
J. World Prehist.	*Journal of World Prehistory*
JA	*Journal des Africanistes*
JAH	*Journal of African History*
JSA	*Journal de la Société des Africanistes*
JSAIMM	*Journal of the South African Institute of Mining and Metallurgy*
Lib. Stud. J.	*Liberian Studies Journal*
NA	*Nyame Akuma*
NADA	*Native Affairs Department Annual (Salisbury)*
No. Rhod. J.	*Northern Rhodesia Journal*
Notes Afr.	*Notes Africaines*
Proc. Roy. Geog. Soc.	*Proceedings of the Royal Geographical Society*
Proc. Royal Soc.	*Proceedings of the Royal Society*
Rev. Cong.	*La Revue Congolaise*

Rev. d'Eth.	*Revue d'Ethnographie*
Rev. Ethngr. et Soc.	*Revue d'Ethnographie et Société*
Rev. Géog. Hum. Eth.	*Revue de Géographie Humaine et d'Ethnographie*
Rhod. Prehist.	*Rhodesian Prehistory*
SA J. Sci.	*South African Journal of Science*
SAAB	*South African Archaeological Bulletin*
TNR	*Tanganyika Notes and Records*
WAJA	*West African Journal of Archaeology*
World Arch.	*World Archaeology*
Zeitschr. f. Ethn.	*Zeitschrift für Ethnologie*

Abiodun, Rowland. 1987. "Verbal and Visual Metaphors: Mythical Allusions in Yoruba Ritualistic Art of Ori." *Word and Image* 3:252–70.

———. 1989a. "Woman in Yoruba Religious Images." *African Languages and Cultures* 2:1–18.

———. 1989b. "The Kingdom of Owo." In *Yoruba: Nine Centuries of Art and Thought*, edited by Henry Drewal and John Pemberton III. New York.

Abrahams, Robert G. 1966. "Succession to the Chiefship in Northern Unyamwezi." In *Succession to High Office*, edited by Jack Goody. Cambridge, Eng.

Achebe, Chinua. 1976. *Morning Yet on Creation Day*. New York.

Adams, Marie Jeanne. 1980. "Afterword: Spheres of Men's and Women's Creativity." *Ethn. Zeitschr.* Zürich 1:163–67.

Adeniji, David. 1977. *Iron Mining and Smelting*, translated and edited by Robert G. Armstrong with the author. Occasional Publication no. 31, Institute of African Studies, University of Ibadan.

Adler, Alfred. 1969. "Essai sur la signification des relations de dépendance personnelle dans l'ancien système politique des Moundang du Tchad." *CEA* 9:441–66.

———. 1982. *La mort est le masque du roi. La royauté sacrée des Moundang du Tchad.* Paris.

Ajuwon, 'Bade. 1989. "Ogun's Iremoje: A Philosophy of Living and Dying." In *Africa's Ogun*, edited by Sandra Barnes. Bloomington, Ind.

Alexandre, Paul, and Jean Binet. 1958. *Le groupe dit Pahouin.* Paris.

Amadiume, Ifi. 1987. *Male Daughters, Female Husbands: Gender and Sex in an African Society.* London.

Ametozion, P. K. n.d. "A Spark of the African Soul." N.p. [Togo]. Mimeo.

Anderson, Martha G., and Christine M. Kreamer. 1989. *Wild Spirits, Strong Medicine: African Art and the Wilderness.* New York.

Angebauer, Karl. 1927. *Ovambo. Fünfzehn Jahre unter Kaffern, Buschleuten und Bezirksamtmännern.* Berlin.

Anjorin, A. O. 1971. "Tin Mining in Northern Nigeria during the Nineteenth and the Early Part of the Twentieth Centuries." *Odù*, n.s. 5:54–67.

Anon. 1956. "God of Iron." *Nigeria Mag.* 49:118–37.

Anquandah, James. 1988. "Life Histories of Akan Terra Cottas." Paper presented at the Conference on African Material Culture, Bellagio, Italy, May 19–28.

Appia, Beatrice. 1965. "Les forgerons du Fouta-Djallon." *JSA* 5:317–52.

Apter, Andrew. 1992. *Black Critics and Kings: The Hermeneutics of Power in Yoruba Society.* Chicago.

Archinard, Louis. 1884. "La fabrication du fer dans le Soudan." *Rev. d'Eth.* 3:249–55.

Ardener, Edwin. [1968]1975. "Belief and the Problem of Women." In *Perceiving Women*, edited by Shirley Ardener. New York.

Ardouin, Claude. 1978. "La caste des forgerons et son importance dans le Soudan occidental." *Et. Maliennes* 24:1–32.

Arens, William, and Ivan Karp, eds. 1989. *Creativity of Power: Cosmology and Action in African Societies.* Washington, D.C.

Arhem, Kaj. 1991. "The Symbolic World of the Maasai Homestead." In *Body and Space: Symbolic Models of Unity and Division in African Cosmology and Experience,* edited by Anita Jacobson-Widding. Stockholm.

Aronson, Lisa. 1989. "Akwete Weaving: Tradition and Change." In *Man Does Not Go Naked,* edited by Beate Engelbrecht and Bernard Gardi. Basel.

Avery, Donald H. 1982. "The Iron Bloomery." In *Early Pyrotechnology,* edited by T. Wertime and S. Wertime. Washington, D.C.

Avery, Donald H., Nicholas J. van der Merwe, and S. Saitowitz. 1988. "The Metallurgy of the Iron Bloomery in Africa." In *The Beginning of the Use of Metals and Alloys,* edited by Robert Maddin. Cambridge, Mass.

Ba, Hampaté, and Jean Daget. 1955. "Notes sur les chasses rituelles Bozo." *JSA* 25:89–97.

Babalola, S. A. 1966. *The Content and Form of Yoruba Igala.* London.

———. 1989. "A Portrait of Ogun as Reflected in Ijala Chants." In *Africa's Ogun,* edited by Sandra Barnes. Bloomington, Ind.

Babcock, Barbara A., ed. 1978. *The Reversible Worlds: Symbolic Inversions in Art and Society.* Ithaca, N.Y.

Baikie, William Balfour. 1867. "Notes of a Journey from Bida in Nupe to Kano in Haussa, performed in 1862." *J. Roy. Geog. Soc.* 37:92–108.

Balandier, Georges. 1968. *Daily Life in the Kingdom of Kongo, from the Sixteenth to the Eighteenth Century,* translated by Helen Weaver. New York.

Baldé, Seikhou. 1935. "Les forgerons au Fouta-Djallon." *L'Education africaine* 90/91:151–55.

Barber, Karin. 1991. *I Could Speak until Tomorrow: Oriki, Women and the Past in a Yoruba Town.* Edinburgh.

Barbot, Jean. 1732. "A Description of the Coasts of North and South Guinea." In vol. 5 of *A Collection of Voyages and Travels,* edited by Awnsham Churchill. 6 vols. London.

Barkindo, Bawuro Mubi. 1989. *The Sultanate of Mandara to 1902: History of the Evolution, Development and Collapse of a Central Sudanese Kingdom.* Stuttgart.

Barley, Nigel. 1983. *Symbolic Structures: An Exploration of the Culture of the Dowayos.* Cambridge, Eng.

———. 1984. "Placing the West African Potter." In *Earthenware in Asia and Africa,* edited by John Picton. London.

Barnes, H. B. 1926. "Iron Smelting among the Ba-Ushi." *J. Roy. Anth. Inst.* 56:189–94.

Barnes, Sandra T. 1986. *Ogun: An Old God for a New Age.* Philadelphia.

———, ed. 1989. *Africa's Ogun: Old World and New.* Bloomington, Ind.

Barnes, Sandra T., and Paula Ben-Amos. 1989. "Ogun, the Empire Builder." In *Africa's Ogun,* edited by S. Barnes. Bloomington, Ind.

Barreteau, D., et al. 1988. "La poterie chez les Mofu-Gudur: des gestes, des formes et des mots." In *Le Milieu et les hommes,* Actes du 2ème Colloque Mega-Tchad ORSTOM BONDY, edited by D. Barreteau and H. Tourneux. Paris.

Barth, Heinrich. 1858. *Travels in North and Central Africa,* vol. 4. London.

Barthes, Roland. 1982. *A Barthes Reader,* edited by Susan Sontag. New York.

Baskin, Judith. 1985. "The Separation of Women in Rabbinic Judaism." In *Women, Religion and Social Change,* edited by Y. Haddad and E. Findly. Albany, N.Y.

Bassani, Ezio. 1987. "Un Cappucino nell'Africa Nera del Seicento." *Quaderni Poro* 4. Milan.

Bastin, Marie-Louise. 1974. "Le haut fourneau *lutengo:* opération de la fonte de fer et rituel chez les Tschokwe du Nord de la Lunda (Angola)." In vol. 3 of *In Memoriam Antonio Jorge Dias.* 3 vols. Lisbon.

Baumann, Hermann. 1935. *Lunda.* Berlin.

———. 1955. *Das doppelte Geschlecht: Ethnologische Studien zur Bisexualität in Ritus und Mythos.* Berlin.

Baumann, Hermann, and Diedrich Westermann. 1957. *Les Peuples et les civilisations de l'Afrique,* translated by L. Homburger. Paris.

Beattie, John. 1960. *Bunyoro: An African Kingdom.* New York.

———. 1970. "On Understanding Ritual." In *Rationality,* edited by Bryan R. Wilson. Oxford.

Bebiano, J. Bacellar. 1960. *Notas sobre a siderurgia dos indigenas de Angola.* Lisbon.

Beidelman, Thomas O. 1962. "Iron-Working in Ukaguru." *TNR* 58/59:288–89.

———. 1966. "Swazi Royal Ritual." *Africa* 36:373–405.

———. 1980. "Women and Men in Two East African Societies." In *Explorations in African Thought Systems,* edited by Ivan Karp and Charles Bird. Bloomington, Ind.

———. 1991. Review of S. Feierman, *Peasant Intellectuals. IJAHS* 24(3):693–95.

Bellamy, Charles V., and F. Harbord. 1904. "A West African Smelting House." *J. Iron and Steel Inst.* 56:99–126.

Bellman, Beryl. 1984. *The Language of Secrecy: Symbols and Metaphors in Poro Ritual.* New Brunswick, N.J.

Ben-Amos, Paula. 1980. *The Art of Benin.* London.

Bent, J. Theodore. 1893. *The Ruined Cities of Mashonaland.* London.

Bérard, M. [1945]1951. "La métallurgie Bassari au Togo français." Première Conférence Internationale des Africanistes de l'Ouest (Dakar). *Comptes rendus* 2:231–35.

Berglund, Axel-Ivar. 1976. *Zulu Thought: Patterns and Symbolism.* Bloomington, Ind.

———. 1991. "Fertility as a Mode of Thought." In *The Creative Communion,* edited by Anita Jacobson-Widding and Walter van Beek. Uppsala Studies in Cultural Anthropology 15. Stockholm.

Berliner, Paul F. 1978. *The Soul of Mbira: Music and Traditions of the Shona People of Zimbabwe.* Berkeley.

Bernhard, F. O. 1963. "Iron-smelting Furnaces on Ziwa Farm." *SAAB* 18:235–36.

———. 1968. "A Ziwa Furnace." *SAAB* 23:16.

Berns, Marla C. 1988. "Ga'anda Scarification: A Model for Art and Identity." In *Marks of Civilization: Artistic Transformations of the Human Body,* edited by Arnold Rubin. Los Angeles.

———. 1989a. "Ceramic Arts in Africa." *African Arts* 22(2):32–37.

———. 1989b. "Ceramic Clues: Art History in the Gongola Valley." *African Arts* 22(2):48–59.

———. 1990. "Pots as People: Yungur Ancestral Portraits." *African Arts* 23(3):50–60.

Bernus, Edmond, and Nicole Echard. 1992. "Les populations actuelles." La Région d'In Gall-Tegidda-n-tesemt (Niger). *Etudes Nigériennes* 52.

Berthier, Paul. 1820. "Examen du fer forgé par les nègres de Fouta Djallon." *Annales des Mines* (Paris), 129–34.

Bertho, J. 1946. "Note sur le haut-fourneau et la forge des Bobo-Oule (Bobo-Rouges) de Dédougou (Haute Côte d'Ivoire)." *Notes Afr.* 30:10–12.

Biebuyck, Daniel. 1956. "Organisation politique des Nyanga. La chefferie Ihana." *Kongo-Overzee* 22:301–41.

———. ed. 1969. *Tradition and Creativity in Tribal Art.* Berkeley.

———. 1973. *Lega Culture: Art, Initiation, and Moral Philosophy among a Central African People.* Berkeley.

———. 1985–86. *The Arts of Zaire.* 2 vols. Berkeley.

Biebuyck, Daniel, and Kahombo Mateene, eds. and trans. 1971. *The Mwindo Epic*. Berkeley.

Binger, Louis Gustave. [1892]1980. *Du Niger au Golfe du Guinée par le pays de Kong et le Mossi*. Paris.

Bird, Charles S., and Martha B. Kendall. 1980. "The Mande Hero: Text and Context." In *Explorations in African Systems of Thought*, edited by Ivan Karp and Charles S. Bird. Bloomington, Ind.

Bischofberger, Otto. 1969. "Die soziale und rituelle Stellung der Schmiede und des Schmiede-Klans bei den Zanaki (Tanzania)." *Paideuma* 15:54–63.

Blacking, John, ed. 1973. *The Anthropology of the Body*. London.

Bledsoe, Caroline. 1992. "The Cultural Transformation of Western Education in Sierra Leone." *Africa* 62:182–202.

Blier, Suzanne P. 1984. "Antelopes and Anvils: Tamberma Works of Iron." *African Arts* 17(3):58–63.

———. 1987. *The Anatomy of Architecture: Ontology and Metaphor in Batammaliba Architectural Expression*. Cambridge, Eng.

Bocoum, Hamady. 1990. "Contribution à la connaissance des origines du Takrur." *Ann. de la Faculté des Lettres et Sciences Humaines* (Dakar) 20:159–78.

Bohannan, Laura [Elenore Smith Bowen]. [1954]1964. *Return to Laughter*. New York.

———. 1975. "Hamlet and the Tiv." *Psychology Today*, July 19:62–66.

Bohannan, Paul. 1954. "Circumcision among the Tiv." *Man*, n.s. 2:5.

Bolakonga, Bobwo. 1989. "Les tabous de la grossesse chez les femmes sakata (Zaïre)." *Annales Aequatoria* 10:41–54.

Borgatti, Jean. 1989. "Atsu Atsogwa: Art and Morality among the Northern Edo of Okpella, Nigeria." In *Man Does Not Go Naked*, edited by Beate Engelbrecht and Bernard Gardi. Basel.

Borgerhoff, R. 1912. "Les industries des Wanande." *Rev. Cong.* 3:278–84.

Boston, John S. 1966. "The Hunter in Igala Legends of Origin." *Africa* 34:116–26.

Bourdieu, Pierre. 1980. *Le Sens pratique*. Paris.

Bourgeois, Robert. 1956. *Banyarwanda et Burundi: III. Religion et Magie*. Acad. Roy. Sci. Col. Brussels.

Bower, J. G. 1927. "Native Smelting in Equatorial Africa." *Mining Mag.* 37(3):137–47.

Boyer, Pascal. 1983. "Le status des forgerons et ses justifications symboliques: une hypothèse cognitive." *Africa* 53:44–63.

Brain, Robert. 1980. *Art and Society in Africa*. New York.

Braithwaite, M. 1982. "Decoration as Ritual Symbol: A Theoretical Proposal and an Ethnographic Study in Southern Sudan." In *Symbols and Structural Archaeology*, edited by Ian Hodder. Cambridge, Eng.

Brelsford, W. V. 1949. "Rituals and Medicines of Chisinga Ironworkers." *Man* 49:27–29.

Breutz, P.-L. 1969. "Sotho-Tswana Celestial Concepts." In *Ethnological and Linguistic Studies in Honour of N. J. Van Warmelo*. Pretoria.

Brincard, Marie-Thérèse, ed. 1990. *Afrique: Formes Sonores*. Paris.

Brock, Beverly, and William Brock. 1965. "Iron Working amongst the Nyiha of Southwestern Tanzania." *SAAB* 20:97–100.

Brown, H. D. 1944. "The Nkumu of the Tumba." *Africa* 14:431–47.

Brown, Jean. 1971. "Ironworking in Southern Mbeere." *MILA* 2:37–50.

Bruel, Georges. 1918. *L'Afrique equatoriale française*. Paris.

Bryant, Alfred T. [1948]1970. *The Zulu People*. New York.

Buckley, Anthony. 1985. *Yoruba Medicine*. Oxford.

Buckley, Thomas, and Alma Gottlieb, eds. 1988. *Blood Magic: The Anthropology of Menstruation*. Berkeley.

Bullock, Charles. 1950. *The Mashona and Matabele*. Cape Town.

Burchell, William. [1824]1967. *Travels in the Interior of Southern Africa.* 2 vols. London.

Burton, John W. 1991. "Representations of the Feminine in Nilotic Cosmologies." In *Body and Space,* edited by Anita Jacobson-Widding. Stockholm.

Burton, W. F. P. 1961. *Luba Religion and Magic in Custom and Belief.* Tervuren.

Bynum, Caroline. 1982. *Jesus as Mother: Studies in the Spirituality of the High Middle Ages.* Berkeley.

Calame-Griaule, Genevieve. 1991. "On the Dogon Restudied." *CA* 32(5):575–77.

——— and Z. Ligers. 1961. "L'homme-hyène dans la tradition soudanaise." *L'Homme* 1(2):89–112.

Cameron, Verney L. [1877]1969. *Across Africa.* New York.

Campbell, J. M. 1909–10. "Native Iron Smelting in Haute Guinée (West Africa)." *Trans. Inst. Mining and Metallurgy* 19:458–62.

Cardinall, A. W. 1931. *Tales Told in Togoland.* Oxford.

Carl, L., and J. Petit. 1955. "Une technique archäique de la fabrication du fer dans le Mourdi (Sahara oriental)." *L'Ethnographie* 50:60–81.

Carroll, Kevin F. 1950. "Yoruba Craft Work at Oyo-Ekiti, Ondo Province." *Nigeria Mag.* 35:344–54.

Carvalho, H. D. de. 1890. *Ethnographia e historia tradicional does povos da Lunda.* Lisbon.

Casalis, Eugène. 1859. *Les Bassoutos.* Paris.

Cashion, Gerald A. 1982. Hunters of the Mande: A Behavioral Code and Worldview Derived from the Study of Their Folklore. Ph.D. diss., Indiana University. 2 vols.

Cavazzi, Giovanni Antonio da Montecuccolo. 1687. *Istorica Descrizione de' tre Regni: Congo, Matamba et Angola.* Bologna.

Célis, Georges. 1987. "Fondeurs et forgerons ekonda (Equateur, Zaïre)." *Anthropos* 82:109–34.

———. 1988. *Introduction à la métallurgie traditionnelle au Rwanda: Techniques et Croyances.* Butare.

———. 1989. "La métallurgie traditionelle au Burundi, au Rwanda et au Buha: Essai de synthèse." *Anthropos* 84:25–46.

———. 1991. *Eisenhütten in Afrika/Les fonderies africaines du fer.* Frankfurt am Main.

Célis, Georges, and Emmanuel Nzikobanyanka. 1976. *La métallurgie traditionelle au Burundi.* Tervuren.

Cerulli, Ernesto. 1956. "L'iniziazione al mestiere di fabbro in Africa." *Studi e Materiali di Storia delle Religioni* 27:87–101.

Chaplin. J. H. 1961. "Notes on Traditional Smelting in Northern Rhodesia." *SAAB* 16:530–60.

Chappel, Tim J. H. 1973. "The Death of a Cult in Northern Nigeria." *African Arts* 6(4):70–74.

Charles, L. 1911. "Les Lobi." *Rev. Ethnogr. et Soc.* 2:202–20.

Chauveau, Jean-Pierre. 1978. "Contribution à la géographie historique de l'or en pays baule (Côte d'Ivoire)." *JA* 48:15–70.

Chikwendu, V. E., and A. C. Umezi. 1979. "Local Sources of Raw Materials for the Nigerian Bronze/Brass Industry (with emphasis on Igbo-Ukwu)." *WAJA* 9:151–65.

"Child Survival: A Moral Imperative." 1989. *Africa News,* May 1:4–7.

Childs, S. Terry. 1991a. "Style, Technology, and Iron Smelting Furnaces in Bantu-Speaking Africa." *J. Arch. Anthro.* 10:332–59.

———. 1991b. "Transformations: Iron and Copper Production in Central Africa." In *Recent Trends in Archaeometallurgical Research,* edited by Petar Glumac. Philadelphia: MASCA Research Papers in Science and Archaeology.

Childs, S. Terry, William Dewey, Muya wa Bitanko Kamwanga, and Pierre de Maret. 1989. "Iron and Stone Age Research in Shaba Province, Zaïre." *NA* 32:54–59.
Christian, Marcus Bruce. 1972. *Negro Ironworkers in Louisiana, 1718–1900.* Gretna, La.
Chukwukere, I. 1982. "Agnatic and Uterine Relations among the Fante: Male/Female Dualism." *Africa* 52:61–68.
Cissé, Youssouf. 1964. "Notes sur les sociétés des chasseurs malinke." *JSA* 34:175–226.
Clapperton, Hugh. [1829]1966. *Journal of a Second Expedition into the Interior of Africa. . . .* London.
Clark, John D. 1974. *Kalambo Falls Prehistoric Site.* 2 vols. Cambridge, Eng.
Clément, Paul. 1948. "Le forgeron en Afrique noire." *Rev. Géog. Hum. Eth.* 2:35–58.
Clifford, James. 1983. "Power and Dialogue in Ethnography: Marcel Griaule's Initiation." In *Observers Observed,* edited by George W. Stocking. Madison, Wis.
———. 1988. *The Predicament of Culture.* Cambridge, Mass.
Cline, Walter. 1937. *Mining and Metallurgy in Negro Africa.* Menasha, Wis.
Clist, Bernard. 1987. "A Critical Reappraisal of the Chronological Framework of the Early Iron Age Industry." *Muntu* 6:35–62.
Clist, Bernard, R. Oslisly, and B. Peyrot. 1986. "Métallurgie ancienne du fer au Gabon: Premiers éléments de synthèse." *Muntu* 4/5:47–56.
Coillard, François. 1886. *Journal Intime.* Paris.
Cole, Herbert. 1989. *Icons: Ideals and Power in the Art of Africa.* Washington, D.C.
Collard, Chantal. 1979. "Mariage 'à petits pas' et mariage 'par vol': Pouvoir des hommes, des femmes et des chefs chez les Guidar." *Anthropologie et Sociétés* 3(1):41–73.
Collett, David. 1985. The Spread of Early Iron-producing Communities in Eastern and Southern Africa. Ph.D. diss., Cambridge University.
Colloques Internationaux du Centre National de la Recherche Scientifique no. 544. 1973. *La Notion de personne en Afrique noire.* Paris.
Comaroff, Jean. 1985. *Body of Power, Spirit of Resistance.* Chicago.
Cooke, C. K. 1959. "An Iron-smelting Site in the Matopo Hills, Southern Rhodesia." *SAAB* 14:18–20.
———. 1966. "Account of Iron-smelting Techniques Once Practised by the Manyubi of the Matopo District of Rhodesia." *SAAB* 21:86–87.
Coquilhat, C. 1888. *Sur le haut Congo.* Brussels.
Cornevin, Robert. 1957. "Etude sur le centre urbain de Bassari (Togo)." *BIFAN* 19:72–110.
———. 1962. *Les Bassari du Nord-Togo.* Paris.
Coronel, P. C. 1979. "Aowin Terracotta Sculpture." *African Arts* 13(1):28–35.
Courlander, Harold. 1983. *The Master of the Forge.* New York.
Cozens, A. B. 1955. "A Village Smithy in the Cameroons." *Nigerian Field* 20:25–34.
Craddock, Paul T., ed. 1980. *Scientific Studies in Early Mining and Extractive Metallurgy.* British Museum Occasional Paper no. 20. London.
Craddock, Paul T., and M. J. Hughes, eds. 1985. *Furnaces and Smelting in Antiquity.* British Museum Occasional Paper no. 48. London.
Crawhall, T. C. 1933. "Iron-working in the Sudan." *Man* 48:41–43.
Cridel, B. 1967. "Technique de construction des cases et artisanat chez les Kabré." Centre d'études et de recherches de Kara. *Documents,* 61–71.
Crowley, Daniel J. 1972. "Chokwe: Political Art in a Plebian Society." In *African Art and Leadership,* edited by D. Fraser and H. Cole. Madison, Wis.
Curtin, Philip. 1975. *Economic Change in Pre-Colonial Africa.* Madison, Wis.
Dacher, Michèle. 1984. "Génies, ancêtres, voisins: Quelques aspects de la relation à la terre chez les Ciranba (Goin) du Burkina-Faso." *CEA* 24:157–92.
Dapper, O. 1668. *Naukeurige Beschrijvinge der Afrikaenshe Gewesten.* Amsterdam.

Dark, Philip J. C. 1973. *An Introduction to Benin Art and Technology.* London.

Darling, Patrick. 1983. "Brief Notes on Iron-Smelting in the Kazaure Hills." *Zaria Archaeology Paper* 5:40–41.

———. 1986. "Fieldwork Surveys in and around Kano State, Nigeria, 1982–1985." *NA* 27:39–41.

David, Nicholas. 1987. "Furnace and Forge: Dokwaza the Smith." Fieldnotes, Mafa.

———. 1988. Comment. African Studies Association Meeting. Madison, Wis.

———. 1990. *Vessels of the Spirit. Pots and People in Northern Cameroon.* Video.

David, Nicholas, and Yves Le Bléis. 1988. *Dokwaza: Last of the African Iron Masters.* Video. Calgary.

David, Nicholas, and Judy Sterner. 1989. "The Mandara Archaeological Project 1988–89." *NA* 32:5–9.

David, Nicholas, Judy Sterner, and Kodzo Gavua. 1988. "Why Pots Are Decorated." *CA* 29:365–89.

David, Nicholas, Robert Heimann, David Killick, and Michael Wayman. 1989. "Between Bloomery and Blast Furnace: Mafa Iron Smelting Technology in North Cameroon." *Afr. Arch. Rev.* 7:183–208.

Davison, S., and P. N. Mosley. 1988. "Iron-Smelting in the Upper Rukuru Basin of Northern Malawi." *Azania* 23:57–99.

de Barros, Philip. 1986. "Bassar: A Quantified, Chronologically Controlled, Regional Approach to a Traditional Iron Production Centre in West Africa." *Africa* 56:148–73.

De Boeck, Filip. 1991a. "Therapeutic Efficacy and Consensus among the Aluund of South-Western Zaïre." *Africa* 61:159–85.

———. 1991b. "Of Bushbucks without Horns: Male and Female Initiation among the Aluun of Southwest Zaïre." *JA* 61:37–71.

Decalo, Samuel. 1976. *Historical Dictionary of Togo.* Metuchen, N.J.

Decle, Lionel. 1898. *Three Years in Savage Africa.* London.

de Grunne, Bernard. 1980. *Terres cuites anciennes de l'Ouest africain.* Louvain-la-Neuve.

de Hemptinne, Msgr. 1926. "Les 'mangeurs de cuivre' du Katanga." Brochure. Brussels. Extract from *Congo* 7:371–403.

de Heusch, Luc. 1954. "Autorité et prestige dans la société tetela." *Zaire* 8:1011–27.

———. 1956. "Le symbolisme du forgeron en Afrique." *Reflets du Monde* 10:57–70.

———. 1975a. "Le roi, les forgerons et les premiers hommes dans l'ancienne société kongo." *Systèmes de Pensée en Afrique Noire.* Paris.

———. 1975b. "What Shall We Do with the Drunken King?" *Africa* 45:363–72.

———. 1980. "Heat, Physiology, and Cosmogony: Rites de Passage among the Thonga." In *Explorations in African Thought Systems,* edited by Ivan Karp and Charles S. Bird. Bloomington, Ind.

———. 1982a. *Rois Nés d'un Coeur de Vache.* Paris.

———. [1972]1982b. *The Drunken King; or, The Origin of the State.* Translated and annotated by Roy Willis. Bloomington, Ind.

———. 1985. *Sacrifice in Africa: A Structuralist Approach.* Translated by Linda O'Brien and Alice Morton. Bloomington, Ind.

———. 1987. "Nkumi et Nkumu: la sacralisation du pouvoir chez les Mongo (Zaïre)." *Systèmes de Pensées en Afrique Noire.* Paris.

———. 1991. "On Griaule on Trial." *CA* 32:434–37.

Delhaise, Comdt. 1909. *Les Warega.* Brussels.

Delisle, F. 1884. "La fabrication du fer dans le Haut Ogowe (Afrique Equatoriale)." *Rev. d'Ethn.* 3:465–73.

de Maret, Pierre. 1980. "Ceux qui jouent avec le feu: la place du forgeron en Afrique centrale." *Africa* 50:263–79.

————. 1985. "The Smith's Myth and the Origin of Leadership in Central Africa." In *African Iron Working*, edited by Randi Haaland and Peter Shinnie. Oxford.

————. 1988. Comments. African Studies Association Meeting. Madison, Wis.

de Maret, Pierre, and Bernard Clist. 1985. "Archaeological Research in Zaïre." *NA* 26:41–42.

de Maret, Pierre, and F. Nsuka. 1977. "History of Bantu Metallurgy: Some Linguistic Aspects." *HA* 4:43–65.

Demolin, Didier. 1990. "The Social Organization of Mangbetu Music." In *African Reflections*, edited by Enid Schildkrout and Curtis Keim. Seattle.

Dennett, Richard Edward. 1906. *At the Back of the Black Man's Mind*. London.

De Rode, Philippe. 1940. "Note sur la fonte de fer." *Aequatoria* 3:103.

De Rop, A. 1954. "Nota's over de smidse van Nkundo." *Aequatoria* 17:1–6.

————. 1956. "Le forgeron Nkundo (Congo)." *Annales de Notre Dame du Sacré-Coeur*, 22–26.

de Rosemond, C. C. 1943. "Iron Smelting in the Kahama District." *TNR* 16:79–84.

de Sousberghe, L. 1955. "Forgerons et fondeurs de fer chez les Ba-Pende et leurs voisins." *Zaïre* 9(1):25–31.

Desplagnes, Louis. 1907. *Le plateau central nigérien*. Paris.

Devisch, René. 1984. *Se recréer femme: Manipulation sémantique d'une situation d'infécondité chez les Yaka du Zaïre*. Berlin.

————. 1988. "From Equal to Better: Investing the Chief among the Northern Yaka of Zaïre." *Africa* 58:261–89.

Dewey, William. 1990. *Weapons for the Ancestors*. Video. University of Iowa.

d'Hertefelt, M. 1962. *Le Rwanda*. In *Les anciens royaumes de la zone interlacustre méridionale*, edited by M. d'Hertefelt, A. A. Trouwborst, and J. Scherer. Tervuren.

d'Hertefelt, M., and A. Coupez. 1964. *La Royauté sacrée de l'ancien Rwanda*. Tervuren.

Dieterlen, Germaine. 1951. *Essai sur la religion bambara*. Paris.

————. 1956. "Parenté et mariage chez les Dogon." *Africa* 26:107–48.

————. 1965–66. "Contribution à l'étude des forgerons en Afrique occidentale." *Annuaire*, Ecole Pratique des Hautes Etudes (Paris) 73:5–28. English translation in *French Perspectives in African Studies,* edited by Paul Alexandre. London, 1973.

————. 1973. "L'image du corps et les composantes de la personne chez les Dogon." *La Notion de la Personne en Afrique Noire*. Colloques Internationaux du C.N.R.S. no. 544. Paris.

Digombe, Lazare et al. 1988. "The Development of an Early Iron Age Prehistory in Gabon." *CA* 29:179–84.

di Leonardo, Micaela, ed. 1991. *Gender at the Crossroads of Knowledge: Feminist Anthropology in the Postmodern Era*. Berkeley.

Dinesen, Isak [Karen Blixen]. [1937]1985. *Out of Africa*. New York.

Dingle, M. E., et al. 1974. "An Attempt to Smelt Iron in a Buisport Type of Furnace." *JSAIMM* 74:268–69.

Dittmer, Karl. 1962. "Schmieden von Eisen." *Encycl. Cin.* Film E 191/1959. Göttingen.

————. 1962. "Senufo-Westafrika (Obervolta), Verhüttung von Raseneisenstein." *Encycl. Cin.* Film E 197/1959. Göttingen.

Dixey, Frank. 1920. "Primitive Iron-Ore Smelting Methods in West Africa." *Mining Mag.* 23:213–16.

Doke, C. M. 1931. *The Lambas of Northern Rhodesia*. London.

Douglas, Mary. 1954. "The Lele of Kasai." In *African Worlds*, edited by Daryl Forde. Oxford.

————. 1957. "Animals in Lele Religious Thought." *Africa* 27:46–57.

————. 1963. *The Lele of Kasai*. London.

————. 1966. *Purity and Danger*. London.

————. 1970. *Natural Symbols: Explorations in Cosmology*. New York.

Doumbia, P. E. N. 1936. "Etude du clan des forgerons." *Bull. Com. Et. AOF* 19:334–60.

Drewal, Henry John. 1977. *Traditional Art of the Nigerian People*. Washington, D.C.

————. 1989a. "The Meaning of Osugbo Art: A Reappraisal." In *Man Does Not Go Naked*, edited by Beate Engelbrecht and Bernard Gardi. Basel.

————. 1989b. "Art or Accident: Yoruba Body Artists and Their Deity Ogun." In *Africa's Ogun*, edited by Sandra Barnes. Bloomington, Ind.

Drewal, Henry John, and John Pemberton III, with Rowland Abiodun. 1989. *Yoruba: Nine Centuries of African Art and Thought*. New York.

Drewal, Margaret Thompson. 1986. "Art and Trance among Yoruba Shango Devotees." *African Arts* 20(1):60–67.

————. 1989. "Dancing for Ogun in Yorubaland and in Brazil." In *Africa's Ogun*, edited by S. Barnes. Bloomington, Ind.

Drost, Dietrich. 1964. "Besondere Verhaltensweisen in Verbindung mit dem Töpferhandwerk in Afrika." In vol. 1 of *Festschrift f. A. E. Jensen*, edited by Eike Haberland et al. Munich.

Du Chaillu, Paul. 1861. *Explorations and Adventures in Equatorial Africa*. New York.

Dugast, Stéphane. 1986. "Le pince et le soufflet: deux techniques de forge traditionnelles au Nord-Togo." Paris: ORSTOM.

Dumett, Raymond I. 1987. "Precolonial Gold Mining in Wassa: Innovation, Specialization, Linkages to the Economy and to the State." In *The Golden Stool: Studies of the Asante Center and Periphery*, edited by Enid Schildkrout. New York.

Duncan, John. 1847. *Travels in Western Africa in 1845 and 1846*. London.

Dupire, Marguerite. 1960. "Situation de la femme dans une société pastorale." In *Femmes d'Afrique noire*, edited by Denise Paulme. Paris.

Dupré, Marie-Claude. 1978. "Comment être femme: Un aspect du rituel mukisi chez les Téké de la République populaire du Congo." *Archives des Sciences Sociales des Religions* 46:57–84.

————. 1981–82. "Pour une histoire des productions: La métallurgie du fer chez les Téké-Ngungulu, Tio, Tsaayi (République populaire du Congo)." *Cah. ORSTOM* 18:195–223.

Dupuis, Annie, and Nicole Echard. 1971. "La poterie traditionnelle Hausa de l'Ader (Rép. du Niger)." *JSA* 41:7–34.

Dupuis Yakouba, A. 1911. *Les Gow, chasseurs du Niger*. Paris.

Durand, O. 1932. "Les industries locales au Fouta." *Bull. Com. Et. AOF* 15:42–71.

Dusseljé, Elso. 1910. *Les Tégués de l'Alima, Congo français*. Anvers.

Dybowski, J. 1893. *La Route du Tchad: du Loango au Chari*. Paris.

Earthy, A. Dona. 1934. "A Short Note on a Kisi Smith." *Man* 34:180.

East, Robert, ed. 1939. *Akiga's Story: The Tiv as Seen by One of Its Members*. Oxford.

Ebin, Victoria. 1982. "Interpretations of Infertility: The Aowin People of South-West Ghana." In *Ethnography of Fertility and Birth*, edited by Carol P. MacCormack. New York.

————. 1989. "Transfers of Power: The King and the Secret Society in a Time of Crisis." In *Creativity of Power*, edited by William Arens and Ivan Karp. Washington, D.C.

Echard, Nicole. 1965. "Note sur les forgerons de l'Ader (pays Hausa, République du Niger)." *JSA* 35:353–72.

————. 1968. *Noces de Feu*. 16 mm film. Paris: Centre de Recherche Scientifique.

————. 1983. "Scories et symboles: Remarques sur la métallurgie hausa du fer au Niger." In *Métallurgies Africaines*, edited by N. Echard. Paris.

————. 1986. "Histoire du peuplement et histoire des techniques: l'exemple de la métallurgie hausa du fer au Niger." *JA* 56:21–34.

————. Forthcoming. "A propos de la métallurgie: Système technique, organisation sociale et histoire." *Et. Nigériennes* 52:1–38.

Eckert, Hans Ekkehard. 1974. "Les fondeurs de Koni." *Géographie. Ann. de l'Université d'Abidjan.* Sér. G. VI:169–89.

————. 1976. "Urtümliche Eisengewinnung bei den Senufo in Westafrika." *Der Anschnitt* 28:50–63.

Eggert, Manfred K. H. 1980. "Der Keramikfund von Bondongo-Lesombo (Région de l'Equateur, Zaïre) und die Archäologie des äquatorialen Regenwaldes." In *Allgemeine u. vergleichende Archäologie*, Beiträge 2. Munich.

————. 1984. "The Current State of Archaeological Research in the Equatorial Rainforest of Zaïre." *NA* 24/25:39–42.

————. 1987. "On the Alleged Complexity of Early and Recent Iron Smelting in Africa: Further Comments on the Preheating Hypothesis. *J. Field Arch.* 14:377–82.

Ekechukwu, L. C. 1989. "A New Furnace Type from the North of Igboland." *NA* 32:20–21.

Eliade, Mircea. [1956]1962. *The Forge and the Crucible*, translated by S. Corrin. Chicago.

Ellis, A. B. 1894. *The Yoruba-speaking Peoples of the Slave Coast of West Africa.* London.

Elshout, Pierre. 1963. *Les Batwa des Ekonda.* Tervuren.

Engelbrecht, Beate, and Bernhard Gardi, eds. 1989. *Man Does Not Go Naked: Textilien und Handwerk aus afrikanischen und anderen Ländern.* Basel.

Eno Belinga, S. M. 1986. "Civilisation du fer und tradition orale bantu." *Muntu* 4/5:11–46.

Essomba, Joseph-Marie. 1985. "Archéologie et histoire au sud du Caméroun: Découverte de hauts fourneaux en pays bassa." *NA* 26:2–4.

————. 1986. "Le fer dans le développement des sociétés traditionnelles du sud Caméroun." *WAJA* 16:1–24.

Estermann, Carlos. 1936. "Les forgerons kwanyama." *Bull. Soc. Neuchâtel Géog.* 44:109–16.

————. 1976. *Ethnography of Southwestern Angola*, edited by G. D. Gibson, vol. 1, pt. 2. New York.

Estermann, Carlos, and Elmano da Cunha e Costa. 1941. *Negros.* Lisbon.

Etienne, Mona. 1980. "Women, Cloth and Colonization." In *Women and Colonization*, edited by Mona Etienne and Eleanor Leacock. New York.

Etienne-Nugue, Jocelyne. 1982. *Artisanats traditionnelles en Afrique Noire: Haute-Volta.* Dakar.

Evans-Pritchard, Edward Evans. 1962. "Heredity and Gestation as the Azande See Them." In *Social Anthropology and Other Essays.* New York.

————. 1967. "Zande Iron-working." *Paideuma* 13:26–31.

Ezra, Kate. 1988. *Art of the Dogon: Selections from the Lester Wunderman Collection.* New York.

————. 1992. *Royal Art of Benin: The Perls Collection in the Metropolitan Museum of Art.* New York.

Fadipe, N. A. [1939]1970. *The Sociology of the Yoruba.* Ibadan.

Fagan, Brian. 1952. "Iron Working with a Stone Hammer among the Tula of Northern Nigeria." *Man* 52:76.

————. 1961. "Pre-European Iron Working in Central Africa with Special Reference to Northern Rhodesia." *JAH* 2:199–210.

————. 1962. "Two Soli Smelting Furnaces from Lusaka, Northern Rhodesia." *SAAB* 17:27–28.

———. 1971. "Kaonde Metalworking." Lecture, Yale University.

Fagg, Bernard. 1984. "Die Terrakotten der Nok-Kultur." In *Afrikanische Keramik*, edited by A. Stössel. Munich.

Fagg, William, and John Picton. 1978. *The Potter's Art in Africa*. London.

Feierman, Steven. 1974. *The Shambaa Kingdom: A History*. Madison, Wis.

———. 1990. *Peasant Intellectuals: Anthropology and History in Tanzania*. Madison, Wis.

Le Fer à travers les âges. 1955. Actes du Colloque International, Nancy, October 3–6. *Annales de l'Est*, Mémoire no. 16, Nancy.

Fernandez, James W. 1982. *Bwiti: An Ethnography of the Religious Imagination in Africa*. Princeton.

———. 1991. "Embodiment and Disembodiment in Bwiti." In *Body and Space*, edited by A. Jacobson-Widding. Stockholm.

Figueiredo Lima, M. Helena. 1977. *Naçao Ovambo*. Lisbon.

Finnegan, Ruth. 1965. *Survey of the Limba People of Northern Sierra Leone*. London.

Forbes, Robert H. 1933. "The Black Man's Industries." *Geog. Rev.* 23:230–47.

———. 1950. *Metallurgy in Antiquity*. Leyden.

Fortes, Meyer. 1962. "Ritual and Office in Tribal Society." In *Essays on the Ritual of Social Relations*, edited by Max Gluckman. Manchester.

Fortier, Joseph. 1982. *Le couteau de jet sacré: Histoire des Sar et leurs rois au sud du Tchad*. Paris.

Fowler, Ian. 1989. "The Oku Iron Industry in Its Regional Setting: A Descriptive Account." Unpublished paper.

———. 1990. "Babungo: A Study of Iron Production, Trade and Power in a Nineteenth-century Ndop Plain Chiefdom (Cameroons)." Ph.D. diss., University of London.

———. 1992 "Sorcery, Secrets, Gender, and Technology." Unpublished paper.

Foy, W. 1890. "Zur Geschichte der Eisentechnik." *Ethnologica* (Leipzig) 1:185–200.

Francis-Boeuf, Claude. 1937. "L'industrie autochtone du fer en A.O.F." *Bull. Com. Et. AOF* 20:403–464.

Franklin, H. 1945. "The Native Iron Workers of Enkeldoorn District and Their Art." *NADA* 22:5–10.

Fraternité Matin (Côte d'Ivoire). 1985. "S.O.S. pour les hauts fourneaux de Koni." July 15.

Freyer, Bryna. 1987. *Royal Art of Benin*. Washington, D.C.

Friede, H. M. 1986. *The Metallurgical Past of South Africa: Distribution, Typology and Characteristics of Traditional Iron Smelting Furnaces*. Occasional Papers 15, University of the Witwatersrand, Archaeological Research Unity. Johannesburg.

Frobenius, Leo. 1909. "Bericht über den Verlauf der Reise von Bamako über Timbuktu nach Togo von April bis Dezember 1908." *Zeitschr. f. Erdkunde zu Berlin*, 122–126.

———. 1910. *The Childhood of Man*. London.

———. 1913. *Und Afrika Sprach*. Vol. 3, *Unter den unsträflichen Aethiopen*. Berlin.

———. 1931. *Erythräa: Länder und Zeiten des heiligen Königsmordes*. Berlin.

Froelich, J.-C. 1954. *Le Tribu Konkomba du Nord-Togo*. Mémoires de l'IFAN 37. Dakar.

Froelich, J.-C., and Paul Alexandre. 1960. "Histoire traditionnelle des Kotokoli et des Bi-Tchambi du Nord-Togo." *BIFAN* 22:211–75.

Fuchs, B. n.d. "Bäle (Bideyat) (Ostsahara, Ennedi): Bau eines Rennofens und Verhüttung von Eisenerz." *Encycl. Cin.* Film E 1212. Göttingen.

Fu-Kiau, A. 1969. *Le Mukongo et le monde qui l'entourait*. Kinshasa.

Fyle, C. Magbaily. 1979. *The Solima Yalunka Kingdom: Precolonial Politics, Economics and Society*. Freetown.

Galloway, Alexander. 1934. "A Note on the Iron-smelting Methods of the Elgeyo Masai." *SA J. Sci.* 31:500–504.

Gardi, René. 1953. "Eisengewinnung bei den Matakam." Institut für den Wissenschaftlichen Film. Göttingen.

———. 1954. *Der schwarze Hephaestus*. Bern.

———. 1969. *African Crafts and Craftsmen*. New York.

Garrard, Timothy F. 1978. "Blacksmithing in Wusuta, Volta Region." Fieldnotes.

Gauthier, J. 1969. *Les Fali de Ngoutchoumi Hou et Tsalo, Montagnards du Nord-Cameroun*. Oosterhout.

Gebauer, Paul. 1950. *Cameroon Brass Casting*. Video.

———. 1979. *Art of Cameroon*. Portland, Ore.

Gehrts, Meg. 1915. *A Camera Actress in the Wilds of Togoland*. Philadelphia.

Gelfand, Michael. [1956]1970. *Medicine and Magic of the Mashona*. Ann Arbor, Mich.

Gennep, Arnold van. 1909. *Rites de Passage*. Paris.

Gentil, P. 1963. "Le forgeron Mossi." *Archives inédites de l'IFAN*. Dakar.

Gibbons, A. St. H. 1897. "A Journey into the Marotse and Masikolumbwe Countries." *Geog. J.* 9:121–45.

Glaze, Anita J. 1981. *Art and Death in a Senufo Village*. Bloomington, Ind.

———. 1986. "Dialectics of Gender in Senufo Masquerades." *African Arts* 19(3):30–39.

Gluckman, Max, ed. 1962. *Essays on the Ritual of Social Relations*. Manchester.

———. 1963. *Order and Rebellion in Tribal Africa*. New York.

———. 1965. *Politics, Law and Ritual in Tribal Society*. Chicago.

Gollnhofer, Otto, and Roger Sillans. 1978. "Le symbolisme chez les Mitsogho: Aspects de l'anthropomorphisme dans la société initiatique du Bwete." In *Systèmes de Signes: Textes Réunis en Hommage à Germaine Dieterlen*. Paris.

Goodall, E. 1946. "Rhodesian Pots with Moulded Decoration." *NADA* 23:37–49.

Goody, Jack. 1967. *The Social Organisation of the LoWiili*. Oxford.

———. 1971. *Technology, Tradition and the State in Africa*. London.

Gosselain, Olivier P. 1992. "Bonfire of the Enquiries: Pottery Firing Temperatures in Archaeology: What For?" *J. Arch. Sci.* 19:243–60.

Gottlieb, Alma. 1982. "Sex, Fertility and Menstruation among the Beng of the Ivory Coast: A Symbolic Analysis." *Africa* 52:34–47.

———. 1988. "Menstrual Cosmology among the Beng of Ivory Coast." In *Blood Magic: The Anthropology of Menstruation*, edited by Thomas Buckley and Alma Gottlieb. Berkeley.

Goucher, Candice. 1984. "The Iron Industry of Bassar, Togo." Ph.D. diss., UCLA.

Gouletquer, Pierre. 1983. "Territoires et technique: le sel et le fer." In *Métallurgies Africaines*, edited by Nicole Echard. Paris.

Graham, C. 1968. "Some Sketches of Katsina from the Past." *Nigerian Field* 33(2):88–90.

Gray, Richard, and David Birmingham, eds. 1970. *Pre-Colonial African Trade: Essays on Trade in Central and Eastern Africa before 1900*. London.

Grébenart, Danilo. 1988. *Les Premiers métallurgistes en Afrique occidentale*. Paris.

Greenberg, Joseph. [1946]1966. *The Influence of Islam on a Sudanese Religion*. Seattle.

Gregory, James R. 1984. "The Myth of the Male Ethnographer and the Women's World." *Amer. Anth.* 86:316–27.

Griaule, Marcel. 1955. "The Problem of Negro Culture." In *Interrelations of Cultures*. UNESCO. Winterthur.

———. 1966. *Dieu d'Eau: Entretiens avec Ogotemmêli*. Paris.

Griaule, Marcel, and Germaine Dieterlen. 1965. *Le Renard Pâle*. Paris.

Grieg, Robert. 1937. "Iron Smelting in Fipa." *TNR* 4:77–81.

Grunderbeck, M. C van, E. Rodie, and H. Doultrelepont. 1983. *La Métallurgie an-*

cienne au Rwanda et au Burundi. Institut de Recherche Scientifique, Publ. 23. Butare.

Guillemin, R. P. 1910. "Die Eisenindustrie der Eingeborenen Kameruns." *Koloniale Rundschau* 1:15–25.

Guillou, Adm. 1950. "L'industrie du fer dans la subdivision de Babimbi." *Et. Cam.* 31/32:207–209.

Gutersohn, A. T. 1920. "Het Ekonomisch Leven van den Mongo-Neger." *Congo* 1:92–105.

Guyer, Jane. 1981. "The Raw, the Cooked and the Half-baked." Boston University, African Studies Center Working Papers.

———. 1984. Research report.

———. 1985. "The Iron Currencies of Southern Cameroon." *Symbols* (Harvard) 2–5:15–16.

———. 1986. "Indigenous Currencies and the History of Marriage Payments: A Case Study from Cameroon." *CEA* 26:577–610.

———. 1988. *Family and Farm in Southern Cameroon.* Boston.

———. 1991. "Female Farming in Anthropology and African History." In *Gender at the Crossroads of Knowledge: Feminist Anthropology in the Postmodern Era*, edited by Micaela di Leonardo. Berkeley.

Haaland, Randi. 1985. "Iron Production, its Socio-Cultural Context and Ecological Implications." In *African Iron Working, Ancient and Traditional*, edited by Randi Haaland and Peter Shinnie. Oslo.

Haaland, Randi, and Peter Shinnie, eds. 1985. *African Iron Working: Ancient and Traditional.* Oxford.

Haberland, Eike. 1962. "Zum Probleme der Jäger und besonderen Kasten in Nordost- und Ost-Afrika." *Paideuma* 7:136–55.

———. 1964a. "Dime. Nordost-Afrika (Süd-Äthiopien): Eisengewinnung." *Encycl. Cin.* E/388/1961. Göttingen.

———. 1964b. "König und Pariah in Afrika." In vol. 1 of *Festschrift für A. E. Jensen*, edited by Eike Haberland et al. Munich.

Hahn, Hans P. 1991a. "Die materielle Kultur der Bassar." Arbeiten aus dem Seminar für Völkerkunde der Johann Wolfgang Goethe, Universität Frankfurt am Main. Bd.24.

———. 1991b. "Eisentechnik in Nord-Togo: Verhüttung und Schmiederei bei den Bassar (Bandjeli), Kabye und Nawdba." Unpub. ms.

Hall, Martin. 1987. *Farmers, Kings, and Traders: The People of Southern Africa, 200–1860.* Chicago.

Hambly, W. B. 1934. "Occupational Ritual in the Ovimbundu." *Amer. Anth.* 36:157–67.

Hammond, Peter B. 1966. *Yatenga: Technology and Culture in a West African Kingdom.* New York.

Hardin, Kris. 1988. "Patterning Change: An Exploration of Technological Style in Weaving and Ceramics." Paper presented to the Conference on African Material Culture, Bellagio, Italy, May 19–28.

Harms, Robert W. 1981. *River of Wealth, River of Sorrow.* New Haven, Conn.

Hartwig, Gerald W. 1971. "Oral Traditions concerning the Early Iron Age in North-western Tanzania." *Afr. Hist. Stud.* 4:93–114.

Hatton, J. S. 1967. "Notes on Makalanga Iron Smelting." *NADA* 9(4):39–43.

Hauenstein, Alfred. 1988. *Examen de motifs décoratifs chez les Ovimbundu et Tchokwe d'Angola.* Coimbra, Portugal.

Herbert, Eugenia W. 1984a. *Red Gold of Africa: Copper in Precolonial History and Culture.* Madison, Wis.

———. 1984b. *Red Gold: Copper Arts of Africa.* South Hadley, Mass. (exhibition catalog).

————. 1986. "The Blooms of Banjeli." *Mount Holyoke Alumnae Quarterly* 69(4):27–28.

————. 1988. "Paradigms of Procreation: Gender and Technology in African Iron Working." Paper presented to the Conference on African Material Culture, Bellagio, Italy, May 19–28.

————. 1990a. *Foundry in the Forest: Iron Smelting at Lopanzo, Zaïre.* Video.

————. 1990b. "Lost-Wax Casting in the Cameroon Grassfields." In *West African Economic and Social History: Studies in Memory of Marion Johnson,* edited by David Henige and T. C. McCaskie. Madison, Wis.

Herbert, Eugenia W., and Candice Goucher. 1987. Resource guide for "The Blooms of Banjeli: Technology and Gender in West African Ironmaking." Amherst, Mass.

Herbert, Eugenia W., and Kanimba Misago. 1990. "Preliminary Report on Research into Traditional Ironworking at Lopanzo, Equateur Province [Zaïre]." *NA* 33:28–29.

Herbert, Eugenia W., and Len Pole. 1989. "African Iron Working on Film and Video." *NA* 31:47–49.

Hilton, Anne. 1985. *The Kingdom of Kongo.* Oxford.

Hinderling, Paul. 1954. *Negerschmiede: Metalltechnik exotischer Völker.* Basel.

————. 1955. "Schmelzöfen und Eisenverarbeitung in Nordkamerun." *Stahl und Eisen* 75:1263–66.

Historical Metallurgy Society of Great Britain. 1985. *Newsletter* 4:1.

Hocart, Arthur Maurice. 1927. *Kingship.* London.

————. 1929. "Coronation and Marriage." *Man* 29:79.

Hodgson, A. G. O. 1933. "Notes on the Achewa and Angoni of the Dowa District of the Nyasaland Protectorate." *J. Roy. Anth. Inst.* 63:123–64.

Holl, Augustin. 1983. "La question de l'âge du fer ancien de l'Afrique occidentale: essai de méthode." Paper presented to the Colloque sur l'Histoire de la Métallurgie du Fer. C.R.A., Paris, March 21–27.

————. 1987. "Le projet archéologique de Houlouf (Nord Cameroun): Campagne de fouilles 1987." *NA* 29:10–13.

Hollis, A. C. 1905. *The Masai, Their Language and Folklore.* Oxford.

Hombert, J.-M. 1981. "Iron Technology in the Cameroon Grassfields." Paper given to the symposium, African Technological Visions, UCLA, May 29–30.

Horton, Robin. 1964. "Ritual Man in Africa." *Africa* 34:85–104.

Housden, John, and Murray Armor. 1959. "Indigenous Iron Smelting at Kalabo." *No. Rhod. J.* 4:135–38.

Huffmann, Thomas N. 1981. "Snakes and Birds: Expressive Space at Great Zimbabwe." *African Studies* 40:131–50.

————. 1989. "Ceramics, Settlements and Late Iron Age Migrations." *Afr. Arch. Rev.* 7:155–82.

Hulstaert, Gustave. 1966. *Notes de botanique mongo.* Brussels.

Hultin, Jan. 1991. "The Conquest of Land and the Conquest of Fertility: A Theme in Oromo Culture." In *The Creative Communion,* edited by Anita Jacobson-Widding and Walter van Beek. Uppsala Studies in Cultural Anthropology 15. Stockholm.

Hunt, Eva. 1977. *Transformation of the Hummingbird.* Ithaca, New York.

Hupfeld. Fr. von. 1899. "Die Eisenindustrie in Togo." *Mitteilungen für Forschungsreisenden u. Gelehrten aus den deutschen Schutzgebieten* 12:175–94.

Imperato, Pascal James. 1970. "The Dance of the Tyi Wara." *African Arts* 4(1):8–13, 71–80.

Inga, Bubu. 1920. "A Native Kiln." *Sierra Leone Studies,* o.s. 16.

Iroko, A.F. 1989. "Les Vestiges d'une ancienne industrie de métallurgie dans la région de Dahomey." *WAJA* 19:1–20, 163.

Izard, Michel. 1985a. *Gens du pouvoir, gens de la terre: Les institutions politiques de l'ancien royaume du Yatenga (Bassin de la Volta blanche)*. Paris.

――――. 1985b. "Le sexe des ancêtres." *JA* 55:85–92.

Jackson, Michael. 1977. *The Kuranko: Dimensions of Social Reality in a West African Society*. London.

――――. 1982. *Allegories of the Wilderness*. Bloomington, Ind.

――――. 1983. "Knowledge of the Body." *Man* n.s. 18:327–45.

Jacobson-Widding, Anita, ed. 1991a. *Body and Space: Symbolic Models of Unity and Division in African Cosmology and Experience*. Stockholm Studies in Cultural Anthropology 16. Stockholm.

――――. 1991b. "The Fertility of Incest." In *The Creative Communion*, edited by A. Jacobson-Widding and Walter van Beek. Uppsala Studies in Cultural Anthropology 15. Stockholm.

Jacobson-Widding, Anita, and Walter van Beek, eds. 1991. *The Creative Communion: African Folk Models of Fertility and the Regeneration of Life*. Uppsala Studies in Cultural Anthropology 15. Stockholm.

Jaggar, Phil. 1973a. "A Kano Blacksmith's Vocabulary." *Kano Studies* 1:99–110.

――――. 1973b. "Kano City Blacksmiths: Precolonial Distribution, Structure and Organization." *Savanna* 2:11–26.

Jaspert, F., and W. Jaspert. 1930. *Die Volkstämme Mittel-Angolas*. Frankfurt.

Jedrej, M. C. 1974. "An Analytical Note on the Land and Spirits of the Sewa Mende." *Africa* 44:38–45.

Jeffreys, M. D. W. 1948. "Stone-age Smiths (Fungom Tribe, Bamenda, Cameroons)." *Arch. f. Völkerkunde* (Wien) 3:1–23.

――――. 1952. "Some Notes on the Bikom Blacksmiths." *Man* 52:49–51.

――――. 1961. "Oku Blacksmiths." *Nigerian Field* 26:137–44.

――――. 1962. "Some Notes on the Kwaja Smiths of Bamenda." *Man* 62:152.

――――. 1971. "Some Notes on the Iron Workers of Bamenda." *Nigerian Field* 36:71–74.

Jemkur, J. F. 1989. "Traditional Iron-Smelting Methods by the Berom of Plateau State, Nigeria." *NA* 32:21–24.

Jensen, A. E., ed. 1959. *Altvölker Süd-Äthiopiens*. With contributions by E. Haberland, A. E. Jensen, Elisabeth Pauli, and W. Schulz-Weidner. Stuttgart.

Johnson, John W. 1986. *The Epic of Son-Jara: A West African Tradition*. Text by Fa-Digi Sisoko. Bloomington, Ind.

Johnson, Marion. 1984. "Two Pottery Traditions in Southern Ghana." In *Earthenware in Asia and Africa*, edited by John Picton. London.

Jonckers, Danielle. 1979. "Notes sur le forgeron, la forge et les métaux en pays minyanka." *JA* 49:103–24.

Jouaux, Catherine. 1989. "Gudur: Chefferie ou royaume?" *CEA* 114:259–88.

Juillerat, Bernard. 1973. "Musique et cycle agraire chez les Mouktélé." In *Les Kirdi du Nord-Cameroun*, edited by Y. Schaller. Strasbourg.

Junod, H. A. 1913. *The Life of a South African Tribe*. London.

――――. 1936. *Moeurs et Coutumes des Bantous*. 2 vols. Paris.

Kaberry, Phyllis M. [1969]1971. "Witchcraft of the Sun: Incest in Nso." In *Man in Africa*, edited by Mary Douglas and P. M. Kaberry. New York.

Kanimba, Misago. 1980. "La naissance des enfants dans la zone d'Ingende." *Anthropos* 75:465–85.

――――. 1988. "La céramique de la dépression de l'Upemba: Etude diachronique étayée des données ethnographiques." Paper presented to the Conference on African Material Culture, Bellagio, Italy, May 19–28.

――――. 1989. "Etat de la recherche sur l'âge des métaux au Zaïre." Africanistique zu Zaïre. *Annales Aequatoria* 7:81–107.

――――. 1991. "Métallurgie du fer à Lopanzo, juillet-août 1989." Unpublished paper.

Kantorowicz, E. H. 1957. *The King's Two Bodies: A Study of Medieval Political Theology.* Princeton.

Karp, Ivan. 1988. Comments. Conference on African Material Culture, Bellagio, Italy, May 19–28.

———. 1989. "Power and Capacity in the Rituals of Possession." In *Creativity of Power,* edited by William Arens and Ivan Karp. Washington, D.C.

Kay, G. and D. M. Wright. 1962. "Aspects of the Ushi Iron Industry." *No. Rhod. J.* 5:28–38.

Kazadi, Ntole. 1988. "Des objets et des hommes: Rapports et transformations dans la culture des Bambala (Zaïre)." Paper presented to the Conference on African Material Culture, Bellagio, Italy, May 19–28.

Kense, François J. 1983. *Traditional African Iron Working.* Dept. of Arch. African Occasional Papers I, University of Calgary. Calgary.

Kent, Susan, ed. 1989. *Farmers as Hunters.* Cambridge, Eng.

Kenyatta, Jomo. 1938. *Facing Mt. Kenya.* New York.

Kiethéga, J.-B. 1983. *L'Or de la Volta Noire: Exploitation traditionnelle: histoire et archéologie.* Paris.

———. 1986. "Le fer ancien au Burkina Faso: technique de production et chronologie." *Connaissances du Burkina* (Ougadougou), nov.–déc. 69–83.

Killick, David John. 1983. Fieldnotes.

———. 1987. "On the Dating of African Metallurgical Sites." *NA* 28:29–30.

———. 1988. "A Comparative Perspective on African Iron-Working Technologies." Paper presented to the African Studies Association. Chicago.

———. 1990. "Technology in Its Social Setting: The Ironworkers of Kasungu, Malawi, 1860–1940." Ph.D. diss., Yale University.

———. 1991a. "Iron Smelting in Natural-Draft Furnaces." *J. Minerals, Metals and Materials* 43(4):62–65.

———. 1991b. "The Relevance of Recent African Iron-Smelting Practice to Reconstructions of Prehistoric Smelting Technology." *Recent Trends in Archaeometallurgical Research,* edited by Peter Glumac. Philadelphia: MASCA Papers in Science and Archaeology 8:1.

Killick, David John, and Robert B. Gordon. 1990. "The Mechanism of Iron Production in the Bloomery Furnace." *Proceedings of the 26th International Symposium on Archaeometry,* edited by R. Farquhar, R. G. Hancock, and L. Pavlish. Toronto.

Kingsley, Mary. [1898]1987. *Travels in West Africa.* London.

Kirby, Jon P. 1986. *Gods, Shrines, and Problem-Solving among the Anufo of Northern Ghana.* Berlin.

Kirk-Greene, A. H. M. 1960. "The Kingdom of Sukur: A Northern Nigerian Ichabod." *Nigerian Field* 25(2):67–96.

Kita, Kyankenge Masondi. 1985. "La technique traditionnelle de la métallurgie du fer chez les Balega de Pangi (Zaïre)." *Muntu* 3:85–100.

Klose, Heinrich. 1899. *Togo unter deutscher Flagge.* Berlin.

———. 1903. "Das Bassarivolk." *Globus* 83(20):309–14.

Knight, Chris. 1991. *Blood Relations: Menstruation and the Origins of Culture.* New Haven, Conn.

Koch, H. 1968. *Magie et chasse au Cameroon.* Paris.

Korse, Piet. 1989. "Le fard rouge et le kaolin blanc chez les Mongo de Basankusu et de Befale (Zaïre)." *Annales Aequatoria* 10:9–39.

Koucky, F. L., and A. Steinberg. 1982. "Ancient Mining and Mineral Dressing on Cyprus." In *Early Pyrotechnology,* edited by T. Wertime and S. Wertime. Washington, D.C.

Krause, R. A. 1990. "Ceramic Practice and Semantic Space: An Ethnoarchaeological Inquiry into the Logic of Bantu Potting." *Antiquity* 64:711–26.

Kreamer, Christine Mullen. 1989. "The Social and Economic Implications of Moba Male and Female Pottery Traditions (Northern Togo)." Paper presented at the Eighth Triennial Symposium of African Art, Washington, D.C.

Krieger, Kurt. 1963. "Notizen zur Eisengewinnung der Hausa." *Zeitschr. f. Ethn.* 88:318–31.

Krige, E. J., and J. D. Krige. [1943]1956. *The Realm of a Rain Queen.* London.

Kuevi, Dovi. 1975. "Le travail et le commerce du fer au Togo avant l'arrivée des Européens." *Et. Tog.*, n.s. 11/12:22–43.

Kuntz, Marthe. 1935. "The Iron-Workers of the Kangwa Tribe." *Man* 35:186.

Kuper, Adam. 1980. "Symbolic Dimensions of the Southern Bantu Homestead." *Africa* 50:8–23.

Kuper, Hilda. 1961. *An African Aristocracy.* London.

Labouret, Henri. 1931. *Les Tribus du rameau Lobi.* Paris.

Laburthe-Tolra, Philippe. 1981. *Les Seigneurs de la foret: essai sur le passé historique, l'organisation sociale et les normes éthniques des anciens Beti du Caméroun.* Paris.

La Fontaine, Jean S. 1978. *Sex and Age as Principles of Social Differentiation.* New York.

———. 1985. *Initiation: Ritual Drama and Secret Knowledge across the World.* Harmondsworth, Middlesex, Eng.

Lafranchi, Raymond. 1991. *The Hands of the Potter: A Film on Pottery in Central Africa.* National Museum of African Art. Video.

Laing, Alexander Gordon. 1825. *Travels in the Timmannee, Kooranko and Soolima Countries in Western Africa.* London.

Lalouel, Médecin-Chef. 1947. "Les forgerons mondjombo." *Bull. Inst. Et. Centr.* 2(1):106–14.

Lanning, E. C. 1954. "Genital symbols on smiths' bellows in Uganda." *Man* 54:167–69.

Larrick, Roy. 1986. "Iron Smelting and Interethnic Conflict among Precolonial Maaspeaking Pastoralists of North-Central Kenya." *Afr. Arch. Rev.* 4:165–76.

Last, J. T. 1883. "A Visit to the Wa-Itumba Iron Workers and the Mangaheri, near Mombia, in East Central Africa." *Proc. Roy. Geog. Soc.* 5:581–92.

La Violette, Adria J. 1987. "An Archaeological Ethnography of Blacksmiths, Potters, and Masons in Jenne, Mali (West Africa)." Ph.D. diss., Washington University.

Laye, Camara. 1953. *L'Enfant noir.* Paris.

Leacock, Eleanor. 1972. Introduction to Frederick Engels, *The Origin of the Family: Private Property and the State.* New York.

Lebeuf, Annie M. D. 1960. "Le rôle de la femme dans l'organisation politique des sociétés africaines." In *Femmes d'Afrique noire,* edited by Denise Paulme. Paris.

Lechaptois, A. 1913. *Aux Rives du Tanganyika.* Algiers.

Lechtman, Heather. 1984. "Andean Value Systems and the Development of Prehistoric Metallurgy." *Technology and Culture* 25:1–36.

Leith-Ross, Sylvia. 1970. *Nigerian Pottery.* Ibadan.

Lestrade, A. 1972. *Notes d'ethnographie du Rwanda.* Archives d'Anthropologie. Tervuren.

Lévi-Straus, Claude. 1966. *The Savage Mind.* Chicago.

———. 1970. *The Raw and the Cooked.* London.

Levtzion, Nehemia. 1973. *Ancient Ghana and Mali.* London.

Lienhardt, R. G. 1961. *Divinity and Experience: The Religion of the Dinka.* Oxford.

Livingstone, David. 1874. *Last Journals.* 2 vols. London.

———. 1961. *Missionary Correspondence* [1841–56], edited by I. Schapera. London.

Lloyd, Peter. 1953. "Craft Organization in Yoruba Towns." *Africa* 23:30–44.

Locko, Michel. 1987. "Les sources archéologiques du fer au Gabon." *NA* 29:23–26.

Lombard, Jean 1957. "Aperçu sur la technologie et l'artisanat Bariba." *Et. Dah.* 18:7–60.

McCaskie, Thomas C. 1992. "People and Animals: Constru(ct)ing the Asante Experience." *Africa* 62:221–47.

MacCormack, Carol P. 1982. "Health, Fertility and Birth in Moyamba District, Sierra Leone." In *Ethnography of Fertility and Birth,* edited by Carol P. Mac-Cormack. New York.

MacCormack, Carol P., and Marilyn Strathern, eds. 1980. *Nature, Culture and Gender.* New York.

McCosh, F. 1979. "Traditional Iron-working in Central Africa with Some References to Ritualistic and Scientific Aspects of the Industry." *Zambezia* 7:155–70.

McCulloch, M. 1957. *The Southern Lunda and Related Peoples.* London.

MacGaffey, Janet. 1975. "Two Kongo Potters." *African Arts* 9(1):28–31.

MacGaffey, Wyatt. 1986. *Religion and Society in Central Africa: The Bakongo of Lower Zaïre.* Chicago.

McIntosh, Roderick J. 1989. "Middle Niger Terracottas before the Symplegades Gateway." *African Arts* 22(2):74–83.

McIntosh, Roderick J., and Susan K. McIntosh. 1988. "From *Siècles obscurs* to Revolutionary Centuries on the Middle Niger." *World Arch.* 20:141–65.

McIntosh, Susan K., and Roderick J. McIntosh. 1988. "From Stone to Metal: New Perspectives on the Later Prehistory of West Africa." *J. World Prehist.* 2:89–133.

McIntosh, Susan K, Roderick J. McIntosh, and Hamady Bocoum. 1992. "The Emergence of Regional Politics in the Middle Senegal Valley." Paper presented to the Society of Africanist Archaeologists, UCLA.

MacKenzie, J. M. 1975. "A Precolonial Industry: The Njanja and the Iron Trade." *NADA* 11:200–220.

McLeod, Malcolm. 1981. *The Asante.* London.

———. 1984. "Akan Terracottas." In *Earthenware in Asia and Africa,* edited by John Picton. London.

McNaughton, Patrick. 1975. *Iron Art of the Blacksmith in the Western Sudan.* West Lafayette, Ind. (exhibition catalog).

———. 1982. "Nyamakalaw: The Mande Bards and Blacksmiths." Unpublished paper.

———. 1988. *The Mande Blacksmith in the Western Sudan.* Bloomington, Ind.

Macrae, F. 1928. "Some Technical Notes on the Tribes of the Mumbwa District of Northern Rhodesia." *NADA* 6:56–67.

Maddin, Robert, ed. 1988. *The Beginning of the Use of Metals and Alloys.* Cambridge, Mass.

Maes, J. 1930. "La métallurgie chez les populations du Lac Léopold II, Lukenie." *Ethnologica* 4:68–101.

Mair, Lucy. 1951. "A Yao Girl's Initiation." *Man* 51:60–63.

Makarius, Laura. 1968. "The Blacksmith's Taboos: From the Man of Iron to the Man of Blood." *Diogenes* 62:25–48.

Malcolm, L. W. G. 1924. "Iron-working in the Central Kamerun. *Man* 24:136–38.

Maluma, E. 1976. "Prehistoric Smelting Furnaces in the Chengwe/Kanakantapa Drainage Area (Central Province of Zambia)." *Archaeologia Zambiana* 18:13–15.

Mandala, Elias. 1990. *Work and Control in a Peasant Economy: A History of the Lower Tchiri Valley in Malawi, 1859–1960.* Madison, Wis.

Mann, O. 1925. "Die Eisengewinnung in Togo und Kamerun." *Afrika Nachrichten* 3:150.

Maquet, Emma. 1965. "Outils de forge du Congo, du Rwanda et du Burundi." *Annales du MRAC,* no. 5. Tervuren.

Maquet, Jean. 1957. *Ruanda: Essai photographique sur une société en transition.* Brussels.

———. 1962. *Afrique: Les Civilisations noires*. Paris.

Margarido, A., and F. Germaix Wasserman. 1972. "Du mythe et de la pratique du forgeron en Afrique noire." *Diogenes* 78:91–122.

Marre, Jeremy, Enid Schildkrout, et al. 1990. *Spirits of Defiance: The Mangbetu of Zaïre*. BBC TV/American Museum of Natural History. Video.

Martin, J.-Y. 1970. *Les Matakam du Nord-Cameroun: dynamiques sociaux et problèmes de modernisation*. Paris.

Martinelli, Bruno. 1982. *Métallurgistes Bassari: Techniques et Formation sociale*. Lomé.

Martins, João Vincente. 1966. *A Idade dos métais na Lunda*. Lisbon.

Martius, A. 1921. "Schmied und Gesellschaft." In *Atlas Africanus*, edited by Leo Frobenius, 2:8.

Marwick, Michael G. 1965. *Sorcery in its Social Setting: A Study of the Northern Cewa*. Manchester, Eng.

Masson-Detourbet, Annie. 1953. "Croyances relatives à l'organisation politique du royaume Lagouané." *JSA* 23:3–34.

Mato, D. 1984. "Terrakotta-Figuren vom Niger und aus dem Niger-Binnendelta." In *Afrikanische Keramik*, edited by A. Stössel. Munich.

Mauny, Raymond. 1961. *Tableau géographique de l'ouest africain*. Dakar.

———. 1971. *Les Siècles obscurs de l'Afrique noire*. Paris.

Mauss, Marcel. [1936]1979. "Body Techniques." In *Sociology and Psychology: Essays by Marcel Mauss*, translated by B. Brewster. London.

Mbot, J. E. 1975. *Eghuhi bifa: Démonter les expressions*. Paris.

Meek, Charles Kingsley. 1925. *The Northern Tribes of Nigeria*. 2 vols. London.

———. [1931]1950a. *A Sudanese Kingdom*. New York.

———. [1931]1950b. *Tribal Studies in Northern Nigeria*. 2 vols. New York.

Meillassoux, Claude. 1980. "Le mâle en gésine, ou de l'historicité des mythes." *CEA* 73–76:353–80.

Melland, F. 1923. *In Witchbound Africa*. London.

Méniaud, J. 1912. *Haut Sénégal-Niger*. 2d series. n.p.

Mercier, Paul. 1968. *Tradition, changement, histoire: Les "Somba" du Dahomey septentrionale*. Paris.

Merlon, R. P. A. 1888. *Le Congo producteur*. Brussels.

Merriam, Alan P. 1974. *An African World: The Basongye Village of Lupupa Ngye*. Bloomington, Ind.

Mertens, Joseph. 1942. *Les Chefs couronnés des Bakongo orientaux*. Brussels.

Mesquitela Lima, A. G. 1971. *Fonctions sociologiques des figurines de culte hamba dans la société et dans la culture tschokué (Angola)*. Luanda.

———. 1977. "Le fer en Angola." *CEA* 66–67:345–351.

Methuen, H. H. 1846. *Life in the Wilderness*. London.

Mévil, A. [c. 1898]. "Les Malinkes—leurs superstitions et leur manière de chercher l'or." In *Au pays du soleil et de l'or*. Paris.

Meyer, Hans. 1910. *Das deutsche Kolonialreich: Ein Länderkunde der deutschen Schutzgebiete*. 2 vols. Leipzig.

Meyerowitz, Eva L. R. 1951. *The Sacred State of the Akan*. London.

Michel-Jones, Françoise. 1978. *Retour aux Dogon*. Paris.

Middleton, John. 1973. "Some Categories of Dual Classification among the Lugbara of Uganda." In *Right and Left: Essays on Dual Symbolic Classification*, edited by Rodney Needham. Chicago.

Miller, Joseph. 1976. *Kings and Kinsmen: Early Mbundu States in Angola*. Oxford.

Mockler-Ferryman, A. F. 1893. "Iron Smelting on the Lower Niger." *J. Iron and Steel Inst.* 44:2. Abstracted from *Up the Niger*, 1892:212–13.

Mohr, Richard. 1964. "Reisenotizen aus Bassari." *Paideuma* 10:39–51.

Moñino, Yves. 1983. "Accoucher du fer; La métallurgie gbaya (Centrafrique)." In *Métallurgies Africaines*, edited by Nicole Echard. Paris.

————. 1984. "Histoire d'houes: Instruments aratoires centrafricaines." *Cah.ORSTOM*, sér. sci. hum. 3/4:585–95.

Moore, Henrietta. 1986. *Space, Text and Gender. An Anthropological Study of the Marakwet of Kenya*. Cambridge, Eng.

————. 1988. *Feminism and Anthropology*. Minneapolis.

Moore, Sally F. 1976. "The Secret of the Men: A Fiction of Chagga Initiation and Its Relation to the Logic of Chagga Symbolism." *Africa* 46:357–70.

Moreau, R. E. 1941. "Suicide by 'Breaking the Cooking Pot.' " *TNR* 12:49–50.

Morgen, Curt von. [1893]1972. *A travers Cameroun du Sud au Nord*, edited and translated by Philippe Laburthe-Tolra. Yaoundé.

Morisseau, Jules. 1910. *Sur le lac Moero*. Brussels.

Mumbanza mwa Bawale na Nyabakombi Ensobato. 1980. "Les forgerons de la Ngiri, une élite artisanale parmi les pêcheurs." *Enquêtes et Documents d'Histoire Africaine* (Louvain) 4:114–32.

Musa, Njavara D. 1990. "Kings of Iron." *West Africa* 3778:88–89.

Musée de l'Homme. 1960. *La Vie du Sahara*. Exhibition catalog. Paris.

Nadel, S. F. 1942. *A Black Byzantium*. London.

National Museum of African Art. 1992. Purpose & [*sic*] Perfection. Pottery as a Woman's Art in Central Africa. (Exhibition)

Ndinga-Mbo, A. 1976. "Quelques reflexions sur la civilisation du cuivre au Congo." *Cah. Cong. Anth. & Hist.* 1:31–34.

Neaher, Nancy. 1976. "Bronzes of Southern Nigeria and Igbo Metalsmithing Traditions." Ph.D. diss., Stanford University.

————. 1979. "Awka Who Travel." *Africa* 49:352–66.

Needham, Rodney, ed. 1973. *Right and Left: Essays on Dual Classification*. Chicago.

Nevadomsky, Joseph. 1984a. "Kingship Succession Rituals in Benin. 2: The Big Things." *African Arts* 27(2):41–47.

————. 1984b. "Kingship Succession Rituals in Benin. 3: The Coronation of the Oba." *African Arts* 27(3):48–57.

Nevadomsky, Joseph, and Daniel E. Inneh. 1983. "Kingship Rituals in Benin. 1: Becoming a Crown Prince." *African Arts* 27(1):47–54.

Newbury, David S. 1981. "What Role Has Kingship?" *Africa-Tervuren* 27(4):89–101.

Niane, Djibril Tamsir. 1960. *Soundjata*. Paris.

Niangoran-Bouah, Georges. 1978. "Idéologie de l'or chez les Akan de Côte d'Ivoire et du Ghana." *JA* 48:127–40.

Nicholson, W. E. 1929. "The Potters of Sokoto, Northern Nigeria." *Man* 29:45–50.

————. 1931. *Man* 31:187–90. (Continuation)

————. 1934. "Bida (Nupe) Pottery." *Man* 34:71–73.

Nicklin, Keith. 1973. "The Ibibio Musical Pot." *African Arts* 7(1):50–55.

Nketia, J. H. Kwabena. 1990. "Dimensions esthétiques des instruments de musique africains." In *Formes sonores*, edited by M.-T. Brincard. Paris.

Nooter, Mary H. 1990. "Secret Signs in Luba Sculptural Narrative: A Discourse on Power." In *Art and Initiation in Zaïre*, edited by C. D. Roy. Iowa Studies in African Art III. Iowa City.

————. 1991. "Luba Art and Polity: Creating Power in a Central African Kingdom." Ph.D. diss., Columbia University.

Nzekwu, Onuora. 1959. "Awka—Town of Smiths." *Nigeria* 61:136–41.

Obenga, Théophile. 1974. *Afrique centrale précoloniale*. Paris.

————. 1976. *La Cuvette congolaise: Les Hommes et les structures*. Paris.

Obeyesekere, Gananath. 1990. *The Work of Culture: Symbolic Transformation in Psychoanalysis and Anthropology*. Chicago.

Odugbesan, Clara. [1969]1971. "Femininity in Yoruba Religious Art." In *Man in Africa*, edited by Mary Douglas and Phyllis Kaberry. New York.

Öhrneman, J. 1929. *Pa Filmfärd till Urskogsfolket*. Stockholm.

Okafor, E. E. 1989. "Eguru Amube Amalla Orba: Blacksmith Clan among the Orba." *NA* 32:24–27.

Okoro, J. Ako. 1990. "Blacksmithing Rituals and Traditions in Northeast Ghana." In *Ancient Myths and Images: The Archaeology of Ideology*, 5–12. Proceedings of the 23rd Annual Chacmool Conf., Calgary, 1990.

O'Neill, Peter, Frank Muhly, Jr., and Winnie Lambrecht. 1988. *The Tree of Iron.* 16 mm film, video.

ORSTOM 1969. *Gabon. Culture et Technique.* Libreville.

Ortner, Sherry, and Harriet Whitehead, eds. 1981. *Sexual Meanings: The Social Construction of Gender and Sexuality.* Cambridge, Eng.

Ottenberg, Simon. 1983. "Artists and Sex Roles in a Limba Chiefdom." In *Male and Female in West Africa*, edited by C. Oppong. London.

Packard, Randall M. 1980. "Social Change and the History of Misfortune among the Bashu of Eastern Zaïre." In *Explorations in African Systems of Thought*, edited by Ivan Karp and Charles S. Bird. Bloomington, Ind.

———. 1981. *Chiefship and Cosmology: An Historical Study of Political Competition.* Bloomington, Ind.

Palau Marti, Montserrat. 1964. *Le Roi-dieu au Bénin.* Paris.

Paques, Viviana. 1956. "Les 'Sanake.'" *BIFAN* 18:369–90.

———. 1967. "Origines et caractères du pouvoir royal au Baguirmi." *JSA* 37:183–214.

Pareles, Jon. 1987. "Music of the Yoruba in Two Concerts." *New York Times*, January 30.

Park, Mungo. 1799. *Travels in the Interior Districts of Africa.* London.

Patokideou, H. K. 1970. "Les Civilisations patriarcales des Kabré face aux programmes modernes de développement économique et social." Ph.D. diss., Lomé.

Paulme, Denise. 1940. *L'Organisation sociale des Dogon.* Paris.

———. 1954. *Les Gens du riz.* Paris.

———, ed. 1960. *Femmes d'Afrique noire.* Paris.

———. 1976. *La Mère dévorante.* Paris.

Pemberton, John. 1975. "Eshu-Elegba: The Yoruba Trickster God." *African Arts* 9(1):20–27.

———. 1986. "Festivals and Sacred Kingship among the Igbomina Yoruba." *National Geographic Research* 2:216–33.

———. 1988. "The King and the Chameleon: Odun Agemo." *Annals of the Institute of Cultural Studies* (Ife) 2:47–64.

———. 1989. "The Dreadful God and the Divine King." In *Africa's Ogun*, edited by S. Barnes. Bloomington, Ind.

Perrot, Claude-Hélène. 1982. *Les Anyi-Ndenye et le pouvoir aux XVIIIe et XIXe siècles.* Abidjan/Paris.

Pfaffenburger, Bryan. 1988. "Fetishised Objects and Humanised Nature: Towards an Anthropology of Technology." *Man* 23:236–52.

Philippe, R. 1954. "Le mariage chez les Ntomb'e Njale." *Aequatoria* 17:129–53.

Phillipson, David W. 1964. "Excavation of an Iron-Smelting Furnace in the Livingstone District of Northern Rhodesia." *Man* 64:178–80.

———. 1966. "Strydom's Farm Iron-Smelting Furnaces. *Man* n.s. 1:560.

———. 1968. "Cewa, Leya and Lala Iron-smelting Furnaces." *SAAB* 23:102–13.

Phimister, Ian R. 1974. "Alluvial Gold Mining and Trade in Nineteenth-Century South Central Africa." *JAH* 15:445–56.

Podlewski, A. 1966. *Les Forgerons Mafa.* Yaoundé.

Poe, Edgar Allan. 1976. "The Gold-Bug." In *The Short Fiction of Edgar Allan Poe*, edited by Stuart and Susan Levine. Indianapolis.

Pole, Len. 1974a. *Iron-smelting in Northern Ghana.* National Museum of Ghana: Occasional Papers no. 6. Accra.

———. 1974b. "Account of an Iron-smelting Operation at Lawra, Upper Region." *Ghana J. Science* 14:127–36.

———. 1975. "Iron-working Apparatus and Techniques: Upper Region of Ghana." *WAJA* 5:11–39.

———. 1982. "Decline or Survival? Iron Production in West Africa from the Seventeenth to the Twentieth Centuries." *JAH* 23:503–14.

———. 1983. "A Ruhr or Rural Industry? The Scale of Iron Production in West Africa." Paper presented to the MEG symposium on metalwork in Africa, Museum of Mankind, London.

Polfliet, Leo. 1985. *Bodies of Resonance: Musical Instruments of Zaïre.* Munich.

———. 1987a. *Anthropomorphische Gefässkeramik aus Zaïre/Anthropomorphic Terracotta Vessels of Zaïre.* Munich.

———. 1987b. *Traditionnelle Gefässkeramik aus Zaïre/Traditional Zaïrian Pottery.* Munich.

Posnansky, Merrick, and N. Grindrod. 1968. "Iron Smelting Furnaces at North Kinangop, Kenya." *Azania* 3:1–5.

Posselt, J. 1926. "Native Iron Workers." *NADA* 4:53.

Powell-Cotton, Diana, and Antoinette Powell-Cotton. 1937. *Mining and Smelting. Angola.* 16 mm film.

Prendergast, M. D. 1978. "Two Nineteenth-century Metallurgical Sites in the Wedza and Gwelo Districts, Rhodesia." *Rhod. Prehist.* 16:11–17.

Preston, George N. 1990. "People Making Portraits Making People: Living Icons of the Akan." *African Arts* 23(3):70–76.

Priddy, Barbara. 1974. *Pottery in Upper Region.* National Museum of Ghana. Occasional Papers no. 7. Accra.

Prins, Gwyn. 1980. *The Hidden Hippopotamus.* Cambridge, Eng.

Pruitt, William F., Jr. 1973. "An Independent People: A History of the SalaMpasu of Zaïre and their Neighbors." Ph.D. diss., Northwestern University.

Quarcoo, A. K., and Marion Johnson. 1968. "Shai Pots: The Pottery Tradition of the Shai People of Southern Ghana." *Baessler Archiv* 16:47–88.

Radimilahy, Chantal. 1985. Contribution à l'Etude de l'ancienne Métallurgie du Fer à Madagascar. Travaux et Documents XXV, Musée d'Art et d'Archéologie de l'Université de Madagascar. Tananarive.

Rattray, Robert S. 1916. "The Iron-Workers of Akpafu." *J. Roy. Anth. Inst.* n.s. 19:430–35.

———. 1923. *Ashanti.* Oxford.

———. 1927. *Religion and Art in Ashanti.* Oxford.

———. 1929. *Ashanti Law and Constitution.* Oxford.

———. 1932. *The Tribes of the Ashanti Hinterland.* 2 vols. Oxford.

Ravenhill, Philip. 1978. "The Interpretation of Symbolism in Wan Female Initiation." *Africa* 48:66–78.

Ray, Reid. 1958. *One Hoe for Kalabo.* National Machine Tool Manufacturers' Association. 16 mm film.

Read, F. W. 1902. "Iron-smelting and Native Blacksmithing in Ondulu Country, South-East Angola." *J. Roy. Anth. Soc.* 32:44–49.

Redinha, Jose. 1949. "Costumas religiosos e feiticistos dos Kiokos de Angola." *Mensario Administrativo* 20/21:27–43.

———. 1953. *Campanha Etnografica ao Tchiboco.* Lisbon.

Reefe, Thomas Q. 1977. "Traditions of Genesis and the Luba Diaspora." *HA* 4:183–206.

———. 1981. *The Rainbow and the Kings.* Berkeley.

Reindorf, C. C. 1895. *History of the Gold Coast and Asante.* Basel.

Renne, Elisha. 1990. "Wives, Chiefs and Weavers: Gender Relations in Bunu Yoruba Society." Ph.D. diss., New York University.

Reynolds, Barrie. 1963. *Magic, Divination and Witchcraft among the Barotse of Northern Rhodesia*. Berkeley.

Richards, Audrey. [1956]1982. *Chisungu: A Girls' Initiation Ceremony among the Bemba of Northern Rhodesia*. London.

Richter, Delores. 1980. "Further Considerations of Caste in West Africa." *Africa* 50:37–54.

Rickard, T. A. 1927. "Curious Methods Used by the Katanga Natives in Mining and Smelting Copper." *Engineering and Mining J.* 123:51–58.

Riesman, Paul. 1986. "The Person and the Life Cycle in African Social Life and Thought." *Afr. Stud. Rev.* 29:71–138.

Rigby, Peter. 1969. *Cattle and Kinship among the Gogo*. Ithaca.

Rivallain, Josette. 1985–86. "Céramiques: les problèmes de l'autochtonie." *Rencontres Archéologiques de Nantes*. Université de Nantes.

Roache-Selk, Evelyn. 1978. *From the Womb of the Earth: An Appreciation of Yoruba Bronze Art*. Washington, D.C.

Robert, J. M. 1949. *Croyances et coutumes magico-religieuses des Wafipa païens*. Tabora.

Roberts, Allen. 1986. "Duality in Tabwa Art." *African Arts* 19(4):26–35.

Roberts, Allen, and Evan Maurer, eds. 1986. *The Rising of a New Moon: A Century of Tabwa Art*. Seattle.

Robertshaw, Peter, ed. 1990. *A History of African Archaeology*. Portsmouth, N.H.

Robins, F. W. 1953. *The Smith*. London.

Robinson, K. R. 1961. "Two Iron-smelting Furnaces from the Chibi Native Reserve, Southern Rhodesia." *SAAB* 16:20–22.

Rogers, Peter. 1990. "The Social Dynamics of Local Iron-Working in Nineteenth-Century Hausaland." M.A. thesis, University of Wisconsin-Madison.

Roscoe, John. 1911. *The Baganda*. London.

———. 1923a. *The Bakitara or Banyoro*. Cambridge, Eng.

———. 1923b. *The Banyankole*. Cambridge, Eng.

———. 1924. *The Bagesu*. Cambridge, Eng.

Rouch, Jean. 1960. *La Religion et la magie Songhay*. Paris.

Roulon, Pauline. 1981. "Rites de fécondité chez les Gbaya-Kara." In *Itinérances en pays peul et ailleurs: Mélanges à la mémoire de P. F. Lacroix*. 2:355–77. Paris: Société des Africanistes.

Routledge, W., and K. Routledge. 1910. *With a Prehistoric People: The Akikuyu of British East Africa*. London.

Rowlands, Michael, and Jean-Paul Warnier. 1988. "The Magical Production of Iron in the Cameroon Grassfields." Paper presented to the Conference on African Material Culture, Bellagio, Italy, May 19–28.

Roy, Christopher D. 1989. "Mossi Pottery Forming and Firing." In *Man Does Not Go Naked*, edited by Beate Engelbrecht and Bernard Gardi. Basel.

Ruskin, John. [1858]1905. *Two Paths*. In *The Complete Works of John Ruskin*, edited by E. T. Cook and A. Wedderburn. London.

Saltman, Carlyn, Candice Goucher, and Eugenia Herbert. 1986. *The Blooms of Banjeli: Technology and Gender in West African Ironmaking*. Video.

Sanday, Peggy R. 1981. *Female Power, Male Domination*. Cambridge and New York.

Sassoon, Hamo. 1962. "Birom Blacksmithing." *Nigeria Mag.* 74:25–31.

———. 1964. "Iron-smelting in the Hill Village of Sukur, Northeastern Nigeria." *Man* 64:174–78.

Sautter, Giles. 1960. "Le Plateau congolais de Mbe." *CEA* 2:5–48.

Sayce, Roderick U. 1933. *Primitive Arts and Crafts*. London.

Schachtzabel, A. 1923. *Im Hochland von Angola*. Dresden.

Schaller, Yves. 1973. *Les Kirdi du Nord-Cameroun*. Strasbourg.

Schildkrout, Enid. 1992. "Revisiting Emil Torday's Congo. 'Images of Africa' at the British Museum." *African Arts* 35(1):60–69.

Schildkrout, Enid, Jill Hellman, and Curtis Keim. 1989. "Mangbetu Pottery: Tradition and Innovation in Northeast Zaïre." *African Arts* 22(2):38–47.

Schildkrout, Enid, and Curtis Keim. 1990. *African Reflections: Art from Northeastern Zaïre.* Seattle and New York.

Schlegel, Alice, ed. 1977. *Sexual Stratification: A Cross-Cultural View.* New York.

Schmidt, Peter. 1978. *Historical Archaeology: A Structural Approach in an African Culture.* Westport, Conn.

———. 1983. "Cultural Meaning and History in African Myth." *Int'l. Jour. of Oral Hist.* 4:167–83.

———. 1988. "Rituals and Reproductive Symbolism of Barungo Smiths." Paper presented to the ASA, Chicago.

———. 1990. "Oral Traditions, Archaeology and History: A Short Reflective History." In *A History of African Archaeology,* edited by Peter Robertshaw. Portsmouth, N.H.

Schmidt, Peter, and Donald H. Avery. 1983. "More Evidence for an Advanced Prehistoric Iron Technology in Africa." *J. Field Arch.* 10:421–34.

Schmidt, Peter, and S. Terry Childs. 1985. "Innovation and Industry during the Early Iron Age in East Africa: The KM2 and KM3 Sites of Northwest Tanzania. *Afr. Arch. Rev.* 3:53–94.

Schmitz, B. 1903. "Les minérais de fer du Haut-Congo." *La Belgique Coloniale* 8:40.

Schomburgk, Hans. 1914. *Im deutschen Sudan.* 16 mm film.

Schulze, Willi. 1971. "Early Iron Smelting among the Northern Kpelle." *Lib. Stud. J.* 3:113–27.

Scott, Joan Wallach. 1988. "Gender: A Useful Category of Historical Analysis." In her *Gender and the Politics of History.* New York.

Scully, R. T. K. 1978. "Phalaborwa Oral Tradition." Ph.D. diss., SUNY Binghamton.

Seikhou, B. 1935. "Les forgerons au Fouta Djallon." *L'Education Africaine* 24:90–91.

Shaw, Rosalind. 1985."Gender and the Structure of Reality in Temne Divination: An Interactive Study." *Africa* 55:286–303.

Shaw, Thurstan. 1984. "Keramik aus Igbo-Ukwu." In *Afrikanische Keramik,* edited by Arnulf Stössel. Munich.

Short, R. V. 1976. "The Evolution of Human Reproduction." *Proc. Roy. Soc. London* 195:3–24.

Shimmin, I. 1893. "Journey to Gambisa's." In F. W. McDonald, *The Story of Mashonaland.* London.

Sieber, Roy. 1972. "Kwahu Terracottas, Oral Traditions, and Ghanaian History." In *African Art and Leadership,* edited by Douglas Fraser and Herbert Cole. Madison, Wis.

Sieber, Roy, and Roslyn A. Walker. 1987. *African Art in the Cycle of Life.* Washington, D.C.

Silla, Ousmane. 1969. "Quelques particularités de la société sénégalaise." *Notes Afr.* 123:36–41.

Simmonds, D. 1984. "Pottery in Nigeria." In *Earthenware in Asia and Africa,* edited by John Picton. London.

Simmons, William S. 1971. *Eyes of the Night: Witchcraft among a Senegalese People.* Boston.

Sinclair, Paul J. J. 1991. "Archaeology in Eastern Africa: An Overview of Current Chronological Issues." *JAH* 32(2):179–220.

Siroto, Leon. 1977. "Njom: The Magical Bridge of the Beti and Bulu of Southern Cameroon." *African Arts* 10(2):38–51.

Skidmore, Cathy. 1992. "Bones and Baptism: Symbols and Ideology in the Career of

Nzinga." Paper presented to the Canadian Association of African Studies, Montreal.

Smets, Georges. 1937. "Quelques remarques sur la technique des Barundi." *Archeion* 19:56–66.

Smith, Edwin W., and Andrew Murray Dale. 1920. *The Ila-Speaking Peoples of Northern Rhodesia.* 2 vols. New York.

Smith, Fred T. 1986. "Compound Entryway Decoration: Male Space and Female Creativity." *African Arts* 19(3):52–58.

———. 1989. "Earth Vessels and Harmony among the Gurensi." *African Arts* 22(2):60–65.

Smith, Michael G., and Mary Smith. 1990. "Kyanship and Kinship among the Tarok." *Africa* 60:242–69.

Smith, Pierre. 1970. "La forge de l'intelligence." *L'Homme* 10(2):5–21.

———. 1973. "Principes de la personne et catégories sociales." In *La Notion de la personne en Afrique noire.* Colloques Internationaux du C.N.R.S. Paris.

———. 1979. "L'efficacité des interdits." *L'Homme* 19(1):5–47.

Smolla, G. 1984. "Anfänge und Struktur prähistorischer Keramikgruppen in Afrika." In *Afrikanische Keramik,* edited by Arnulf Stössel. Munich.

Soppelsa, Robert T. 1987. "*Assongu:* A Terracotta Tradition of Southeastern Ivory Coast." *Africa* 57:51–73.

Spande, Dennis. 1977. *A Historical Perspective on Metallurgy in Africa: A Bibliography.* Waltham, Mass.

Sperber, Dan. 1975. *Rethinking Symbolism,* translated by Alice Morton. Cambridge, Eng.

Spiess, C. 1899. "Die Schmiedekunst im Evhelande (Togo)." *Globus* 75:63–4.

Spindel, Carol. 1989a. "Kpeenbele Senufo Potters." *African Arts* 22(2):66–73.

———. 1989b. *In the Shadow of the Sacred Grove.* New York.

Stanley, G. H. 1931. "Some Products of Native Iron Smelting." *SA J. Sci.* 28:131–34.

Stannus, H. 1914. "Nyasaland: Angoni Smelting Furnaces." *Man* 14:131–32.

Staudinger, Paul. 1911. "Zinnschmelzen afrikanischer Eingeborener." *Zeit. f. Ethn.* 43:147–53.

Stayt, H. A. [1931]1968. *The BaVenda.* London.

Stern, R. 1910. "Die Gewinnung des Eisens: Überlieferungen bei den Nyamwezi." Appendix to F. Stuhlmann's *Handwerk und Industrie in Ostafrika.* Hamburg.

Sterner, Judy. 1989. "Who is Signalling Whom? Ceramic Style, Ethnicity and Taphonomy among the Sirak Bulahay." *Antiquity* 63:451–59.

Stewart, J. 1881. "Lake Nyasa and the Water Route to the Lake Region of Africa." *Proc. Roy. Geog. Soc.* 3:258–74.

Stocking, George, ed. 1983. *Observers Observed: Essays on Ethnographic Fieldwork.* Madison, Wis.

Stoller, Paul. 1992. *The Cinematic Griot.* Chicago.

Stössel, Arnulf, ed. 1984. *Afrikanische Keramik: Traditionnelle Handwerkskunst südlich der Sahara.* Munich.

Stow, G. W. 1905. *The Native Races of South Africa.* London.

Strother, Zoë. 1989. "Does a Leopard Eat Leaves?" Unpublished paper.

———. 1992. "Inventing Masks: Structures of Artistic Innovation among the Central Pende of Zaïre." Ph.D. diss., Yale University.

Stuhlmann, F. 1894. *Mit Emin Pasha ins Herz von Afrika.* Berlin.

———. 1910. *Handwerk und Industrie in Ostafrika. Abhandlungen des Hamburgischen Kolonialinstituts* 1:49–80.

Sulzmann, Erika. 1983. "Orale Tradition und Chronologie (Bolia)." In *Mélanges de Culture et de Linguistique africaines,* edited by C. Faik-Nzuji Madiya and Erika Sulzmann. Berlin.

Sundstrom, Lars. [1965]1974. *The Exchange Economy of Pre-Colonial Africa.* New York.

Sutton, J. E. G. 1985. "Temporal and Spatial Variability in African Iron Furnaces." In *African Iron Working: Ancient and Traditional,* edited by Randi Haaland and Peter Shinnie. Oslo.

Tait, David. 1961. *The Konkomba of Northern Ghana.* London.

Tamari, Tal. 1991. "The Development of Caste Systems in West Africa." *JAH* 32(2):221–50.

Taylor, G. 1926. "Native Iron-workers." *NADA* 4:53.

Tegnaeus, H. 1950. *Le Héros Civilisateur: Contribution à l'Etude Ethnologique de la Religion et de la Sociologie Africaine.* Stockholm.

Telfair, Peter. 1987a. "Notes on the Construction and Operation of a Low Shaft Iron Making Furnace at Bengoue Camp, Mekambo District, Gabon in 1957." Unpublished.

————. 1987b. "Techniques de pointe chez les Bakota." In *Aethiopie, vestiges de gloire.* Exhibition catalog, Fondation Dapper. Paris.

Temple, O., and C. L. Temple. [1919]1922. *Notes on the Tribes, Provinces, Emirates and States of Northern Provinces of Nigeria.* Lagos [Cape Town].

Terray, Emmanuel, ed. 1978. "L'or dans les sociétés akan." *JSA* 48.

Tessmann, Gustav. 1913. *Die Pangwe.* 2 vols. Berlin.

————. 1934. *Die Baja.* Stuttgart.

Theuws, Thomas. 1960. "Naître et mourir dans le rituel Luba." *Zaïre* 14(2/3):115–73.

Thomas, N. W. 1918. "Nigerian Notes, II. Metal Work." *Man* 18:184–86.

Thompson, Robert Farris. 1969. "Àbátàn: A Master Potter of the Ègbádò Yorùbá." In *Tradition and Creativity in Tribal Art,* edited by Daniel Biebuyck. Berkeley.

————. 1970. "The Sign of the Divine King." *African Arts* 3(3):8–17, 74–80.

————. 1981. *The Four Moments of the Sun.* Washington, D.C.

————. 1983. *Flash of the Spirit.* New York.

Thomson, Joseph. 1886. "Sketch of a Trip to Sokoto by the River Niger." *J. Manchester Geog. Soc.* 2:1–18.

Todd, Judith. 1985. "Iron Production by the Dimi of Ethiopia." In *African Iron Working. Ancient and Traditional,* edited by Randi Haaland and Peter Shinnie. Oslo.

————. n.d. "The Dim Blacksmith." Fieldnotes.

Torday, Emil. 1924. "Note on Certain Figures of Forged Iron Formerly Made by the Bushongo of the Belgian Congo." *Man* 24:17.

————. [1925]1969. *On the Trail of the Bushongo.* New York.

Torday, Emil, and T. A. Joyce. 1911. *Notes ethnographiques sur des peuples communément appelés Bakuba ainsi que les peuples apparentées, les Bushongo.* Brussels.

Travelé, Moussa. 1928. "Note sur les coutumes des chasseurs Bambara et Malinke du Cercle de Bamako (Soudan français)." *Rev. d'Eth.* 34–36:207–12.

Tremearne, A. J. N. 1910. "Pottery in Northern Nigeria." *Man* 10:57, 102–103.

————. [1914]1968. *The Ban of the Bori.* London.

Trowell, Margaret, and Karl P. Wachsmann. 1953. *Tribal Crafts of Uganda.* London.

Troy, Lana. 1986. *Patterns of Queenship.* Stockholm.

Tucker, J. T. 1933. *Angola, the Land of a Blacksmith Prince.* London.

Turner, Victor W. 1953. *Lunda Rites and Ceremonies.* Occasional Papers of the Rhodes-Livingstone Museum, n.s. no. 10. Livingstone, Zambia.

————. 1962. "Ndembu Circumcision Ritual." In *Essays on the Ritual of Social Relations,* edited by Max Gluckman. Manchester, Eng.

————. 1967. *The Forest of Symbols.* Ithaca, N.Y.

Udvardy, Monica. 1991. "Gender, Power and the Fragmentation of Fertility among the Giriama of Kenya." In *Body and Space,* edited by Anita Jacobson-Widding. Upssala.

van Beek, Walter. 1982. "Eating like a Blacksmith: Symbols in Kapsiki Ethnozoology." In *Symbolic Anthropology in the Netherlands*, edited by E. Schwimmer and P. E. Josselin de Jong. The Hague.

———. 1991. "Dogon Restudied: A Field Evaluation of the Work of Marcel Griaule." *CA* 32(2):139–67.

van der Merwe, Nikolas, and Donald H. Avery. 1987. "Science and Magic in African Technology: Traditional Iron Smelting in Malawi." *Africa* 57:143–72.

Van Noten, Francis. 1985. "Ancient and Modern Iron Smelting in Central Africa: Zaire, Rwanda and Burundi." In *African Iron Working: Ancient and Traditional*, edited by Randi Haaland and Peter Shinnie. Oslo.

Van Noten, Francis, and E. Van Noten. 1974. "Het Ijzersmelten bij de Madi." *Africa-Tervuren* 20(3/4):57–60.

van Overbergh, C. 1907. *Les Bangala*. Brussels.

Vansina, Jan. 1955. "Initiation Rituals of the Bushongo." *Africa* 25:138–53.

———. 1964. *Le Royaume kuba*. Tervuren.

———. 1966. *Kingdoms of the Savanna*. Madison, Wis.

———. 1969. "The Bells of Kings." *JAH* 10(2):189–97.

———. 1972. "Ndop: Royal Statues among the Kuba." In *African Art and Leadership*, edited by Douglas Fraser and Herbert Cole. Madison, Wis.

———. 1973. *The Tio Kingdom of the Middle Congo: 1880–1892*. London.

———. 1978. *The Children of Woot*. Madison, Wis.

———. 1983. "Is Elegance Proof? Structuralism and African History." *HA* 10:307–48.

———. 1984. *Art History in Africa*. New York.

———. 1990. *Paths in the Rainforests: Toward a History of Political Tradition in Equatorial Africa*. Madison, Wis.

———. "Kings in Tropical Africa." Unpublished paper.

Vaughan, James. 1973. "Nyagu as artists in Marghi society." In *The Traditional Artist in African Societies*, edited by Warren d'Azevedo. Bloomington, Ind.

Vergiat, A. 1937. *Moeurs et coutumes des Mandja*. Paris.

Vermot-Mangold, R. 1977. *Die Rolle der Frau bei den Kabre in Nord-Togo*. Basel.

Vidal, Pierre. 1976. *Garçons et filles. Le passage à l'âge d'hommes chez les Gbaya-Kara*. Recherches Oubangiennes 4. Nanterre.

Viditz-Ward, Vera. 1991. *Photographing the Paramount Chiefs of Sierra Leone*. Exhibition brochure. Washington, D.C.

Visser, Leontien E. 1982. "The Social Meaning of White, Red and Black among the Ahouan of Ivory Coast (West Africa)." In *Symbolic Anthropology in the Netherlands*, edited by E. Schwimmer and P. E. Josselin de Jong. The Hague.

Volavka, Zdenka. 1977. "Voania Muba: Contributions to the History of Central African Pottery." *African Arts* 10(2):59–66.

———. 1989. "The Art of Making a Leader." In *World Art: Themes of Unity in Diversity*. Acts of the XXVI International Congress of the History of Art. Edited by I. Lavin. University Park, Penn.

von Luschan, Franz. 1909. "Eisentechnik in Afrika." *Zeit. f. Ethn.* 41:22–59.

———. [1919]1968. *Die Altertümer von Benin*. New York.

Wagner, Gustave. 1954. "The Abaluyia of Kavirondo (Kenya)." In *African Worlds*, edited by Daryl Forde. Oxford.

Wahlman, Maude. 1972. "Yoruba Pottery Making Techniques." *Baessler Archiv*, n.s. 20:312–46.

Wallace, William. 1896. "Notes on a Journey through the Sokoto Empire and Borgu in 1894." *Geog. J.* 8:211–21.

Wannyn, R. 1961. *L'Art ancien du métal au Bas-Congo*. Champles-par-Wavre.

Warnier, J.-P., and Ian Fowler. 1979. "A Nineteenth-century Ruhr in Central Africa." *Africa* 49:329–51.

Wauters, G. 1937. "L'institution du 'Nkumi." *Annales de Notre-Dame du Sacré-Coeur,* 152–60.

Weeks, John H. 1913. *Among the Congo Cannibals.* London.

Weissenborn. 1888. "Die Eisenbereitung bei den Jaunde-Leute." *Mitteilungen aus den deutschen Schutzgebieten* 1:61–63.

Welbourn, A. 1984. "Endo Ceramics and Power Strategies." In *Ideology, Power and Prehistory,* edited by D. Miller and C. Tilley. Cambridge, Eng.

Wembah-Rashid, J. A. R. 1973. *Iron Working in Ufipa.* Dar-es-Salaam.

Wente-Lukas, Renate. 1972. "Eisen und Schmied im südlichen Tschadraum." *Paideuma* 18:112–43.

———. 1977. "Fer et forgeron au sud du lac Tchad." *JA* 47:107–22.

Werbner, Richard. 1990. "The Fugue of Gender: Bwiti in Reflection." *Journal of Religion in Africa* 20:63–91.

Wertime, T. A., and J. D. Muhly, eds. 1980. *The Coming of the Age of Iron.* New Haven, Conn.

Wertime, T. A., and S. F. Wertime, eds. 1982. *Early Pyrotechnology: The Evolution of the First Fire-using Industries.* Washington, D.C.

Westermarck, Edward. 1926. *Ritual and Belief in Morocco.* 2 vols. London.

Whyte, Susan R. 1981. "Men, Women and Misfortune in Bunyole." *Man* 16(3):350–66.

Willett, Frank. 1967. *Ife in the History of West African Sculpture.* New York.

———. 1984. "Ein hochkulturliches Zentrum der Frühgeschichte: Ife und seine Nachbarschaft." In *Afrikanische Keramik,* edited by Arnulf Stössel. Munich.

Williams, Denis. 1974. *Icon and Image.* New York.

Willis, Roy G. 1974. *Man and Beast.* London.

———. 1977. "Pollution and Paradigms." In *Culture, Disease and Healing: Studies in Medical Anthropology,* edited by D. Landy. New York.

———. 1981. *A State in the Making: Myth, History and Social Transformation in Precolonial Ufipa.* Bloomington, Ind.

———. 1991. "The Body as Metaphor: Synthetic Observations on an African Artwork." In *Body and Space,* edited by Anita Jacobson-Widding. Stockholm.

Wilson, Monica. 1957. *Rituals of Kinship among the Nyakyusa.* London.

———. 1977. *For Men and Elders.* New York.

Wise, R. 1958. "Some Rituals of Iron-making in Ufipa." *TNR* 50:106–11; 51:232–38.

Wolfe, A. 1961. *In the Ngombe Tradition: Continuity and Change in the Congo.* Evanston, Ill.

Wright, Bonnie L. 1989. "The Power of Articulation." In *Creativity of Power,* edited by W. Arens and I. Karp. Washington, D.C.

Wright, Marcia. 1985. "Iron and Regional History: Report on a Research Project in Southwestern Tanzania." *Afr. Econ. Hist.* 14:147–65.

Wyckaert, R. P. 1914. "Forgerons paiens et forgerons chrétiens au Tanganyika." *Anthropos* 9:371–80.

Wylie, Diana. 1990. *A Little God: The Twilight of Patriarchy in a Southern African Chiefdom.* Hanover, N.H.

Yandia, Félix. 1988. "Métallurgie centrafricaine: Données ethnographiques et Implications archéologiques." Mémoire de maîtrise, Université Paris X, Nanterre.

Young, Iris M. 1984. "Is Male Gender Identity the Cause of Male Domination?" In *Mothering,* edited by J. Treblicot. Totowa, N.J.

Zacharias, S., and H. G. Bachmann. 1983. "Iron-Smelting in West Africa: Ivory Coast." *J. Hist. Met. Soc.* 17:1–3.

Zahan, Dominique. 1960. *Sociétés d'initiation Bambara: Le n'domo, le kore.* Paris.

————. 1963. *La dialectique du verbe chez les Bambara.* Paris.

————. 1980. *Antilopes du soleil: Arts et rites agraires d'Afrique noire.* Vienna.

Zech, Julius von. 1898. "Vermischte Notizen über Togo und das Togohinterland." *Mitteilungen aus den deutschen Schutzgebieten* 11:89–161.

INDEX

EUGENIA W. HERBERT is E. Nevius Rodman Professor of History at Mount Holyoke College. The author of *The Artist and Social Reform: France and Belgium, 1885–1898, The Private Franklin: The Man and His Family,* and *Red Gold of Africa: Copper in Precolonial History and Culture,* she has also collaborated on several films on African metal working and belief systems.